John Mackintosh

Historic Earls and Earldoms of Scotland

John Mackintosh

Historic Earls and Earldoms of Scotland

ISBN/EAN: 9783741187568

Manufactured in Europe, USA, Canada, Australia, Japa

Cover: Foto ©ninafisch / pixelio.de

Manufactured and distributed by brebook publishing software (www.brebook.com)

John Mackintosh

Historic Earls and Earldoms of Scotland

HISTORIC EARLS

AND

EARLDOMS OF SCOTLAND

BY

JOHN MACKINTOSH, LL.D.

Author of "The History of Civilisation in Scotland;" "The Story of Scotland;" "The Revolution of 1688 and Viscount Dundee;" "History of the Valley of the Dee," etc., etc.

ABERDEEN:
W. JOLLY & SONS

Preface.

The substance of this volume originally appeared in the columns of the "Aberdeen Weekly Journal," but it has been carefully revised and important additions made. From the variety of matter, and number of personages treated in the work, it may be interesting to a wide circle of readers.

I have not deemed it necessary to burden the pages of this volume with a multiplicity of references and foot-notes, as the original sources of information are often indicated in the text itself.

It may be well, however, to state that I have long been familiar with the national records of Scotland, such as the "Scots Acts of Parliament," "Exchequer Rolls," "Register of the Great Seal," "Register of the Privy Council," "National Manuscripts," "Burgh Records," and many other registers and important historic records too tedious to mention.

Touching the sources of information more specially relating to this volume, I have consulted the family histories, charters, and papers, connected with the families treated. Amongst others, the volumes of the Old and New Spalding Clubs have been used, especially the "The Antiquities of the Shires of Aberdeen and Banff," edited by the late John Stuart, LL.D.; and also the volumes of the "Miscellany" of the Old Club; "The Records of

Aboyne," edited by the Marquis of Huntly, and issued in 1894, which are of high historic value; "Historical Papers Relating to the Jacobite Period, 1699-1750," which has been admirably edited by Colonel James Allardyce, LL.D., and issued in 1895-96, these are of great historic value and interest; the two volumes containing the writings of the distinguished Latin scholar, Dr. Arthur Johnston, present a number of interesting historic references to personages who lived in the first half of the seventeenth century; these volumes have been carefully edited by Sir William D. Geddes, LL.D., and issued in 1892-95.

The Right Hon. John Francis Erskine, Earl of Mar, communicated interesting information touching the Earldom of Mar in recent times, which I gratefully acknowledge.

ABERDEEN, *April*, 1898.   J. M.

CONTENTS.

PAGE

INTRODUCTION, ... 17-18

CHAPTER I.
EARLDOM AND EARLS OF MAR.
SECTION I.

Ruadri, First Earl of Mar—Morgund, Second Earl—Gilchrist, Third Earl, endowed the Priory of Monymusk,—Gratney, Fourth Earl—Duncan, Fifth Earl, made grants to the Priory of Monymusk—Dispute between Mar and Thomas Durward—Earldom of Garioch—William, Sixth Earl, conflict with Alan Durward—Mar, Great Chamberlain—His Death—Donald, Seventh Earl, taken prisoner—Gartney, Eighth Earl—Donald, Ninth Earl.—Castle of Kildrummy, ... 19-26

SECTION II.

Thomas, Tenth Earl of Mar—Chamberlain of Scotland—Visits England and France—His Death—Margaret, Countess of Mar and Garioch—James, Earl of Douglas and Twelfth Earl of Mar—His Death—Isabel, Countess of Mar and Garioch—Intrigues, Margaret Stewart, Countess of Angus—Isabel Countess of Mar—Sir Thomas Erskine—Robert III.—Death of the Countess's husband—Alexander Stewart captured the Countess—He became Earl of Mar, ... 26-33

SECTION III.

Alexander Stewart, Earl of Mar—Battle of Harlaw—Mar appointed Admiral—His son, Thomas—Death of the Earl—Sir Robert Erskine claimed the Earldom—His struggle with the Government, ... 33-41

SECTION IV.

Lordship of Garioch given to the Queen—Death of Sir Robert Erskine—Sir Thomas, Lord Erskine—His efforts—His claim to the Earldom rejected—James II. granted the

Earldom to his son—James III. granted the Earldom to his brother—The Earldom granted to John—His Death—No Earls of Mar for a long period—Portions of the Earldom granted to vassals of the Crown, . . . 41-49

SECTION V.

James Stewart, Earl of Mar—The Earldom of Mar and Lordship of Garioch Restored to John, Lord Erskine—Earl John elected Regent of Scotland—His Death—John, Twentieth Earl of Mar—He Joined the Party opposed to the King's favourites—" Raid of Ruthven "—Lord Maxwell—The banished Earls pardoned—Efforts of Earl John to recover the lands of the Earldom, Act of Parliament in his favour, protests against it, ... 49-57

SECTION VI.

Earl John raised Actions and Processes in the Court of Session to recover the Lands of the Earldom—He was Lord Treasurer of Scotland—His Death—John, Twenty-first Earl of Mar—He protested for higher Precedence—Decreet of Ranking of the Peers—Protests of the Earls of Mar for higher Precedence—Death of Earl John, . 57-63

SECTION VII.

John, Twenty-second Earl—Charles, Twenty-third Earl—He was a Jacobite—John, Twenty-fourth Earl of Mar—Appointed Secretary of State for Scotland—He offered his service to George I.—Dismissed from the Office of Secretary—He projected a Rising—Meeting at Braemar—Meeting at the Castle of Aboyne—The Standard of Revolt raised—Movements of the Insurgent Army, Perth taken—the Accession of James VIII. Proclaimed—Battle of Preston—Battle of Sheriffmuir—Arrival of James VIII. (Pretender)—Duke of Argyle's March—Retreat of the Insurgents—Flight of the Pretender and Earl of Mar, ... 63-69

SECTION VIII.

Effects of Mar's Rising—Many persons forced to join it—Estates of the Forfeited Earl of Mar—His Death—Thomas, Lord Erskine, Lady Frances Erskine—The Title of Earl of Mar restored to John Francis Erskine, Twenty-seventh Earl of Mar—John Thomas, Twenty-eighth Earl—John Thomas Miller, Twenty-ninth Earl

Contents.   ix

of Mar, and Earl of Kellie—His Death—John Francis Erskine, Thirtieth Earl of Mar—Claim of Lord Kellie to the Earldom of Mar—Opinion of the Committee of Privileges—Debates in the House of Lords touching the Earldom of Mar—Act of Parliament, . . 70-77

CHAPTER II.
EARLDOM AND EARLS OF BUCHAN.
SECTION I.

Mormaers, and Early Earls of Buchan—Colbain, Earl of Buchan—Roger, Earl—Fergus, Earl—Marjory, Countess of Buchan—Comyns—William Comyn, Earl of Buchan—He was Justiciary of Scotland, and founded the Abbey of Deer—Alexander Earl of Buchan, Justiciary, and High Constable of Scotland—Old Castles erected by the Comyns—Earl of Buchan one of the Guardians of Scotland—John Comyn, Lord of Badenoch, claimed the Crown of Scotland—John Comyn, Earl of Buchan—Edward I.—John Baliol and Robert Bruce, . . . 78-85

SECTION II.

Perilous state of the Kingdom—Earl of Buchan invaded England—Edward I. invaded Scotland—Battle of Dunbar—Earl of Buchan submitted to Edward I.—John Comyn, Lord of Badenoch, Guardian of Scotland—Edward I. in Caerlaverock Castle—Scottish Ambassadors to France—Great Invasion of Scotland by Edward I.—Submission of the Lord of Badenoch and the Scots, ... 85-91

SECTION III.

The Earl of Buchan loyal to Edward I.—Castles of the Lord of Badenoch—Robert Bruce—Slaughter of the Lord of Badenoch—Bruce crowned King—He was defeated by the English, and suffered extreme privation—Death and ruin befell many of his adherents—At last Bruce defeated a body of English cavalry—He marched into Aberdeenshire, at Barra—He completely defeated the Earl of Buchan, and utterly subdued the Comyn Clan, 91-99

SECTION IV.

Beaumont, Earl of Buchan—Edward Baliol in Scotland—He defeated the Scots—Edward III.—The Earl of Buchan captured, but permitted to return to England—Alexander

Stewart, Earl of Buchan—His sons- John Stewart, Earl of Buchan, and Constable of France—Murdoch Stewart, Earl of Buchan; after his execution, the Earldom reverted to the Crown — James Stewart erected Earl of Buchan—He fought on the side of James III. at the Battle of Sauchie Burn—Alexander, Second Earl of Buchan—John, Third Earl—Christian, Countess of Buchan—James Douglas, Fifth Earl of Buchan—Mary, Countess of Buchan—James Erskine, Sixth Earl of Buchan—James, Seventh Earl—William, Eighth Earl—David Erskine, Lord Cardross, Ninth Earl of Buchan—Henry David, Tenth Earl—His sons—David Stewart, Eleventh Earl—Henry David, Twelfth Earl—David Stewart, Thirteenth Earl, . . . 99-107

CHAPTER III.

EARLDOM AND EARLS OF HUNTLY.

SECTION I.

Early Notice of the Gordons—Sir Adam Gordon joined Wallace—He fought at Bannockburn—He was the first Gordon who obtained Lands in the North—His Death—Sir Adam—He was engaged at the Battle of Culblean—John was taken prisoner at the Battle of Durham—His Death—Sir John, he fought in the Battle of Otterburn—His two sons—Sir Adam—Elizabeth Gordon, married Sir William Seton; their son, Alexander inherited the Gordon Lands—He was created a Lord of Parliament, 108-114

SECTION II.

Alexander, Second Lord Gordon, and First Earl of Huntly—His marriages—A Contract between him and Sir William Keith—Conflict between the King and the Earls of Douglas—Huntly appointed Lieutenant-General of the Kingdom—Battle of Brechin—Huntly endeavoured to strengthen his position by bonds of Manrent—His Death—George, Second Earl of Huntly—He married thrice—Expedition against the Earl of Ross—His Submission—Bonds of Manrent given to Huntly—He was Justiciary for the North—Duncan, Chief of the Mackintoshes, 114-121

SECTION III.

George, Second Earl—A Marriage Contract—A Tragic Scene—The King Imprisoned—Attitude of Huntly—He was

Contents.

made a Privy Councillor, and Lieutenant of the North—Bonds of Manrent—A Marriage Contract—Disturbance in the Highlands, the Lord of the Isles forfeited—Huntly, Lord Chancellor—Perkin Warbeck in Scotland—He married Lady Catherine Gordon—Bog of Gight—Death of Huntly, ... 121-128

SECTION IV.

Alexander, Third Earl of Huntly—He was Commissioned to restore peace in the Highlands—Donald Dubh—Huntly received grants of lands for his services—He was created hereditary Sheriff of Inverness—Bonds of Manrent—John, Lord Gordon — Battle of Flodden — Huntly supported the Duke of Albany's Government—Henry VIII.—Death of the Earl of Huntly, ... 128-134

SECTION V.

George, Fourth Earl of Huntly, a minor—Distracted State of the Kingdom—The Earl of Angus seized the young King—Earl of Huntly's Marriage—Bonds of Manrent—Huntly created Hereditary Sheriff of Aberdeen—Disturbance on the Borders, an army mustered—Death of James V.—The Earl of Huntly received a Commission of Lieutenancy of the North—He entered into a bond with the Earl of Crawford—Huntly supported Cardinal Beaton—Disturbance in the Highlands, Donald Dubh—Huntly appointed Lord Chancellor, taken a prisoner at the Battle of Pinkie, ... 134-140

SECTION VI.

George, Fourth Earl of Huntly, a prisoner in England—His contract with the Duke of Somerset—His escape—Quarrel between Huntly and the Chief of Clan Chattan, Mackintosh executed—Disturbance in the Highlands, Huntly failed to restore peace and returned home—His attitude toward the Lords of the Congregation—Meeting of Catholics—Quarrel between the Gordons and Ogilvies, 140-146

SECTION VII.

George, Fourth Earl of Huntly—The Queen's Progress to the North—Strathbogie Castle—Lord James Stewart created Earl of Moray—Huntly's attitude—Sir John Gordon—The Countess of Huntly—Battle of Corrichie—Death of Huntly—His titles and estates forfeited—George, Lord vention of Estates—The Duke of Gordon declined to surrender the Castle—Excitement in the Convention—Viscount Dundee—Surrender of the Castle by the Duke of Gordon, ... 193-198

Section XVI.

George, First Duke of Gordon—He visited the Court of James VII.—He was repeatedly imprisoned—His Death—Alexander, Second Duke of Gordon—He joined the Rising of 1715—He was a good Landlord—His Death—His Family—Cosmo—George, Third Duke of Gordon—Lord Lewis Gordon joined the Rising of 1745, and escaped to France—Ballad to his memory, . . 199-204

Section XVII.

Death of Cosmo—George—Alexander, Fourth Duke of Gordon—Elected a Representative Peer—His Marriage—Elevated to the Peerage of the United Kingdom—A nobleman of energy and public spirit—He raised two regiments of Fencibles—He was elected Lord Chancellor of the University and King's College, Aberdeen—Burns' Visit to Gordon Castle—"The Reel o' Bogie"—William Marshal—The Duke was a kind Landlord—His Death—His Family, ... 204-208

Section XVIII.

George, Fifth Duke of Gordon—He joined the army—He raised the 92nd Highlanders, was appointed Colonel Commandant of the Regiment—Sketch of the Services of the 92nd, in Egypt, Portugal, and Spain—Heroic Action of the 92nd at Quatre Bras and Waterloo, . 209-214

Section XIX.

George, Fifth Duke of Gordon—His Marriage, Huntly Lodge—He was Keeper of the Great Seal of Scotland, and Governor of Edinburgh Castle—He was a considerate Landlord—His Death—The Duchess of Gordon returned to Huntly Lodge—She erected the Gordon Schools in Huntly—Her Death—The Dukes of Richmond and Gordon as Landlords, ... 214-218

Section XX.

ABOYNE BRANCH OF THE HUNTLY FAMILY.

John, Viscount Aboyne, George, Viscount, James, Viscount—Charles Gordon, First Earl of Aboyne—His Marriage—

Contents.

His Death—Charles, Second Earl—Charles, Third Earl—Charles, Fourth Earl—He greatly improved his estates—His marriage—His Death—George, Fifth Earl—Elected a Representative Peer—Created a Peer of the United Kingdom—Succeeded to the title of Marquis of Huntly— His Family— His Death— Charles, Tenth Marquis of Huntly, and Sixth Earl of Aboyne—Charles, Eleventh Marquis of Huntly, and Seventh Earl of Aboyne, ... 218-223

CHAPTER IV.

EARLDOM AND EARLS OF ERROLL.

SECTION I.

Tradition of the Hays—William Hay of Erroll—David Hay of Erroll—Gilbert Hay—Nicholas Hay, Lord of Erroll—Sir Gilbert Hay of Erroll—He joined Bruce, and accompanied the King in his wanderings and difficulties—He was appointed Hereditary Lord High Constable of Scotland, ... 224-228

SECTION II.

Office of High Constable—Death of Sir Gilbert—Sir David, Second High Constable of the Erroll line—Sir Thomas, Third High Constable—His Marriage—His Death—Sir William, Fourth High Constable—Sir William, Fifth High Constable, and First Earl of Erroll—His Marriage—Nicholas, Second Earl of Erroll—William, Third Earl—Bonds of Manrent. 228-234

SECTION III.

A Combat between a Frenchman and Scotsman—William, Fourth · Earl of Erroll—Battle of Flodden—Earl of Erroll slain—William, Fifth Earl—His Marriage—Bonds of Manrent—Death of Earl William—William, Sixth Earl — George, Seventh Earl — Bonds of Manrent—Officers at arms, ... 234-239

SECTION IV.

George, Seventh Earl—Appointed Lieutenant—His Death—Andrew, Eighth Earl—An Agreement between the Earl and Tulidef—Francis, Ninth Earl—Bond of Friendship between him and the Earl of Huntly—Letter from the King—Bonds of Manrent, ... 239-244

xvi   Contents.

SECTION V.

Francis, Ninth Earl—Differences between the High Constable and Earl Marischal—Feud between the Gordons and the Hays—Gordon of Gight's proceedings—His trial, adjourned, resumed, and again adjourned—Settlement of the Feud. 245-250

SECTION VI.

The Earl relieved from restraint—Dispute between Lord Hay and Lord Keith—Commission issued by Charles I.—Death of Earl Francis—William, Tenth Earl—Visit of Charles I. to Scotland—Ceremony of the King's Coronation—Death of Earl William—Gilbert, Eleventh Earl, Coronation of Charles II. 250-255

SECTION VII.

Gilbert, Eleventh Earl—Fine imposed on him by Cromwell's Commissioners—Restoration of Charles II.—Death of Earl Gilbert—John, Twelfth Earl—Revolution of 1688—Erroll elected Chancellor of University and King's College, Aberdeen—His Death—Charles, Thirteenth Earl—Territories of the Earldom, ... 256-261

SECTION VIII.

Charles, Earl of Erroll was opposed to the Union—He was suspected as a Jacobite—Coronation of George I.—Death of Earl Charles—Mary, Countess of Erroll, recognised as Hereditary High Constable of Scotland, her deputy acted at the Coronation of George II.—Her Death—James, Lord Boyd—William, Fourth Earl of Kilmarnock—Charles, and William Boyd. . . 261-266

SECTION IX.

Boyd Family—James, Lord Boyd, and Fifteenth Earl of Erroll—His Family—He officiated at the Coronation of George III.—Elected a Representative Peer—His Death—George, Sixteenth Earl of Erroll—William, Seventeenth Earl—Knight—Marischal, a Representative Peer—His Family—His Death—William George, Eighteenth Earl—His Marriage—His Family—When George IV. visited Scotland, the High Constable discharged the functions of his office—He was elevated to the Peerage of the United Kingdom—He received many honours—

Contents. xvii

His Death—William, Harry, Nineteenth Earl—Charles Gore, Twentieth Earl of Erroll. 266-270

CHAPTER V.

KEITHS, GREAT MARISCHALS OF SCOTLAND, AND EARL MARISCHALS.

SECTION I.

Legend and Tradition of the Keiths—Early Great Marischals, Hervey de Keith—Sir Philip Keith—Sir Hervey Keith—Sir John—Sir Robert—Sir Robert, he led the Scottish cavalry at the Battle of Bannockburn—He received a grant of lands and the office of Marischal from Robert I.—He was slain at the Battle of Dupplin—Sir Robert, Great Marischal, he was Sheriff of Aberdeen—Sir Edward, Great Marischal—His Family—His Death—Sir William, His Marriage—He took an active part in public affairs—He erected the Castle of Dunnottar—His Death—Sir William, Great Marischal—He rendered important service to the Government, . . . 271-276

SECTION II.

William, First Earl Marischal—William, Second Earl Marischal—He officiated in the Parliament of 1488—His Family—William, Third Earl Marischal—Two of his sons fell in the Battle of Flodden.—He officiated at the Coronation of James V., and was one of the Guardians of the young King—William, Fourth Earl Marischal—He accompanied James V. to France, and was one of the Keepers of the infant Queen Mary's person—His Marriage—He fought at the Battle of Pinkie—Master of Marischal—The Queen Regent on her death-bed and the leaders of the Reform movement, ... 276-281

SECTION III.

William, Fourth Earl Marischal, moved the Adoption of the Confession of Faith in Parliament—Later Part of his Life—His Death—George, Fifth Earl Marischal—Early Part of his Life, he Travelled and Studied Abroad—He was Ambassador to the Court of Denmark to arrange the Marriage between James VI. and the Princess Anne—He took an active Part in Public Affairs—He was Charged to Appear before the Privy Council, . 281-286

Contents.

Section IV.

George, Fifth Earl Marischal—His Foundation of Marischal College—Later part of his Life—His Death—William, Sixth Earl Marischal—He took an Interest in Public Affairs—He acted at the Coronation of Charles I.—His Family—His Death—William, Seventh Earl Marischal—He joined the Covenanters—He mustered the Covenanters of Angus and Mearns—In 1645 he joined the King's Party—He was Engaged at the Battle of Preston—He officiated at the Coronation of Charles II.—He was taken Prisoner by Cromwell's Officers and imprisoned—How the Regalia was Preserved. . 286-293

Section V.

William, Seventh Earl Marischal, liberated from prison—His family—His death—George, Eighth Earl Marischal—He was nominated on the Commission to visit the Universities—His death—William, Ninth Earl Marischal—He endowed a Chair of Medicine in Marischal College—He was opposed to the Union between Scotland and England—His family—His Death—George, Tenth Earl Marischal—He joined the Rising of 1715, and took an active part in it—He escaped, but was attainted—James Francis Edward Keith attained distinction in the Russian Army, ... 293-298

Section VI.

General Keith's Career in Russia—He entered the service of Frederick the Great of Prussia—Made Field-Marshal—His service in the Prussian army—His Death, and Character—Earl Marischal in the service of Prussia—He visited Scotland, became heir to the Earldom of Kintore—He returned to Prussia—His Death, . . . 298-306

CHAPTER VI.

EARLDOM AND EARLS OF FINDLATER, AND SEAFIELD.

Section I.

Territory of the Earldom—Early notice of the Ogilvies—Sir Walter Ogilvie—Sir Walter of Auchleven—His son, Sir Walter—Sir James Ogilvie—His family—Sir James—Sir Alexander—He settled the estates on Sir John Gordon—Quarrel between the Gordons and Ogilvies—

Contents. xix

PAGE

James Ogilvie—Sir Walter Ogilvie, first Lord Deskford
—James, second Lord, ... 307-312

Section II.

James, First Earl of Findlater—He joined the Covenanters—
He obtained a new patent—Sir Patrick Ogilvie, second
Earl of Findlater—He supported the Royal cause—His
Death—James, Third Earl of Findlater—His family—
His death—James, Fourth Earl of Findlater, and First
Earl of Seafield—A distinguished nobleman—A member
of Parliament, Secretary of State, President of Parliament, Lord High Chancellor, and created Earl of Seafield—Elected a Representative Peer, he moved that the
Union be dissolved—His family—His Death—James,
Fifth Earl of Findlater and Second Earl of Seafield—
Cullen House ransacked, ... 312-317

Section III.

James, Fifth Earl of Findlater and Second Earl of Seafield—
Marriage of his daughter to the Chief of Grant—Death
of Earl James—James, Sixth Earl of Findlater and Third
Earl of Seafield—He made efforts to introduce improvements—His Death—James, Seventh Earl of Findlater
and Fourth Earl of Seafield—His Marriage—Burns at
Cullen—Death of Earl James—Succession of Sir Lewis
Alexander Grant, ... 318-322

Section IV.

Early notice of the Grants—Their Territories—Chiefs of Grant,
—Sir Duncan Grant, Laird of Freuchie—John Grant of
Freuchie—His family—His Death—James Grant of
Freuchie—John of Freuchie—His family—John Grant
of Freuchie—Dispute between the Grants and Mackintoshes—Sir John Grant, Sixth Laird of Freuchie—
James Grant of Carron—Death of Sir John. . . 322-327

Section V.

James Grant, Seventh Laird, joined the Covenanters—His
death—Ludovick, Eighth Laird—His marriage—A
member of Parliament—Took an active part in the Revolution of 1688—He raised a Regiment—Battle of Cromdale—He received a charter incorporating all his lands
into a regality—Castle Grant—Death of Ludovick—
Colonel Alexander Grant—His death, . . . 327-332

Contents.

Section VI.

Sir James Grant of Grant—His marriage—A member of Parliament—His death—Sir Ludovick Grant of Grant—A member of Parliament—Castle Grant occupied by the Insurgents in 1746—Death of Sir Ludovick—Sir James Grant of Grant—He travelled abroad—He founded Grantown—He raised two Regiments—His Death, tributes to his memory, ... 332-338

Section VII.

Sir Lewis Alexander Grant of Grant, Fifth Earl of Seafield, Viscount Reidhaven, and Lord Ogilvie of Deskford and Cullen—A member of Parliament—He retired from public life—His death—Sir Francis William, Sixth Earl of Seafield—A Kind Landlord—Cullen House—Rebuilding of Cullen—A Representative Peer—His family—His death—John Charles Grant Ogilvie, Seventh Earl of Seafield, ... 338-342

Section VIII.

John Charles Grant Ogilvie, Seventh Earl of Seafield—He was elevated to the Peerage of the United Kingdom—Great rejoicings in Strathspey—He was a good Landlord, and made many improvements—His Death—Tributes to his memory—Ian Charles Grant Ogilvie—Eighth Earl of Seafield, and Second Baron of Strathspey—He joined the army—His Death—James Ogilvie Grant, Ninth Earl of Seafield—His Family—His Death—Francis William Ogilvie Grant, Tenth Earl of Seafield—His Death—James Ogilvie Grant, Eleventh Earl of Seafield, . 343-347

HISTORIC EARLS

AND

EARLDOMS OF SCOTLAND.

INTRODUCTION.

THERE were no Earls in Scotland until the twelfth century. The people were in the earlier periods organised under the tribal form of government. But from the eighth century to the close of the eleventh, society in Scotland was in a progressive and transitional stage.

In the year 844 Kenneth M'Alpin mounted the Coronation Stone at Scone, and became the real founder of the historic Kingdom of Scotland. This important event has to be interpreted as the result of the long struggle of the chief tribes. The accumulating force of circumstances and the necessities of life, and the new influence of a common religion, all naturally tended to a greater concentration of power under some one of the leading tribes. The foundation of the monarchy marked two distinct steps of advance:— (1) It concentrated more power in the original centre, Scone, whence the historic kingdom was gradually extended outward to the north-east, the west, and the south; (2) it supplied a continuous influence, which operated effectively, though slowly, in developing the loose elements of separate tribal communities into a nationality.

Prior to the twelfth century the Mormaers were the rulers of districts or territorial divisions in Scotland. The Mormaer's power over the inhabitants of the district was vested in the tribe of the land, and the succession to the Mormaership seems to have been limited to the descendants of the founder of the tribe. Thus the Mormaer was the ruler of all the people within the territory of the tribe. In early fragments of Chronicles and in the Book of Deer notices of the Mormaers of Athole, Angus, Moray, Mar, Buchan, and other districts occur. The official called the Toshach seems to have had military functions, but in early times the powers of the Mormears and all officials were limited by usage and custom. Before the end of the eleventh century, the central Government had obtained some control over the Mormaers and local tribes between the Forth and the Spey.

After the eleventh century the title of Mormaer began to fluctuate, and was shortly superseded by the title of Comes or Earl. In the twelfth century charters were introduced, and feudal tenor, under which direct grants of territory were given by the King. In this way great changes were effected in connection with the land.

There were four periods in which remarkable changes took place in the ownership and possession of the land of the country:—(1) From the early part of the twelfth century to about 1265 ; (2) during the War of Independence a large portion of the land passed into the hands of new owners, and new names and families came into influence and power ; (3) in the sixteenth century considerable tracts of the best land in the country passed into the possession of new owners ; (4) from the middle of the seventeenth century to about 1750 many changes were effected in territorial possessions, mainly caused by the Civil War, the Revolution of 1688, and the risings of 1715 and 1745.

The rise and vicissitude of great families are associated with many important historic events and touching incidents ; and the utmost effort will be made to render this series instructive and interesting.

CHAPTER I.

Earldom and Earls of Mar.

SECTION I.

RUADRI, FIRST EARL OF MAR—MORGUND—GILCHRIST—GRATNEY
— DUNCAN— WILLIAM— DONALD— GARTNEY— DONALD—
CASTLE OF KILDRUMMY.

THE old district of Mar was very extensive. It commenced in the neighbourhood of Aberdeen, and extended to the border of Badenoch, comprising nearly the whole of the valleys of the Dee and Don and the territory lying between them. As mentioned in the Introduction, in Celtic times the Mormear was the ruler of the tribe of the land; and the old Earls of Mar were descended from the Celtic Mormears, and can be traced from the tenth century onward.

In 1014 Donald, son of Emin, was Mormaer of Mar, and in that year he proceeded to Ireland to assist the Irish in repelling the attacks of the Danes, and he fought and fell in the battle of Clontarf. In the reign of Alexander I. Ruadri was Mormaer of Mar, and he became the first Earl of Mar. He was one of the Earls who gave consent to the foundation charter of the Abbey of Scone by Alexander I., in 1120. He was also a witness to the important charter of David I. to the monks of Dumfermline, about 1126.

Ruadri was succeeded by Morgund, second Earl of Mar. Between the years 1165 and 1171 he granted the church of Tarland to the canons of St Andrews, with its tithes and oblations, land and mill, and also the second tithes of the Earl's land, and timber from his woods for building purposes. This grant was confirmed by a charter of William the Lion. Earl Morgund and Agnes, his countess, also granted the church of Migvie to the canons of St. Andrews.

Morgund was succeeded by Gilchrist, third Earl of Mar. It seems probable that he built the Priory of Monymusk, and by charter he granted to it the churches of St Marnan of Leochel, St. Wolock of Ruthven, St. Andrew of Alford, and Invernochty in Strathdon. He contested the claims of the patronage of the church of St Marnan, of Aberchirder, with William the Lion and the Bishop of Moray, and granted it to the monks of the Monastery of Arbroath.

Gilchrist was succeeded by Gratney, fourth Earl of Mar, of whom little is known. But he appeared, with his son Malcolm, as a witness of charters, under the title of Earl of Mar, and one at least of these charters was confirmed by William the Lion. About the year 1224 he was succeeded by Duncan, fifth Earl of Mar. Earl Duncan granted St Andrew's Church, in Braemar, to the Priory of Monymusk, with an acre of land on the other side of the Water of Clunie. He also confirmed some of the grants made by his father, Earl Morgund.

A dispute arose between the Earl of Mar and Thomas Durward touching the legitimacy of Earl Morgund and his son Duncan. Durward asserted that Morgund and his son were illegitimate, and on that ground he claimed the Earldom of Mar, in right of his mother, of whom little is known, except that she was the wife of Malcolm Lundin, the King's hereditary door-keeper. It is pretty certain, however, that the King supported the claim of his doorkeeper, with the aim of breaking up this old Celtic earldom. The dispute for a time was settled by a compromise under which Thomas Durward obtained his great domains in Mar—stretching from Invercanny, on the banks of the Dee, to Alford, on the Don, and from Coull, on the West, to Skene, on the east. Yet the Durwards were not satisfied, and subsequently Thomas Durward's son claimed the whole

Earldom of Mar, and made the utmost efforts to obtain possession of it. This family took the name of Durward from their hereditary office of doorkeepers to the King, and for a time they rose rapidly to power and influence.

This seems the proper place to touch briefly on the origin of the Earldom of the Garioch, which afterwards became connected with the Earldom of Mar. The Earldom of the Garioch was created by William the Lion, and granted by him to his brother, David, Earl of Huntingdon. This new earldom mainly consisted of the territory surrounding the old fort of Dunideer, and lying between the Don and its tributary, the Water of Ury. Earl David, the first historic Earl of the Garioch, was a singularly important personage, inasmuch as he was the ancestor of the subsequent Royal line of Scotland, and also remotely of Great Britain.

He was born in 1144—the third grandson of David I. He married a sister of Randolph, Earl of Chester, and by her he had three sons and four daughters. His eldest daughter, Margaret, married Alan of Galloway, and it was through her issue that John Baliol claimed the Crown of Scotland. His second daughter, Isabella, married Robert de Bruce of Annandale. His youngest daughter, Ada, married Henry de Hastings. And it was the descendants of these daughters of Earl David, who, after the death of Alexander III. and his granddaughter, the Maid of Norway, claimed the Crown of Scotland.

Earl David died about 1219. Two of his sons, Henry and David, predeceased him; and his third son, John, "the Scot," succeeded to the earldom of the Garioch. On the death of his mother he became Earl of Chester. After the death of Earl John, the earldom of the Garioch reverted to the Crown; and it was eventually granted as a lordship to the Earls of Mar.

Returning, Duncan, Earl of Mar, was one of the witnesses to a charter by Alexander II. to Ness, his physician, of the lands of Banff, in the fief of Alyth, which was dated at Aberdeen on the 9th of October, 1232. Earl Duncan was succeeded by his son, William, sixth Earl of Mar. He is mentioned among the great barons of Scotland in the letter of fealty granted by Alexander II. to Henry III. of England in 1244.

This Earl, during the minority of Alexander III., came into conflict with Alan Durward, who was Justiciary of Scotland, and son of Thomas Durward mentioned before. Durward had married a natural daughter of Alexander II., by whom he had several daughters; and it was alleged in 1252 that he was endeavouring to obtain from the Pope the legitimation of his wife, so in the event of the death of the boy Alexander III., his daughter would be the heiress to the Crown of Scotland. Thus Alan was a great and aspiring personage. He assumed the title and style of Earl of Athole from 1233 to 1235; and not content with the very large part of the Earldom of Mar which his father had obtained for him, in 1257, he claimed the whole Earldom of Mar. In that year a papal rescript was issued, directing an inquest to be held, proceeding on the narrative that "Our beloved son, the nobleman Alan, called the Durward, hath signified to us that, whereas the nobleman William of Mar, of the diocese of Aberdeen, hath withheld the Earldom of Mar, of right belonging to the aforesaid Alan, and the same doth occupy to the prejudice of the said Alan, and that Morgund and Duncan, deceased, to whom the said William asserts his succession to the said earldom, were not begotten in lawful matrimony." Notwithstanding Alan's great efforts, Earl William continued in possession, and Durward failed in his aim and ambition.

Earl William was one of the most powerful barons of his time in Scotland. He was one of those who were removed from the Government of Scotland by Henry III. of England, in September, 1255, while his opponent, Alan Durward, was one of those who replaced him. Mar was, however, recalled to the king's councils in the beginning of the year 1257. In November, 1258, he appears, along with Alan Durward, as one of those whom Henry III. undertook to support in the government of the kingdom. He was named among the barons of Scotland to whom Henry III. bound himself to deliver up the child that his daughter Margaret, queen of Alexander III., was about to give birth in England.

He held the office of Great Chamberlain of Scotland in 1252, and again from 1263 to 1266. In 1270 he was sent to England, accompanied by the Abbot of Dunfermline, on a mission for the recovery of the Earldom of Huntingdon.

By a charter dated at Falkland on the 23rd of January, 1268, witnessed by his sons, Donald and Duncan, he confirmed to the canons of St Andrews the grants made to them by his grandfather, Morgund, Earl of Mar, of the church of Tarland, and by his grandmother, Countess of Mar, of the church of Migvie; and, further, granted an acre of land, lying between the church and the castle of Migvie, for a manse to the vicar serving the cure. One clause in his charters touches on the questions which had been raised as to the legitimacy of Earl Morgund.

Earl William died in 1273, and was succeeded by his eldest son, Donald, seventh Earl of Mar. He was present at the meeting of the Estates held at Scone on the 5th of February, 1284, in which the barons and bishops bound themselves in the name of the nation to acknowledge the king's granddaughter, Margaret, the Maid of Norway, as the heir of the Crown of Scotland.

After the death of the Maid of Norway, in September, 1290, it appears that the Earl of Mar became a supporter of the claims of Robert Bruce of Annandale to the Crown of Scotland. In 1291, Donald, Earl of Mar, one of the seven Earls of Scotland, and the king's freemen of Moray, appealed from William, Bishop of St Andrews, and John Comyn, Lord of Badenoch, Guardians of Scotland, to

Edward I. for redress of wrongs done to them by under-wardens of Scotland, who had wasted and plundered their towns and lands in Moray, burned their barns, carried away their goods, and slain men and women.

The Earl of Mar was present in the chapel of the Castle of Berwick, on the 3rd of August, 1291, when Edward I. protested that his consent to try the claims of the candidates for the Scottish Crown within the realm of Scotland, should not prejudice the exercise of his right as Lord Superior of Scotland, within the kingdom of England. The same year, on the 24th of July, he was present in the Church of the Friars at Perth, when Edward I. received the fealty of Mary, Queen of Isle of Man, and Countess of Strathearn.

Earl Donald fought at the battle of Dunbar, on the 26th of April, 1296; and shortly after he was taken a prisoner by the English.

He married Muriel, a daughter of the Earl of Strathearn, by whom he had issue. He died in 1297, and was succeeded by his son, Gartney, eighth Earl of Mar. He married Christian Bruce, a sister of Robert I.; while Robert I. married Isabel, a sister of Earl Gartney. The Earl received with his wife the lordship of Garioch, to be held in free regality. He died in 1305, and was succeeded by his son, Donald, ninth Earl of Mar, who was then a boy; and Edward I. ordered that the heir of Mar should be kept in the Castle of Bristol; and soon after ordered that Donald, Earl of Mar, is to be with the king in his own household. He was detained a prisoner in England till after the battle of Bannockburn.

Earl Gartney left two daughters—Ellen of Mar, the eldest, and Janet. Ellen married Sir John Monteith; their daughter, Christian Monteith, married Sir Edward Keith, Great Marischal of Scotland; and their daughter, Janet Keith, married Sir Thomas Erskine; their son, Sir Robert Erskine, as a descendant of Ellen of Mar, became heir to the Earldom of Mar, and claimed it in the following century.

Earl Donald returned to Scotland in 1314, but it appears that he occasionally revisited England. He led one of the divisions of the Scottish army which invaded England in the summer of 1327. After the death of Robert I., the Earl of Mar joined the cause of his cousin, the young Prince David II. On the death of the Earl of Moray, the Regent of Scotland, in 1332, the Earl of Mar was elected Regent of the Kingdom. Shortly after he was slain at the disastrous battle of Dupplin. He was succeeded by his son, Thomas, tenth Earl of Mar.

From an early period the Castle of Kildrummy was the principal seat of the Earldom of Mar. It is one of the oldest castles in Scotland, and in its time was a great stronghold. Probably part of the castle was built about the middle of the thirteenth century. The castle, with its fortifications, covered about three Scotch acres of ground; but it has for long been ruinous. The castle has been repeatedly burned and defaced. It was in the form of a square, opening toward the south, and consisted of six or seven towers and a chapel. It is built of dressed freestone, and the ruins show that the masonry has been excellent. The walls are about eighteen feet thick, with rooms within them, and a passage through them, and small holes for watching, which runs round the structure. In the last century one of the towers, called the "Snow Tower," was standing. It consisted of seven vaulted storeys, each about twenty feet in height, making the total height of the tower 140 feet. In the top storey there was then a breach toward the north-east, locally called the "Devil's Gap," touching which various traditions were current. In the bottom of the tower there was a draw-well, whence water was drawn to the top through a round opening in the centre of each storey. There was also another draw-well in the close. There was an underground vaulted passage which led to a small stream upon the north side of the castle. The great hall was on the north side of the close in the form of an oblong square, and over sixty feet in length and forty feet in breadth, with large arched windows. On the north-east side there was a chapel and a burial ground.

This great castle is associated with many important and interesting historic events and touching incidents, which I will subsequently narrate in connection with the personages and chief actors in these events and scenes. In the summer of 1296, when Edward I. was returning southward on his triumphal progress through Scotland, he stayed a night or two at Kildrummy Castle, and thence marched to Brechin. Again, in 1303, when returning southward on his second progress through the kingdom, he stayed some time at the Castle of Kildrummy, and thence proceeded southward by Brechin.

As we have seen, Robert Bruce was a brother-in-law of Gartney, Earl of Mar. Thus Bruce was the uncle of Donald, who became Earl of Mar in 1306, but was a prisoner in England, so in this way it happened that Bruce had command of the Castle of Kildrummy when he entered on the great enterprise of re-taking the kingdom of Scotland.

SECTION II.

THOMAS, EARL OF MAR—MARGARET, COUNTESS OF MAR AND GARIOCH — ISABEL, COUNTESS OF MAR — ALEXANDER STEWART.

David II., in 1358, granted to Earl Thomas a charter of confirmation of the Lordship of the Garioch to him and his heirs. In 1356 Thomas, Earl of Mar, granted a charter to William Chalmer of the lands of Easter Ruthven, in Cromar, for three yearly suits at the earl's head courts at Migvie. In 1359 he granted a charter to William Leith, burgess of Aberdeen, of the lands of Rothney, Hareboggs, and Blackeboggs, in the regality of the Garioch, and with common pasture in the earl's forest of Benachie. This charter was confirmed the same year by David II. The same year he granted a charter to William Fentoun of the lands of Upper Towie, Nether Towie, and Culquhork, in Strathdon.

In 1359 Earl Thomas was Chamberlain of Scotland. But in 1361 there was a strife between him and David II., his cousin. The King besieged the Castle of Kildrummy and took it; and appointed Sir Walter Moigne temporary keeper of the castle. A Parliament, which met at Perth in 1370, found that the Earl of Mar had contumaciously absented himself.

The Earl married Margaret Stewart, the eldest daughter of Thomas Stewart, Earl of Angus. Earl Thomas was often in England and France. In March, 1359, he had a passport through England for himself and thirty persons in his retinue, and three merchants; while in August, 1359, he had a safe conduct for himself and one hundred horsemen in his train. The same year, in October, he had a passport to France with twenty-four horsemen. In November, 1362, he had a safe conduct to the shrine of St. Thomas à Becket at Canterbury for himself and twelve horsemen. He had passports for himself and twelve horsemen in February, 1363, in March the same year, and in February, 1365. In July, 1365, he had a licence to send eight horsemen to Newcastle-on-Tyne with one hundred and twenty oxen, which he had sold to merchants in that city. In October, 1368, he had a passport for himself and twelve gentlemen on their way through England in pilgrimage to St. Amiens, in France. He was the last in the male line of the old Celtic Earls of Mar, having died in 1377, leaving no issue.

His only sister, Margaret, who had married William, first Earl of Douglas, then became Countess of Mar and Garioch in her own right. She had a son and a daughter to her husband, who died in 1384. He was succeeded by his son James, second Earl of Douglas, and also twelfth Earl of Mar and Garioch in right of his mother. Earl James, on the 27th of July, 1388, confirmed a grant of his father

William, to the monks of Melrose of the patronage of the parish church of Cavers. Thirteen days later he fell, leading the Scots at the battle of Otterburn. He having left no legitimate issue, his sister, Isabel, then succeeded to the Earldom of Mar and the Lordship of the Garioch, her mother's heritage, and she also succeeded to the unentailed lands of the House of Douglas.

This Isabel, Countess of Mar and Garioch in her own right, and also the owner of many other estates of wide extent, naturally became the victim of many intrigues. In short, a network of plots was woven around her. Margaret Stewart, Countess of Angus in her own right, the widow of Thomas, late Earl of Mar, Isabel's uncle, was an exceedingly active agent in these plots. She was a woman of great energy, and quite unscrupulous. In her youth she had a son to William, first Earl of Douglas—her brother-in-law. This natural son, her only child—George Douglas, was thus the Countess Isabel's illegitimate brother. The Countess of Angus (who, in virtue of her late husband, continued to take the style of Countess of Mar), in her passion for the aggrandisement of her only son, was ready to attempt anything. In 1389 she resigned the Earldom of Angus, with the Lordships of Abernethy and Bonkill, in favour of her son, George Douglas, which was confirmed by a charter of Robert II. Yet this lady was far from satisfied with the position of her son, the Earl of Angus. She still continued to make the utmost efforts to obtain settlements of the unentailed lands of the House of Douglas in favour of her son. Above all, she concentrated her longing eyes upon the wide territorial possessions of the Countess Isabel—the Earldoms of Mar and Garioch. Of course, George Douglas, now Earl of Angus, naturally seconded his mother's plots.

Isabel, Countess of Mar and Garioch, married Sir Malcolm Drummond, a brother of Annabella, Queen of Robert III. But there was no issue of the marriage. It appears that Drummond acted in concert with those who were interested in opposing and defeating the prospective claim of the Erskine family to the Earldom of Mar. Sir John Swinton married Margaret, Countess of Mar, after the death of her first husband, William, first Earl of Douglas; and she, too, became involved in the plots through the action of her second husband. On the 18th of March, 1391, Sir Thomas Erskine appeared before the King in a Parliament sitting at Scone, and addressed him thus:—" My Lord the King, it has come to my knowledge that there is a certain contract made between Sir Malcolm Drummond and Sir John Swinton upon the lands of the Earldom of Mar and the Lordship of the Garioch, of which Earldom and Lordship Isabel, the said Sir John Malcolm's wife, is the real and lawful heir, and failing of the heirs of her body, the half of the forementioned Earldom and Lordship pertains to my wife of right and heritage. Therefore I require you, for God's sake, as my Lord and my King, as lawful attorney to my said wife, that in case of any such contract to be made in prejudice of my said wife of that which ought of right and of law to pertain to her in fee and heritage, failing, the said Isabel, as is before said, that ye grant no confirmation thereupon contrary to the common law of the country and of my wife's right." To this the King replied, " that he thought the request was reasonable," and promised that he would do nothing to prejudice Sir Thomas's wife's right or his own. Sir Thomas Erskine had a notary public present, who formally executed an instrument recording the requisition and the engagment.

Again, on the 22nd of November, 1395, Robert III, declares in a letter to Sir Thomas Erskine that he will not receive any resignation or alienation which Isabel Douglas, Countess of Mar and Garioch, may wish to make of these Earldoms in prejudice of the true heirs, namely— the heirs of the said Thomas Erskine.

Two years later, the weak King, Robert III., lent his

aid to the great plotter, Margaret Stewart, ex-Countess of Mar and Countess of Angus, mentioned before. At Edinburgh, on the 24th of May, 1397, the King entered into an indenture with "Margaret, Countess of Mar and Angus, undertaking that, in consideration of George Douglas, her son, Lord of Angus, shall marry one of the King's daughters, then the King shall give him all the lands of the Earldom of Angus in free regality, heritable to the said George and his daughter, and to the longest liver of them and to their male heirs. And also our Lord the King shall confirm, approve, and ratify under his great seal all gifts, settings, and consignations made or to be made by Isabel, Countess of Mar, to the said George, her brother, of all the lands, rents, and possessions which she has, or may have, within the kingdom of Scotland; and also our Lord the King shall receive all resignations that the said Isabel likes to make, and with all haste he shall give charter and heritable possession to the said George and his daughter. Also the King truly promises not to receive any resignations made by the Countess Isabel of any lands, rents, or possessions, nor give confirmation, but only to the use and profit of the said George her brother," even although he has given any letter to Sir Thomas Erskine. Such was the state of the question of the Earldom of Mar and Garioch towards the close of the fourteenth century. But startling surprises were not far off.

In 1390, Robert III. granted to his brother-in-law, Sir Malcolm Drummond, Lord of Mar in right of his wife, the Countess Isabel, a licence to erect a tower on the lands of Castletown of Braemar. The King, in 1393, granted to Sir Malcolm by charter, forty pounds sterling per annum from the great custom of Aberdeen, until the King shall give him forty pounds worth of lands.

When Sir Malcolm was residing in his own castle in 1402, he was attacked by a band of ruffians, instigated by Alexander Stewart (the hero of Harlaw), overpowered, and thrown into a dungeon, where the cruel treatment he received ended in his death. Tytler, the historian, says—"There seems to have been little doubt that the successful wooer and the assassin of Drummond was one and the same person."

After the murder of her husband, Isabel was residing at the castle of Kildrummy, the chief seat of the Earldom of Mar, a widow, childless, and quite unprotected. In the summer of 1404, Alexander Stewart, a leader of broken men and the terror of the country, swooped down upon the castle and his victim. He captured the Countess's castle, and seized her person, and then extorted from her under a covenant of future marriage a charter, dated the 12th of August, 1404, by which she gifted to Alexander Stewart the Earldoms of Mar and Garioch, and all the other lands and superiorities belonging to her by hereditary right. The immediate effect of this charter was to cut off the Erskines, and others who had hopes of succeeding to the Earldom of Mar.

This daring outrage upon the Countess's person and property and extortion of the charter were too flagrant to stand altogether unredressed. But Stewart's relation to the Royal Family, being a natural son of the late Alexander Stewart, Earl of Buchan, the "Wolf of Badenoch," and the power of his uncle, the Duke of Albany, appears to have saved him from any actual punishment. Accordingly a compromise was arranged, by which the interests of other parties were secured. The matter assumed a dramatic form.

On the 9th of September, 1404, the Countess, accompanied by Alexander, Bishop of Ross; Sir Andrew Leslie, Walter Ogilvie, and other gentlemen of the district, and a multitude of the people, proceeded to a meadow outside the great gate of Kildrummy Castle. And then Alexander Stewart came out of the castle, advancing to where the Countess stood, and in the presence of the assemblage delivered over to her the castle with its charters, the silver vessels, and other jewels, and everything therein, placing the keys in her hands, to dispose of the castle as no longer under any constraint. This having been done, the Countess, holding the keys in her hands, then made choice of Alexander Stewart as her husband before all the people; and gave him in free marriage the Castle and the Earldoms of Mar and Garioch, and all the lands which she possessed. Immediately after this interesting ceremony the charter of the 12th of August was renounced by Alexander Stewart in favour of the Countess, to be reconveyed by her to him, which was done by a similar charter of the 9th of December; but with reservation to the longest liver. and ultimate destination in case of there being no issue from the marriage, to Isabel's heirs. This was confirmed by a charter of Robert III. on the 21st of January, 1405, under the Great Seal. Thus Alexander Stewart became Earl of Mar.

The Countess Isabel, the unhappy victim of many intrigues, and such violence as indicated above, died about three years after her marriage, and left no issue by Alexander Stewart. But he continued to hold the Earldom, and endeavoured to secure the succession to his natural son, Thomas Stewart.

The new Earl of Mar lived in grand style, and often travelled abroad. On the 3rd of September, 1406, John Stele and William Stewinson, chaplains of the Earl of Mar, had a safe conduct till Easter to pass to and from Bruges, in connection with Mar's affairs. In April, 1406, Henry IV. granted letters of safe conduct to Alexander, Earl of Mar, and Lord of the Garioch, with forty persons in his train, to go into England to a passage-of-arms with Edmund, Earl of Kent, in the presence of the King. The same year, on the 5th of September, he had another safe conduct for himself and seventy persons for a passage-of-arms with the Earl of Kent. He had also adventures in France.

On the 24th of December, 1409, Alexander, Earl of Mar and Garioch, granted a charter to Alexander Forbes of Brux, conveying to him the lands of Glencoure and the Orde, in the lordship of Strathdon, for one penny yearly at the south door of the Church of Invernochty. In 1410 the Earl granted a charter to Sir Alexander Irvine of Drum of the lands of Davachindore and Fidlemouth, in the Earldom of Mar, for one penny yearly at the south door of the Parish Church.

It appears that Sir Alexander Irvine was one of the Scottish knights who took part in the exploits of the Earl of Mar at the siege and conflicts of Liege in 1408. On this occasion the cause for which Mar fought was to place a worthless man in a bishop's see against the majority of the people.

SECTION III.

ALEXANDER STEWART, EARL OF MAR—BATTLE OF HARLAW—CLAIM OF LORD ERSKINE TO THE EARLDOM—HIS PROCEEDINGS.

AFTER Alexander Stewart became Earl of Mar, he was an active supporter of his uncle, the Duke of Albany, who was then Regent of Scotland. He was a man of great energy, but a very unscrupulous character, and never relinquished the characteristics of his original aims as a leader of broken men upon the hills. This appeared in his restless visits to England and France with a train of armed retainers, ready to engage in any daring exploit.

In 1411, the family quarrel between Donald, Lord of the Isles, and the Duke of Albany came to a crisis, solely owing to the determination of the latter to ignore the lawful claim of Donald, Lord of the Isles, to the Earldom of Ross, in right of his wife, Margaret Leslie. Legally and morally, Albany, the grasping Regent of Scotland, was on the wrong side in this family quarrel, and desired to aggrandise his own family in defiance of law and justice. He wanted the Earldom of Ross for his own son—the Earl of Buchan. Albany found an admirable agent for his purpose in the person of his nephew—Alexander Stewart, Earl of Mar; and the Regent entered into a bond with him for mutual support, and commissioned Mar to lead the local army of the counties of Aberdeen, Kincardine, and Forfar, and the citizens of the burghs of Aberdeen and Dundee. Indeed, Mar was recognised as an able and brave leader of men.

All hope of a peaceful settlement of the quarrel having vanished, at last the Lord of the Isles resolved to try issues with the Regent, and enforce his right to the Earldom of Ross by the sword. He mustered his vassals and followers, and at the head of about six thousand men he crossed the water to the mainland. He marched through the Earldom of Ross, in which he received much support, and greatly increased the strength of his army. Proceeding southward, he advanced through Moray, crossed the Spey, and continued his advance through Banffshire and the higher grounds of Strathbogie and the Garioch, and pitched his camp on the Hill of Benachie. There he posted his army, and awaited the attack of his adversary—the Regent Albany; but this grasping schemer had not the courage to face the man whom he had been the cause of bringing so far from home. It is said that Donald's army numbered ten thousand men. On the other side the Earl of Mar was at the head of the chief men and their followers of the three counties mentioned above, and a considerable number of the citizens of Aberdeen and Dundee. Although not quite so numerous as Donald's host, they were much better armed and equipped. The leading men of the north-east of Scotland were on the field—the Forbeses, the Irvines, the Burnetts, the Leslies, the Hays, the Gordons, Ogilvies, Leiths, and others; Robert Davidson, the provost of Aberdeen, and Sir James Scrimgeour, the hereditary constable of Dundee. The battle was fought on the 24th of July, 1411, upon a moor edging up the Hill of Benachie. The action was long and furiously contested, many fell on both sides, and night put an end to the desperate struggle. There was no great victory on either side, but Donald and his followers retreated, leaving a great number of slain men. Many of the Lowland barons and their followers, and the citizens of Aberdeen and Dundee, were slain on the field. Thus locally, the Battle of Harlaw was a great and important event, and was commemorated in an early ballad.

Yet no important event in Scottish history has been more strangely misinterpreted than the Battle of Harlaw. For it was entirely a personal and family quarrel in its origin, cause, and effect. It had not the slightest national or racial significance; it was a mere family quarrel from beginning to end, of which the Duke of Albany was the instigator. Further, the Duke of Albany failed to attain his aim, for Donald of the Isles retained possession of the Earldom of Ross, and his son Alexander succeeded him in 1420. In 1424 James I. granted a charter to Alexander, Lord of the Isles, confirming to him the right to the Earldom of Ross. On the 27th of May, 1425, when Murdoch, Duke of Albany, (the late Regent's son) was tried in the Castle of Stirling, and sentenced to be executed, Alexander, Earl of Ross and Lord of the Isles, was one of the jurymen on the trial. These facts speak for themselves, touching the cause and effect of the Battle of Harlaw.

The Earl of Mar was appointed Admiral of the Realm of Scotland. It appears that he attacked and despoiled English vessels at sea between Berwick and Newcastle. On the 16th of November, 1420, he entered into an agreement with Murdoch, Duke of Albany, and Governor of Scotland. In this bond, the earl, and his son, Sir Thomas Stewart, were bound always to act on the Governor's side before and against all men, except the King alone. The Governor bound himself to give the earl one-half of the profits of the Justiciary Courts of Aberdeen, Banff, and

Inverness. The Governor was to give his letters patent that he would stand by the earl—as the late Governor had done—in all disputes and quarrels. The Governor undertook to confirm the grant by the earl to his son, Sir Thomas Stewart, of the lands of Mar and Garioch, if the earl could show a charter by the King, confirming the lands of Mar and Garioch to himself and his heirs. The Governor would not consent to the marriage of his son and heir apparent, Walter Stewart, with the daughter of Sir Robert Erskine, without the consent and assent of the Earl of Mar. The Governor had given to the earl the profits of the lands of Badenoch, Urquhart, and Strathown, until they could be let to advantage, when the Governor was to receive one half of the profits, and the earl the other half for life.

Shortly after the return of James I., Mar resigned the Earldom into his hands, and on the 28th of May, 1426, the King granted a charter to his cousin, Alexander Stewart, and his natural son, Sir Thomas Stewart, of the Earldom of Mar, and the Lordship of the Garioch, to be held by him during his life, and after his death by Sir Thomas and his heirs lawfully begotten, whom failing, to revert to the Crown. On the 9th of January, 1427, James I. granted a charter to Alexander, Earl of Mar, of the lands of the Lordship of Badenoch, in the Sheriffdom of Inverness, during the period of his life. It seems doubtful, however, if he derived much profit from the Lordship of Badenoch. In 1431, Donald Balloch, a cousin of the Lord of the Isles, completely defeated the Earl of Mar in a pitched battle at Inverlochy, in Lochaber. About this time Mar was appointed by the King Lieutenant of the North.

The Earl of Mar had no legitimate children, and he made the utmost efforts to secure the succession of his natural son Sir Thomas to the Earldom. Sir Thomas married Margaret, Countess of Buchan, a daughter of Archibald, fourth Earl of Douglas, the widow of John, Earl of Buchan (the Regent Albany's son), and only an heir seemed necessary to render the succession to the Earldom of Mar secure. But the fates were against the Earl and his son. Sir Thomas Stewart died childless in the lifetime of his father; and on the death of Earl Alexander himself, in 1435, the King annexed the Earldom of Mar and the Lordship of the Garioch to the Crown. After his death, John of Clat, a canon of Brechin and Aberdeen, and prebendary of Cloveth, bequeathed a sum of money to celebrate a mass annually at the altar of St. Catherine in the Cathedral of Aberdeen, for the repose of the soul of Alexander, Earl of Mar.

James I. ignored the claim of Sir Robert Erskine, a son of Sir Thomas Erskine and Janet Keith, who was the nearest heir of Isabel, the late Countess of Mar and Garioch. Sir Robert was a determined though a prudent man, and he had no intention of tamely yielding to the royal will; yet he wisely refrained from remonstrating with James I. The chief aim of the policy of James I. was to reduce the power of the barons. In his short reign he annexed the Earldoms of Fife, Monteith, March, and Mar to the Crown.

In 1435 Sir Robert Erskine and his son and heir, Thomas Erskine, entered into a contract with Sir Alexander Forbes, afterwards first Lord Forbes, by which it was agreed that Sir Alexander should do all in his power to help Sir Robert Erskine and his son to obtain all their right of the Earldom of Mar and Lordship of the Garioch. And for his help, counsel, and trouble on their behalf, Sir Robert and his son undertook for themselves and their heirs to give Sir Alexander and his heirs the Lordship of Auchindor, with the patronage of the Church, the Buck, and Cabrach, and a half davach in free forest, lying within the Earldom of Mar and Sheriffdom of Aberdeen—granting a charter of these lands to him in fee and heritage within forty days after the recovery of the Earldom of Mar.

After the murder of James I. at Perth, in 1437, Sir Robert Erskine took the requisite legal steps in the usual form to secure his right of succession to the Earldom of Mar and Lordship of the Garioch. As a descendant from Ellen, the eldest daughter of Gratney, Earl of Mar, a sister of Donald, Earl of Mar and Regent of Scotland, Sir Robert Erskine maintained that after the death of the Countess Isabel, he was the nearest and lawful heir to the Earldom of Mar. In 1438 Sir Robert obtained two special retours of service, the first of which was dated the 22nd of April. The inquest was summoned and presided over by Sir Alexander Forbes, Sheriff-Depute of Aberdeen; and among the names of the jurors on the inquest were—Sir Alexander Irvine of Drum, Sir Gilbert Hay, a brother of the Lord High Constable of Scotland; Sir John Forbes and Sir William Forbes; Alexander Keith of Inverugie, Alexander Meldrum of Fyvie, and other twelve. These jurors, after making the usual inquiry, found that—" Isabel, Countess of Mar and Garioch, had died in the peace and faith of the King, vested and seized in the lands of the Earldom of Mar and Lordship of the Garioch; that her cousin, Sir Robert Erskine, was her nearest legitimate heir in the half of the said lands and lordship; that he is of lawful age; that the lands of the Earldom of Mar are held of the Crown by ward and relief, and the lands of the Lordship of Garioch in free regality; that the half lands of Mar are now in the hands of the King through the death of the late Alexander Stewart, Earl of Mar; and further, that the lands of the regality of Garioch are in the hands of Elizabeth, Countess of Buchan, wife of Sir Thomas Stewart." The second retour was dated the 16th of October, 1438, and was also presided over by Sir Alexander Forbes, Sheriff-Depute, and excepting five of the names, the jurors were those who had been on the first inquest. The finding and report of the jurors were similar to that of the first retour.

In virtue of these retours it appears that Sir Robert was infefted in the Earldom. Subsequently he assumed the title of Earl of Mar and Lord Erskine, under which he granted a number of charters to vassals of the Earldom. On the 26th of June, 1439, Robert, Earl of Mar and Lord Erskine, granted a charter to Sir Alexander Forbes of the half of the Lordship of Strathdee, in the Earldom of Mar. He was at once recognised as Earl of Mar in Aberdeen, as appears from an entry in the records of the city, dated the 28th of December, 1439, when he was made a free burgess and member of the guild, as "a noble and powerful Lord, Robert of Erskine, Earl of Mar and Lord Erskine." On the 10th of May, 1440, he granted a charter to Alexander Irvine of Drum, confirming to him the lands of Davachindore and of Fidlemouth, in the Earldom of Mar.

But the Government soon began a struggle with the Earl, which was protracted and tantalising. During the minority of James II. various arrangements were entered into between Lord Erskine and the Government, the drift of which was to delay a final settlement of his claim to the Earldom until the King attained his majority. At Stirling, on the 10th of August, 1440, it was agreed between the Government and Lord Erskine that the Castle of Kildrummy should be delivered to Lord Erskine and kept by him for the King's behoof until he be of age. Lord Erskine promised to lay his claims before the King and Parliament to be decided. In the meantime Lord Erskine was to receive all the rents of the half of the Earldom of Mar which he claimed. Whenever Erskine got possession of the Castle of Kildrummy he was to deliver up the Castle of Dumbarton to the King. It appears that Lord Erskine surrendered the Castle of Dumbarton to the King, but he was not put in possession of Kildrummy Castle.

On the 9th of August, 1442, Lord Erskine appeared before the King and council in Stirling Castle, and complained that Crichton, the Lord Chancellor, had refused to retour him to the Lordship of the Garioch, or put him in possession of the Castle of Kildrummy; he then protested that "he might and should be free to intromit, at his own hand, with the whole lands of Mar and Garioch." Accordingly, he immediately after besieged and took the Castle of Kildrummy, and the King then seized Erskine's Castle of Alloa.

James II., on the 12th of May, 1447, by letters patent, charged Lord Erskine and his son Thomas to deliver up the Castle of Kildrummy for the King's reception, when he visited these quarters of the kingdom, under the penalty of rebellion. In June, 1448, another agreement was made between Lord Erskine and the King and Council, by which Erskine undertook to deliver up the Castle of Kildrummy before the 3rd of July to anyone appointed by the King to keep it till the King attain his majority; and then to deliver it up to either of them whom Parliament found to have a right to it. The King and Council undertook that as soon as the Castle of Kildrummy was delivered up, the King should deliver up to Lord Erskine his Castle of Alloa, with all its furniture and warlike stores.

It appears, however, that the Government had not fulfilled the above conditions. For on the 4th of April, 1449, Sir Thomas Erskine, the eldest son of Lord Erskine, in the name and on behalf of his father and himself, appeared before the King and Parliament at Stirling, and declared that he was willing to fulfil the agreements between the King and his father and himself touching the lands of the Earldom of Mar and the Castle of Kildrummy, and to abide by the judgment of Parliament. He protested against the unjust detention of the revenues of the Earldom. On the 26th of January, 1450, Sir Thomas again appeared before the King and Parliament, and asked that justice should be done to his father touching the Earldom of Mar, which belonged to him by hereditary right, and was unjustly withheld from him by the King. To this the Lord Chancellor of Scotland replied that, by an Act of a General Council, it was enacted that until the King came of age he should possess all the lands and lordships in which his father died vested and seised; and that he was ready, "by his Privy Council, to hear the claim of Lord Erskine, as well as the claim of the King, to the Earldom."

SECTION IV.

LORDSHIP OF GARIOCH GRANTED TO THE QUEEN—DEATH OF ROBERT, EARL OF MAR AND LORD ERSKINE—EFFORTS OF THOMAS, LORD ERSKINE—HIS CLAIMS TO THE EARLDOM DECIDED IN A COURT IN ABERDEEN.

IN 1452 James II. granted the lordship of the Garioch to Mary of Gueldres, his Queen, by charter, for life. Sir William Leslie of Balquhain was Bailie of the Regality of Garioch, and he continued to act for the Queen in discharging the functions of this office. The Queen died on the 16th of November, 1463.

Robert, Earl of Mar, and Lord Erskine, died about the beginning of 1453. But his son, Sir Thomas, Lord Erskine continued to insist on his claim and right to the Earldom of Mar. At Edinburgh, on the 21st of March, 1453, Thomas, Lord Erskine, appeared before the King and the three estates of the realm, and presented a petition asking that justice should be done to him touching the lands of the Earldom of Mar and the Lordship of the Garioch. Then Sir William Crichton, Lord Chancellor of Scotland, rose and said that the King intended to be in the northern districts of his kingdom, soon after Whitsunday, and that he would there do justice to Lord Erskine. This promise was long in being fulfilled. It was four years afterwards ere the King and his Privy Council thought fit to do justice to the claim of Lord Erskine.

On the 15th of May, 1457, Lord Erskine's claim touching the Earldom of Mar came before a Justiciary Court, held in the Town Hall of Aberdeen, at which the King was present as prosecutor in his own cause, and Sir William Crichton, the Lord Chancellor, as his advocate. The record proceeds in the names of John, Lord Lindsay of the Byres, High Justiciary of Scotland north of the Forth, and of Walter Lindsay, acting on this occasion as Sheriff of Aberdeenshire on behalf of David, Earl of Crawford—the hereditary sheriff of the county, who was then a minor. A great assemblage of bishops, barons, and freeholders crowded the hall, among whom were George, Bishop of Brechin; John, Bishop of Moray; William, Earl Marischal; William, Earl of Erroll, the hereditary High Constable of Scotland; Alexander, Earl of Huntly; Robert, Lord Fleming; George, Lord Leslie; Sir John Ogilvie of Lintrathen; Sir Walter Ogilvie of Deskford: Sir William Leslie of Balquhain; Sir William Cranstoun of Corsbie; Sir Walter Stewart of Strathaven; William Moray of Tullibardine; Ninian Spot, comptroller of the Royal household, and many others.

The proceedings commenced by reading the summons issued by the King's Chancery to seven of the men who had been jurors on the inquest of 1438, commanding them to appear before the King and his councillors to answer for their error, and response in favour of the late Robert, Lord Erskine, to the Earldom of Mar in the Sheriffdom of Aberdeen. The names of these seven men were—James Skene of Skene, John Mowat of Loscragy, Andrew Buchan, Thomas Allardyce of Allardyce, Ranald Cheyne, Walter Barclay of Tolly, and John Scroggs. These men having appeared in the court, Lord Erskine appeared in person for his interest, and adduced evidence from written documents showing that the jurors had been guilty of no error in returning as they did. The seven men were then removed to a separate chamber, and the King, accompanied by the chief personages mentioned above, also went into this chamber, where the men were examined; while the body of the spectators remained in the hall.

John Scroggs was called first. After admitting that he was on the service and retour of 1438, he was asked what he knew about the late Countess Isabel, he replied that he had no personal knowledge of her. Asked in what degree of kin Robert, Lord Erskine, stood to Isabel, he answered that neither at the time of the inquest, nor since, had he known anything about the point at all. Asked whether any person on the inquest had objected to the tenor of the retour, and if so, how many, he replied that five persons had objected, of whom Gilbert Menzies and John Wans were two, but he could not recollect the names of the other three. He then asserted that "he and other persons on the inquest were seduced into acting as they did by the bland words and lies of John Haddington, and other counsel of Lord Erskine; but that he now clearly knew, on consideration of the letters and right of our Lord the King, that he and the other jurors had erred, and delivered an unjust award on the subject of the half of the lands of the Earldom of Mar; for which error he most humbly implored the King's pardon, throwing himself upon the King's mercy for the remission of his guilt.

James Skene of Skene was next called and examined on the preceding points. He said that he knew that the late King James was in possession of the Earldom of Mar after the death of Earl Alexander; but he added that if he had known of the charters, letters, and rights of the King as he did now, he would not have decided against the King's right as he did: that he was well aware that he and other jurors on the inquest had erred and rendered an unjust award, for which he besought the King's mercy and pardon.

Andrew Buchan, on being called and interrogated on the points premised, replied as Skene had done, and said that the late Thomas Stewart of Garioch had died vested and seised as of fee in the Earldom of Mar, and that Elizabeth, Countess of Buchan, his wife, had the third part of the lands of the Earldom as terce through her husband's death. Ranald Cheyne gave evidence similar to Buchan's; and Barclay of Tolly gave the same testimony as Skene and

Buchan did, and added that he was present and acting as a servant to Alexander, Lord Gordon, who personally delivered state possession, and hereditary seisin to Thomas Stewart of the lands of the Earldom of Mar. Although Thomas Allardyce of Allardyce and James Mowat of Loscragy were summoned and appeared in court, there is no record of their examination or evidence.

It appears that Lord Erskine was not permitted to cross-examine the evidence of the above witnesses. Indeed, it seems probable that he was not admitted into the chamber at all when the evidence was taken.

On the King and the lords returning from the chamber to the hall, Lord Erskine was called, and appeared in the presence of the King, bishops, barons, lords, and many freeholders of the Sheriffdom of Aberdeen and other Sheriffdoms. The Lord Chancellor then rose and said that Lord Erskine had repeatedly, in Parliament, demanded justice from the King, and that brieves of inquest should be given him from the Royal Chancery, and he now wanted to know what more Lord Erskine asked for in respect to the lands of the Earldom of Mar. Lord Erskine replied that he desired nothing more than a brieve of inquest, and execution and service, as on former occasions he had repeatedly stated.

The Lord Chancellor again rose and said:—" I, as Chancellor of our Lord the King here present, and on his part, grant to you the said brieve of inquest and execution thereof, and completion of justice in the said lands, so that you may have no just cause hereafter for complaint against our Lord the King, nor against me as Chancellor, on the ground of failure in the execution of justice." Lord Erskine immediately left the hall to advise with his counsel whether he should at once have the brieve served or not; and after consideration, he returned to the court and presented the brieve of inquest formerly obtained by him for its immediate execution.

The jurors of the inquest were immediately chosen and

impanelled, with the consent of Lord Erskine, and consisted of William, Earl of Erroll; Alexander, Lord Montgomery; John, Lord Lindsay of the Byres; George, Lord Leslie; Robert, Lord Fleming; Sir William Leslie of Balquhain; Sir Alexander Home of Home; Sir Walter Stewart of Strathaven; Sir John Ogilvie of Lintrathen; Sir Walter Ogilvie of Deskford; Walter Barclay of Tolly, Alexander Fraser of Philorth, Alexander Dunbar, James Skene of Skene, Andrew Buchan, Andrew Menzies, Ronald Cheyne, Richard Vans, David Dempster of Auchterless, John Scroggs, and Thomas Allardyce of Allardyce. Under the presidency of Walter Lindsay, Sheriff-Depute of Aberdeen, these jurors deliberated and reported.

Then Lord Erskine, with Archibald Stewart and Alexander Graham as his advocates, asked that the brieve of inquest should be publicly read, which was done. Thereupon he asserted "1. That the late Robert, Lord Erskine, his father, had died last vested and seised as of fee, at the peace and faith of our Lord the King, of the half of the Earldom of Mar. 2. That Thomas was the nearest and lawful heir of his father in the said lands, and that these lands were in the hands of the King, according to law, through the death of Robert, his father, and in consequence of the fact that he himself had not prosecuted his right for about four years."

To this the Lord Chancellor replied, in the name of the King—"That what Lord Erskine asserted in the first of the above points was contrary to the truth, for Robert, Lord Erskine, did not die vested and seised in the Earldom of Mar; as our Lord the King was vested in the said lands, and in lawful and peaceful possession of them at the time of the death of Robert, Lord Erskine, through the decease of the late King, his father. Touching the second point of inquest, though Lord Erskine was the nearest and lawful heir of his father, yet this was never the case in regard to the lands in question. Concerning the points, in whose hands the lands now are, the truth is that these lands are in the King's hands; as the late King died vested and in the lawful possession of them as his heritage and property, our Lord the present King received investiture and possession of them at the moment when he received his Royal crown, and thus held possession of them by the same right as his father. So the brieve sought by Lord Erskine could in no way be served. The Chancellor asserted that Lord Erskine stood in no degree of kinship whatever to Isabel, Countess of Mar; and that no person now alive knew if the late Robert, Lord Erskine, was in fact related to Isabel, and it was on such relationship that Robert based his right to the half of the Earldom. Therefore Thomas, Lord Erskine, could never obtain these lands, nor have lawful entry to them by a brieve of inquest, because after the death of Isabel, Thomas Stewart, Earl of Buchan, died vested and seised as of fee, at the peace and faith of the King, in these lands of the Earldom of Mar. That his widow, the Countess of Buchan, obtained the third part of the lands of the Earldom of Mar as her terce."

The Chancellor, continuing, asserted that the retour of service of 1438, which Robert, the late Lord Erskine, had obtained, could be of no validity, on account of the causes already stated. Consequently the seisin which followed upon this retour was quite invalid. On these grounds and many others, in the name of the King, the Lord Chancellor declared that Thomas, Lord Erskine, had no right to the lands of the Earldom of Mar, or any part of them.

Yet Erskine produced the Countess Isabel's charter of the 9th December, 1404, which was confirmed by Robert III., and offered various reasonings on his own behalf in connection with it. This was confronted by the charter of the 12th of August, 1404, which was extorted from Isabel, subsequently renounced by Alexander Stewart, and never confirmed. There was no question as to which of the charters was valid; but the King's side, of course, prevailed, and Lord Erskine's claim to the Earldom was rejected.

In 1459 the gross money rental of the Earldom of Mar was £396 10s, with thirty head of cattle, for each of which 5s was allowed, and two chalders and four bolls of "custom oats," for each of which 4d. was allowed.

James II. in 1459 granted the Earldom of Mar to his own youngest son, John, then an infant. He became a manly and promising prince. In 1475 John, Earl of Mar and Garioch, granted a charter to Duncan Forbes, son of Alexander Forbes of Brux, of the lands of Over Towy, Nether Towy, and Culfork, in the Earldom of Mar. In 1477 he ordered his bailies—William Leith of Bernis, and Alexander Abercromby, to give seisin of the lands of Johnstoun, in the regality of the Garioch, to Alexander Johnston, grandson and heir of Gilbert Johnston of Johnston, and to his wife, Agnes Glaster.

But somehow the Earl of Mar became obnoxious to the favourites of his brother—James III.; and Earl John was arrested and imprisoned in the Castle of Craigmillar, where it is said that he was bled to death. Earl John having died unmarried, and the Earldom lapsed to the Crown.

In 1482 James III. granted the Earldom to his brother, the Duke of Albany. But he was involved in a conspiracy against the Crown and the liberty of the nation; and when this became publicly known, he was forced to retire to England. Edward IV. of England died on the 9th of April, 1483, and this event and others which followed upset Albany's schemes. On the 24th of June a Parliament met at Edinburgh, to which the Duke of Albany and Earl of Mar was summoned to appear and answer to a charge of treason; as he failed to appear, his estates were forfeited to the Crown, and also the lands of his chief adherents. Albany crossed the English Channel, and settled in France. In 1485, he was killed by the splinter of a lance while looking on at a tournament in Paris. James III. then granted the Earldom of Mar to his third son, John, a mere boy; and he died at the age of 17. The Earldom again reverted to the Crown, and continued in its possession for a period of upward of 60 years, during which there were no Earls of Mar.

In 1504 James IV. granted to Sir Alexander Gordon of Midmar a five years' lease of the lands of Strathdee and Cromar, and appointed him bailie of these lands, and empowered him to hold courts and administer the law within these lands. In 1405 James IV. appointed William Forbes of Towie, Chamberlain of the lands and Lordships of Mar and Garioch, and empowered him to collect the King's rents and profit of these lands and make account thereof, and to hold Chamberlain's courts. In the following year Forbes was made bailie within the lands and bounds of Mar and Garioch, "which he has in take of the King's highness, he making account in the Exchequer of the escheats thereof, to continue for three years and longer during the King's will."

But large portions of the lands of the Earldom were from time to time granted to favourite vassals of the Crown. Alexander Elphinstone, son and heir apparent of Sir John Elphinstone of Elphinstone, and his wife Elizabeth Berlay, the Queen's servant, who had come to Scotland with the intention of residing there all the days of her life, received a charter from James IV., in 1507, of the lands of Invernochty, Ballebeg, with the mill, meadow, woods, and glens of Glennochty, Invernethy, Ledmakcy, Culquhony, and Culquhary, in Strathdon; Mekle Migvie, Easter Migvie, Tillypronie, Blalok, and Correcreif, in Cromar, and in the Earldom of Mar; and the lands of Duncanston, Glandirston, Rochmureall, and Tillefoure, in the Lordship of the Garioch, which were all to be erected into the barony of Invernochty. The same year the King granted another charter to Alexander Elphinstone and his wife of the above lands, and adding the lands of Skellatar, with the Forest of Corgarf;

the lands of Fenclost, Bolquham, and Balnabooth, in Glenbucket; Balnabooth, in Kilbethok; Ballintamore, &c., with the Forest of Badenyone and Kilvalauch; Easter Clova, with Corrykeynsane; Contelauch, with Braidshaw, and the east half of Glenlos; Kinclune, in the Lordship of Strathdon, which was then to be united to the barony of Invernochty, in exchange for the lands in Cromar and those in the Lordship of the Garioch mentioned before. Elphinstone and his wife received from the King several other charters of lands in the Earldom of Mar; and in 1510 James IV. granted to him and his heirs the barony, town, and the Castle of Kildrummy.

Alexander Elphinstone in 1410 was created a Lord of Parliament under the title of Lord Elphinstone.

SECTION V.

JAMES STEWART, EARL OF MAR—THE EARLDOM OF MAR AND LORDSHIP OF GARIOCH RESTORED TO JOHN, LORD ERSKINE.

QUEEN MARY granted to her natural brother, James Stewart, Prior of St. Andrews, what remained of the lands of the Earldom of Mar in the hands of the Crown, and on the 7th of February, 1562, created him Earl of Mar. For a short time he was called Earl of Mar. Afterward, however, the Queen became aware of the claim of the Erskine family to this Earldom and Lordship of the Garioch. Accordingly she resolved to restore them to the legitimate heirs, who were then represented by John, sixth Lord Erskine.

The first requisite to restoration was to establish Lord Erskine's status as heir of the last legitimate holder of the Earldom of Mar. This was done in the usual way by a retour of service upon a brieve issued from the Royal Chancery, which was addressed to the Sheriffs of the counties of Aberdeen, Stirling, and Clackmannan, assembled in the Town Hall of Edinburgh. The inquest under the presidency of these sheriffs was held on the 5th of May, 1565; and among the fifteen jurors who gave the verdict were the following: David, Earl of Crawford; Sir James Douglas of Drumlanrig; Patrick, Lord Lindsay of the Byres; James Stirling of Keir, John Grant of Freuchie, John Home of Blackadder, James Cockburn of Stirling; and Robert Drummond of Carnock. The verdict of the jurors was that Robert, late Earl of Mar and Garioch, and Lord Erskine—grandfather of Alexander, Lord Erskine, and great grandfather of John now Lord Erskine—had died in the peace and faith of James II., and that John, now Lord Erskine, was the legitimate and nearest heir of the late Robert, Earl of Mar and Garioch.

Lord Erskine's status having been established as heir to Earl Robert, on the 23rd of June, 1565, Queen Mary granted a charter under the Great Seal, which stated that— Isabel Douglas, Countess of Mar and Garioch, having died without issue, and the late Robert, Lord Erskine, having been duly served as the nearest and lawful heir of the Countess Isabel in the Earldom of Mar and Lordship of the Garioch—John, now Lord Erskine, who was served as nearest and lawful heir to the late Robert, Lord Erskine, the heir of the Countess Isabel, had an undoubted hereditary right to the Earldom of Mar and Lordship of Garioch, notwithstanding that his predecessors were debarred from the possession of them; therefore granting to John, Lord Erskine, his heirs and assignees, the Earldom of Mar and the lands of the Lordship and Regality of the Garioch. The precept for the infeftment was issued on the 24th of June, the day after the charter. Thus John, Lord Erskine, became Ninteenth Earl of Mar.

Among the lands specified in the charter as being in the Earldom of Mar are Strathdon, Strathdee, Braemar, and Cromar, being portions of the Earldom then in the hands of the Crown. But seeing that the barony and Castle of Kildrummy, the chief seat of the Earldom, had been alienated by the Crown, as before indicated, the Manor of Migvie was declared to be a proper place for the infeftment in the Earldom of Mar, while the old castle of Dunnideer was to serve the same purpose for the Lordship and Regality of the Garioch. The Earl immediately recovered possession of the lands still in the hands of the Crown, but many years elapsed ere the other lands of the Earldom of Mar could be recovered, and large portions of them were never recovered.

On the 27th of June, 1565, John, Earl of Mar, signed an agreement between himself and Robert Stewart, a natural son of James V., and Abbot of Holyrood, in which the Earl promised that he would never claim any right to the lands of Cabrach, the lands and barony of Cluny, and the lands of Logy and Dawane, parts of the Earldom of Mar, granted by the Queen to her half-brother, Robert, usually styled Lord Robert.

John, Earl of Mar, was appointed guardian of the infant King, James VI. The charter restoring to him the Earldom was ratified by an Act of Parliament on the 19th of April, 1567.

He married Annabella, a daughter of Sir William Murray of Tullibardine, by whom he had issue.

On the death of the Regent Lennox in 1571, the Earl of Mar was elected Regent of Scotland. The Regency of Mar was of short duration. He died on the 28th of October, 1572.

He was succeeded by his son, John, Twentieth Earl of Mar, and seventh Lord Erskine. This Earl was a man of great energy and ability; and he made determined and prolonged efforts to recover the lands of the Earldom. He was a supporter of the Regent Morton; and he entered into a bond with the party of the Barons who were opposed to the Duke of Lennox and Sir James Stewart, Earl of Arran— the King's favourites. At length the plot against the

King's favourites was ripe for execution. The King was very fond of hunting, and on the 22nd of August, 1582, his Majesty by invitation proceeding to the grounds of Ruthven Castle, in the neighbourhood of Perth, to enjoy his favourite amusement. When the sport of the day was concluded, he went to the Castle of Ruthven as the welcome guest of the Earl of Gowrie. Everything had passed off in the most pleasing style, and his Majesty at last retired to rest. The following morning, when the King arose and looked abroad, he was greatly alarmed by the throng of armed men around the castle ; and on wishing to depart, he discovered that he was a prisoner. The Earl of Arran was immediately seized and imprisoned, and the Duke of Lennox was warned to leave the country without delay. This exploit is known in history as " the Raid of Ruthven."

The King was permitted to step about, although he was attended by a body of well-armed men, to preserve his royal person from danger. In a few days he was removed to Stirling, and in October he was conveyed to Edinburgh. A Parliament was then held at Edinburgh, on the 19th of October, and an Act of Indemnity—or, rather, a vote of thanks—to the chief actors in the enterprise was passed. This was a game which parties of the Scottish Barons often played, with varying success.

Despite the vigilance of his keepers, the young King contrived to escape in the end of June, 1583, and threw himself into the Castle of St. Andrews. Soon after, the power of the Ruthven party was terminated. The King issued a proclamation on the 30th of July, touching " the Raid of Ruthven," and announced that he had resumed his independent authority. Referring to the raid, he expressed his willingness to forget the offence and grant forgiveness to all concerned in it, if they should timeously profess their penitence ; and for a time several of the Barons implicated in the raid continued members of the Privy Council. But it so happened that on the 23rd of August the Earl of

Arran reappeared in the council, and soon resumed his influence and power in the Government. Indeed he instigated the young King to prosecute to the utmost all those concerned in "the Raid of Ruthven," and at last, on the 31st of March, 1584, it was denounced as "high treason." By this time, a number of those implicated in it had been tried, one by one or collectively, and sentenced to banishment or imprisonment, and disgrace.

But the hatred of Arran's rule had become general, and a new plot, sanctioned by a bond, was formed against him, in which the Earls of Mar, Angus, and Gowrie, Lord Lindsay, the Master of Glamis, Claud Hamilton, John Hamilton, and others were associated. They resolved to seize Stirling Castle, and then raise an insurrection. On the 10th of April, the Earl of Mar and the Master of Glamis, with a strong body of their followers, captured Stirling Castle. But on the 15th of April the Earl of Gowrie was arrested by Colonel Stewart at Dundee, and immediately conveyed to Edinburgh. This somewhat disconcerted the insurgent barons. At the same time the Earl of Arran, with a strong force, advanced against them; and on the 24th of April they fled from Stirling, leaving a garrison of only 25 men in the castle. The following day a royal proclamation was issued for the pursuit and capture—dead or alive—of the Earls of Mar and Angus, the Master of Glamis, and other rebels; but they escaped by Lanark to Kelso, and crossed the Border into England. When the King and his army appeared before Stirling Castle, the small garrison left by the Barons surrendered, and on the 28th of April their captain and other three were hanged.

On the 2nd of May, 1584, the Earl of Gowrie was tried for treason in Stirling Castle by a jury of his peers, including the Earls of Argyll, Arran, Crawford, and others. He was convicted and beheaded the same day beneath the castle wall. The same month an act of Parliament was passed for disinheriting all his posterity; and in August an Act of

Forfeiture was passed between the Countess of Gowrie. From May, 1584, till midsummer, 1585, the Earl of Arran was the supreme ruler of Scotland. His policy was clearly manifested in the two short sessions of what is known as the "running Parliament," and the proceedings of the Privy Council during the brief period of his sway—in which a series of extremely despotic acts were passed.

This action and reaction at short intervals, always issuing in sudden and unexpected changes at the centre of authority, is a striking characteristic of Scottish history. Lord Maxwell had been for several generations the leading local personage in Dumfries and its neighbourhood; and he had frequently held the office of Warden of the Western March. On the 29th of April, 1581, John, Lord Maxwell, was appointed to this office by the King and Council. He was a supporter of Lennox and Arran, and immediately after the execution of Morton, the regent, Maxwell was created Earl of Morton. The new-made Earl was at feud with John Johnston of Johnston, a powerful Border laird, and formerly a Warden of the Western March; and, on the 26th of May, 1582, a royal proclamation ordered them not to appear with their armed followers in Edinburgh— "to a day of law appointed to be held on the last day of May." On the 19th of November the Earl of Morton was deprived of the Wardenship of the Western March, while his rival Johnston was appointed to the office. Subsequently, the Earl of Morton was charged with many misdemeanours, and at last denounced as a rebel. In the winter of 1584, he appeared as a leader of a Border revolt against Arran's Government; and in April a muster of the loyal vassals of the Crown was ordered to proceed against him; while the gift to him of the Earldom of Morton was revoked. Therefore he was at war with the King and his Government.

Maxwell had 1000 armed men in the field. The banished Earls of Mar and Angus and other lords at once

saw their opportunity, and joined Maxwell. In the
beginning of November, 1585, they returned, and having
mustered their adherents, met Maxwell at Selkirk. Thence
they marched on Stirling with a force of 8000 men. The
King and Arran were in Stirling when the earls and lords
appeared before it. Arran immediately fled towards the
Highlands, while the King, notwithstanding all his craft,
had no alternative but to receive the proffered homage of
his rebellious barons, and pardon them.

Thus the forfeitures of the Earls of Mar, and Angus and
other lords were revoked, and their lands and titles restored
to them. Subsequently the Earl of Mar acted with the
Catholic Earls—Huntly, Crawford, Erroll, Angus, and
others.

Touching the recovery of the alienated lands of the
Earldom of Mar and Lordship of Garioch, Earl John took
the first important step in the year 1587, when he presented
a supplication to the King and Parliament, narrating that
Isabel Douglas, Countess of Mar, having been lawfully
infeft at the time of her death in the Earldom of Mar and
Lordship of Garioch, holding immediately from the King's
predecessors; and that the late Robert, Earl of Mar and
Lord Erskine, having been served heir to Isabel, Countess
of Mar; and that John, Lord Erskine and Earl of Mar, the
petitioner's father, having been lawfully retoured as heir to
the Earl Robert, therefore John, now Earl of Mar, was heir
by progress to the Countess Isabel, and heritably entitled
to the possession of the Earldom and its territories, although
his ancestors had been "wrongfully debarred from the
possession of the lands of the said Earldom and Lordship,
partly by the troubles which occurred and intervened, and
partly from the iniquity of the time and stifling of the
ordinary course of justice by the partial dealing of such
persons as had the Government of our Sovereign Lord's
predecessors and realm, and offices for the time," notwithstanding the frequent protests of his predecessors in

Parliament and Council. "And seeing for the said Earl's better security, and that his highness' dearest mother's good intention may take better effect toward the possession of the said lands, it is necessary that he should be served heir to his predecessor who died last vested and seised in the said Earldom and Lordship, and that a sufficient right of action be established in his person and his heirs for recovering these lands, and the possession thereof, notwithstanding the length of time which has intervened—considering that by the laws and customs of the realm the right of blood nor any heritable title falls under prescription, nor is taken away by whatsoever length of time or lack of possession." Therefore the Earl desired the King and Parliament to examine the rights and evidence under which the Countess Isabel, Robert, Earl of Mar, and his father, John, Earl of Mar, held the Earldom.

The above statement and points being heard, seen, and considered by the King and Parliament, and after careful examination had been made, the King and the three Estates of Parliament found the rights above specified to be lawful, valid, and sufficient to prove the points of the supplication, and ratified, approved, and confirmed the same. "And declares the aforesaid rights to have as great force and effect in the person of John, Earl of Mar, as the same had or might have in the person of the late Countess, Isabel Douglas, or the late Robert, Earl of Mar and Lord Erskine, her heir, and that he should have full right as heir by progress to all the lands in which they died vested, seised, and retoured . . . notwithstanding any exception of prescription or lack of possession that may be alleged to the contrary. Always without prejudice to all other lawful defences competent to the parties having interest.

This Act was passed on the 29th of July, 1587. On that day the master of Elphinstone, in name and behalf of his father, Robert, Lord Elphinstone, appeared before the King and Parliament and protested that this Act in favour of John, Earl of Mar, touching the Earldom of Mar and Lordship of the Garioch, should not hurt or prejudice Lord Elphinstone in his possession of the lands and Lordship of Kildrummy.

The same day, George, Earl of Huntly, Lord of Gordon and of Badenoch, and Lieutenant of the North, appeared in the presence of the King and Parliament, and protested that this Act in favour of John, Earl of Mar and the Lordship of Garioch, should be no hurt or prejudice to him or his friends touching their rights and titles to whatsoever lands within this Earldom of Mar and Lordship of Garioch: and that they should be permitted to adduce reasons and defences, whensoever they or their successors happened to be called upon touching their rights of their lands and possessions.

SECTION VI.

John, Twentieth Earl of Mar—Decreet of Ranking of the Peers—John, Twenty-First Earl.

EARL JOHN having obtained great and exceptional powers, as indicated in the preceding section, in 1593 he commenced proceedings in the Court of Session against William Forbes of Corse, the representative of his great-grandfather, Patrick Forbes, a younger son of the second Lord Forbes to whom the lands of Corse and Kincraigie were granted, by charter of feu-farm to be held of the Crown, by James III., in 1482. Mar called for this charter to be reduced and annulled, and the right to the lands declared to belong to him. He qualified his claim as lawful heir to the Countess Isabel in the lands of Strathdee and Braemar, in which the lands in question lay. The court sat on the 28th of January, 1593, and Mr. John Preston of Fentonbarns; Mr. Thomas Craig, the well-known feudal lawyer; and Mr. John Nicholson appeared as counsel for the Earl of Mar; and Mr. John Russel, and Sir John Skene of Currihill, a distinguished lawyer, and afterwards a judge of the Court of Session, appeared for Forbes. The matter was entered into, and the court disallowed Forbes's defences, and admitted the Earl's reasons. Mar, however, refrained from further prosecution of the case at that time.

But he revived the process in 1620. William Forbes of Corse was then dead, and the suit was renewed against Patrick Forbes, his son and heir, the highly esteemed and amiable Bishop of Aberdeen. The case was ably presented and debated on both sides. The final judgment in Mar's favour was given on the 23rd of June, 1621. This decision was founded upon the ground that neither James III., nor his predecessors and successors had any right of property in the Earldom of Mar subsequently to the charter of Robert III., dated the 21st of January, 1405, which confirmed Isabel's charter of the 9th of December, 1404.

The Earl of Mar next directed his attention to the recovery of Kildrummy, originally the chief seat of the Earldom. Proceedings against Lord Elphinstone and his son, the Master of Elphinstone, whose ancestors (as I have shown before) had been in possession of Kildrummy for 110 years, were commenced by summons issued in 1621. It was a great and complicated case, and it caused much alarm in the north-east of Scotland and in other quarters of the kingdom. All those directly interested in opposition to the Earl of Mar's claim, joined with the Elphinstones in this case. The process continued for four years, and the Earl of Mar was represented by Mr. Thomas Hope, Mr. Andrew Ayton, and Mr. Thomas Nicolson; while Lord Elphinstone's counsel was Mr. Lewis Stewart, a very able lawyer; and Mr. James Oliphant, advocate-Depute, with His Majesty's special warrant for His Majesty's interest in the matter.

The King's interest was alleged on five points, namely—any right that he might pretend to the lands of Kildrummy as part of the Earldom of Mar and Lordship of Garioch; in his character as apparent heir to Alexander Stewart,

Earl of Mar, or his son Thomas; as heir of blood to any of the Kings, his predecessors; as pretending right as heir of provision to Alexander, Earl of Mar; and, lastly, as having right thereto by bastary, last heir, or otherwise. The counsel for the parties in the case were heard at length, and point after point was ably argued and debated on both sides. The final decision was delivered on the 1st of July, 1626, by which the lands and estates of Kildrummy were declared to belong to John, Earl of Mar by heritable right from Sir Robert Erskine, the legitimate heir of Isabel, Countess of Mar and Garioch.

After this decision, Lord Elphinstone and the Master of Elphinstone agreed to an arrangement whereby John, Earl of Mar, undertook to pay to them 48,000 merks, on receipt of which the Elphinstones should ratify the terms of reduction, and renounced all right to the castle and lands of Kildrummy.

There were, however, many other estates and rights of superiority which had been alienated from the Earldom of Mar and Lordship of Garioch by preceding Kings of Scotland, and also by crown vassals. The Earl, therefore, pushed on proceedings for the recovery of these possessions and rights. As he had succeeded so far, he resolved to widen the scope of his claims. He now procured five general retours by which he was served nearest and lawful heir, on the 22nd of July, 1628, to Donald, Grateny, Donald, and Thomas, Earls of Mar of the old Celtic line. Having thus established his status on the widest basis, he was fully prepared for legal action.

Accordingly, the process which ensued embraced prosecutions against upwards of 150 proprietors in possession of lands or superiorities within the Earldom of Mar and the Lordship of the Garioch, and amongst these may be mentioned—the Earls of Crawford, Kinghorn, and Earl Marischal; Lord Forbes, the Master of Forbes; Lord Deskford, and Lord Wemyss; Irvine of Drum, Burnett of

Leys, Leslie of Balquhain ; Scrymgeour of Dudhope, the heriditary constable of Dundee ; many Gordons, Forbeses, Leslies, Leiths, and many other persons of note, some of whom were resident in France, Germany, Holland, Poland, Denmark, Sweden, and Ireland. These persons were called upon to produce their charters of possession either from the Erskines up to Robert, Lord Erskine and Earl of Mar ; or from Isabel, Countess of Mar: or Margaret, Countess of Mar ; or Thomas, Earl of Mar ; or Donald, Earl of Mar ; or Gratney, Earl of Mar ; or Donald, Earl of Mar. All these were to be reduced, so far as the lands specified were parts and dependencies of the Earldom of Mar.

It is no wonder that there was a great stirring up of rights and claims, much anxious searchings in the massive iron chests, with their complicated locks and secret drawers which were the repositories of the charters in the old Scottish castles and towers. Some of those involved in the process had possessed their lands for centuries, and many for several generations. A considerable number succeeded in proving their right to the property in question, or to the superiority and property both ; but in the majority of cases the superiority was found to belong to the Earl of Mar. In a few cases the Earl withdrew his claim. The interest of these cases consisted in the application of the laws of feudal tenure.

Earl John held the office of Lord Treasurer of Scotland from 1615 to 1630. He died on the 17th of December, 1635, at the age of seventy-seven. Three months after his death, the final decision in the above processes of reductions was given. He was succeeded by his son John, twenty-first Earl of Mar, and eighth Lord Erskine. The Earl married Christian Hay, a daughter of Francis, Earl of Erroll, and had issue. The fortune and influence of the family had reached the zenith in his time.

It was this Earl who commenced a series of protests for higher precedence in the roll of Peers. This was a point

Earls of Mar. 61

very highly valued by the nobles of Scotland, as is manifest in the records of Parliament. At the opening of almost every session for upward of a century a number of Earls and Lords protested regarding the precedency of their names and titles on the rolls of Parliament. Bitter contentions arose between many of the Scottish Peers touching their precedency; and in 1587, Parliament issued an Order, intended to allay these feelings, which had no effect. James VI. issued a Royal Commission under the Privy Seal in 1605, for examining and settling the disputed questions of precedency among the peers. Among the names of the commissioners for " Ranking the Nobility" were the following:—John Graham, Earl of Montrose, who held the office of Lord High Chancellor from the 15th of January, 1599 to 1604; Francis Hay, Earl of Erroll; George, Earl Marischal; Alexander Seton, president of the Court of Session in 1593—created Lord Fyvie on the 4th of March, 1598, and Earl of Dunfermline on the 4th of March, 1606, and appointed Lord High Chancellor in 1604; Lord Elphinstone, Sir Thomas Hamilton of Monkland, a Lord of Session in 1592, and subsequently Lord President—created Earl of Haddington in 1619, he was an able lawyer and a notable antiquary; Sir David Lindsay, the Lord Lyon King of Arms; Sir John Skene, a Lord of Session, and Keeper of the Public Records, and a few others.

These commissioners were empowered to call before them the whole of the Peers of the kingdom, and in accordance with the documents and evidence laid before them to determine every man's rank and place. Accordingly the commissioners summoned the Peers by name to appear and adduce whatever evidence they could, in the form of writs and documents and oral evidence, touching their claims of precedency, "to be seen and considered by the commissioners, and to hear and see their ranks and places of priority and precedency appointed and set down to them according to the antiquity of their productions, and that which should be verified in their presence." The ranking thus to be settled was to stand in force in each instance "until a decreet before the ordinary judge be recovered and obtained." Most of the Peers appeared before the commissioners personally or by counsel, and after the evidence was produced "at diverse meetings, and very carefully sighted, examined, and considered by the Commissioners," they issued their decreet on the 5th of March, 1606. But the ranking of the decreet was in no case final, being open to reductions before the Court of Session by aggrieved parties. Naturally the decreet was not satisfactory to all the nobility of Scotland. As a matter of fact it was a somewhat hasty attempt to settle a series of rather difficult historic questions associated with personal titles, family interests, and hereditary rights. Nevertheless the Decreet of Ranking and the Schedule of Evidence, upon which the precedency were based, are important historical documents; and with the corrections made upon it by the decisions of the Court of Session, and the additions made to it by the creation of new peers between 1606 and 1707, it forms what has been called the Union Roll of the Scottish Peerage.

According to the ranking of 1606, the Earl of Angus was placed first. Argyle second, not on the ground of the date of the Earldom, which was 1457, but because he held the hereditary office of Master of the Household and Justiciary-General. The Earl of Crawford was ranked third on the roll. The Earl of Erroll, the hereditary Lord High Constable of Scotland, was placed fourth. His office in Parliament as constable was to keep order and guard outside the walls of the House. Earl Marischal was ranked fifth; his office as Marischal was next in grade to the High Constable. The Earl of Sutherland stood sixth on the roll; his ancestor having been created Earl in 1347. The Earl appeared before the commissioners, and produced a charter of David II. to William, Earl of Sutherland, and Margaret his wife, the "King's sister." John, Earl of Mar, adduced evidence before the commissioners commencing with the charter of Isabel, Countess of Mar and Garioch, of 9th December, 1404, and concluded with an extract of the retours of 1589; he was placed seventh on the roll.

But his son John, Earl of Mar, was not satisfied with his place on the roll. In 1639 he protested in Parliament for higher precedency than that assigned to him by the Decree of Ranking in 1606. His protest was to this effect—"That his sitting in this Parliament do no ways prejudge him of that place and precedency in Parliament and other public and private meetings due to him by his rights and infeftments; but that it shall be lawful to him to claim the same by virtue of his right according to law," that is, before the Court of Session. The succeeding Earls repeated the protests for higher precedency in 1661, 1681, 1689, 1696, 1698, 1702, 1704, and 1705.

The Earl of Mar adhered to the Royal cause in the Civil Wars of the seventeenth century. In consequence of this, the family suffered serious loss, as the debts contracted in the cause of Charles I. and Charles II. necessitated the sale of many of their estates. Earl John died in 1654 and was succeeded by his son John, Twenty-second Earl of Mar and ninth Lord Erskine.

SECTION VII.

JOHN, EARL OF MAR—CHARLES, EARL—JOHN, EARL—SECRETARY OF STATE FOR SCOTLAND—RISING OF 1715—ARRIVAL OF JAMES VIII—HIS PROGRESS SOUTHWARD—RETREAT—FLIGHT.

THE Earl first married Mary Scott, a daughter of Walter, first Earl of Buccleuch; and secondly, Mary Mackenzie, a daughter of the Earl of Seaforth. He died in 1665, and was succeeded by his son Charles, Twenty-third Earl of Mar and tenth Lord Erskine. The Earl married Mary, a daughter of George, Earl of Panmure, and had issue. This

Earl was a Jacobite, and was almost ruined by his attachment to the Stuart dynasty. He died in 1689, and was succeeded by his son John, Earl of Mar and eleventh Lord Erskine.

Earl John was an able politician. Although, like his predecessors, he was at heart a Jacobite and distrusted by William of Orange; yet, in the reign of Queen Anne, in 1706, Mar was appointed Secretary of State for Scotland; and he assisted the Government to carry the Treaty of Union through the Scottish Parliament. Sir George Lockhart of Carnwath said:—" Mar gained the favour of all the Tories, and was by many of them esteemed an honest man, and well inclined to the Royal Family. Certain it is that he vowed and protested so much many a time; but no sooner was the Marquis of Tweed-dale and his party dispossessed than he returned as the dog to his vomit, and promoted all the Court of England's measures with the greatest zeal imaginable. . . . His great talent lay in the cunning management of his designs and projects, in which it was hard to find him out." The Jacobites made the utmost efforts in Parliament and the country to obstruct and defeat the passing of the Treaty of Union; and they were extremely enraged at the Earl of Mar for assisting the Government to pass it.

Mar continued Secretary of State for Scotland; and in the latter years of the reign of Queen Anne, it appears that the Jacobites had been very active, and were gaining ground. The Queen died on the 1st of August, 1714. Thereupon the Elector of Hanover was proclaimed King, under the title of George I. The Earl embraced the earliest opportunity of offering his service to the new King, but somehow he did not receive His Majesty's commands. On the 24th of September, 1714, he was dismissed from the office of Secretary of State for Scotland, and the Duke of Montrose appointed to it. Yet Mar remained for some time about the Court in London; no special favour, however, was granted to him by the new King; and at last the Earl resolved to be revenged.

He left London in the beginning of August, 1715, and landed in Fifeshire. Then he proceeded to Braemar, issuing intimations, as he advanced northward, to the Highland Chiefs and his friends to join him at a great hunting party in the forest of Mar. He reached Invercauld Castle on the 19th of August, and immediately commenced operations for the memorable gathering, which met on the 26th of August, at Braemar. The party then assembled round the Earl of Mar included the Marquis of Huntly, eldest son of the Duke of Gordon; the Marquis of Tullibardine, eldest son of the Duke of Athole; Earl Marischal, the Earls of Erroll, Seaforth, Southesk, Linlithgow, Carnwath, Traquair, and Nithsdale; the Lords Duffus, Rollo, Drummond, Stormont, Strathallan, Ogilvie, and Nairn; the Viscounts Kenmure, Kilsyth, and Kingston; Gordon of Glenbucket, the lairds of Auldbar and Auchterhouse; and about twenty men of note and influence in the Highlands. The number of men assembled at Braemar was nearly eight hundred.

There were palpable indications of the coming rising in other places. In Aberdeen, early on the morning of the 11th August, 1714, even before the accesion of George I. had been proclaimed in the city, two fiddlers playing Jacobite tunes, and accompanied by a number of young men, marched through the streets; and on reaching the Castlegate, they gathered round a well and drank the health of James VIII. Tidings of this reached the Government in London, and the Magistrates were commanded to give an account of the incident to the Lord Justice Clerk. On the 21st of August, the Earl of Mar, who was then Secretary for Scotland, wrote to the magistrates asking for particulars of the affair. Similar incidents occurred in other places.

On the 3rd of September, 1715, a special meeting was held at Aboyne Castle to deliberate on the projected rising

At this meeting there were present—the Marquis of Tullibardine, Earl Marischal, the Earl of Southesk, and Lord Huntly; Glengarry from the Clans, Glenderule from the Earl of Breadalbane and the gentlemen of Argyleshire; Lieutenant-General Hamilton, Major Gordon, and a few others.

The final resolution having been taken at Aboyne, the die was cast. On the 6th of September, the standard was raised in Castletown of Braemar, on the spot where the Invercauld Arms Hotel now stands. From this originated the spirited Jacobite song, adapted to the reel tune called "The Braes o' Mar." A stanza or two of the ballad may be quoted :—

> The standard on the Braes of Mar
> Is up and streaming rarely;
> The gathering pipe on Lochnagar
> Is sounding lang an' sairly.
>
> The Highland men,
> Frae hill and glen,
> In martial hue,
> Wi' bonnets blue.
> Wi' belted plaids,
> An' burnished blades,
> Are coming late and early.
>
> Wha wadna' join our noble chief,
> The Drummond and Glengarry,
> Macgregor, Murray, Rollo, Keith,
> Panmure and gallant Harry?

. . . . . .

A large number of the Braemar men, and men from other quarters of the country, joined the rising. There is evidence, however, that a considerable number of those who joined the rising had no choice, but were forced to follow their feudal superiors. Even John Farquharson of Invercauld entirely disapproved of Mar's movement, and was extremely unwilling to join it; but he had no alternative, as the Earl was his feudal superior.

Mar himself assumed the rank of commander-in-chief of the insurgent force; and his followers, and those of the barons and chiefs, immediately commenced to move southward by the Spital of Glenshee. They marched through Moulin and Logierait to Dunkeld, receiving reinforcements as they proceeded; and at Dunkeld the army numbered 5000 men. On the 16th of September, a detachment took possession of Perth; and to this centre the whole army marched, and Mar made it his headquarters.

Meanwhile the accession of James VIII. was being proclaimed in the cities and burghs of the north. On the 20th of September, Earl Marischal entered Aberdeen with a party of men and proceeded to the Cross on the Castlegate, where Patrick Sandilands, the depute sheriff, read the document which proclaimed the accession of James VIII. to the throne of his ancestors. At night the city was illuminated, and the bells of St. Nicholas Church were rung in honour of the memorable occasion. The following day Earl Marischal and his company were hospitably entertained by the members of the Incorporated Trades; and on the departure of the Marischal in the evening they accompanied him to Inverugie House. The trades and the professors of the Colleges were thorough Jacobites; but the magistrates were inclined to continue loyal to the Government. They were, however, suddenly assailed by a mob, overpowered and forced to yield; and the Jacobite party obtained command of the town. On the 28th of September Earl Marischal returned to Aberdeen; and a few days later a head court of the burgh was held in St. Nicholas Church; and a Jacobite Council was elected, with Patrick Bannerman as Provost. Thus the city was placed under the reign of James VIII.

The Earl of Mar ordered the new Council of Aberdeen to supply three hundred Lochaber axes for the army; and imposed a tax of upwards of two hundred pounds for supplies, and conveying the press and types of James Nicol, the town's printer, to Perth; and also imposed on the citizens a requisition for £2000 sterling—the first instalment of £500 to be immediately paid, under the penalty of rebellion.

As the rising spread, some of the leading Jacobites in the North of England joined it. By the month of November, there were fourteen thousand men in arms for the Stuart cause. Mar himself, however, had little military skill or energy, and remained too long inactive in Perth. The body of the insurgents, mainly consisting of Scots and some Englishmen, who were operating in England, under the command of Forster, were overtaken by the royal troops at Preston. On the 12th of November, a severe battle was fought, in which the insurgents were completely defeated, and many of the Scots and their leaders taken prisoners. Among others, John Farquharson of Invercauld was taken and imprisoned. He was confined till 1717, when by the efforts of the Rev. Mr. Ferguson, minister of Logierait, who had once been minister of Crathie, Invercauld was liberated. Mr. Ferguson was the father of Dr. Adam Ferguson, the philosopher and historian.

Mar at last made a movement from Perth southward; and on the 13th November, his force and the royal army, under the Duke of Argyle, met and fought the Battle of Sheriffmuir, near Dunblane, which was indecisive. As the loss of men on each side was nearly equal, both claimed the victory. The actual result, however, was that Mar retired with his army to Perth, where his force began to melt away.

James VIII. landed at Peterhead on the 22nd of December, 1715. On the following day he passed through Aberdeen, only staying to take some refreshments in Skipper Scott's house in the Castlegate. Thence he proceeded to Fetteresso, where the professors of the Colleges of Aberdeen presented him with loyal addresses; and Provost Bannerman received from His Majesty the honour of knighthood. James was suffering from attacks of ague in his progress southward, and he reached Perth on the 6th of January,

1716. His presence inspired no new hope, as this representative of the Stuart line had not the mien of a man likely to lead an army to victory and glory. Preparations were made, however, for his coronation at the historic burgh of Scone, on the 23rd of January. But ere that day came the Stuart King was seriously thinking of retiring from the advance of his enemies.

The Duke of Argyle was lying at Stirling Castle with the royal army. On the 23rd of January he commenced his march upon Perth, but his progress was very slow, owing to the depth of snow upon the ground.

At midnight on the 30th of January the insurgent army commenced to retreat, crossed the Tay on the ice and marched to Dundee, and thence by Arbroath to Montrose. There, on the 3rd of February, the Pretender, the Earl of Mar, and a few other persons went aboard a small vessel and sailed for France. This incident caused a stir and much indignation in the army, and a number of the men left for their homes. General Gordon was left in command, and marched the fast diminishing army northward. On reaching Aberdeen, on the 7th of February, the remainder of the army dispersed. But a large number of those who joined the rising never returned to their homes, being either slain or taken prisoners.

Comparatively lenient feelings towards the insurgents prevailed in Scotland. But the English Government took the punishment of the prisoners and those implicated in the rising, into their own hands. Many of the prisoners were executed at Carlisle and other places, and hundreds were sent to the plantations to drag out a wretched life in slavery. Several persons of rank made their escape from prison and fled for their lives, amongst whom were Forster, Lord Nithsdale, and Mackintosh of Borlum. The estates of over 40 families in Scotland were forfeited to the Crown.

SECTION VIII.

EFFECTS OF MAR'S RISING—ESTATES OF THE FORFEITED EARL—HIS DEATH—THE TITLE OF EARL OF MAR RESTORED TO HIS GRANDSON, JOHN FRANCIS.

Naturally the Episcopal clergy in Scotland had always leaned to the side of the exiled line of Kings. When the temporary restoration came, they could scarcely resist the temptation, and some of them openly sided with the Pretender, and expressed their sentiments by praying for his success. The Government proceeded to prosecute them. Those who occupied chapels were summoned in groups before the magistrates and tried under the Toleration Act: their chapels were shut, and a number of them imprisoned until they complied with the provisions of the Act. Any of the old Episcopal ministers who still occupied parish churches were summoned before the Presbyteries, and if found guilty of praying for James VIII., or otherwise favouring him or his cause, they were deposed. In the Presbytery of Alford five ministers were deposed from parishes churches—Mr. Jaffery, minister of Alford; Mr. Livingstone, of Keig; Mr. Alexander, of Kildrummy; Mr. Robertson, of Strathdon; and Mr. Law, of Kearn. The four first named were incumbents at the Revolution of 1688, and had command in their charges. In the Synod of Aberdeen about 30 ministers were deposed.

In Aberdeen the Jacobite Town Council, during its short reign, made niney-four new burgesses. Amongst those were William Meston, Professor of Philosophy in Marischal College; Lord Drummond, a son of the Duke of Perth; and Gordon of Glenbucket. But, under an Act of the Privy Council, on the 10th of April, 1716, a new town council was elected, and, on the 12th the magistrates and council despatched a loyal address to His Most Gracious Majesty George I. The same day the new council rescinded all the new acts of the late Jacobite council. Thus, in Aberdeen, the rising of 1715 was renounced.

After the suppression of the rising, clear evidence came to light that many persons were forced to join it. On the 15th March, 1716, a justice of peace court was held at the Kirkton of Alford by Sir William Forbes of Craigievar, Arthur Forbes of Breda, and Archibald Forbes of Putachie, having met under a warrant from the Duke of Argyle, for disarming the country, David Lumsden of Cushnie appeared before the court and asked that witnesses should be examined to prove—that Henry Lumsden and Robert Reid, vassals of the Earl of Mar in the Lordship and Regality of Kildrummy; also Alexander Gordon, Jerom Dunbar, Robert Grant, James Rae, William Mare, William Davidson, Robert Henderson, Thomas Cook, William Gray, Francis Ferguson, John Finnie, and Thomas Forbes: all of whom were tenants of the said David Lumsden, who is also a vassal of the Earl of Mar within the Lordship and Regality of Kildrummy; that these men were all taken prisoners at the battle of Preston, in November, 1715; that they were forced to join the rising by the threats of those acting under Mar. The court deemed the request reasonable and called witnesses.

William Tough, a married man, over 70 years of age, was called and sworn. He deponed "that he knew all the persons named in the above list; and that they resided in the Lordship and Regality of Kildrummy; and that they were compelled to go out in the unhappy Rebellion much against their inclination. And that they did, to be free of the same, flee from their houses for several days; and that by my Lord Mar's order, parties were sent, who did set fire to their houses and corn yards. And that after they had absconded for several days, they were taken prisoners and conveyed to Braemar, where my Lord Mar then was. That he lives in the neighbourhood and knows all to be true, being an eye-witness of the same. And this is the truth as he shall answer to God."

Other six men who were living in the neighbourhood appeared before the court; and on being sworn and interrogated as to what they knew of the above-named persons, and whether they were forced to join in the Rebellion, all the six witnesses gave clear evidence corroborating the testimony of the first witness—William Tough. There also appeared several other witnesses who lived in the neighbourhood of the above-named persons, "now prisoners, who were taken at Preston." The witnesses declared that these prisoners "were all pressed and forced into the Rebellion." The justices concluded that force had caused these unhappy prisoners to be in the Rebellion.

After the suppression of the rising, troops were sent into Braemar and other parts of the Highlands, and measures were adopted for securing the peace of the country. An Act was passed for disarming the Celtic inhabitants, embracing the countries to the north of the Forth and the Highland districts of the West. This Act, however, failed to attain its object. As it merely imposed penalties, rising to transportation, against those found guilty of appearing in arms, and no means were provided for enforcing disarmament, the Act was inoperative. In 1725, another disarming Act was passed, which ordered each clan to be summoned to appear at a specified place, and there deliver up their arms. The execution of this Act was entrusted to General Wade, who imagined that he had performed the task effectively; and he also informed his Majesty the King that the Highlanders had now become simple peasants, with their staffs in their hands. He also stated that if the system of roads and fortresses proposed by him were made, any future rising in the Highlands would be impossible; but subsequent events proved that the general's sanguine anticipations were utterly futile.

Although the Earl of Mar saved his life by sailing from

Montrose to France with James VIII., all his estates and titles were forfeited to the Crown. After a time, however, the clemency of the Crown and the Government was extended to the members and friends of the family of Mar, not immediately descended from the attainted Earl. They were permitted to repurchase the forfeited estates at a price much below their market value, and to settle them under trust for the benefit of the lineal heirs of the house. The purchasers and trustees were Lord Grange, the forfeited Earl's younger brother, and David Erskine of Dun—a Lord of the Court of Session; and on the 26th of July, 1725, this transaction was confirmed by a charter from the Crown, upon which infeftment followed. Lord Grange and Lord Dun having before, on the 23rd of March, 1723, executed "a back bond," specifying the conditions under which they agreed to hold the property—expressing in a deposition and entail "that the benefit of the purchase should be for the behoove of Thomas Lord Erskine, only son of the forfeited Earl." The two trustees, Lord Grange and Lord Dun, proceeded to sell the estates of the Earldom, and to pay the debts and incumbrances upon them; and having completed their work in 1739, they then executed a disposition and entail of the residue of the Earldom of Mar, on the following lines of succession:—"(1) Thomas, Lord Erskine, and his heirs male; whom failing to the heirs whatsoever descending of Thomas, Lord Erskine; (2) the preceding heirs having failed, on Lady Frances Erskine, Thomas' sister, and her heirs male, whom failing, to the heirs whatsoever descending of her, whom all failing, then on James Erskine—Lord Grange." The lands of the Earldom in Aberdeenshire were all sold.

John, the forfeited Earl, lived for the most part in France, and attended the Court of James VIII., the Pretender, at St. Germains, near Paris. It appears that he had incurred the suspicion and displeasure of James, and finally had to leave the Court. He died at Aix-la-Chapelle in May, 1732.

He left an only son, Thomas, Lord Erskine, mentioned above, and a daughter, Lady Frances Erskine. Lord Erskine died in 1766, leaving no issue. Lady Frances then became heir of the Earls of Mar. She married her cousin, James Erskine, a son of Lord Erskine—the forfeited Earl's younger brother. Lady Erskine died in 1776, and left a son by her husband, John Francis Erskine : and to him, when an old man, in 1824, the title of Earl of Mar was restored by an Act of Parliament. He was a grandson of the forfeited Earl, and twenty-seventh Earl of Mar. He died in 1825, and was succeeded by his son, John Thomas, twenty-eighth Earl of Mar. He died in 1828, and was succeeded by his son, John Thomas Miller, twenty-ninth Earl of Mar. He also claimed the title of Earl of Kellie, which was adjudged to him in 1835. Thenceforth he bore the title of the Earl of Mar and Kellie. The Earl died in 1866, leaving no issue, and was succeeded by his nephew, a son of his sister, John Francis Erskine Goodeve, thirtieth Earl of Mar. He succeeded as heir-general to his uncle, according to the law of Scotland, which had prevailed at least for five or six centuries. He did not obtain any of the lands of the Earldom of Mar ; the remaining lands of the Earldom are in the possession of Lord Kellie. He voted repeatedly as Earl of Mar at Holyrood ; while the Earl of Kellie, his cousin, always addressed him as Earl of Mar. But in 1867, the Earl of Kellie commenced to lodge cases in the House of Lords, claiming to be the Earl of Mar. It was long, however, ere he was ready to proceed with these cases. The Earl of Mar at once presented a petition as Earl of Mar, asserted his right to the title, and protested against the claim of the Earl of Kellie. In January, 1872, the Earl of Kellie died ; but his son and successor continued to prosecute a claim to the title of Earl of Mar. At last, in 1874, the Earl of Kellie's claim was referred to the Committee of Privileges, that is a committee of a certain number of the Peers, who usually consider and give an opinion on petitions and claims relating to peerages, which is subsequently reported to the House of Lords. The opinion of the committee in this case, was recorded on the 25th of February, 1875, and was as follows :—

"Resolved, that it is the opinion of this Committee that the claimant, Walter Henry, Earl of Kellie, Viscount Fenton, Lord Erskine, and Lord Dirleton, in the Peerage of Scotland, has made out his claim, &c., to the honour and dignity of Earl of Mar in the Peerage of Scotland, created in 1565 ; that report thereof be made to the House." This opinion was reported to the House, and on the 26th of the same month, it was sent to the Lord Clerk Register in Edinburgh. After this, the Earl of Mar attended at an election of Representative Peers at Holyrood, and offered his vote as a Scottish Peer ; but the Lord Clerk Register refused it. This caused a stir among a number of Scottish Peers, which was not surprising in the circumstances created by the opinion of the Committee of Privileges, and the rather hasty decision of the House of Lords on one of the oldest Earldoms in the island.

An interesting series of debates touching the subject of the Earldom of Mar and who should have the right to the title of Earl of Mar, came off in the House of Lords. One on the 9th of July, 1879, on the motion of the Duke of Buccleuch to the effect—" That this House should order that at all future meetings of the Peers of Scotland, under a Royal Proclamation, for the election of Peers to represent the Peers of Scotland in Parliament, the Lord Clerk Register, officiating, do call the title of Mar in the Roll of Peers of Scotland, in the order of precedence to which it has been declared by the resolution of this House on the 26th of February, 1875, to be entitled, according to the date of the creation of that Earldom."

The Duke spoke briefly in support of his motion. His main point being that according to the judgment of the House of Lords, the Earl of Kellie had proved his claim to

"Earldom of Mar, created by Queen Mary in 1565," therefore his precedence should be in accord with the date of the creation of the Earldom. The Marquis of Huntly addressed the House at some length and to the points in question; and moved the previous question to the Duke's resolution. After speeches by the Earls of Redesdale, Mansfield, and Selborne, and the Lord Chancellor, the Duke withdrew his resolution.

On the 11th of July, 1879, the Marquis of Huntly raised a debate on several questions touching the Earldom of Mar. One of his questions was this: "Can the Lord Clerk Register call that new Earldom of Mar which was created in 1565 in any place upon the roll at all, when the resolution of the Committee of your Lordships' House says that the order of precedence must never be altered?" Several Peers delivered speeches, but nothing definite was done.

Another long debate took place on the 14th of June, 1880, on resolutions moved by the Earl of Galloway. He delivered an able and well-reasoned speech, and concluded by moving the following resolutions:—" That, whereas the Select Committee appointed to consider the matter of the petition of the Earl of Mar and Kellie, presented on the 5th of June, 1877, (the prayer in which petition was that the title of Earl of Mar should be brought down to the date 1565 from its existing place on the Union Roll) and the precedents applicable thereto, reported to the House on the 27th of July, 1877, that they had not been able to discover any precedent of orders made by the House for altering the order of precedence of the Peers of Scotland on the Union Roll; and that they were not disposed to recommend that any order should be made on the petition of the Earl of Mar and Kellie. In order to give due effect to the recommendation contained in this report, it is incumbent upon this House to rescind the order of the 26th February 1875," &c. The House by a majority of eight adopted the resolution that the order of the 26th of February, 1875, should be rescinded. But the House did not rescind this order. Accordingly, on the 21st of the same month, the Marquis of Huntly put a question to the Lord Chancellor whether any intimation of this resolution had been made to the Lord Clerk Register. The Lord Chancellor replied thus:—

"I believe no intimation has been made, and that none properly can be made, to the Lord Clerk Register with regard to this resolution. Before the House can rescind that Order, there must be a motion and a vote to do so. There has been no such vote passed; and if any noble lord should propose one, I must assume that he would come prepared to recommend to the House the adoption of what he may consider a more proper form of Order to be substituted for that which has been made. The Order that was made was consequential on a judicial act of the House, founded on a report of the Committee of Privileges; and if that be rescinded, beyond all question some other must be made. I hope that any one who moves such an Order will consider whether it shall be in a form which will not put on the Union Roll of Scotland two Earldoms of Mar, or in the form which, leaving only one Earldom of Mar, will change its precedence, and whether there are not objections of the gravest character to either of these courses."

Thus the finding of the Committee of Privileges of 1875 raised grave doubts whether the ancient dignity of Earl of Mar had not been surrendered to the Crown. To remove these doubts an Act of Parliament was passed in 1885, in which the old title of Earl of Mar was confirmed to John Francis Erskine Goodeve, dating from 1404; while, according to these decisions, Walter John Francis Erskine bears the title of Earl of Mar created in 1565. Thus, at present, there are two men with the title of Earl of Mar.

CHAPTER II.

Earldom and Earls of Buchan.

SECTION I.

NOTICE OF MORMAERS AND EARLY EARLS—EARLY NOTICE OF THE COMYNS—WILLIAM, EARL OF BUCHAN—ALEXANDER, EARL—JOHN, EARL—JOHN, LORD OF BADENOCH, CLAIMS THE CROWN OF SCOTLAND.

THE ancient district of Buchan, commenced on the north side of the lower stretch of the Don, and from the mouth of the Don swept round the coast to the mouth of the Deveron at Banff, running along the south bank of the Deveron, and including the parishes of King-Edward and Turriff, thence striking southward, bounded by the Garioch, and onward to the Don.

In early times Ellon was the chief seat of justice for the Earldom. When John, the son of Uthred, about 1209, received the lands of Tedrett and Ardindrach from Fergus, Earl of Buchan, he became bound to attend personally thrice a year at the Earl's Chief Courts at Ellon. According to ancient usage, the Earl, with the Dempster of Buchan, sat on the Moot Hill to dispense justice among his vassals; and it appears that this was also the place where the Earl received formal investiture of the Earldom.

In the Book of Deer, the names of seven Mormaers of Buchan are recorded. Donald, son of Ruadri, was Mormaer of Buchan in the reign of Malcolm II. He was succeeded by Donald, son of MacDubhacan; and he was succeeded by his brother Canneach. He was succeeded by his son, Gartnait, in the reign of Alexander I. Gartnait's daughter, Eva, became heiress, and married Colbain, who then assumed the title of Earl of Buchan. Colbain and Eva, his wedded wife, made a grant of land to the Monastery of Deer. They had a son, Roger, who succeeded to the Earldom. Earl Roger was succeeded by his son Fergus. He had an only daughter, Marjory, and she became Countess of Buchan in her own right—a circumstance which will again be referred to.

William Comyn was an active and able churchman, and came from the north of England to Scotland in the early part of the twelfth century. He soon gained the favour of David I., was much trusted by him, and at last he was appointed Lord High Chancellor of Scotland. He died about 1161. David I. granted to Richard Comyn, a nephew of the Chancellor, the manor of Linton Roderick, in Roxburghshire. Richard Comyn married a granddaughter of Donald Bane, a brother of Malcolm III., Canmore; and thus allied himself with the Royal Family of Scotland. He became a great favourite of William the Lion, who in many ways advanced his interests.

Richard's son William was born in 1163. William was twice married. By his first wife, he had two sons, Richard and Walter; both were men of note in their day, and extended the territory and influence of the family. About 1229 Walter Comyn became Lord of Badenoch. In 1231 he married the heiress of Monteith, and then obtained that Earldom with its extensive territories. He was present at the coronation of Alexander III. on the 13th of July, 1249. During the minority of the King, the Lord of Badenoch and Earl of Monteith played a leading part in the Government of Scotland. He died in 1258, leaving no issue by his countess; and the family of his elder brother succeeded to his estates. For several generations the Lords of Badenoch held wide territories, and wielded great influence in the Government of the Kingdom.

William Comyn, father of the above Lord of Badenoch, married, as his second wife, Marjory Countess of Buchan, only daughter of Earl Fergus—mentioned before; and thus

Comyn became Earl of Buchan. So he was the common ancestor of the Lords of Badenoch and the Earls of Buchan— of the Comyn line. He was appointed Justiciary of Scotland. In 1222 Alexander II. appointed him guardian of the Earldom of Moray. He founded the Cistercian Abbey of Deer, which was dedicated to St. Mary. Earl William died in 1233, and was succeeded by his son, Alexander, second Earl of Buchan of the name of Comyn. After the defeat of Haco and the wreck of his fleet, when the tidings of his death in Orkney on the 15th of December, 1263, reached Alexander III., he immediately resolved to reduce the Western Isles to the subjection of the Crown. Accordingly an army was mustered and placed under the command of the Earls of Mar, Buchan, and Alan Durward, and the army proceeded to the Isles. On the approach of the army many of the chiefs fled; some of them were captured and executed for the support which they had given to Haco's expedition; while others were expelled or fined. The Earls secured much booty, and then returned to the mainland.

The Earl of Buchan held the offices of Justiciary of Scotland, and High Constable of the Kingdom. He was also hereditary Sheriff of the county of Banff; and in 1265 he was baillie of the town of Dingwall.

In 1262 he founded a hospital in Turriff for twelve poor men. He also founded a hospital at Newburgh in the parish of Foveran.

A number of the old castles and towers in Buchan are believed to have been erected by the Comyns. The old castle of King-Edward is said to have been the chief feudal seat of the Earldom. It stood near the burn of King-Edward, on the south side and some distance from the river Deveron. It seems to have been a great stronghold, and in its time commanded the lower stretch of the beautiful and fertile valley of the Deveron. It has long been in ruins, and only some traces of it remain.

The old Castle of Slains is also said to have been a seat of the Comyns, Earls of Buchan; and, at a later period, once the residence of the Erroll family. The ruins of this castle stand on the top of a rock jutting out into the sea, at an elevation of over a hundred feet. Before the introduction of cannon, it would have been almost impregnable, as the only approach to it is a narrow defile on the north side, which a few determined men might have held against any attacking force. Little but its massive ruins now remain.

The old Castle of Dundarg stood upon a peninsular rock of red freestone, over sixty feet above the beach below. Though now in ruins, there are traces of a large court and extensive buildings, and it had been a place of great strength in its time. It is in the parish of Aberdour. In the parish of Rathen there are two old castles, Cairnbulg and Inverallochie. The castle of Cairnbulg was restored by Mr. Duthie, the proprietor of the estate, in 1897.

The old castle of Inverugie, called the old Craig of Inverugie, which is about two miles westward from Peterhead, and is seen from the railway, seems to have been a place of considerable strength, but it is now in ruins. It was once the seat of the Cheyne family, and subsequently of the Earls Marischal.

Alexander, Earl of Buchan, was present at the great meeting of the Estates, held at Scone on the 5th of February, 1284, in which the King's granddaughter, Margaret, the Maid of Norway, was declared to be heiress of the Crown of Scotland. On the death of Alexander III. in 1286, the Earl of Buchan was appointed one of the Guardians of Scotland for the districts on the north of the Forth: while John Comyn, Lord of Badenoch, was elected one of the Guardians of the kingdom on the south of the Forth. At this time the Comyns were the most powerful family in Scotland. Buchanan says, in his History of Scotland, that "the power of this family has never been equalled in Scotland, either before or since."

Earl Alexander died in 1289, and was succeeded by his son John, third Earl of Buchan of the Comyn line. He attended and took part in the Parliament which met at Brigham in March, 1290, and sanctioned the marriage between King Edward's son and the Maid of Norway, and other important matters. This treaty provided that the rights, laws, and liberties of Scotland should continue entire and untouched; no native was to be called to answer for any crime or cause at any court out of the kingdom; no Parliament was to be held beyond the boundaries of Scotland to discuss Scottish affairs. In a word, the complete independence of the nation was recognised and strictly guarded by this treaty.

The direct line of heirs to the Kingdom of Scotland failed, upon the death of the Maid of Norway on her way to Scotland in the end of September, 1290. As soon as the tidings of the young Queen's death became known in the country, several of the leading Earls began to muster their followers, and move through the country intently looking for more supporters. A number of claimants for the Crown of Scotland appeared, amongst whom was Sir John Comyn, Lord of Badenoch. Comyn claimed the Crown of Scotland as a descendant on the maternal side from Donald Bane; and even the mere fact of his publicly asserting his claim to the throne gave him more power and influence among the people.

At the meeting appointed by Edward I. on the 24th of June, 1291, which assembled on a green plain opposite the Castle of Norham, eight claimants for the Crown of Scotland appeared, namely :—John Baliol, Lord of Galloway ; Robert Bruce, Lord of Annandale ; Lord John Hastings ; Sir John Comyn, Lord of Badenoch ; Patrick Dunbar, Earl of March ; Florence, Count of Holland ; John Vesy, for his father, Nicholas Soulis ; and William Ross, and they were accompanied by many of the Scottish nobility and clergy. None of the claimants were very near in relationship to the Royal line of the Scottish Kings, but the three first names on the list stood nearest, thus:—David, Earl of Huntingdon, was a grandson of David I. and a younger brother of Malcolm, IV. and William the Lion; and Earl David had three daughters, Margaret, Isabella, and Ada, and Baliol claimed as a grandson of Margaret, the eldest daughter; Robert Bruce claimed as a son of Isabella, the second daughter; and John Hastings claimed as a grandson of Ada, the youngest daughter. At an early stage of the proceedings it was seen that the real contest for the Crown would lie between these three claimants. But, if the contest had taken the form of a struggle in arms between the first four claimants within Scotland itself, it seems probable that Sir John Comyn, Lord of Badenoch, would have secured the Crown and mounted the throne. For at this time the Comyns were the most powerful clan in Scotland. The Lord of Badenoch, however, did not persist long in the prosecution of his claim in King Edward's Court when he saw that there was no chance of success.

The Bishop of Bath began the business of the meeting by reading King Edward's speech, which, after referring to the unhappy state of Scotland, proceeded in a flowing style to characterise the benignity of the illustrious Prince who had seen fit to come to her rescue. He then said that his Royal master had allowed three weeks to the nobles and clergy of Scotland to bring forward whatever they could to impugn King Edward's right of superiority over that kingdom, and they had adduced nothing to invalidate it. Thus, all disturbing questions being brushed aside, Edward I. announced that his title of Lord Superior was undisputed, and, therefore, he intended to act in that character. Robert Bruce was asked whether he was willing to prosecute his claim to the Crown of Scotland in the court of the Lord Superior, and Bruce, in the presence of the meeting, expressly recognised Edward I. as Lord Superior, and agreed to abide by his decision. The same question was put to each of the claimants, and they all consented without reserve to the demand of Edward.

Many meetings were held at which the claimants for the Crown of Scotland appeared before Edward I. The claims of Bruce and Baliol were heard and argued at great length; and Hastings also insisted that he was entitled to a third part of the kingdom of Scotland. At last, on the 17th of November, 1292, in the Castle of Berwick, and in the presence of a great assemblage, Edward I. delivered judgment in favour of Baliol. The vassal king then rendered homage to his Lord Superior, and orders were issued to invest him in his feudal fief. Baliol proceeded to Scone to be crowned, with a warrant from his Lord Superior authorising the ceremony, which was accordingly performed on the 30th November. Shortly after, he passed into England, and there concluded the last act of the drama by rendering homage to Edward I. as the invested vassal King of Scotland.

Edward I. soon placed Baliol in a very humiliating position. Upon disputes arising among the Scots touching money matters and lands on which the courts had given decisions, some of the defeated parties appealed to the Court of Edward I. Baliol remonstrated, but Edward told him that he had determined to exercise direct dominion over the Kingdom of Scotland "whenever and wherever he thought fit." He was summoned to appear before the English Parliament and answer to an appeal touching lands of the Earl of Fife. On the 15th of October, 1293, the appeal came before Parliament, and Baliol was asked what defence he had to offer; but he declined to answer. "What means this?" said Edward: "you are my vassal, you have done homage to me, and you are here in consequence of my summons." Baliol still declined to make any answer to the appeal; so Parliament declared that he was a contumacious offender, and accordingly resolved to deprive him of the means of wrong-doing by taking three of the chief castles of Scotland into the hands of the Lord Superior until his vassal, King John, should render proper satisfaction.

SECTION II.

THE EARL OF BUCHAN INVADES ENGLAND—COMYN, LORD OF BADENOCH, GUARDIAN OF THE KINGDOM—EDWARD I.—SURRENDER, TERMS OF SUBMISSION.

SCOTLAND was fast drifting into a perilous position. In 1294 Edward I. was entering on a war against the King of France; and he summoned Baliol and the Scottish nobles to assist him in the French war. But they disobeyed, and held a meeting of Parliament at Scone. In October, 1295, a defensive and offensive treaty was concluded between France and Scotland. In March, 1296, the Scots mustered an army, and under the command of John, Earl of Buchan, and High Constable of Scotland, they invaded Cumberland and wasted the country. Shortly after, the Earl of Buchan led another raid into Northumberland.

In April, 1296, Edward I. invaded Scotland. He attacked Berwick, and ruthlessly massacred eight thousand of the inhabitants, sparing neither age nor sex. The town was utterly ruined. Edward formed a ditch, and threw up defensive works round Berwick. Thence he proceeded towards Dunbar, the key of the Eastern Marches. The Scots had mustered to defend the Castle of Dunbar; but on the 26th of April they were attacked, defeated, and dispersed, and many of them slain and taken prisoners. The Castle of Dunbar was seized by Edward; and the Earls of Athol, Monteith, and Ross, and a number of other barons submitted to him. All the prisoners of rank were conveyed to England and imprisoned.

Edward I. proceeded rapidly with his work. The castles of Roxburgh, Jedburgh, and others on the line of his march were surrendered to him. He reached Edinburgh on the 6th of June, immediately attacked the castle with all the appliances at his command, and pelted it day and night for a week, after which it capitulated. He continued his triumphal progress to Linlithgow, and onward to Stirling, crossed the Forth unopposed, and, proceeding by Perth, passed the Tay and entered Forfarshire. Baliol had fled before the advance of Edward's army; and at the Castle of Brechin, on the 10th of July, 1296, he came like a criminal suing for mercy, and submitted to Edward's pleasure. He was at once degraded and dispossessed of his fief (kingdom) and conveyed to England a prisoner.

At Montrose, John Comyn, Earl of Buchan, submitted to Edward I., and was sent into England a prisoner. In 1297, he was permitted to return to Scotland. For some time he worked against Wallace and supported the English. But after the battle of Falkirk, the Earl again turned against the English, which was no doubt owing to his kinsman being elected one of the Guardians of the Kingdoms. Sir John Comyn, called the Red Comyn, was a son of John Comyn, Lord of Badenoch, one of the Guardians of Scotland in 1286, and a Claimant for the Crown as before stated. He married a sister of John Baliol, the now deposed King; thus the Red Comyn was a nephew of Baliol. The Lord of Badenoch, father of the Red Comyn, was one of the ablest and most powerful men in Scotland of his time. He died in 1300 at an advanced age, and was succeeded by his son, John. These family connections throw light on an important series of subsequent events.

Wallace resigned the Guardianship of Scotland shortly after the Battle of Falkirk in 1298; and Sir John Comyn (the Red) afterwards Lord of Badenoch, and John de Soulis were elected Guardians, associated with Robert Bruce, Earl of Carrick, and William Lamberton, Bishop of St. Andrews. Bishop Lamberton was a warm personal friend of Wallace and Bruce.

In July, 1299, at a meeting of the Guardians and some

of the nobles, held at Peebles, a rather serious scuffle occurred, which originated in a proposal touching the property of Sir William Wallace, who was then in France:—
"And upon that each of these knights gave the lie to the other, and they drew their daggers; and the Earl of Buchan and Sir John Comyn thought because Sir David de Graham is with Master John Comyn, and Malcolm Wallace with the Earl of Carrick, that some quarrel was begun with intention to deceive them, and Master John Comyn leaped upon the Earl of Carrick and took him by the throat, and the Earl of Buchan upon the Bishop of St. Andrews, and they held them fast, until the Steward and others went between them and stopped the scuffle."

So far as known, it appears that Comyn, Lord of Badenoch, as chief Guardian of Scotland, acted loyally on behalf of his country. In 1300, Edward I. invaded Scotland, took several castles in Dumfriesshire; and then besieged Caerlaverock Castle, which, after a heroic defence against his whole army, at last surrendered. It was here that Edward I. was obliged to listen to one of the most severe attacks that has ever been made upon him touching his claims of feudal superiority over the Kingdom of Scotland. About the end of August, the Archbishop of Canterbury, acting as the Pope's legate, placed a Bull from Boniface VIII. in the hands of Edward I., which was read aloud in the presence of his assembled barons and knights. Boniface charged Edward I. with violating all the rights and liberties of Scotland, and stated " that neither he nor any of his predecessors held over Scotland any superiority; since, when, in the wars between your father Henry and Simon de Montfort, he requested the assistance of Alexander III., King of Scotland, he acknowledged by letters patent that he received such assistance, not as due to him, but as a special favour. Moreover, when you yourself invited King Alexander to attend your coronation, you made the requests as a matter of favour and not of right. When the King of Scotland rendered homage to you for his lands in Tynedale and Penrith, he publicly protested it was rendered not for his Kingdom, but for these lands only, since, as King of Scotland, he was independent. Yea, further, when Alexaner III. died, leaving an heiress to his Crown, a granddaughter in her minority, the wardship of this infant was not given to you, which it would have been if you had been Lord Superior, but it was given to certain nobles of Scotland elected for the office." Touching the negotiations for the proposed marriage between the Prince of Wales and the Maid of Norway, the Pope reminded Edward I. "that he had acknowledged the independence of Scotland; and it was singular that he submitted to negotiate if he had a right to command. Regarding the changes lately made on the rights and liberties of Scotland, with the consent of a divided nobility, or the person Edward had placed in charge of the kingdom, these ought not to continue, as all had been extorted by force and intimidation. The Pope then exhorted Edward, in the name of God, to at once liberate the bishops and clergy whom he had imprisoned, and to remove all the offices and officials whom he had thrust upon the Scottish nation. On the conclusion of the reading of the Bull, Edward started up, and exclaimed—" I will not be silent or at rest either for Mount Zion or Jerusalem; but, as long as there is breath in my nostrils, I will defend what all the world knows to be my right." The result, however, was that he disbanded his army for a time, though not for long.

In 1303, Edward I. was making the utmost efforts to prevent the King of France from giving any encouragement to the Scots. In the spring, the Earl of Buchan, Sir John Soulis, and the Steward of Scotland were sent to France as Ambassadors; but ere they reached Paris, a truce was arranged between England and France, in which all reference to the Scots was excluded. In the final treaty of peace, ratified at Paris in May, 1303, no reference to the Scots occurred. Yet, through the craft of Edward I., abetted by the King of France, the Scottish envoys were induced to remain at the French Court by base and false professions. On the 25th of May they communicated with Comyn, the Guardian, in the following sentences :—" Be not alarmed that the Scots are not included in the treaty. The King of France will immediately send Ambassadors to divert Edward from war, and to procure a truce for us until the two Kings can have a personal conference in France. At that conference, a peace will be concluded beneficial to our nation; of this the King of France has himself given the most positive assurance. . . . Marvel not that none of us return home at present; we would all have willingly returned, but the King of France will have us to remain till we bring home intelligence of the result of the business; wherefore, for the Lord's sake, despair not; but if ever you acted with resolution, do so now. . . . The French ambassadors will be empowered to treat of peace, as well as to negotiate a truce." The men thus detained at the French Court were John Soulis, one of the Guardians; the Earl of Buchan, the Steward of Scotland, and Ingram Umfraville; so with these men absent, and the defection of Bruce, Earl of Carrick, there were few persons of ability and rank left in Scotland to offer resistance to the ruthless invader.

Edward I. was now free from embarrassment abroad and at home, and having made ample preparations for the final conquest of Scotland, he commenced his march upon the doomed country in the middle of May, 1303. His army was arranged in two divisions—one under himself and the other under the Prince of Wales. Edward advanced by Morpeth, and reached Roxburgh on the 21st of May, where he was joined by the followers of Bruce, Earl of Carrick. The Prince of Wales entered Scotland by the Western Marches, but his advance was checked at several points by Wallace; he therefore deviated from his intended route and marched through Roxburghshire, advancing northward in the rear of his father. Edward reached Edinburgh on the

4th of June, marched by Linlithgow and thence to Stirling, crossed the Forth, and on the 10th of June entered Perth. Comyn, the Guardian, with the small force under his command, could not venture to face the great hosts of the invader or contest his advance with any hope of success. Edward stayed in Perth till the middle of July, then proceeded to Dundee, and thence to Montrose. At this stage he summoned Sir Thomas Maule to surrender the Castle of Brechin, but Sir Thomas declined. Edward then marched from Montrose to Brechin with his war engines, and besieged the castle. Sir Thomas made a heroic defence; but at last he was fatally wounded and expired, and the garrison surrendered, though not till five waggon loads of lead had been thrown into the castle.

Resuming his progress northward, he marched by the Castle of Kincardine, and arrived at Aberdeen on the 24th of August. He stayed in the city about a week. Thence he marched through Buchan, and reached Banff on the 4th of September; whence, marching northward, he crossed the Spey and advanced through Moray, reaching Kinloss on the 20th of September. Edward advanced into Badenoch and occupied for several days the Castle of Lochindorb—one of the strongholds of the Comyns, Lords of Badenoch. He returned by Kinloss, thence moving southward by Kildrummy Castle, whence to Brechin, and onward to Dunfermline, where he stayed through the winter of 1304.

Comyn, Lord of Badenoch, the Guardian of Scotland, was encamped at Strathord; and in the end of December, 1303, negotiations were commenced with him for his submission to Edward I. The conditions offered by Edward virtually implied the surrender of national liberty; and the negotiations were tedious and protracted. The terms of submission were agreed to on the 9th of February, 1304, in which it was stipulated that their lives should be spared, and that they should retain their lands, but subject

Earls of Buchan.

to such fines as Edward might think fit to impose upon them. But the following persons were specially excluded from the above terms :—Wishart, Bishop of Glasgow ; Sir John Soulis, the Steward of Scotland, Sir Simon Fraser, Sir William Wallace, David de Graham, and Alexander de Lindsay : to all those the chance of preserving their lives was offered on certain terms, mostly stated periods of banishment from Scotland, except Wallace. " As for William Wallace, it is convenanted that he shall render himself up at the will and mercy of the King, if it shall seem good to him." There is evidence that Edward was earnestly requested to offer reasonable terms to Wallace; but he absolutely declined to listen to such a proposal. The narrative of Wallace's capture and fate is well known. After the surrender of Stirling Castle, Sir William Oliphant, its governor and heroic defender, was sent to the Tower of London and executed ; and the garrison, numbering one hundred and forty men, were despatched to various prisons in England.

It then seemed that all was over, and Scotland utterly subdued. But surface appearances are often deceptive. A worthy successor to Wallace immediately took the field, and made heroic and supreme efforts to recover the kingdom.

SECTION III.

THE EARL OF BUCHAN LOYAL TO EDWARD I.—ROBERT BRUCE.—SLAUGHTER OF RED COMYN—BRUCE CROWNED—DEFEATED—BRUCE ATTACKS THE EARL OF BUCHAN AND THE COMYNS AND VANQUISHES THEM.

AFTER the surrender and submission of Comyn, the late Guardian, there is no doubt that the Earl of Buchan had resolved to continue loyal to Edward I. His Earldom and its extensive territory were secure, and virtually his feudal powers within it remained in his own hands as before;

therefore he had little occasion to feel grieved at the change. There is evidence that the Lord of Badenoch was content to remain a loyal vassal of Edward I., as his lands and feudal powers were still in his own hands. Thus, after what had taken place in Scotland during a few past years, he had good grounds for being content.

    The Lords of Badenoch had a number of strong castles in their Highland territories, most of which were erected by the Comyns. The Castle of Ruthven, once a great stronghold, stood on a high isolated bank on the south side of the upper stretch of the Valley of the Spey. The island fortress of Lochindorb is on the islet in deep water in the centre of the loch. Lochindorb is two miles long and about half a mile in breadth. The islet is about an acre in extent, which is all occupied by the curtain walls and the dilapidated towers of the castle. In its time it had been a strong place. The old Castle of Raits was another stronghold of the Comyns in Badenoch, the site of which is now occupied by a large modern building, called Belleville House. The old Castle of Roy was also one of the sites of the Comyns. It is placed on an eminence a short distance to the east of the Water of Nethy, and near the Free Church of Abernethy. It is a large structure in the form of a quadrangle with high walls, but it is now in ruins. These and other castles attest the power of the Comyns in this extensive Highland region; while the strongholds of the Earl of Buchan, (already mentioned,) show clearly that the Comyn clan was one of the most powerful in Scotland at the beginning of the fourteenth century.

    Robert Bruce, Earl of Carrick, had assisted Edward I. in his last campaign, and supplied him with a battering-ram for the siege of Stirling Castle. He was a grandson of the Bruce who had fought out the contest in Edward's court, for the Crown with the now deposed John Baliol. He was a young man, little over thirty years, and hitherto had shown a rather vacillating character. On the death of his father in the spring of 1304, he succeeded to the large family estates in England and Scotlamd, and was Lord of Annandale as well as Earl of Carrick. In June, 1304, he entered into a compact with Bishop Lamberton, in which they mutually agreed to assist each other against all their enemies. It appears that somehow this compact became known to Edward I., and Bruce, when attending the English Court, was questioned concerning it. He at once saw that his life was in danger, and one morning he mounted his horse and rode swiftly to Scotland.

Bruce arrived at his Castle of Lochmaben early in February, 1306. On the 12th of February, as a freeholder of the county, he attended the English judges who were holding their courts at Dumfries, and there he met the Lord of Badenoch, John Comyn, the late Guardian of Scotland—sometimes called "The Red Comyn." Bruce and Comyn entered the Greyfriars convent to have a private interview touching public affairs; and their conversation waxed warm. Bruce referred to the miserable state of Scotland—once an independent kingdom, and now nothing but a province of England. He then proposed that Comyn should take his lands and help him to be king; or if Comyn preferred it, Bruce was to take his lands and help him to be king. But Comyn demurred to such proposals, and professed loyalty to Edward I. Bruce charged him with betraying important secrets of his; their talk became bitter and hot, and at last Bruce drew his dagger and stabbed Comyn. He immediately turned from the convent, and rushed into the street shouting for a horse. His friends asked if anything was amiss. "I doubt," said Bruce, "I have slain Comyn." Instantly Kilpatrick, one of his followers, ran into the convent and slew the wounded man outright, and also killed his uncle, Sir Robert Comyn.

It may be that the murder of Comyn was unpremeditated; yet it removed the only competitor for the throne of Scotland whom Bruce had reason to fear. Comyn had claims to the Crown as his mother was a sister of John Baliol; and he was also a descendant of Donald Bane, a brother of Malcolm III., as before indicated. This relation to the old line of Celtic Kings would have given him a great advantage in the eyes of the people in the event of any struggle between the two for the throne of Scotland. Bruce had rashly committed himself and could not recede. He had assassinated one of the most powerful men in the kingdom, and incurred the bitter enmity of all his kin and numerous followers.

Immediately after these tragic deeds, Bruce drove the English judges and officials out of Dumfries and across the border. The news soon spread; the people of Galloway assumed a threatening attitude, and many of Edward's officials fled from the kingdom. Bruce soon resolved on a bold step. He mounted the throne and was crowned King at Scone, on the 27th of March, 1306. But his followers were few in number, and consisted of—The Bishops of St. Andrews, Glasgow, and Moray, and the Abbot of Scone; his four young and stalwart brothers; his nephew, Thomas Randolph of Strathdon, and his brother-in-law, Christopher Seton; the Earls of Athol, Lennox, and Monteith; Gilbert Hay of Erroll and his brother Hugh, Nigel Campbell of Argyle, David of Inchmarten, Robert Boyd of Kilmarnock, Sir John Somerville of Linton, David Barclay of Cairns, Alexander Fraser, Sir James Douglas, and Robert Fleming. This small party—the forlorn hope of the Scottish nation—had arrayed against it the hosts of England, the numerous followers of the Comyns, and many of the Scotch nobles.

The desperate nature of the enterprise on which Bruce had embarked soon appeared. His small force could not face the English army in the field; and he encamped in the wood of Methven, six miles from Perth. On the 19th of June, 1306, the English under Pembroke attacked Bruce, and, after a severe encounter, completely defeated him. Indeed Bruce himself narrowly escaped, while many of his followers were slain or taken prisoners. Edward I. ordered the prisoners to be immediately executed. Accordingly they were hanged and quartered. Bruce, with about two hundred of his followers, retired into the forest of Athole. But they were pursued as outlaws, and they soon began to feel the extreme miseries of their position. Bruce was forced to leave Athole to save his followers from starvation; and with great difficulty he moved by unfrequented tracts to Aberdeenshire. At Aberdeen he was joined by his wife and other ladies; but on the approach of a numerous body of the enemy, led by the Earl of Buchan, Bruce and his company betook themselves to the mountains of Breadalbane.

Amid these wilds they suffered extreme privation. As food was very scarce, they gathered wild berries; some of them hunted, and others fished, in order to preserve their lives; while their clothing was often in tatters, through living day and night for weeks and months exposed to the open air in these high altitudes. Bruce, with a number of his friends, had reached the head of the Tay, and were approaching Argyleshire—the district of the Lord of Lorne. This chief was related through marriage to the "Red Comyn," and, naturally, he was eager to vent revenge upon Bruce. Lorne, at the head of a strong body of his followers, attacked Bruce and his small company in Strathfillan. A severe encounter ensued; but Bruce's company were overwhelmed by numbers and fell back. Gilbert Hay of Erroll and James Douglas were wounded, and many of their horses were killed. To avert the total destruction of his small band, Bruce commanded them to retreat through a narrow pass while he brought up the rear himself, and repeatedly turned his horse and drove back the assailants, till at last the pursuit of the enemy ceased.

Winter was approaching, and they could not then subsist in this mountainous region. The Queen and a few attendants were conveyed, under an escort of mounted men, to the Castle of Kildrummy, which they reached in safety.

Bruce had only two hundred men on foot, and with these he resolved to seek refuge in Cantyre or some of the islands; and Sir Neil Campbell was sent forward to provide vessels and provisions for the voyage. The King and his men proceeded in the direction of Cantyre, but they were reduced to the utmost extremities for want of provisions. While wandering amongst the hills and woods in search of food, they met the Earl of Lennox, who, since the battle of Methven had heard nothing of the fate of Bruce, and the two men feelingly embraced each other. Lennox supplied his friends with provisions, and by his assistance they reached Cantyre, where Neil Campbell joined them. Angus, Lord of the Isles, warmly welcomed Bruce and his followers, and treated them with much hospitality; and also gave them the Castle of Dunaverty to live in and enjoy themselves after their wanderings and privations. Yet the emissaries of Edward I. and the Comyns were so numerous and so alert in their efforts to capture Bruce that he, with the fate of Wallace before him, did not deem himself safe, even in this castle, from the bitter and determined pursuit of his enemies. Accordingly, in the end of the year, 1306, Bruce, with a few of his followers, passed over to the small isle of Rathlin, on the northern coast of Ireland, and stayed there during the winter.

But death and ruin befell many of Bruce's supporters and friends. The English troops scoured the country, and seized all suspected persons. Bruce's wife and daughter were captured and imprisoned in England. The Countess of Buchan, a daughter of the Earl of Fife, had married John Comyn, Earl of Buchan. Because this lady had dared to assist at the coronation of Bruce, she was taken and conveyed to Berwick, and placed in a cage specially built for her; which hung in one of the centre turrets of the Castle of Berwick, where she could be seen by the people passing by.

The Castle of Kildrummy was besieged by the English

and the Comyns. After a determined and heroic defence by Nigel Bruce, the King's brother, it was taken. Nigel Bruce was conveyed in fetters to Berwick and there executed. The Earl of Athole and Sir Simon Fraser were carried to London and executed as traitors, and their heads placed upon London Bridge beside that of Wallace. Many others were seized and executed with all the shocking cruelties of the period; further, many of the people were struck down and slain without trial, evidence, or question; and for several years a frightful scene of bloodshed and cruelty prevailed throughout the kingdom.

In the spring of 1307 Bruce returned to Scotland, and recommenced the task of recovering the kingdom in his own district of Carrick and Ayrshire. For some time his position was very perilous. The emissaries of Edward I. and the Comyns were constantly hunting him, and he had several very narrow escapes. Subsequently he was joined at Cumnock, in Ayrshire, by Sir James Douglas, who had collected a body of men in his own barony. With his followers thus increased, Bruce resolved to give a good account of himself.

Early in May, Pembroke, the English commander, advanced into Ayrshire at the head of three thousand cavalry, with the intention of extinguishing Bruce. The young king, however, in his wanderings had acquired some experience, and he fixed on a position at Loudon Hill. After inspecting the ground, he limited the space for the evolutions of the English cavalry and at the same time protected both his flanks by three deep trenches on each side of his position. Beyond these trenches the ground was marshy. Having thus prepared the ground, he posted his six hundred spearmen, and coolly awaited the attack of the English cavalry. On the 10th of May the English cavalry, under Pembroke, advanced in two lines; and the first line, at full gallop, charged the Scottish spearmen. But they stood firm and unhorsed many of their assailants. The cavalry reeled and then broke, and retired in disorder upon the second line. Instantly the Scots, with their spears levelled, followed them at the double, and completely defeated them. Pembroke fled to the Castle of Ayr, and reported his defeat. After this, Bruce gained ground step by step.

In 1308 Bruce crossed the Tay and advanced northward to Aberdeenshire, with the object of reducing Comyn, the Earl of Buchan, who upheld the English authority in this quarter of the country. But he was attacked by a severe illness caused by the exposure and privation which he had endured; and the war operations were somewhat delayed. Bruce's army proceeded by Inverurie, and in the march northward several skirmishes took place between his troops and the followers of the Comyns. His army retired into Strathbogie to obtain a supply of provisions and afford Bruce some rest. When he had partly recovered, the army returned to Inverurie.

At the same time the Earl of Buchan was in the field with a force numbering over a thousand men, and had advanced to the neighbourhood of Oldmeldrum. Comyn's ally, Sir David Brechin, with a small party, rapidly advanced on Inverurie, and surprised some of Bruce's outposts. When tidings of this reached the King, it greatly roused him. He instantly rose from his bed, called for his horse, and mounted, and led his army direct to Comyn's position, which was on an eminence at Barra, in the parish of Bourtie. A severe battle ensued. But Comyn's army was completely defeated, and his retreating followers hotly pursued for miles, and many of them slain. Bruce then proceeded with extreme severity to waste and destroy the possessions of the Comyns in Buchan. The Earl himself escaped to England, but the power of his kin and followers was utterly broken; and he was the last Earl of Buchan of the name of Comyn. Indeed, the very name of Comyn was for a time proscribed. As indicated in a preceding paragraph, the Earl of Buchan married Lady Isabel, daughter of Duncan,

Earl of Fife, by whom he had a son, John, and two daughters. The Earl himself died in England in 1313, his son having died before him. His eldest daughter, Alice, married Henry, Lord Beaumont, and in right of his wife, he claimed the Earldom of Buchan.

The "Red Comyn" left a son, John, who was brought up with the children of Edward I.; and he accompanied Edward II. to Bannockburn, where he was slain when fighting against the Scots.

SECTION IV.

BEAUMONT, EARL OF BUCHAN—ALEXANDER STEWART—JOHN—MURDOCH—JAMES—JOHN—CHRISTIAN, COUNTESS OF BUCHAN—JAMES DOUGLAS, EARL—MARY, COUNTESS — ERSKINES, EARLS OF BUCHAN.

AFTER the extinction of the Comyns and the departure of Henry Beaumont, there were no Earls of Buchan for some time. The extensive territory of the Earldom was much broken up, and divided among other families. None of the subsequent Earls wielded such power and influence in the district and in the government of the kingdom as the Comyns had done.

Henry Beaumont's claim to the Earldom of Buchan was admitted in 1323. It appears, however, that he failed to obtain possession of the Earldom till after the death of Randolph, Earl of Moray and Regent of Scotland, which occurred on the 20th of July, 1332. Eleven days after the death of Randolph, Edward Baliol appeared in the Firth of Forth with a fleet, and immediately landed his troops on the coast of Fifeshire. His force numbered three thousand men on foot and four hundred cavalry; and his most ardent supporters were Henry Beaumont, who claimed the Earldom of Buchan, Lord Wake of Liddel, and Henry Percy. Among Baliol's Scottish supporters, the most notable was the Earl of Athole, whose territories in Athole and Strathbogie were forfeited by Robert I. There were many others under Baliol's banner hungering for land in Scotland, and pretending that they had claims to it. Thus Baliol's followers were animated by strong motives. Accordingly, they marched to Strathearn with remarkable rapidity and spirit, surprised the Scottish army under Mar, the Regent, at Dupplin on the 11th of August, and completely defeated the Scots. Mar himself, Robert Bruce, Earl of Carrick, the Earl of Monteith, and many of the Scots were slain. The following day Baliol took possession of Perth.

On the 24th of September Baliol was crowned at Scone. He then proceeded southward to Roxburgh, surrendered the independence of Scotland to Edward III., and gave up Berwick and the territories on the border to his Lord Superior. To support Baliol and ruin Scotland—Edward III., within five years, led in person four successive invasions into the Kingdom. In his last invasion, 1336, at the head of a great army he proceeded to Perth, thence marched to Aberdeen, wasting the country, and burning villages and towns along his route. He advanced through the counties of Aberdeen and Banff, crossed the Spey, and marched onward till he reached Inverness. Sir Andrew Moray, the Regent, wisely avoided a battle, but he harassed the enemy most effectively; and Edward III. returned to England without subduing Scotland. Baliol, when left to his own resources, soon disclosed his nakedness. He became an object of hatred, suspicion, and contempt among all classes of the Scots, and in 1339 he finally fled from the kingdom, and assumed his natural position as a pensioned dependent on England.

In 1335 Henry Beaumont, Earl of Buchan, was staying in his Castle of Dundarg, when he was captured by the Scots. But, on the payment of a very large ransom he was permitted to return to England.

The next Earl of Buchan was Alexander Stewart, the third son of Robert II., who was also Lord of Badenoch.

He was a restless and fierce man, and earned for himself the name of "The Wolf of Badenoch." Among other oppressive acts he took possession of some lands which belonged to the Bishopric of Moray. For this he was excommunicated; but he retaliated by advancing with a body of his followers in 1390, and burned down the grand Cathedral of Elgin and a part of the city. Yet the Church of that day was too strong for him, and he was compelled to do penance for his reckless outrage. He died in 1394, leaving no legitimate issue; but he left several natural sons.

Shortly after the burning of the cathedral, one of his sons, Duncan Stewart, led a party of his followers across the mountains which divide the counties of Aberdeen and Forfar, and plundered the Lowlands. In 1392 Duncan made another raid; and the landed men of the district, headed by Sir Walter Ogilvie, Sheriff of Angus, mustered and met him at Gasklune, near the Water of Isla; but he completely defeated them. Ogilvie, the sheriff, his brother, and others were slain. The Government, in a general council held at Perth, ordered Duncan Stewart and his accomplices to be proclaimed outlaws for the slaughter of Walter Ogilvie and others. Another son of the Lord of Badenoch and Earl of Buchan, was Alexander Stewart, Earl of Mar, and hero of Harlaw, who has been characterised in preceding sections.

After the death of Alexander Stewart, the Earldom of Buchan was conferred on John Stewart, a son of the Duke of Albany. This Earl gained distinction as an officer in the service of France. He fought in the French army at the battle of Beauge against the English, who were under the command of the Duke of Clarence. In this action, Clarence was slain, the Earl of Buchan having stunned and unhorsed him by a blow of his mace; and the English were defeated. For this Charles VII. conferred on the Earl of Buchan the sword of the Constable of France. He was killed at the battle of Verneuil, on the 27th of August, 1424. He left no legitimate issue, and the Earldom went to his brother, Murdoch, Duke of Albany and Regent of Scotland.

But after the return of James I. in 1424, he resolved to punish the Albany branch of his own kindred. On the 13th of May, 1424, Sir Walter Stewart, eldest son of the Duke of Albany; Malcolm Fleming, brother-in-law of Albany; and Thomas Boyd, a member of the Kilmarnock family, were arrested and imprisoned; and towards the end of this year, the Earl of Lennox, father-in-law of Albany, and Sir Robert Graham, were seized and imprisoned. This was the prelude to a desperate move and tragedy meditated by the King.

He summoned a Parliament, which met at Perth on the 12th of March, 1425. On the ninth day of the Parliament, the Duke of Albany and his son, Sir Alexander Stewart; the Earls of Douglas, March, and Angus; William Hay of Erroll; Sir Alexander Seton of Gordon; Sir Alexander Irvine of Drum; and others—in all thirty barons and knights—were arrested. At the same time the King seized the castles of Falkland and Doune, and imprisoned Albany's wife in the castle of Tantallon. These proceedings astonished the Scottish barons and knights; but the move was specially directed against the Duke of Albany and his family, so the other barons were released after a very short imprisonment.

In May, Parliament reassembled at Stirling, and prepared to settle the doom of Albany and his family. A court was held in Stirling Castle on the 26th of May, 1426. Walter Stewart, the eldest son of Albany, was tried before the King and a jury of twenty-one barons; he was found guilty, condemned, and immediately beheaded. The following day, the King's own cousin, the Duke of Albany, and his son, Alexander, and the aged Earl of Lennox, were tried, convicted, and sentenced to death. They were all executed before the Castle of Stirling. Albany and his sons were men of stalwart and commanding presence, and their hard fate at the hands of the King excited much sympathy amongst the people.

After the execution of the Duke of Albany, the Earldom of Buchan reverted to the Crown; and it remained in the hands of the Crown till after the death of James II., and in 1469 James III. conferred the Earldom of Buchan on James Stewart, the second son of Sir James Stewart, "the Black Knight of Lorne," by Joan Beaufort, the widow of James I. Thus the new Earl was the King's uncle. The Earl married Margaret Ogilvie, the heiress of Sir Alexander Ogilvie of Auchterhouse, by whom he had issue; and he took the titles of Earl of Buchan and Lord Auchterhouse.

In 1467, James III. granted to his uncle and his wife the lands of the Baronies of Strathalva and Down, with the Castle of Banff, and the fishings of the water of Deveron.

When the southern barons entered into a conspiracy against the King, the Earl of Buchan naturally continued loyal. The King crossed the Forth, and passed into the north-eastern counties, where a strong force rallied round him. He then marched southward, and came in sight of the rebellious barons at Blackness in West Lothian, and the Earl of Buchan attacked and drove back the left wing of the insurgent army. Negotiations were opened, and the Earl of Buchan insisted on severe measures against the insurgent nobles; but the Earls of Huntly and Erroll were opposed to this, and they retired to the north. It was evident, however, that Buchan's view was right. A pacification was arranged in May, 1488, in which the barons promised to return to their allegiance and maintain the rights of the Crown and the peace of the kingdom; and thereupon the King disbanded his army and returned to Edinburgh.

But the disaffected barons remained in arms, with the young Prince James at their head, against his father. The King again mustered an army, and advanced towards Stirling to secure the passage of the Forth, but the gates of the castle were closed against him, as the governor had joined the insurgent barons. On the 11th of June, 1488, the two armies approached each other at a small brook called the Sauchie Burn, about a mile from the field of Bannockburn. An engagement ensued. Although the Royal troops were greatly outnumbered, the action was fiercely contested; but at last the king's men were driven back and defeated by the charges of the border spearmen. The King, in retiring from the field, was thrown from his horse, and some of the rebels came up and killed him. Thus fell James III., in the thirty-seventh year of his age, and the twenty-eighth of his reign.

The victorious barons passed the night on the field of battle. On the following morning they proceeded to Linlithgow, issued a proclamation, and immediately seized the Royal treasure and the reins of Government. The Earls of Buchan, Huntly, and Lennox, Lord Forbes and others, who fought for James III., were summoned to appear before Parliament and answer to a charge of treason. Parliament met at Edinburgh on the 6th of October, 1488, and proceeded to consider the position of those who had been summoned for treason. The Earl of Buchan appeared and tendered his submission; and he was pardoned and restored to power. None of the others who was cited appeared, and consequently their possessions were placed at the disposal of Parliament.

In 1489 the Earls of Huntly and Lennox, Lord Forbes, and others, rose in arms against the party in power. But after a short struggle the rising was suppressed. The new King, James IV., was not at all inclined to treat harshly those who had supported his father; and the young ruler soon became popular.

The Earl of Buchan died in 1499, and was succeeded by his son, Alexander, second Earl of Buchan. He died in 1508, and was succeeded by his son, John, third Earl of Buchan. He married Margaret, daughter of James Scrymgeour of Dudhope, Constable of Dundee, by whom he had issue. John Stewart, Master of Buchan, fought and fell on the disastrous field of Pinkie, in 1547. Earl John was succeeded by his grand-daughter, Christian, Countess of Buchan, in 1551. She married Robert Douglas, second son of Sir Robert Douglas of Lochleven, and in 1574 a charter of the Earldom, together with Earlshill, was granted to him and the Countess. Their son, James Douglas, was served heir to his father in 1583, and to his mother in 1588, as fifth Earl of Buchan. He married Margaret Ogilvie, a daughter of Lord Deskford. The Earl died in 1601, leaving an only daughter as heiress—Mary Douglas, Countess of Buchan.

She married James Erskine, a son of John, twentieth Earl of Mar. Thus James Erskine in right of his wife became sixth Earl of Buchan. He was one of the Lords of the Bedchamber to Charles I., and usually resided in England. The Countess died in 1628, leaving an only son and two daughters. Earl James died in 1640, and was succeeded by his son, James, seventh Earl of Buchan. He died in 1664, and was succeeded by his only son, William, eighth Earl of Buchan. At the Revolution of 1688, the Earl supported the cause of James VII., and appeared in arms against the new Government. He was captured and imprisoned in Stirling Castle, but was not brought to trial. He died in Stirling Castle in 1695, leaving no issue.

His kinsman, David Erskine, fourth Lord Cardross, succeeded to the Earldom as ninth Earl of Buchan. After the succession of George I. he was elected a representative peer in 1715, 1722, and 1727. In 1697 he married Frances, a daughter and heiress of the honourable Henry Fairfax of Hurst, in the county of Berks, and by her he had three sons and two daughters. He died in 1745, and was succeeded by his eldest surviving son, Henry David Erskine, tenth Earl of Buchan.

He was born on the 17th of April, 1710: and married Agnes, a daughter of Sir James Stewart, Baronet, of Good-trees, by whom he had issue—David Erskine, Lord Cardross, Henry of Almonddell, and Thomas. His second son, Henry, was born in November, 1746. He studied law, and was called to the Scottish bar in 1768.

He was a man of remarkable talents, and soon obtained a wide practice. He was appointed Lord Advocate in 1783, but had to resign office the same year on a change of Government. He was elected Dean of the Faculty of Advocates in 1786. In 1806, on the return of the Whigs to office, he was again appointed Lord Advocate. He was much esteemed for amiability, brilliant wit, and legal knowledge.

Thomas, the Earl's youngest son, was born in 1750. He served for a short time both in the army and navy; but resigned his commission and directed his attention to the study of law, and was called to the English bar in his twenty-eighth year. He soon took a foremost place at the bar, and some of his speeches are fine specimens of English forensic oratory. In 1783 he entered Parliament as member for Portsmouth; but his success in the House of Commons was not remarkable. In 1806 he was appointed Lord Chancellor, and received the title of Baron Erskine. He held the Great Seal only for a short time, as he had to retire on the dissolution of the Whig Government in the spring of 1807. In 1817 he published a political fragment entitled "Armata," which contains some good remarks on constitutional law and history.

John Stockdale had published a defence of Warren Hastings, composed by the Rev. John Logan, which it was alleged contained a libel upon the House of Commons, and Erskine undertook the defence of Stockdale. The trial took place on the 9th December, 1789, and the following quotation from Erskine's speech on the occasion refers to the government of India :—

"Gentlemen, I think I can observe that you are touched with this way of considering the subject, and I can account for it. I have not been considering it through the cold medium of books, but have been speaking of man and his nature, and of human dominion, from what I have seen of them myself amongst reluctant nations submitting to our authority. I know what they feel, and how such feelings can alone be suppressed. I have heard them in my youth from a naked savage, addressing the Governor of a British colony, holding a bundle of sticks in his hand, as the notes of an unlettered eloquence. 'Who is it' said the jealous ruler over the desert, encroached upon by the restless foot of English adventure, 'who is it that causes the river to rise in the high mountains and empty itself into the ocean? Who is it that causes to blow the loud winds of winter, and that calms them again in summer? Who is it that rears up the shade of these lofty forests, and blasts them with the quick lightning at his pleasure? The same Being who gave to you a country on the other side of the waters, and gave ours to us; and by this title we will defend it,' said the warrior, throwing down his tomahawk upon the ground, and raising the war sound of his nation. These are the feelings of subjugated men all round the globe; and, depend upon it, nothing but fear will control where it is vain to look for affection." Erskine died in 1823.

Earl David died in December, 1767, and was succeeded by his eldest son, David Stewart Erskine, eleventh Earl of Buchan. He married Margaret Fraser, a daughter of William Fraser of Fraserfield, in 1771. The Earl engaged little in public affairs; but he took a keen interest in antiquarian and literary subjects.

He died on the 19th of April, 1829, without issue, and was succeeded by his nephew, Henry David Erskine, twelfth Earl of Buchan. In 1809 he married Elizabeth, youngest daughter of Sir Charles Shipley, and by her had issue. He died in 1857, and was succeeded by his son, David Stewart Erskine, thirteenth Earl of Buchan.

CHAPTER III.

Earldom and Earls of Huntly.

SECTION I.

EARLY NOTICE OF THE GORDONS—ADAM GORDON JOINED WALLACE —HE WAS THE FIRST OF THE NAME WHO OBTAINED LANDS IN THE NORTH—ALEXANDER SETON, FIRST LORD GORDON.

TRADITION carries the origin and surname of Gordon far back into bygone ages. It is said that there was a tribe in Gaul called Gordon before the Christian era : and that there was a Roman Emperor of the name of Gordonius.

There appear, however, to have been families of the name of Gordon in France at an early period. The Gordons settled in Scotland in the early part of the twelfth century. It seems that they first obtained lands in Berwickshire, to which they gave the name of the barony of Gordon. In this district, another of their possessions was called Huntly, which the family at a subsequent period assumed as the title and name of their Earldom in the North, and adopted the name in Strathbogie.

About the year 1160 Richard de Gordon granted to the monks of the Abbey of Kelso a right of pasture, an acre of land at Todlaw, and an acre of meadow in Huntly-Strother, in the barony of Gordon. He was succeeded by his son, Sir Thomas de Gordon. In 1170 Sir Thomas confirmed his father's grant of lands to the monks of Kelso. He was an ardent supporter of the policy of William the Lion ; and ably assisted him in his conflicts with the people of Galloway, Ross, and other quarters of the kingdom.

Sir Thomas died in 1215, and was succeeded by his son,

Earls of Huntly.

Thomas, who was knighted by Alexander II. He confirmed the grants of his father and grandfather to the Abbey of Kelso; and made some additional grants of lands, with a portion of his peatry of Brunmoss, and with the liberty of taking timber from his woods and pulling heather on his estates, for which privileges Gordon obtained the right of burial in the cemetery of the Abbey of Kelso. He died in 1258, leaving an only child, a daughter, called Alice de Gordon. She married Sir Adam Gordon, a descendant of a younger branch of the family; and thus united the estates of Gordon and Huntly, in the Merse. Sir Adam was a man of great energy. He was one of the company who left Scotland to assist Lewis IX. of France in an expedition to the Holy Land. But disaster overtook this expedition, and Sir Adam and many others perished before reaching the Holy Land. His widow survived him for several years. She died in 1280, and was succeeded by her son, Sir Adam Gordon.

In the spring of 1296, Sir Adam Gordon, with his tenants, joined the army led by John Comyn, Earl of Buchan, which invaded and wasted the North of England. Gordon's lands were plundered by Edward I. on his march through Berwickshire, and forfeited to the English Crown. Sir Adam was present at the battle of Dunbar on the 26th of April, 1296, and fell in that disastrous action. He was succeeded by his eldest son, Sir Adam de Gordon. After the defeat of the Scots at Dunbar, Sir Adam, with a few other Scotsmen, retreated northward, until he was forced to surrender to Edward I. at Elgin, on the 28th of July, 1296.

In the spring of 1297, Sir William Wallace raised the standard against Edward I., and Sir William Douglas and Sir Adam Gordon were amongst the first who joined him. Sir Adam fought bravely at the battle of Stirling Bridge; and also, against fearful odds, at the battle of Falkirk, where the Scots were overwhelmed and defeated by the weight of superior numbers.

This was a period of rapid changes in Scotland. After the capture of Wallace in the summer of 1305, Sir Adam Gordon surrendered to Edward I. Shortly after, he was appointed one of the Justiciaries of Lothian, with an annual fee of forty merks. He continued on the English side; and in 1309, Edward II. granted to him the lands of Stichel. He adhered till 1313, to the English cause, which had then become well-nigh hopeless. Accordingly Sir Adam offered his allegiance and service to Bruce, which was gladly accepted; and he immediately joined Randolph, Earl of Moray. At the battle of Bannockburn, Randolph led the centre division of the Scottish army, and Sir Adam fought heroically under him on that memorable field.

On the 20th of April, 1320, Parliament met in the Abbey of Arbroath, and drew up a spirited and remarkably constitutional address to the Pope, which represented to His Holiness the real state of the Scottish nation. Parliament selected Sir Adam Gordon and Sir Edward Mabuisson to carry this address to Rome, and plead its prayer before the Pope. When they arrived at Rome, they were rather coldly received. But, aided by two of Sir Adam's sons, John and Thomas, who were in holy orders, they at last obtained an interview with the Pope, and presented the address from the Scottish Parliament. They succeeded so far, as the severe papal edicts against Scotland were suspended.

When Sir Adam returned home, he advised Robert I. to send Randolph, Earl of Moray, as ambassador to the Pope. Accordingly, Randolph proceeded to Rome in 1323, and he succeeded in persuading the Pope to give Bruce the title of King of Scotland, and remove all cause of quarrel.

Robert I. granted a charter of the barony of Strathbogie to Sir Adam Gordon, which had been forfeited from David Strathbogie, Earl of Athole, by an act of Parliament in 1319. He was the first of the Gordons who obtained territory in Aberdeenshire and the north. He died about 1325, and was succeeded by his son, Sir Adam Gordon. But the

Gordons were not secure in their possession of Strathbogie till after the death of the Earl of Athole.

As stated in a preceding chapter, after the death of Randolph, the Regent, Edward Baliol, at the head of an English party, invaded the kingdom, and claimed earldoms and lands in Scotland. David Strathbogie, Earl of Athole, who had married one of the heiresses of the disinherited Comyns, seized possession of Strathbogie, which had been granted by charter to Sir Adam Gordon's father. At last the Earl of Athole besieged the Castle of Kildrummy, which had been held for some years by Sir Andrew Moray's wife, Christian Bruce, the heroic sister of Robert I., on behalf of her nephew, David II. When Sir Andrew Moray, the Regent, received tidings of Athole's attack on Kildrummy, he immediately marched northward to raise the seige. He was accompanied by William Douglas, Sir Adam Gordon of Strathbogie, the Earl of Dunbar, Ramsay of Preston, and other men of note; his army numbered about eight hundred fighting men. Athole's followers were probably more numerous, as his territorial power was very extensive. He prepared to face the Regent; and, leaving Kildrummy, he marched his army to a position on the wooded slope of Culblean, in the valley of the Dee. The battle was fought on the 30th of November, 1335. William Douglas led the vanguard, with a company of stalwart men, and advanced with consummate tact, watching his opportunity, and at the proper moment ordered his men to couch their spears and charge the centre of the enemy's line. A furious hand to hand combat ensued. Sir Andrew Moray then rapidly advanced with the main body of his men, and assailed the enemy in flank with irresistible fury. The contest raged hotly for a short time. Athole fell on the field, and his followers were completely defeated, and fled in confusion.

This battle was an exceedingly important national event. It formed a turning-point, as the national party at the time were reduced to dire extremity; while Athole was the most powerful baron in Scotland, owing to his wide territorial possessions and his connection with the disinherited Comyns. Thus his continued opposition would have proved ruinous to the national cause. The battle also restored Sir Adam Gordon to his estates in Strathbogie; and secured the lands of a considerable number of other families, who would have lost their possessions if Athole and the English party had prevailed.

John Gordon, son of Sir Adam, was taken a prisoner at the battle of Durham in 1346. Sir Adam died in 1351, and was succeeded by his son, John, who was confined, with David II., and a number of other Scots prisoners, in the Tower of London by Edward III. for a period of eleven years. In 1357 the enormous ransom extorted by Edward III. for the Scottish king was adjusted, and he was released, and returned to Scotland. At the same time Sir John Gordon was liberated, and he, too, with many other prisoners, had to pay ransoms for their liberty.

In 1358 the King granted a charter confirming to John Gordon the grant which Robert I. gave to his grandfather, Sir Adam, of the lands of Strathbogie. During the rest of his life he usually resided at Strathbogie, putting his estates in order, which had been much impaired by hostile raids. He died about the year 1374, and was succeeded by his son, Sir John.

Robert II., in 1376, granted to Sir John Gordon, a charter confirming the grant made by Robert I. to his great-grandfather of the lands of Strathbogie. Sir John was a man of great activity. In 1388 he was present and fought in the battle of Otterburn, in which he distinguished himself. In 1391 he was appointed Justiciary for settling disputed marches.

Sir John died in 1394, unmarried, but left two natural sons, by Elizabeth, a daughter of Cruickshank of Aswanley, in the parish of Glass. His two sons, John and Thomas, were usually called, in the traditions of Strathbogie and the

Valley of the Deveron, "Jock and Tam," The lands of Aswanley lay on the south side of the beautiful valley of the Deveron; and the old house stood on the south bank, a few paces from the river, in a well sheltered and fertile spot, with a small brook on the east side rippling to the Deveron. It is about half a mile east from the Church of Glass.

It appears that Sir John Gordon made ample provision for his two sons. John Gordon was Laird of Essie, in the parish of Rhynie, and from him were descended the Gordons of Lesmore and other branches of the Gordons. Thomas Gordon was Laird of Daach and Ruthven, in the parish of Cairnie, and from him were descended the Gordons of Hallhead, in Cushnie, and Esslemont, in Ellon, and other branches of the old line of the Gordons of the north.

Sir John Gordon was succeeded by his brother, Sir Adam. He married Elizabeth Keith, fourth daughter of Sir William Keith, Great Marischal of Scotland, by whom he had issue. He was for a short time Warden of the East Marches. He was at the battle of Homildon, and fell while leading a charge against the English, on the 14th of September, 1402.

He was succeeded by his son, John Gordon of Huntly and Strathbogie. He married Lady Agnes Douglas, a daughter of Lord Dalkeith. By her, it appears, he had no issue. He died in 1408, and was the last of the male line of the Gordons of Strathbogie. The succession then fell to his sister, Elizabeth, who became the heiress of her father, Sir Adam Gordon.

In 1408 Elizabeth Gordon married Alexander Seton, the second son of Sir William Seton of Seton. The same year Elizabeth Gordon resigned her lands in Parliament at Perth, and on the 20th of July, she and her husband received a charter from the Regent Albany of "all the lands and baronies of Gordon and Huntly within the sheriffdom of Berwick, the lands of Fogo and Fauns, and the lands of Strathbogie and Beldygordon, in Aberdeenshire," to be held by them and their heirs. Thus Alexander Seton obtained the Gordon territories.

He was one of the commissioners appointed to treat for the liberation of James I. in 1423. The following year, on the 28th of May, he became surety for 400 merks of the King's ransom. In 1436 he was created a Lord of Parliament under the title of Lord Gordon.

In 1437 Lord Gordon drew the rents of Aboyne and Cluny. These territories appear to have come through Elizabeth Keith, the wife of Sir Adam Gordon, and from her to Lord Gordon's wife.

Alexander Seton, first Lord Gordon, had three sons and one daughter by Elizabeth Gordon, his wife—Alexander, Master of Gordon, and subsequently created Earl of Huntly; William, ancestor of the Setons of Meldrum; and Henry. His daughter Elizabeth married Alexander, Earl of Ross and Lord of the Isles. Lady Seton Gordon died at Strathbogie on the 16th of March, 1436, and was interred at St. Nicholas Church in Aberdeen. Lord Gordon died in 1440, and was succeeded by his eldest son, Alexander.

SECTION II.

ALEXANDER, SECOND LORD GORDON—FIRST EARL OF HUNTLY— APPOINTED LIEUTENANT GENERAL OF THE KINGDOM—GEORGE, SECOND EARL.

ACCORDING to some of the genealogies, Alexander, Lord Gordon, first married Jean Keith, a daughter of Sir William Keith, Great Marischal of Scotland, and she is said to have died without issue. There seems, however, to be some doubt as to this marriage. In 1425 Lord Gordon married Egidia Hay, a daughter and heiress of John Hay of Tullibody. The following year, on the 8th of January, the King, upon the resignation of Egidia, granted to them and their heirs the lands of the barony of Tullibody; also the forests of Boyne and Enzie, and barony of Kilsaurle; and the lands of Kinmundy in the barony of King-Edward. By this lady he had a son, Alexander, who succeeded to the lands of Tullibody, his mother's heritage, and he became the ancestor of the Setons of Abercorn. Lord Gordon divorced Egidia Hay, a proceeding which seems to have been effected without any bad feeling on either side.

Lord Gordon next married Elizabeth, a daughter of Sir William Crichton, Lord High Chancellor of Scotland, and by her he had three sons and three daughters—George, his successor; Alexander of Midmar, and Adam Dean, of Caithness; his eldest daughter, Janet, married James Dunbar, Earl of Moray; Elizabeth married, first, Nicol Hay, second, Earl of Erroll; and she married, secondly, John, Lord Kennedy; Christian married William, Lord Forbes.

Alexander, Lord Gordon, resigned his lands into the King's hands for new infeftment on the 3rd of April, 1441, and on the same day he and Elizabeth his wife received a charter of the lordships of Gordon and Strathbogie; the lands of Aboyne, Glentanner, Glenmuick, and others.

So large a portion of the Keith lands having come into the possession of Lord Gordon, a dispute arose between him and Sir William Keith, Great Marischal of Scotland. A meeting to settle matters was held at Cluny on the 1st of August, 1442, at which Lord Gordon and Sir William Keith, Walter Ogilvie of Beaufort, Sir Alexander Irvine of Drum, Sir Andrew Ogilvie, of Inchmartin, and others were present. After careful deliberation, Lord Gordon granted a deed stating that—" From natural affection, nearness of kin, and for services done to him, he and his heirs renounced, and discharged all rights and claims that he or they had, or may have in time to come, in favour of Sir William Keith, Marischal of Scotland, of all lands, offices, or any part of them, in possession of Sir William Keith. Lord Gordon also promised to make Sir William and his son,

Sir Robert, sure of the said lands and offices. He further bound himself and his heirs to pay the penalties named in an agreement between his deceased father and mother and himself on the one part, and the said Sir William Keith and his wife on the other part, if he or his heirs broke the conditions of this contract; and has sworn the bodily oath and touched the Holy Book, that he and his heirs shall keep and fulfil these conditions. Amen."

On the 5th of October, 1443, Alexander, Earl of Ross, Lord of the Isles, and Justiciary beyond the Forth, granted the barony of King Edward and the patronage of all the benefices within it to Alexander Seton, Lord Gordon, for his life-time; and commanded all the tenants to obey him.

The exact date of the creation of the Earldom of Huntly has not been ascertained. The date usually given is the year 1449, but there is some evidence that the Earldom was conferred on Lord Gordon in 1445. Anywise, the new Earl rapidly rose to a commanding position in the government of the kingdom. The great political question of the time was the fierce and determined struggle which raged between the Crown and the House of Douglas. In this contest the first Earl of Huntly acted a very important and decisive part on the side of the Stuart line. For nearly ten years the nation from day to day knew not whether Stuart or Douglas would triumph.

In 1449 the Earl of Huntly was the King's tenant in the lands of Buchrom, Kinnimond, and Abergeldie. On the 28th of April, 1451, he received for his services to the Crown, a charter from James II. of the Lordship of Badenoch and the Castle of Ruthven.

The tragic death of the Earl of Douglas by the hands of the King in Stirling Castle in February, 1452, was the signal for civil war, which raged from the Borders to Inverness. The vassals of the Douglases and their allies—the Earls of Crawford and Ross—were very numerous and daring, and the King was in great difficulty and imminent peril. He immediately appointed the Earl of Huntly, Lieutenant-General of the kingdom. But Huntly himself was in an extremely difficult position. On the north side of him were the Earl of Ross, and the two Douglas, Earls of Moray and Ormond, while on the other was the powerful and fierce Earl of Crawford. Huntly soon mustered a strong force from the valley of the Deveron, Strathbogie, the valley of the Dee, and other quarters of the north.

The King had resolved to join Huntly, and marched to Perth. But the Earl of Crawford, who was at the head of an army, determined to prevent Huntly from joining the King; and he took up a strong position about two miles north-east from Brechin. Huntly marched southward, and on the 18th of May, 1452, the two armies came in sight of each other. A fierce and severe battle ensued. The Lindsays fought bravely, and for a time the issue seemed doubtful. Both sides displayed great bravery, Crawford himself made many desperate efforts to win the day. At last he was completely defeated, and fled to his Castle of Finhaven, hotly pursued by Calder of Aswanley. The loss was severe on both sides. Two of Huntly's brothers—William and Henry—were slain, and a considerable number of his vassals. One of Crawford's brothers and many of his followers fell upon the field.

The highest point of the rising ground on the north side of the battlefield is called "Huntly's Hill," and upon it there is a large stone, known as "Huntly's and Bardie's Stone." Huntly had to return north to chastise the Earl of Moray and his men, who had invaded and wasted Strathbogie during his absence at Brechin. He crossed the Spey, and advanced into Morayshire, and inflicted severe punishment upon the followers of Douglas, Earl of Moray. The final struggle between the King and the Douglases took place in the south of the kingdom.

When at Aberdeen on the 7th of September, 1456, James II. granted a remission to the Earl of Huntly and his son, Sir George Seton, Master of Gordon, for their depredations on the Earldom of Mar. The Earldom was then in dispute between the King and Lord Erskine; and Huntly had occupied the lands of Kildrummy and Migvie in 1452-53.

In 1464 the Earl received from the King a charter erecting the town of Kingussie, in the Lordship of Badenoch, into a free burgh of barony. In 1467 the King granted Huntly a charter of certain lands in Elgin.

The Earl of Huntly, during the latter part of his life, endeavoured to strengthen his position by entering into bonds of manrent. On the 8th of July, 1468, William, Lord Forbes, "becomes man of special fealty, retinue, and service to an high and mighty Lord, Alexander, Earl of Huntly, and Lord of Badenoch, to serve him leal and truly for all the days of my life, both in peace and war, before and against all them that live or die, my allegiance to my sovereign only excepted." This bond, at the same date and in similar terms, was repeated in favour of George, Lord Gordon, son and heir-apparent to the Earl of Huntly; and thereupon the Earl of Huntly granted to Lord Forbes and his heirs the lands of Abergarden, in the barony of Aboyne, the lands of Tulyfour, in the Lordship of Tough and the barony of Cluny, and other lands, all within the Sheriffdom of Aberdeen. "And if I (Lord Forbes) shall happen to die, as God forbid, without issue by Christian Gordon, my wife, daughter of the Earl of Huntly, and sister of Lord Gordon, through which the succession to my heritage fall into the hands of any other of my kin, male or female, whatsoever they be that shall succeed me in my heritage of the lands of the Lordship of Forbes, the heirs succeeding to me shall likewise be men of special service, manrent, and retinue, as I am to my foresaid Lords."

In this way the succeeding Earls of Huntly, following the common practice of the times, made many efforts to secure and extend their power.

Alexander, first Earl of Huntly, died at Strathbogie on

the 15th of July, 1470, and was interred at Elgin. His kinsman, Richard Forbes, Dean of Aberdeen, mortified certain lands to the altar of St. Mary for the repose of his soul and that of his Countess, Elizabeth Crichton. Buchanan's lines on the Earl may be quoted :—

> Enclosed within this tomb lies
> ALEXANDER GORDON,
> Who has added new lustre to an ancient name.
> Comely, strong, and in his course of life
> by ill unsubdued ;
> Rich, shunning extravagance, hospitable to all ;
> Loving peace, ready for war.
> Having gone the round of all the blessings
> of a happy life ;
> He rendered up his soul to heaven, his dust to earth.

He was succeeded by his son George, second Earl of Huntly. While Lord Gordon, under a strictly fenced and guarded matrimonial contract, dated the 20th of May, 1455, he married Elizabeth Dunbar, Countess of Moray, and widow of Archibald Douglas, Earl of Moray, who was slain at the battle of Arkinholm on the 1st of May the same year. This marriage did not continue long. As the parties were within the forbidden degree of relationship, a divorce was obtained. There was no issue of the marriage.

Huntly next married the Princess Annabella, a daughter of James I., in 1458, by whom he had issue, four sons and four daughters. But in July, 1471, he was divorced from her on account of his marriage with the Countess of Moray, his first wife, as both ladies were within the third and fourth degrees of relationship. Their descendants, however, were legitimated.

The Earl married, thirdly, Elizabeth Hay, a daughter of William, first Earl of Erroll, and by her he had issue, three daughters.

Although a truce with England was concluded in October, 1474, to continue for seventeen years, yet Edward IV. was not friendly to Scotland. He harboured the forfeited Earl of Douglas, and entered into negotiations with John, Earl of Ross and Lord of the Isles, with whom he concluded a treaty. When the terms of the treaty became known to the Government, the Earl of Ross was summoned to appear before Parliament in Edinburgh and answer to several charges of treason; but he failed to appear, and sentence of forfeiture was passed against him. Preparations were then made to invade his territories and reduce him to subjection.

The Earls of Crawford and Athole led an expedition against the Earl of Ross. The Earl of Huntly also mustered his vassals, and captured the Castle of Dingwall. He then led his force into Lochaber, and induced the Earl of Ross to tender his submission and petition for pardon. The Earl followed Huntly's advice, and though the Earldom of Ross was annexed to the Crown, and the districts of Cantyre and Knapdale and the Castles of Inverness and Nairn were taken from him, at the intercession of the Queen, the rest of his lands were restored by royal charter. He was also created a Lord of Parliament under the title of Lord of the Isles.

On the 27th of March, 1476, the King sent a letter to the Earl of Huntly, warmly thanking him for the part he had taken in the subjection of the Earl of Ross. Shortly after, the King promised to secure by charter and seizin to the Earl and his heirs 100 merks worth of land in convenient places in the north parts of the kingdom.

In 1472 Sir Alexander Dunbar of Westfield gave his letters of faith to "become man to a noble and mighty lord, my Lord George, Earl of Huntly, Lord of Gordon and Badenoch, in leal and true manrent and service, in peace and in war, against all deadly in all the points contained in the oath of manrent, my allegiance to our Sovereign Lord the King alone excepted. This my manrent and service to endure for all the days of my life, all fraud and guile excluded and put away. "At Huntly, the 30th day of

June, before these witnesses—Ranald of Wenton, George Leslie of Quhitecorse; Hugh the Ross, son and heir-apparent to Hugh the Ross of Kylrawak; William of Seteoun, and many others.

The Earl of Huntly was Keeper of the castles of Inverness and Redcastle. In 1479 he was appointed Justiciary north of the Forth. Thus it came within his functions to use his authority for the suppression of feuds between families. Duncan, the chief of the Mackintoshes, was accused for breach of contract touching the lands of Glenmoriston; and at Perth, on the 25th of July, 1481, he became bound to obey the judgment of his Lord Superior, "and make amends if any breach was proved."

SECTION III.

GEORGE, SECOND EARL OF HUNTLY.—WARBECK IN SCOTLAND—LADY CATHERINE GORDON.

IN 1481 a contract of marriage between William, son of Earl Marischal, and Elizabeth, daughter of the Earl of Huntly, was concluded as follows:—"That is to say, that for great favours and kindness which has been between the said Lords, and to be continued among the same (God willing)—William, son and apparent heir to Earl Marischal, shall marry and have to wife Elizabeth Gordon, daughter of the said Earl of Huntly. For which marriage, to be solemnised in the face of the Holy Kirk, the said George, Earl of Huntly, his heirs and assignees, shall pay to the said William, Earl Marischal, his heirs, executors, or assignees, the sum of sixteen hundred marks, usual money of Scotland, at the terms under written, that is to say—at the term of Whitsunday, beginning in the year of God 1481, one hundred marks; and at the term of Martinmas in winter following, another hundred marks, and so forth, year by year and term by term, two hundred marks yearly without any interruption until the said sum of sixteen hundred marks be fully paid. . . . And, further, it is appointed between the parties that William, Earl Marischal, shall infeft by charter and possession the said William, his son, and Elizabeth, his spouse, and to their heirs male, one hundred marks worth of lands to be held of the King, of his lands of the barony of Aden, lying within the Sheriffdom of Aberdeen, and in due form at the sight of the Earl of Huntly, and the expense thereof to be evenly divided between the two Lords. And if their writs be misty and not clear in anything, that they shall be corrected at the sight of the friends of both parties, and especially of William, Earl of Erroll, William, Lord Forbes, Alexander Gordon of Midmar, Master Gilbert de Hey of Ury, James Wishart of Pitarow, and Robert Arbuthnot of that Ilk."

The Earl of Huntly was among the Barons who accompanied the King and his army to the Borders in 1482. The army was well equipped, and Cochrane, one of the King's favourites, was appointed to command the artillery. When the army reached Lauder a tragic scene occurred. The Barons, headed by the Earl of Angus, met in a church, and after some deliberation they resolved to seize the King and sweep off his favourites. While they were considering how to execute their resolution, a knock was heard at the door; it was Cochrane with a message from the King. When Cochrane entered, the Earl of Angus instantly seized him, and pulled the gold chain from his neck, saying that "a rope would befit him better." "My lords," said Cochrane, "is it jest or earnest?" He was told that it was earnest, and he was quickly bound and placed under guard. A party of the Barons, who were despatched to the royal tent, immediately seized the King's musician, Rogers, and the rest of the royal favourites. These were then led, along with Cochrane, to the Bridge of Lauder, where they were all hanged. After these executions the Barons disbanded the army, returned to the capital with the King, and imprisoned him in the Castle of Edinburgh.

In the subsequent proceedings of the Duke of Albany, the Earl of Huntly took the side of the King. When the conspiracy of the southern Barons reached a crisis, in 1488, Huntly supported the King. And after the King's death, Huntly opposed the party of the Barons at the head of the Government for some time; but he became a favourite with James IV., and opposition to the party in power soon ceased. Huntly was made a Privy Councillor; and on the 13th of May, 1491, he was appointed Lieutenant of the North until the King attained twenty-five years of age, and thereafter during His Majesty's pleasure.

Alexander Home of that Ilk gave his bond of manrent to the Earl of Huntly in 1486, in these terms:—"I, Alexander Home, have become man, by the faith and truth in my body, for all the days of my life, to a right noble and mighty Lord, and my dearest Lord, George, Earl of Huntly, Lord Gordon and Badenoch, counter and against all that live or die, may, my allegiance to our Sovereign Lord the King only excepted. In witness of this my manrent, I have put my seal, with the subscription of my hand." In 1490, Home, who was then Great Chamberlain of Scotland, gave anew his bond of manrent to Alexander Gordon, Master of Huntly.

The same year, Sir John Rutherfurd of Tarland gave his bond of manrent to Lord Gordon, Master of Huntly, thus—"I, Sir John Rutherfurd of Tarland, to be bound and strictly obliged, and by the faith of my body leally and truly, bind and oblige myself, in the straitest style of obligation, to a noble and mighty Lord, Alexander, Lord Gordon, in true manrent, homage, and service, for all the days of my life; that I shall be ready to ride and pass with my Lord at his warning, in all his lawful and honest quarrels, and give leal and true counsel . . . and abide and remain with his Lordship against whosoever, my allegiance to our Sovereign and my service of law only excepted, because my said Lord is bound to defend me, and give me a fee at his pleasure. . . . In witness of which I have affixed my seal to this at Aberdeen, the 8th of December, 1490."

At Perth, on the 21st of February, 1491, a contract of marriage between the Earl of Bothwell and a daughter of the Earl of Huntly was arranged. It was agreed between "the right noble and mighty Lords, George, Earl of Huntly, and Alexander, Lord Gordon, his son, on the one part, and Patrick, Earl Bothwell and Lord Hailes, on the other part, in form and effect as follows:—that Earl Bothwell shall marry, God willing, and have to wife one of the two daughters of the Earl of Huntly—Margaret or Catherine—whichever pleases him best . . . Between the date of this agreement and the 20th day of April next, and thereafter as hastely as it may be lawfully, shall solemnise and complete, in the face of the Holy Kirk, this marriage . . . For which marriage to be completed, God willing, the Earl of Huntly, and Lord Gordon, their heirs, executors, and assignees, shall be thankfully content and pay to the Earl Bothwell, his heirs, executors, and assignees, the sum of two thousand marks of usual money of Scotland, at the following terms—at the fest of Witsonday, two hundred marks, at the fest of St Martin in the winter following, other 200 marks, and so forth till the 2000 marks be fully paid." At the same time the parties for themselves and their friends agreed to a bond of alliance to continue for all the days of their lives, and that they would assist each other to the utmost of their power "in all their actions, causes, and quarrels, moved and to be moved, with their persons, goods, castles, strengths, kin, men, and friends, and all that will do for them, against all men that live and die may, their allegiance to the King excepted; and they shall fortify, supply, maintain, and defend each other in men, kin, and friends, in their honours, lands, heritages, conquests, goods, and all other matters whatsoever, without dissimulation, to the utmost of their power; that when any of them shall know, hear, or see, scath or personal grievance to the honours, heritages, or goods of the others, then they should tell and show it to them, and do the utmost to defend them."

Alexander Innes of Aberchirder gave a bond of manrent to Alexander, Lord Gordon, Master of Huntly, on the 8th of September, 1491, which was witnessed by Kenneth Mackenzie of Kintail, Alexander Seton of Meldrum, John Leslie of Wardes, Thomas Gordon of Kennardy, and Duncan Thomson of Auchinhamper.

The Earl of Huntly often had difficulties with the chiefs and people on the Highland territories over which he was Lord Superior. After the forfeiture of the Earl of Ross, in 1476, there was much fighting in the Highlands; and part of the Earldom of Ross was wasted. Repeated attempts were made in the name of John, Lord of the Isles, to recover the Earldom of Ross. Alexander of Lochalsh, a natural brother of the Lord of the Isles, could command a considerable number of followers. In 1491 he made a raid into the counties of Inverness and Ross, and wasted the country; but, at last he was defeated by the Mackenzies. The Mackenzies, however, paid little respect to the officers of the Crown; and the Earl of Huntly had to issue a commission of fire and sword against them. In a Parliament held at Edinburgh in May 1493, John, Lord of the Isles, was forfeited. Shortly after he surrendered to the King, and then retired to the monastery of Paisley, where he died in 1498, and was interred in the tomb of his Royal relative, King Robert III.

The Earl of Huntly sometimes accompanied the King in his expeditions to the north. In 1497 Huntly was appointed Lord High Chancellor of Scotland.

In the year 1495 a remarkable character appeared in Scotland—Perkin Warbeck—who, according to some authorities, was a son of a Florentine Jew; but, according to his own confession, he was a native of Tournay, in Flanders. This man was persuaded by the Duchess of Burgundy, a sister of Richard III. of England, to personate her nephew, Richard, a brother of Edward V. Thus Perkin, accompanied with six hundred men, attempted to land at Kent in July, 1495; but he was repulsed, and one hundred and fifty of his men were captured and executed. He next made an effort to obtain a footing in Ireland, but failed. Undaunted by these failures, Perkin pursued his mission, and, with his retinue, he arrived at Stirling Castle on the 20th of November, 1495. James IV. was a remarkably romantic character himself, and he at once received Perkin as "Prince Richard of England," and conducted him to apartments in Stirling Castle. Immediately letters were despatched to the Earls of Athole, Strathearn, Huntly, and Earl Marischal, and the barons of Angus, commanding them to meet the King at Perth, that they might have the honour of being presented to Prince Richard. As it was intended to wage war on behalf of the claims of this prince to the throne of England, letters were sent to the sheriffs ordering wappenschaws to be held throughout the kingdom. Perkin soon became a favourite of the King. A personal allowance of £1200 a year was granted to him; while his followers were quartered and maintained among the burghs. He moved through the kingdom in the style of a prince, staying at Perth, Falkland Palace, Aberdeen, Stirling, Linlithgow, and Edinburgh, as suited his pleasure.

Favoured by the King, a marriage was arranged between Perkin and Catherine Gordon, a daughter of the Earl of Huntly, a lady of rare beauty and attraction. The marriage was celebrated, and Perkin then assumed the title of Duke of York.

The King resolved to support the Duke's claim to the throne of England, and ordered the Crown vassals to muster at Lauder. The preparations for the invasion of England were completed on the 12th of September, 1496. On the 14th the King and the Duke of York made their offerings in the Chapel of Holyrood, and ordered a trental of masses for the success of the undertaking, and then marched south-

Earls of Huntly. 127

ward. The Scots crossed the border and entered Northumberland; and the Duke of York then issued a manifesto to his subjects, declaring that he had come to deliver them from the usurpation and tyranny of Henry VII; but the English people showed no signs of enthusiasm for a new King introduced by a Scottish army. The army plundered Northumberland, and returned to Scotland. On the 8th of October, the King and the Duke had returned to Edinburgh.

After this failure, the Duke's followers soon fell away. James IV. at last discovered that Perkin's cause was unpopular among the people, and resolved to send him away. A ship, called the Cuckoo, was equipped at Ayr, and amply stored with provisions. In the middle of July, 1497, the Duke and his Duchess and about thirty attendants sailed from the port of Ayr, under the care of Robert Barton, a skilful mariner; and on the 26th of July he arrived at Cork, where he was coldly received. Thence he sailed, with three small vessels, for Cornwall, and landed at Whitesand Bay on the 7th of September. He assumed to title of Richard IV., and raised his standard. About 3000 men joined him, and he attacked Exeter; but he was captured on the 5th of October, and carried to London. He was executed at Tyburn on the 28th of November, 1499.

Lady Catherine Gordon accompanied her husband when he was defeated in Cornwall. She was taken prisoner at St. Michael's Mount. But she was kindly treated. Henry VII. took a great interest in the beautiful prisoner; and after the execution of her husband she lived at the English Court. Subsequently she married thrice. She died in 1537, and was interred in Fyfield Church, where a monument was erected to her memory.

In March, 1500, the Earl of Huntly held a Justiciary Court at Jedburgh, and fined the Earl of Bothwell, who was Warden of the West Marches, £500. This sum represented the pledges or bail for a number of persons dwelling in Liddesdale who had failed to appear in court.

The Earl founded the Castle of Bog of Gight (Gordon Castle) and repaired the Castles of Strathbogie and Aboyne. He died at Stirling in 1500, and was interred at Cambuskenneth.

SECTION IV.

ALEXANDER, THIRD EARL OF HUNTLY—HE WAS COMMISSIONED TO RESTORE PEACE IN THE HIGHLANDS.

EARL GEORGE was succeeded by his son Alexander, Third Earl of Huntly. He married Jean Stewart, a daughter of the Earl of Athole, and by her he had four sons and several daughters. He married, secondly, Elizabeth Gray, by whom he had no issue.

Soon after he succeeded to the Earldom he was appointed Sheriff of Elgin and Forres. He had a tack of the Crown lands of Brachlie, Balnacrief, Calloquhy, and Culmore. In December, 1500, he received from the King a grant of wide territory in Lochaber, which had been in the hands of the Crown since the forfeiture of the late Earl of Ross and Lord of the Isles.

In 1503 the Earl of Huntly was commissioned to proceed to Lochaber to let the King's lands to loyal men, and to expel broken men from the district. At the same time the Earl of Argyle was appointed Lieutenant-General of the Isles, and empowered to let the lands of the Islands, and to expel all those whom he pleased. These proceedings led to a rebellion of the Islesmen in 1503.

A grandson of the late Lord of the Isles, known under the name of Donald Dubh, was captured by the Earl of Athole and given up to the Earl of Argyle, who threw him into prison. Donald, however, made his escape from Argyle in 1501; and in 1503 he assumed the title and position of Lord of the Isles. The Government proclaimed him and his supporters rebels. Nevertheless, the Islesmen invaded Badenoch, Lochaber, and the islands of Bute and Arran.

The Earls of Huntly, Argyle, and Crawford were ordered to lead an army against them; and a naval demonstration was also made to cow the Islesmen. Parliament met at Edinburgh on the 11th of March, 1503, and with the sanction of Parliament, the King then proclaimed that—" If any one should apprehend and bring to the King, Maclean of Lochbuy, great Macleod of Lewis, or Macneil of Barra, and others named, they should receive half of these rebels' lands; and if they capture and bring to the King any other chief, or any Highlandman whatsoever connected with the rebellion, they shall be rewarded therefor according to the value of the lands and goods of the persons taken." A naval and a land attack was made upon the Islesmen, and they for a time were quelled.

When the Earl of Huntly returned from the expedition, the King, for the special and faithful service which he had rendered, granted to him and his heirs the lands of Mamore, in the Lordship of Lochaber.

Yet, in 1505 the Islesmen again revolted. The Earl of Huntly was commanded to march against them from the north, while the King himself, at the head of an army, advanced from the south. A number of the chiefs submitted; but Macleod of Lewis held out, and Huntly besieged and stormed his Castle of Stornoway. Donald Dudh was captured and imprisoned in the Castle of Edinburgh.

In 1505 the Earl of Huntly resigned the lands of the Earldom, and the King re-granted them to him and his heirs, " creating, uniting, and incorporating these lands into one free Barony and Earldom, to be named the Barony and Earldom of Huntly, and the chief messuage of the same, which was formerly called Strathbogie, to be in all future times named the Castle of Huntly." At the same time he received charters of the barony of Fothergill and others in Perthshire; and also the Castle of Inverlochy. In 1506 the King granted to him the lands of Cullarlies, in Aberdeenshire, and the Forest of Cabrach, for his faithful service.

On the 16th of January, 1509, the Earl of Huntly was created hereditary Sheriff of Inverness, which then embraced a jurisdiction over the counties of Inverness, Ross, Sutherland, and Caithness. He had to appoint deputies at Tain, Dingwall, Wick, Inverlochy, and Kingussie. He was also custodier of the Castle of Inverness, and was empowered to erect fortalices and appoint captains.

The Earl made efforts to strengthen his position and influence by bonds of manrent. In 1502 Huntly obtained a bond of manrent from Alexander Seton of Tullibody—" And I shall keep service and manrent to my said Lord, in all his actions, matters, and quarrels . . . . and I shall keep his counsel secret, &c." In 1503 Alexander Crome of Inverernane gave his bond of manrent and became a true man and servant to Alexander, Earl of Huntly—" for all the days of my life." And " I shall keep his counsel if he shows it to me, and if he desires my counsel, I shall give him the best for his honour and profit that I can."

In 1506 Sir William Scott of Balnery gave his bond of manrent to Alexander, Earl of Huntly, "for all the days of my lifetime." And " I shall ride and go with him, and take part in all his matters, actions, causes, and quarrels, in peace and in war, before all living men." This bond is dated at Edinburgh, and witnessed by Robert Innes of Invermerkie, Thomas Copland of Udach, Mr. James Strachin, John of Seton, Mr. John Davidson, and others.

Alexander Reid, laird of Dallaquharny, gave a bond of manrent to Huntly on the 17th of April, 1508. In 1509, William Robertson, laird of Strowane, became "bound to a noble and mighty lord—Alexander, Earl of Huntly, Lord Gordon and Badenoch—that I shall be a true man and servant to him, and shall be ready to ride and go with him in peace and in war, with my kin and friends, before and against all others except the King, and John, Master of

Athole." Robertson had a bond of manrent with the Master of Athole.

On the 30th of November, 1509, at Elgin, John Grant of Freuchie gave his bond of manrent to the Earl of Huntly—" In friendship and service to the said Earl, to honour, assist and serve him, with all the kin, friends, servants, dependants, and partakers that I may make—in all and whatsoever his actions, causes, questions, and quarrels, against all persons whatsoever."

At Inverness on the 10th of March, 1511, Doul Ranaldson gave his bond of manrent to Alexander, Earl of Huntly, thus:—" I, Doul Ranaldson, the son and heir of Ranald Alanson of Alanbigrin . . . bind and oblige myself to a noble and mighty Lord and my Lord Alexander, Earl of Huntly, for his reward, help and supply given to me, that I become and shall be his man and servant, and shall continue his manrent and service during all the days of my life." The same year, at Huntly, on the 25th of June, Duncan Thomson of Auchinhamper gave his bond of manrent to the Earl of Huntly, thus:—" Forasmuch as my said Lord has given me his letter of maintenance, therefore I bind and oblige myself to become a true man and servant to my Lord for all the days of my life."

In 1519, John, Earl of Athole, gave his bond of manrent to the Earl of Huntly. He bound himself to give Huntly true counsel when he asked it, and to assist him in peace and war, with his kin, servants, and friends. The bond is dated at Perth.

Huntly's brother, Adam Gordon, had married Elizabeth, a daughter of John, Earl of Sutherland; and a dispute arose touching the succession to the Earldom of Sutherland. Owing to Huntly's position of hereditary Sheriff of Inverness, it was in his court and before him that his brother Adam tried to get his wife served as heir to her father in the Earldom of Sutherland. This, however, could hardly be effected, as Elizabeth had two brothers, John and Alexander, then living. Nevertheless, the power and influence of Huntly ultimately prevailed; and Adam Gordon's grandson, John, on the death of his grandmother in 1535, succeeded to the Earldom of Sutherland.

In 1510, John, Lord Gordon, married Margaret Stewart, a natural daughter of James IV., by Margaret Drummond. The Earl, his father, granted to him and his wife certain lands in the lordship of Badenoch, and also the lands of Fothergill in Perthshire. Lord Gordon died at Kinloss on the 5th of December, 1517, and was interred before the high altar of the Abbey. He left two sons—George, who afterwards became fourth Earl of Huntly, and Alexander, Bishop of the Isles and Galloway.

At the battle of Flodden the Earl of Huntly and Lord Home commanded the left wing of the Scots, consisting of the northern clans and the borderers, numbering six thousand men. They attacked the English vanguard and drove it back in disorder; but the English reserve then advanced and kept Huntly in check. After a long and desperate struggle, in which the Earls of Lennox, Argyle, Crawford, Montrose, and many others were slain, the right and left wings of the Scots were completely routed.

Meantime the King and the Earl of Surrey were wrestling in a fierce hand-to-hand combat in the centre. The King placed himself at the head of his spearmen and fought with the utmost fury and bravery, and the English ranks were repeatedly broken and Surrey's standard threatened. At last the King and his division were completely surrounded by the enemy; still the Scots fought in a circle with their spears extended outward, and repelled their assailants. The King himself fell, mortally wounded in the head, within a spear's length of the Earl of Surrey. Even yet the Scots continued to fight till night put an end to the contest. The Earl of Huntly escaped from the field, but the Laird of Gight and many of the Gordon clan were slain. In short, there was scarcely a family of note in the kingdom but had lost some of its members on the fatal field of Flodden.

After the battle, Huntly took an active part in the Government of the country, and endeavoured to preserve order, which was a difficult task. The Queen was appointed Regent by Parliament, and Huntly was to assist her in the government of the kingdom. But her frothy disposition speedily led her into actions which rendered this arrangement nugatory, as she married the young Earl of Angus in 1514, which immediately deprived her of the Regency.

A party of the barons were looking to the Duke of Albany as a likely personage to take the reins of Government. As a member of the Royal Family, after the infant King, he was next heir to the throne. He was requested to assume the functions of Governor of Scotland; but the state of society in Scotland offered comparatively few attractions to a man habituated to the gay and fashionable society of France, and he seems to have been very loth to leave the enjoyments of his adopted country, even in exchange for the highest office in the Council of Scotland.

In May, 1515, the Duke of Albany arrived in Scotland, and received a warm welcome from the people. He began his government with bold and severe measures. Lord Home and his brother were apprehended, tried, condemned, and executed for treason. Their lands in the lordship of Gordon, on the Borders, were forfeited; and on the 26th of October, 1516, these lands were granted by the Regent Albany to Alexander, Earl of Huntly.

When Albany returned to France in 1517, he appointed the Earl of Huntly Lieutenant-General of Scotland, excepting the West Highlands, over which Argyle held a commission. As stated in preceding paragraphs, Huntly was firmly allied with the Earl of Athole and many of the lairds in the north, and he was then the most powerful man in the kingdom. But there was much disorder in the country, which was greatly increased by the persistent interference of Henry VIII. with the internal affairs of Scotland. He appears to have had a special animus at the Duke of Albany. He endeavoured to get the young King, James V., into his hands by encouraging his sister to flee into England with her children; he kept a number of paid spies and agents in Scotland for the express purpose of exciting tumults, private quarrels, and rekindling the jealousy of the nobles, in order to distract and discredit the Government of the Regent Albany.

Owing to the able control of the Earl of Huntly, there was less disorder in the north than in the southern quarters of the kingdom. In 1521 Huntly proceeded to Ross, accompanied by many of his allies, to settle his affairs and prevent disorder in that district. He stayed in the Castle of Dingwall for some time, where he granted charters to a number of his adherents.

Huntly was with the army mustered by Albany, the Regent, in September, 1522. Albany marched at the head of the army to the Scottish Border on the Solway; but it appeared that the Earl of Huntly was opposed to an invasion of England in the interest of France; and, on the advice of Huntly, Argyle, and the Earl of Arran, a truce was concluded between Lord Dacre and Albany. The Scottish army was then disbanded.

Albany again resolved to invade England in October, 1523, and the northern clans were commanded to meet Huntly at Stirling. It appears that Huntly was seized with a severe illness, and was unable to accompany the army. He died at Perth on the 16th of January, 1524.

SECTION V.

GEORGE, FOURTH EARL OF HUNTLY—HUNTLY CREATED HEREDITARY SHERIFF OF ABERDEEN.

EARL ALEXANDER was succeeded by his grandson George, a boy of ten years, the eldest son of John, Lord Gordon.

Earls of Huntly. 135

His lot was cast in a stirring and important period of the nation's history. He succeeded to a high position, with its many responsibilities and great opportunities, amid difficult circumstances.

During his minority the young Earl frequently resided at Court, where he had many opportunities of observing the proceedings of personages in high circles and at the centre of authority. For some time after the departure of the Regent Albany there was an intense struggle of factions and divided counsels at the head of affairs. The Earl of Angus at last seized the young King James V., and shortly concentrated all the power of the Crown in his own hands. Angus kept the King in close constraint, and, revelling in his usurped power, he exercised a severe tyranny on all who dared to oppose him. Two attempts were made to rescue the King from the grasp of the bold and daring noble, in one of which the Earl of Lennox lost his life; while the chains of the captive were more firmly riveted than before. The Douglases were complete masters of the position—Angus himself was Lord High Chancellor, his uncle was Treasurer, and they compelled the King to sign all deeds which they presented to him. At last, with the assistance of Archbishop Beaton and others, the King escaped from Angus in May, 1528, and from that time to the end of his reign he pursued the Earl and his associates with relentless severity.

It appears that the young Earl of Huntly was seduced from his allegiance by the Earl of Angus, and that he accompanied Angus in his flight into England. Afterwards Huntly offered his fealty and homage to the King, who warmly received him, as they had been often together as playmates. In 1529 the Earl of Huntly received a charter from the King of the lands of the Lordship of Strathdee and Cromar, excepting Migvie, for a rent of £180, twenty marts (cattle), and six bolls of oats.

In 1530 the Earl of Huntly contracted to marry Elizabeth

Keith, a sister of William, fourth Earl Marischal. This contract is remarkably minute in details; and contains careful provisions against the contingency of divorce. The Marischal promised to give Elizabeth five thousand merks as a tocher; on the other hand, the Earl of Huntly undertook to infeft Earl Marischal in forty pounds worth of land in the barony of Huntly, under a letter of reversion. The marriage was consummated, and the Earl by Elizabeth had nine sons and three daughters.

On the 26th of June, 1532, the Earl of Huntly received a bond of manrent from Hector Mackintosh, captain of Clan Chattan, which was dated at Pitlurg, and witnessed by George Gordon of Gight, John Gordon of Longar, Robert Innes, brother of the laird of Innes, and others. The captain and his men had wasted the lands of the Earl of Moray—James Stewart, a natural son of James IV.—and taken possession of the castles of Darnaway and Halhill. In 1534, Huntly, as Lieutenant-General of the North, had to execute a commission of fire and sword against Hector Mackintosh and his men, in which Huntly was assisted by Grant, the laird of Freuchie.

In 1533 friendly relations between the Gordons and the Forbeses were broken. It appears that during the absence of Lord Forbes, his tenants had made depredations on Huntly's forest of Corennie. The Earl demanded reparation, and summoned the offenders. The unfortunate feud between the Forbeses and the Gordons frequently led to distressing conflicts.

In 1536 Huntly received a number of bonds of manrent. James Garioch of Kinstair and his son John gave their bond of manrent to the Earl; and Robert Duguid of Auchinhove. in Lumphanan. They bound themselves to serve their lord within the kingdom of Scotland in all his actions and quarrels. In December Hector Maclean of Duart, and M'Kinnon of Strathardale, visited Strathbogie to arrange about a wadset, which Earl Alexander had from Maclean's father, of lands in Lochaber. Having amicably settled this matter, they gave Huntly a bond of manrent.

On the 25th of June, 1537, at Lenturk, Duncan Davidson of Auchinhamper gave his bond of manrent to the Earl of Huntly. The following year, George, Lord Hume, became bound by the truth and faith in his body "to a noble and mighty Lord, George, Earl of Huntly, Lord Gordon and Badenoch, Chancellor of Scotland, and Knight of the most noble order of St Michael. . . . That we, our kinsmen and friends, shall serve and take a full part, and be for the said Earl, his kin and men, in all his and their good causes, quarrels, and just opinions and actions, honest and lawful, as faithfully as any lord or servant serves his lord and master within this realm, against all others dedly." In 1541, John Leslie of Syde, son and heir-apparent to William Leslie of Balquhain, became bound to the Earl of Huntly— "For as much as my said Lord has given me the sum of four hundred merks, usual money of Scotland, therefore I am become a true man and servant to my said Lord, and shall, with my kin, friends, servants, allies, and tenants, serve, go, and ride with him against all persons, excepting the King and George, Earl of Rothes." This bond is dated at Aberdeen on the last day of July, and witnessed by Alexander Irvine of Drum, William Wood of Bonetown, Alexander Irvine of Coull, Robert Carnegie of Kynnard, and others.

The Earl of Huntly was Hereditary Sheriff of Inverness and Governor of the Castle of Inverness, as stated in a preceding section; and on the 3rd of March, 1540, Earl George was by charter created Sheriff of Aberdeen upon the resignation of David Lindsay, Earl of Crawford; and he was also Heritable Baillie of the lands belonging to the Bishop of Aberdeen.

In the summer of 1542 Huntly was sent by the King to the Borders with a force to prevent the English from pillaging the country. The Earl made efforts to secure peace; but the demands of Henry VIII. soon became insufferable. The King mustered an army, and advanced towards the Borders, with the intention of invading England. But the Earl of Huntly and other nobles declined to cross the Border, and the King was forced to disband the army; and shortly after he died.

After the death of James V., Cardinal Beaton made an effort to obtain the chief place in the Government. But the Earl of Arran, as next heir to the Crown, was named Regent, and the Earls of Huntly, Moray, and Argyle were nominated as the Council of the infant Princess, Mary. The Earl of Huntly was strongly opposed to the domineering policy of Henry VIII., and for a time declined to follow the steps of the weak-kneed Regent of Scotland.

On the 31st of March, 1543, Huntly received a commission of Lieutenancy of the North. By this commission his right extended from the Mearns to the Western Sea, embracing the whole of the northern districts of Scotland, all the islands within Inverness-shire, and those of Orkney and Shetland. The authority given to him was very comprehensive. He had the power of governing and defending the people within these limits, and, if necessary, of raising armies and commanding the people to join them. He was empowered to raise the Royal banner, and to make such statutes for the preservation of order as he deemed necessary. He might invade those who rebelled against his authority with fire and sword; imprison, punish, and execute them; and, if necessary, he was empowered to treat with the rebels and bring them again to obedience and order. He held the King's castles of Inverness and Inverlochy, and in his own territories he had the castles of Strathbogie, Bog of Gight, Aboyne, Ruthven in Badenoch, and Drummin in Glenlivat; and also a number of castles in the possession of members of his own family, or parties on whom he could place reliance.

In January, 1543, at Edinburgh, Huntly entered into a

Earls of Huntly. 139

bond with David, Earl of Crawford, for their mutual support of each other; and in March he received a bond of manrent from Lord Saltoun. The same year, in May, he had a bond from Hugh Fraser, Lord Lovat, who bound himself with his men, kin, friends, servants, allies, and adherents to take part in all the Earl's actions and quarrels, in peace and in war, &c. He also received bonds from Ewin Allanson, captain of the Clan Cameron; and Willian Mackintosh, captain of the Clan Chattan.

The Earl of Huntly supported the policy of Cardinal Beaton against the English and the aggression of Henry VIII. In the beginning of September, 1543, the Cardinal and Huntly met at Stirling. Shortly after, a conference between Beaton and the Regent Arran was held, and they became reconciled. Arran then agreed to act with the Cardinal, and to oppose the party of the nobles who supported the claims of Henry VIII.

Serious disturbance had arisen in the Highlands. Donald Dubh, after a long period of imprisonment, had escaped, and immediately assumed the character of Lord of the Isles, and soon gathered a large number of followers. In October, 1544, he invaded and wasted the lands of Urquhart, Glenmoriston, and Lochaber. On the 8th of December, 1544, Huntly met the barons and chiefs of the north at Elgin, and they entered into a bond to assist him in the execution of his office of lieutenant. Among the names of those who subscribed the bond were the following :—John, Earl of Sutherland ; John, Earl of Athole; Alexander Fraser, Lord Lovat; William Mackintosh of Dunnochton ; James Grant of Freuchie; John Mackenzie of Kintail; Hugh Ross of Kilravock ; John Grant of Ballnadalloch ; and a number of others. Huntly led his army against the Islesmen, and wasted the lands of the Camerons of Lochiel; and in March, 1545, Donald Dubh came to terms, and promised to visit the Queen at Stirling. But, instead of appearing at Stirling, he entered into a correspondence with Henry VIII.

While Huntly was lying with his army at Inverness, Donald Dubh again wasted the lands of Urquhart and Glenmoriston and carried off a great booty. On the 11th of June the Lords of Council issued a proclamation against Donald and his men, which threatened to utterly destroy them. But Donald and his followers treated those threats with scorn, and continued negotiations with England. He assumed the title of Earl of Ross and Lord of the Isles, and mustered a force of eight hundred men to assist Henry VIII., who granted him a pension of two thousand crowns. He died soon after, and was succeeded by James Macdonald of Islay and Dunivaig, as Lord of the Isles. The new lord gave Huntly much trouble.

Huntly was appointed Lord Chancellor of Scotland on the 2nd of June, 1546. On returning north, he mustered the whole force of the counties of Nairn, Cromarty, and Inverness, and marched into Lochaber at the head of a strong army. Assisted by his kinsman the Earl of Sutherland and William Mackintosh, captain of the Clan Chattan, he apprehended Ewin of Locheil, captain of the Clan Cameron, and Ranald Macdonald Glass of Keppoch, two of the leaders in the late conflicts. They were imprisoned in the Castle of Ruthven, in Badenoch, and afterwards conveyed to Elgin and tried for treason, convicted, and beheaded; and a number of their followers were hanged.

The Earl of Huntly fought on foot at the battle of Pinkie, and was taken a prisoner and conveyed to England.

SECTION VI.

GEORGE, FOURTH EARL OF HUNTLY—A PRISONER IN ENGLAND—
HIS ESCAPE—INVITES QUEEN MARY TO LAND AT ABERDEEN.

THE Earl of Huntly was a prisoner in England and strictly guarded. The Duke of Somerset, Governor of England, was well aware of the power and influence of the Scottish personage who had unfortunately fallen into his hands. Accordingly, it appears that Somerset made the utmost efforts to bring Huntly over to the side of the English party. The Earl was very anxious to obtain his liberty and return to Scotland, therefore he was constantly tempted with promises of release, if he would only undertake to support the English interest. This will appear from the following:—On the 5th December, 1548, it was agreed between the Duke of Somerset and the Earl of Huntly that the Earl was to have a licence to go to Scotland and stay there for two months and a half after his departure from the burgh of Berwick; and, in the meantime, he was to deliver the Countess of Huntly, his wife; Alexander, Lord Gordon, his eldest son; George Gordon, his second son; William Gordon, his third son; and Alexander Gordon, his brother, as hostages for his return at the appointed time. Also that he should pay the ransoms of certain prisoners for which he was responsible.

The following day another contract was drawn, which declared that the first one was of no effect, nor "binding on any of us—but was devised by me, the said Earl, to be carried with me into Scotland at my going thither, to be shown to the Governor and others in Scotland, for a covert of our proceedings, and to the intent that, by pretence thereof, I might better promote the King's affairs, and advance such purposes as I have promised to the Duke, to do my best to bring to pass." By the second contract the Earl agreed to return to England within ten weeks, and to leave as hostages the persons named in the first contract. Yet there seems to have been some suspicion in Somerset's mind of Huntly's sincerity. Though the Earl was permitted to proceed under a guard to Berwick, instructions were sent to detain him at Newcastle. Huntly, on the other hand, distrusted the good faith of Somerset, and therefore resolved to make an effort to escape.

Huntly reached Morpeth on the 22nd of December,

where he was to await the arrival of his Countess and the other hostages. The Earl, however, aided by George Kerr of Heton, who provided relays of horses, escaped from Morpeth and arrived at Edinburgh in the beginning of February, 1549. On his arrival he was warmly welcomed. For his faithful services he received the Earldom of Moray and the Sheriffdom of Elgin and Forres.

In 1550 a quarrel arose between the Earl of Huntly and William Mackintosh, chief of the Clan Chattan. There is no clear evidence of the cause of this quarrel. He held the office of deputy-lieutenant under the Earl of Huntly, and he was deprived of this office, apprehended, and imprisoned. On the 2nd of August, 1550, he was tried by a jury at Aberdeen. He was accused of conspiring against the Earl of Huntly, Her Majesty's Lieutenant of the North, convicted, and sentenced to death. His execution was delayed for some time, and he was conveyed to Strathbogie Castle, where he was executed. On the 14th of December, 1557, by an Act of Parliament, the sentence against Mackintosh was reversed as illegal.

In 1552 the Queen-mother, accompanied by the Regent Arran, made a judicial progress through the kingdom as far as Inverness. Huntly entertained the party at the Castle of Strathbogie in such a grand style that the Frenchmen of the Court suggested to the Queen that such a great noble should not be tolerated in so small a kingdom as Scotland, and that "his wings should be clipped."

Huntly was ordered to curb the lawless actions of the Camerons and John of Moidart, who was elected by the Clan Ranald as their chief, excluding the rightful heir. In September, 1553, Huntly met John of Moidart at Ruthven Castle, in Badenoch; and the Earl then received the said John, captain of the Clan Ranald, and his son Allan, "their kin, friends, and allies, remitting them and heartily forgiving all offences, wrongs, and disobedience in times past to the said Earl, or any of his, and especially the last

Earls of Huntly.

offence and brake made by them, their friends, and allies, upon his good friend, Lord Lovat." Moidart, his son, and their allies, promised to keep good rule within their bounds, to obey authority, and to continue to be true servants to the Earl of Huntly. They also promised to endeavour to bring Donald Gormson and all the captains and chiefs of the North Isles to pass to the Queen and council as becoming true subjects.

But disturbance again broke out; and in 1554 the Queen Regent commissioned Huntly to bring John of Moidart to justice. The Earl mustered an army, chiefly composed of the Clan Chattan and his own vassals, and advanced into the territory of Clan Ranald. Moidart and his followers retreated without coming to an engagement; and the Mackintoshes declined to follow them into their fastnesses. They then raised such a tumult in the camp that the Earl was forced to retire, and returned home.

Huntly's opponents at once seized the opportunity to magnify his failure; and the Queen Regent caused him to be imprisoned at Edinburgh. The Earl was deprived of the Chancellorship, and compelled to resign his tacks of the Earldoms of Ross, Mar, and Moray. He was confined for some time, and had to pay heavy fines to the Government before he obtained his liberty. After his imprisonment he usually resided upon his own estates.

In 1557 Huntly was again restored to favour. On the 5th of August he was appointed Lieutenant-General of the Kingdom. At this time the Earl of Huntly was recognised as the head of the Roman Catholic party in Scotland. He gave a general support to the Queen Regent in the struggle between her and the Reformers, and occasionally interposed between her and the Lords of the Congregation to prevent hostilities. Huntly disapproved of the presence of the French troops in Scotland, and regarded them as a disturbing element in the kingdom. He had a great stake in the country, and accordingly acted with caution amid the revolutionary movement.

Naturally Huntly became suspicious of the good faith of the Lords of the Congregation, and asked them to promise that they would maintain him and his friends in their lives and possessions. To this they replied that they were obliged to defend each other in the event of attack, and that they would defend him if he joined them. Upon this assurance, on the 25th of April, 1560, Huntly rode into the camp. The Queen Regent and the Lords made efforts to come to terms, but could not agree.

Huntly was not present at the Parliament which was held at Edinburgh in 1560, and which abolished the Roman Catholic religion in Scotland. It also appears that the proceedings of Lord James Stewart, and the Earls of Argyle and Athole, raised a suspicion in his mind that they had formed some plot against him; and, indeed, these Earls entered into a bond "to bridle the Earl of Huntly if he intended any mischief."

When it became known that Queen Mary of Scots, after the death of her husband, the King of France, had resolved to return to the home of her ancestors, there were many indications of the approaching struggle for office and power. Lord James Stewart, Prior of St. Andrews, was appointed by Parliament to proceed to France on a mission to Queen Mary; while at a secret convention of the Catholic nobles, headed by the Earl of Huntly, John Lesly, the parson of Oyne, and afterwards Bishop of Ross, was deputed, in April, 1561, to proceed to France, and represent the views of the Catholic party to Queen Mary. They earnestly entreated her to land at Aberdeen, where she would find an army of 20,000 men ready to protect her and convey her in triumph to Edinburgh. But before embarking, the Queen intimated to the leading men in Scotland that she expected them to exercise the virtue of mutual forbearance, and not fly at each other's throats.

Mary landed at Leith on the 19th of August, 1561; and the Earl of Huntly came post with sixteen horses to welcome her. As Lord Chancellor, he was present at the meetings of the Privy Council. On the 22nd of December he was present at the Convention in which the questions affecting the ecclesiastical revenues were discussed. Lord James, the Queen's half-brother, was placed at the head of the Government, and Maitland of Lethington was appointed Secretary of State.

The quarrel between the Gordons and the Ogilvies of Findlater reached a crisis in July, 1562. Alexander Ogilvie of Ogilvie and Findlater married Elizabeth Gordon, a daughter of Adam Gordon, Dean of Caithness, third son of Alexander, first Earl of Huntly. Alexander Ogilvie, owing to the conduct of his son, James of Cardell, thought fit to disinherit him. Accordingly, he granted to Sir John Gordon, third son of George, Earl of Huntly, the Barony of Ogilvie and Findlater, reserving his own and wife's life rent. Sir John Gordon was to assume the name and arms of Ogilvie, and, failing his male issue, the succession was to devolve to his brothers, William, James, and Adam, with remainder to Sir Walter Ogilvie of Boyne, Sir Walter Ogilvie of Dunlugas, and James, Lord Ogilvie.

After the death of Alexander Ogilvie, Sir John Gordon married his widow, Elizabeth Gordon. This marriage appears to have been an unhappy one. James Ogilvie thought that he was unjustly disinherited. In July, 1562, the case was to come before the Court in Edinburgh, and Sir John Gordon was there, and met James Ogilvie in the street. A fight ensued, in which Ogilvie was wounded. Gordon was imprisoned; but on the 25th of July he escaped from prison. This affair became associated with the series of incidents and events which issued in the eclipse and overthrow of the Huntly family for a time.

Huntly had not changed his religion, and various incidents and circumstances indicated that Lord James

Stewart, the Queen's half-brother, had resolved to crush him. It became known that the Earldom of Moray was to be detached from Huntly's possessions and conferred on Lord James. The Queen was in the hands of Lord James and the Protestant Lords. Huntly was coldly treated by the Queen; and in the winter of 1562 he retired from the Court to the north.

In the beginning of the year 1562 the Queen intimated her intention to visit the north; and in January the Town Council and Magistrates of Aberdeen discussed the question of raising money for the decoration of the city.

SECTION VII.

GEORGE, FOURTH EARL OF HUNTLY (CONTINUED)—THE QUEEN'S PROGRESS TO THE NORTH—GEORGE, FIFTH EARL—LANDS AND TITLES RESTORED TO HIM.

IN August, 1562, the Queen, accompanied by Lord James and a number of the nobles, started on her progress to the north. The Queen reached Old Aberdeen on the 27th of August, where she was met by the Countess of Huntly. She had come to intercede for her son, Sir John Gordon, and was informed by the Queen that nothing could be done for him unless he surrendered and entered into ward at Stirling Castle. The Countess promised that he would do this; and, accordingly, Sir John submitted; but, finding that his keeper was to be Lord Erskine, the uncle of Lord James Stewart, the enemy of his family, he declined to entrust himself in the custody of Erskine, and retired to one of his own castles. This conduct seems to have greatly offended the Queen and caused her to treat Sir John severely.

The Earl and Countess of Huntly invited Queen Mary to visit them at Strathbogie Castle, and made great preparations for her reception; but she declined. She permitted the Earl of Argyle and the English Ambassador, Randolph, to visit Strathbogie, and the latter wrote—" Huntly's house is the best furnished of any house I have seen in this country; his cheer is marvellously great; and his mind then such, as it appeared to us, as ought to be in any subject to his Sovereign."

On leaving Old Aberdeen, the Queen proceeded northward, passing through the parishes of Drumblade and Forgue, and over the west shoulder of the Foreman Hill to Rothiemay House. At Rothiemay the Queen was again requested by Huntly to visit Strathbogie, but she refused unless Sir John Gordon returned to his obedience. The Queen proceeded northward through Moray, and on arriving at Darnaway Castle she held a council, and summoned Sir John Gordon to surrender his castles of Findlater and Auchindoun. She then invested her half-brother, Lord James, in the Earldom of Moray. On the following day she proceeded to Inverness, but found the gates of the castle closed against her. Next morning the gates of the castle were opened, but Alexander Gordon, captain of the castle, and other five of the garrison were executed. Alarming reports were spread, and the local Crown vassals were ordered to muster to assist the Queen. When returning to Aberdeen, the Queen was refused admittance to Findlater Castle, which intensified her distrust of the Gordons.

When the Queen returned, and made her entry into Aberdeen, she received a warm and hearty welcome from the citizens. She resolved to stay forty days in the city, or till peace and order were restored in the surrounding district.

Captain Hay, the royal messenger, appeared at the Castle of Strathbogie, and he was treated with the utmost respect. There was a cannon which always stood in the centre of the court of the Castle of Strathbogie, and the Queen demanded the surrender of this cannon. The Earl replied, that "not only the cannon, which was her own, but also his body and goods were at her disposal. He considered it strange that he should be so hardly treated, because he was not a party to the offence of his son, and offered to hazard his life in the capture of the Castles of Findlater and Auchindoun if she only commanded him to this effect. He desired these things to be reported to his Sovereign from her most humble and obedient subject as none more, nor never would be than he." The Countess also desired the Royal messenger to inform the Queen that Huntly was ever her obedient subject. These declaratious were treated with scorn; and when Huntly sent the keys of the castles of Findlater and Auchindoun they were not received, and the bearer was imprisoned.

The Earl and his son, Sir John, were commanded to appear before the Queen and Council at Aberdeen. Naturally, Huntly declined to place himself in the power of his enemies, yet he offered to surrender for trial by his peers in Parliament. He again sent his Countess to intercede with the Queen; but she was not permitted to see the Sovereign.

Troops were sent to attack Huntly in his stronghold of Strathbogie; but the Earl eluded them and escaped. On the 21st of October, Sir John Gordon attacked and defeated a company of troops under Captain Stewart, who was attempting to take possession of Findlater Castle. Two days later the Gordons were proclaimed rebels, and immediate surrender of the Castle of Strathbogie was demanded, but refused.

For his own protection and defence, Huntly mustered an army and advanced towards Aberdeen, marching well up along the higher ground to the Hill of Fare in Midmar; and on the 28th of October, 1562, he was met by the Earls of Moray and Athole at the head of about two thousand men. An engagement ensued, in which the Gordons were defeated, and the Earl's sons, Sir John and Adam, surrendered. The Earl himself fell from his horse and died of apoplexy immediately after his capture. Two days after the battle, five gentlemen of the Gordon clan were executed on the Castlegate of Aberdeen; and, three days later, Huntly's son, Sir John Gordon, was executed at the same place. But Adam Gordon, the younger son, was spared.

Strathbogie Castle was then rifled. Many of its rich furnishings and ornaments were taken to Edinburgh, and others of them were carried by Moray to the Castle of Darnaway to fit up his newly-acquired residence in this ancient Earldom. Those who assisted Huntly were fined to the amount of £3542 6s 8d.

Huntly's body lay for some time in Aberdeen, and was embalmed by Robert Henderson, a surgeon; and subsequently it was carried to Edinburgh by sea. The body was placed in Holyrood, and on the 29th of May, 1563, it was brought into the Council Chamber, in a chest, when the sentence of forfeiture was passed by Parliament. The arms were torn and struck out of the Herald's book. The Countess of Huntly protested against the sentence. Huntly's remains lay in Holyrood until the 21st of April, 1566, when they were conveyed to Strathbogie, and interred at Elgin.

George, Lord Gordon, the late Earl's oldest surviving son, married Anna Hamilton, a daughter of the Duke of Chatelherault, by whom he had issue. In 1562, when his father and brothers were up in arms, he was living quietly with his wife's friends—the Hamiltons; yet he was included in the doom of forfeiture passed against the family. The Duke, his father-in-law, was commanded to deliver him up; and in the afternoon of the 28th of November, 1562, he was taken in the Duke's lodging, in the Kirk of Field Wynd, and imprisoned in Edinburgh Castle. On the 8th of February, 1563, he was tried and convicted of treason. A few days after, he was sent in " free ward " to the Castle of Dunbar. In May he was ordered to attend the Parliament, to hear the sentence of forfeiture passed upon his father's body ; and, he was again sent to Dunbar, where he remained until 1565. On the 3rd of August it was proclaimed at the Market Cross of Edinburgh that the horning against him was remitted ; and he might go where he pleased. He soon presented himself before the Queen and was kindly received.

On the 8th of October, 1565, by a Royal proclamation, Huntly was restored to all the lands held by his father, and to all the family titles. On the 24th of February, 1566, Huntly's sister Jean was married to the Earl of Bothwell in the Abbey of Holyrood, and the event was celebrated with great splendour. The contract of marriage between the parties shows that it was consented to by Huntly and his mother, and also by Queen Mary. The Queen took a keen interest in this marriage, she signed the contract, "and gave the bride a wedding dress of cloth of silver."

The Earls of Huntly and Bothwell were in their chambers in Holyrood, on the evening of the 9th of March, 1566, when they were suddenly alarmed by the clang of arms in the courtyard of the Palace. This was Lord Ruthven and his band of conspirators in search of David Rizzio, the Queen's foreign secretary. They found their victim sitting with his cap on his head in Her Majesty's presence, along with a small social party in the Queen's supping-room. Some sharp talk passed between the Queen and Ruthven, but more of the conspirators rushed in. Instantly the table and chairs were overturned in the scuffle, and David Rizzio was seized and dragged to an outer room, and there stabbed to death. A guard was placed over the Queen : but several gentlemen escaped, and warned the citizens of Edinburgh. The alarm-bell was rung, and the citizens rushed to the palace with torch lights. They demanded the instant deliverance of the Queen ; but she was not permitted to speak to them. Darnley appeared and assured the people that the Queen was quite safe, and commanded them to go home. Lord Ruthven placed armed men to watch the gates and all the private passages ; but in spite of the utmost vigilance of the conspirators, the Earls of Huntly and Bothwell managed to escape during the night.

Mary soon disengaged her husband from the nobles who had murdered her favourite; and Darnley was duped by the Queen as well as by the conspirators. He had not the ability, the resolution, nor even the recognised rough honesty of his day, to carry him through such a plot. He fled with the Queen to Dunbar Castle, where they were joined by Huntly.

Huntly was appointed Lord High Chancellor in place of the Earl of Morton, who was forced to flee for his part in the slaughter of Rizzio.

The Earl of Huntly accompanied the Queen on her visit to Jedburgh in October, 1566. He was also present at the conference in Craigmillar Castle in December, when the Lords advised the Queen to divorce Darnley, which she declined to do.

The plot to remove Darnley, which seems to have originated with Maitland of Lethington, the Secretary of State, was soon concocted. According to custom, a bond was drawn up by Sir James Balfour, an experienced lawyer and a firm friend of Bothwell. This bond declared that Darnley "was a young fool and tyrant, and unworthy to rule over them." They therefore bound themselves to remove him by some means or another, and each engaged to stand true to the other in this deadly enterprise. The bond was subscribed by the Earls of Argyle, Bothwell, and Huntly, Lethington, the Secretary of State, Sir James Balfour, and others. Their victim had become sick, and was visited by the Queen at Glasgow, whence he was conveyed to Edinburgh on the last day of January, 1567.

SECTION VIII.

GEORGE, FIFTH EARL OF HUNTLY—MURDER OF DARNLEY—
HUNTLY'S ACTION—ESCAPE OF THE QUEEN—HUNTLY LIEU-
TENANT-GOVERNOR OF THE KINGDOM.

WHEN Darnley was brought to Edinburgh he was put into a house close to the city wall, called Kirk-of-Field, and here the Queen was very attentive to him, and for several nights before the murder she slept in the room immediately below his. At last everything seems to have been prepared, and the evening of Sunday the 9th of February, 1567, was fixed for his murder. When that day came, everything at the Court was going on in the most natural and joyful fashion; the Earl of Moray had left to join his wife at St. Andrews, and on the evening fixed for the dismal deed, a marriage was to be celebrated between two of the Queen's servants. Meanwhile, the agents of Bothwell and the Earl himself were intently engaged in making the final preparations for the horrible deed. The conspirators had resolved to blow up the house with powder. After dark they placed a large quantity of this destructive element in the room below the King's, Bothwell himself superintending the operations. About ten o'clock in the evening the Queen arrived from Holyrood to join her husband, and, passing the door of her own bedroom, entered the apartment of the King. Some agreeable conversation passed between them; and then the Queen recollected that she had promised to attend the ball to be held that night in honour of her two servants' marriage. She bade the King farewell and departed, with Bothwell and the Earl of Huntly and her attendants, to Holyrood; and apparently only two of the conspirators stayed behind at the King's lodgings. In spite of all the care that had been taken by the contrivers of this dolesome plot, there appears to have been a hitch in their proceedings. It is pretty evident that Darnley and his servants had discovered their danger and attempted to escape, and had got some distance away when they were caught in the garden and strangled. Bothwell, with a number of his followers, returned from the palace about midnight, and joined the two conspirators, who had already lighted the train. The explosion shook the earth, and the inhabitants of Edinburgh were aroused from their sleep. The murderers had to escape swiftly, Bothwell ran to his apartments in the palace and immediately went to bed, only to be awakened as if from slumber half an hour afterwards by a message informing him of the tragedy. He then, like an innocent man, shouted "Treason! treason!" and along with the Earl of Huntly called on the Queen to tell her what had happened.

It was well known at the time that Bothwell was the chief actor in this great crime, but at the moment no one would have been safe to accuse him. A few days after the murder, Bothwell himself, surrounded by fifty armed men on horseback, paraded the streets of Edinburgh, and, with hideous and furious gestures, openly declared that "if he knew who were the authors of the bills accusing him, he would wash his hands in their blood."

Rumours immediately began to arise that the Queen was about to marry Bothwell.

Parliament met at Edinburgh on the 14th of April, and Bothwell bore the crown and sceptre before the Queen when she rode to the Parliament House. A considerable number of Acts were passed, mostly relating to ratifications of grants of lands and reductions of forfeitures. John, Lord Erskine, got a ratification of the Earldom of Mar and Lordship of the Garioch, and other lordships. Ratifications of grants of lands to the Earls of Huntly, Moray, Crawford, Morton, Rothes, and other barons were passed; and also formal reductions of the forfeitures against the Earls of Huntly and Sutherland, and a number of gentlemen of the name of Gordon were passed, Bothwell received a grant of lands with the Castle of Dunbar.

On the 21st of April the Queen went to Stirling to visit her son, and stayed two days. When returning to Edinburgh on the 24th, the Queen—accompanied by the Earl of Huntly, Lethington, the Secretary, Sir James Melville, and others—at the Bridge of Almond was met by Bothwell at the head of an armed force of his retainers, who conveyed her and her party to the Castle of Dunbar. Sir James Melville said that Bothwell boasted that he would marry the Queen, "who would or who would not: yea, whether she would herself or not." The Queen was kept for about a week a close prisoner in Dunbar Castle; but the exact character of the acts which occurred between Mary and Bothwell during these days can never be fully known; yet there is evidence that the Queen was disgracefully treated by him.

Lady Jean Gordon, the Earl of Bothwell's wife, was a sister of the Earl of Huntly. No doubt this lady was anxious to be released from such a man as Bothwell. Accordingly, on the 26th of April, 1567, she formally entered a process of divorce against him upon the ground of adultery. Bothwell also, on the 27th of April, entered a process of divorce from his wife on the ground of consanguinity, and his divorce was pronounced on the 7th of May.

Bothwell brought the Queen from Dunbar Castle to Edinburgh Castle on the 29th of April. Preparations for their marriage were rapidly pushed forward. The banns of their marriage were proclaimed on the 12th of May; and on the 15th of the month the marriage was celebrated in the Palace of Holyrood. For three weeks after their marriage, they stayed at Holyrood.

On the 7th of June, the Queen and Bothwell left Edinburgh, and fled to Borthwick Castle, and thence with extreme difficulty escaped to Dunbar Castle. There they issued a proclamation commanding the Crown vassals to muster immediately. Meantime a party of the barons took possession of Edinburgh, and, having come to an understanding with Sir James Balfour, the Governor of Edinburgh Castle, the confederate barons at once assumed all the functions of the Government. The leading men in this movement were the Earls of Morton, Athole, Glencairn, Lord Lindsay, and Lord Home. On the 11th of June they issued a proclamation ordering the people to muster and assist in rescuing the Queen from thraldom. The Queen and Bothwell had mustered about 2000 men, and advanced upon Edinburgh. The confederate barons resolved to meet them, and, marching from the capital, the two armies came in sight of each other near Musselburgh. Bothwell had posted his men on Carberry Hill. After a day's manœuvring and treating, the Queen surrendered to the confederate Barons, and Bothwell was permitted to ride off in the direction of Dunbar. The Queen was conveyed to Edinburgh; and when she at last saw herself a prisoner in the hands of a party of the Barons, she was extremely vexed. She surrendered on the 15th of June, and on the 17th she was carried a captive to Lochleven, and there imprisoned in the island fortress.

On the 29th of June, the Earls of Huntly and Argyle and others met at Dumbarton, and entered into a bond to make all reasonable efforts to secure the Queen's liberty. But Huntly and Argyle soon after retired to their own districts, and for a time stood aloof.

Huntly was present at the Parliament which met in December, 1567, and bore the sceptre. He was pardoned by the Regent Moray for all offences committed since the 10th of June. In February, 1568, he was ordered, as Sheriff of Aberdeen, to prevent the theft of lead from the Cathedrals of Elgin and Aberdeen.

On the 2nd of May, 1568, Queen Mary escaped from Lochleven, and proceeded to Hamilton. Her chief supporters were the Earls of Huntly, Argyle, Rothes, and Cassillis; the Lords Harris, Livingston, Fleming, and the Hamiltons. Huntly immediately mustered his vassals, and marched to her assistance. After the defeat and flight of the Queen, Huntly held out for her.

For a time Huntly held Justice Courts, and executed those who would not obey him as lieutenant under the Queen's authority. He also levied taxes in the north. He held Aberdeen and the north for the Queen.

About the end of January, 1569, the Earls of Huntly and Argyle proceeded to Glasgow and issued a proclamation that all men between the ages of sixteen and sixty should be ready at an hour's warning with twenty days' victual, to resist the Earl of Moray, Regent, and their old enemies the English. The Regent got notice of this move, and nothing came of it. But Huntly continued active in the Queen's cause, and he got bonds from a number of the northern lairds, who undertook to assist him to the utmost of their power. Amongst those were—Sir Alexander Ross of Balnagown, Robert Munro of Foulis, Sir George Gordon of Shives, John Gordon of Cluny, George Gordon of Lesmore, Robert Innes of Invermarkie, Lachlan Mackintosh of Dunnachtan, Alexander Leslie of Arderay, Alexander Leslie of Pitcaple, John Mortimer of Craigievar, John Leslie of Leslie, James Innes of Draunie, John Hay of Perke, Alexander Abercrombie of Pitmedden and others.

The Regent was hard pressed. The Laird of Grange, Governor of Edinburgh Castle, and Maitland of Lethington, left him and threw in their lot with the Queen's cause. On the 13th of January, 1570, the Regent was shot by Hamilton of Bothwellhaugh; and a civil war raged in the kingdom for several years.

Huntly was appointed Lieutenant-Governor of the kingdom by Queen Mary. On the 13th of June he issued a proclamation at Aberdeen commanding all men to hold themselves ready and well armed for war, to advance against "the rebellious faction who conspired for their sovereign's murder, and brought strangers to waste her realm." Huntly occupied Aberdeen, and raised men in the surrounding country. He ordered the northern lairds to meet him at Brechin on the 8th of August; but the Regent (Lennox) resolved to disperse this gathering. The Earl of Morton advanced on Brechin with a number of horsemen, who attacked and defeated Huntly's party, and executed forty prisoners. Huntly returned to Aberdeen, and met the representatives of the Duke of Alva, who had come to negotiate with the Queen's party. After this meeting, Huntly and Argyle sent Lord Seton with a letter to the Duke of Alva, informing him of the Queen's imprisonment in England, and Queen Elizabeth's extreme hostility to Mary's party, and therefore requesting assistance.

In the month of August, 1570, Huntly attended a meeting of his party at Dunkeld. Immediately after, he entered Angus at the head of eight hundred men, and destroyed mills, and burned houses. On the 3rd of September he, along with others, signed a bond to Queen Elizabeth to abstain from fighting for two months, in order that the treaty between her and Queen Mary might proceed more rapidly. The English Queen had heard of Lord Seton's mission to the Duke of Alva, and she proposed this treaty to delude Mary's foreign friends; for the Regent Lennox protested that any negotiations with Mary would be disastrous to Elizabeth and King James. The result was that neither party adhered to the agreement.

SECTION IX.

GEORGE, FIFTH EARL OF HUNTLY (CONTINUED)—HUNTLY'S COMMUNICATIONS WITH QUEEN ELIZABETH—HIS DEATH—GEORGE, SIXTH EARL.

THE Regent insisted that, as Huntly and the Duke of Chatelherault were the chief persons then holding out, they should be reduced to the King's authority. In March he issued a proclamation commanding the Crown vassals to muster at Perth. The castle of Dumbarton was taken from the Queen's party on the 5th of April, 1571, which weakened Mary's adherents, as Archbishop Hamilton was among the prisoners who surrendered. He was tried, condemned, and executed on the 9th of April. He was the last of the Roman Catholic Bishops of St. Andrews.

There was much skirmishing between the King's and Queen's parties about Edinburgh, which had little result. Both parties issued proclamations and counter-manifestoes; and the Regent Lennox summoned a Parliament, which met at Stirling on the 25th of August. About the same time the Queen's party held their Parliament in Edinburgh, in which sentences of forfeiture were passed against the Earl of Morton and other leading men of the King's party; while in the King's Parliament Acts were passed in favour of the Earl of Morton and Lord Lindsay, as a reward for their resistance to the open enemies of the King, and also in favour of those who had taken the Castle of Dumbarton from the enemy. While the King's party were thus mutually helping and congratulating each other, a body of 300 of the Queen's adherents, under the command of the Earl of Huntly, Buccleuch, and Lord Hamilton, marched from Edinburgh upon Stirling, and on the morning of the 4th of September completely surprised them and slew the Regent Lennox. The consequences would have been more serious if the citizens of Stirling had not come to the rescue of the King's party and saved them from being carried off prisoners.

While Huntly was fighting for the Queen in the south, his brother, Sir Adam Gordon of Auchindoun, held the north for her. Unhappily the feud between the Gordons and the Forbeses became intensified in this struggle. On the 17th of October, 1571, the two clans encountered each other at Tullyangus, where the Forbeses were defeated, and lost 120 men. Afterwards the Master of Forbes and his allies met the Gordons at the Crabstane, Aberdeen, and a furious conflict ensued, in which many were slain, and the Master of Forbes and 200 of his men were taken prisoners.

Sir Adam Gordon continued his career of warfare. In June, 1572, he entered into the Mearns and surprised the Castle of Douglas of Glenbervie, wasted his lands, and carried off his goods. Early on the morning of the 5th July, at the head of 1600 men, he surprised the King's forces at Brechin, and took several of the leaders and 200 men prisoners. But, after haranguing them about the wrongs inflicted upon his family through the death of his father and the execution of his brother, he dismissed them. Gordon marched to Montrose and imposed a ransom of £2000 and two tuns of wine upon the town.

A truce between the King's party and the Queen's adherents was agreed to at the end of July, 1572, to continue for two months. In the following October the Regent Mar died, and the Earl of Morton was then proclaimed Regent. Proposals were made to Huntly for his submission, which he rejected; but on the 18th of December he agreed to a renewal of the truce. He sent the Laird of Esslemont on a mission to France requesting aid to continue the struggle. In the winter of 1573 Huntly seems to have seen that the struggle against the King's party was hopeless. Accordingly he resolved to make the best terms he could for himself and his friends.

Huntly had an interview with the Regent Morton at Aberdour on the 18th of February, 1573. A few days after an agreement was concluded, under which Huntly and the Hamiltons were to receive a remission, for past offences and the murders of the late Regents, a discharge for all the damage done by them during the late troubles; and they were also to be secured in their estates and titles. The Master of Forbes and John Glen of Bar, who had been taken prisoners by Sir Adam Gordon, were to be immediately liberated. Huntly was to discharge his armed men, and the forfeiture standing against him was to be reduced.

The Earl of Huntly became a firm supporter of the policy of the Regent Morton, and often corresponded with Queen Elizabeth and her Ministers. Towards the end of April, 1573, the sentence of forfeiture pronounced against him was reduced by Parliament.

In June, 1574, Huntly wrote from Leith to Queen Elizabeth, and earnestly assured her that all the reports circulated against him were quite unfounded. Yet suspicion was so strong that, on the 11th of July, Alexander Seton, younger of Meldrum; Patrick Cheyne of Esslemont; and Alexander Drummond of Medhope, became sureties for him that he should enter the district of Galloway before the 22nd inst., and stay there until liberated. On the 30th of July the Earl wrote a long letter to Queen Elizabeth, assuring her that there was no cause for offence in his behaviour, seeing that his brother Sir Adam was in France, and for his actions there he was not responsible. Moreover, he trusted that his brother was innocent of the charges alleged against him.

The Earl returned from Galloway to Hamilton in September; and in November he gave surety to the Lords of the Privy Council that he would return to ward when required. On the 25th of July, 1575, Sir Adam Gordon returned from France to Scotland, with twenty of his companions. He was immediately seized, and imprisoned in Blackness Castle. In January, 1576, he was released, on the Earl of Huntly becoming surety, for the relief of his cautioners—Hugh, Earl of Eglinton, Lord Elphinstone, and others—that he would enter into ward in the town of Kirkcudbright.

On the morning of the 24th of October, 1576, the Earl was in good health. In the afternoon, he went out to play a game of football, and, after kicking the ball once or twice, he fell upon his face. He was immediately conveyed to his room in Strathbogie Castle, where he died three hours later. His body was embalmed by William Urquhart, a surgeon from Aberdeen, and, after lying a few days in the castle chapel, was interred in Elgin Cathedral.

By Lady Anna Hamilton, his countess, he had three sons and one daughter. These were—George, who succeeded him; Alexander of Stradoun; William, who became a monk of the Order of St. Bennet, and died in France; and Jean, who married George, fifth Earl of Caithness.

During the minority of George, sixth Earl of Huntly, his uncle, Sir Adam Gordon of Auchindoun, managed his affairs, and sent him to France to complete his education.

The latter part of the sixteenth century was remarkable for bitter feuds amongst the Scottish nobility, which sprang from many causes and circumstances. The sad feud between the Gordons and the Forbeses broke out afresh in 1579, owing to contentious expressions between George Gordon of Gight and Alexander Forbes, younger of Towie, uttered in the King's presence. There was, however, a more tangible cause of quarrel between the two families— the possession of the lands in the Barony of Keig and Monymusk, granted to the fourth Earl of Huntly by Cardinal Beaton. The Forbeses maintained and complained that these lands were granted to Huntly over their heads, as they were "the old kindly tenants and possessors"; but now the Earl endeavoured to have them removed, which in the circumstances they resisted. The interference of the authorities was disregarded for some time. The Laird of Gight was slain, and a party of the Gordons rose up in arms to avenge his death; and there were forays and bloodshed from the valley of the Dee to Strathbogie. For a time the Gordon lairds and the Forbes lairds mustered their retainers, and the struggle proceeded until the Privy Council ordered the chiefs of both parties to sign such assurances as should be presented to them within twenty-four hours, under the penalty of rebellion. They were commanded to appear in Edinburgh, accompanied by forty of their retainers, to settle the terms of an agreement, on the

23rd of April, 1580; and they then made a submission, by which they became bound to abide by the decision of the Privy Council.

The same year, on the 24th of October, the Earl of Huntly gave a bond to the Laird of Grant, in which he promised that the remission he was to obtain from the King for Lachlan Mackintosh of Dunachton should not take effect until Lachlan desisted from disturbing Grant in the possession of Rothiemurchus, Laggan, and Dalfour in Badenoch.

Huntly took an active part in the suppression of the abortive rising of the Earls of Mar, Angus, Gowrie, and others in the spring of 1584. He was one of the jury at the trial of the Earl of Gowrie. This year he obtained bonds of manrent from Mackenzie of Kintail, Monro of Foulis, Macleod of Lewis, Macdonald of Glengarry, Macgregor of Glenstrae, and Drummond of Blair.

In 1585 the Earl was engaged in settling difficulties which had arisen between his kinsmen the Earls of Sutherland and Caithness. He entered into a lawsuit with the Countess of Moray and Argyle, which involved him in serious trouble. The following year, in November, Huntly, through his friendly relations with the Drummonds of Blair and the Menzies' of Weem, came into conflict with the Earl of Athole. He declined to make peace with Athole until the latter gave assurance that he would cease from assisting the forays made upon the lands of Drummond and Menzies. Huntly arrested some of Athole's servants, and tried them before his own courts, which resulted in Athole's tenants being exempted from Huntly's jurisdiction.

In 1587 Huntly received, for his good services, a grant of the lands of the Abbey of Dunfermline from the King. He was also appointed High Chamberlain of Scotland. Huntly was present at the meeting of the Estates in May; and on the 15th of May he attended the great banquet at which King James attempted to reconcile many of his nobles who were at feud with each other.

An extraordinary meeting of the General Assembly was held at Edinburgh in February, 1588, for the purpose of arousing the nation to a sense of danger from the threatening Spanish Armada. The alarming character of the crisis had attracted a great assemblage of members who were animated by one spirit. They drew up an extremely dark picture of the state of the kingdom. Strong complaints against Jesuits and seminary priests, who were permitted to seduce the people and spread their poisonous doctrine, was made in the Assembly. In the north, where the Earl of Huntly was supreme, the Reformed religion had taken comparatively little hold upon the people.

James Gordon, a celebrated Jesuit, and an uncle of the Earl of Huntly, was living at Strathbogie. In February, 1588, he accompanied Huntly to the Court, and was introduced to the king. James VI. considered himself a great authority on religious and theological subjects, and he conversed with the famous Jesuit for some time, and then ordered him into confinement. Shortly after Huntly, Lord Claud Hamilton, and others met at Linlithgow to concert measures in the interest of the Roman Catholics in Scotland. The King, on hearing of this meeting, asked an explanation, and Huntly protested that he and his associates had no intention of forming a conspiracy. Huntly soon returned to Edinburgh, and slept in Holyrood Palace.

SECTION X.

GEORGE, SIXTH EARL AND FIRST MARQUIS OF HUNTLY—AN ARMY MARCHED AGAINST HIM—FEUD WITH THE EARL OF MORAY—SLAUGHTER OF MORAY—WAR IN THE NORTH.

ON the 21st of July, 1588, Huntly's marriage with Lady Henrietta Stewart, a sister of Ludovic, Duke of Lennox, was celebrated at Holyrood with great mirth and rejoicing. The King himself took a keen interest in the marriage; and the ceremony was performed by Archbishop Adamson of St. Andrews.

The Earl was often solicited by the ministers to join the Reformed Church, and this greatly annoyed him. Yet, on the 30th of November, 1588, "Huntly submitted to the Church, publicly confessed his errors, and solemnly protested his desire to become a faithful and obedient subject, promising hereafter by word and deed to defend the professed religion to the utmost of his power—not from any fear of loss, hope of honour or favour, but of mere conscience and zeal to the truth, detesting all superstition and Papistry."

In December Huntly proceeded with the King on a visit to Kinneil, and subsequently resided with him at Holyrood. But Queen Elizabeth sent a letter to the King accusing the Earl of Huntly of a conspiracy, which came before the Privy Council on the 27th of February, 1589. It was alleged that he had been corresponding with the Duke of Parma and the King of Spain, and transcripts of letters said to have been intercepted were produced. Huntly denied that he had entered into any conspiracy, and protested that the letters were forgeries, concocted by his enemies. The meeting of Council closed amid a scene of intense excitement; and Huntly was conveyed up the High Street and imprisoned in Edinburgh Castle. Touching these letters, such evidence as exists points to the conclusion that they were forgeries. Huntly was liberated on the 6th of March.

Huntly was in high favour with the King and often in his company. But, on the 9th of March, Patrick Gordon of Achindoun and others warned Huntly that the Lord Chancellor, Maitland, had formed a plot to slay him; and he immediately proceeded to the north, accompanied by the Earls of Erroll and Crawford. On their way north they encountered the Master of Glamis at the head of a company of armed men, but they took him prisoner and carried him with them. At this time there was a strong movement to put down Jesuits and seminary priests, who were protected by the Earl of Huntly and other nobles; and in January a meeting of the leading Reformed ministers was held at Edinburgh, to devise and recommend measures to the Government. This meeting petitioned the Government to purge the kingdom of all Jesuits and priests.

On the 7th of April, 1589, the King issued orders for an armed muster of the Crown vassals. The King in person, at the head of an army, commenced to march northward. Huntly, Erroll, and Angus, also assembled their vassals and friends, and advanced to the Bridge of Dee. They were summoned to appear at Edinburgh, but they treated the Royal herald with scorn, and tore the proclamation in pieces. The King continued to advance northward, and Huntly and his allies retired and disbanded their men. The King reached Aberdeen on the 20th of April, and stayed a day or two in the city, and slept in Charles Mowat's house. But the King was offended because Huntly did not come personally and submit to him. Accordingly, he resolved to proceed to the Castle of Strathbogie.

The King arrived at Strathbogie on the 26th of the month; and on the night of his arrival the Master of Glamis captured the Earl of Huntly, but instead of bringing him before the King, he was conveyed to the tower of Torriesoul under a strong guard. The following morning he was sent away to Aberdeen, under a numerous guard of horsemen. There is evidence, however, that the King had no intention of subjecting Huntly to any severe punishment.

Huntly petitioned that his trial might take place, or that he might be allowed to go into voluntary banishment, and offered caution that he would not return without the permission of the King. To the latter proposal his opponents would not listen; they insisted that he should be tried for treason. The English agents proposed that the Council should be bribed to execute him; but the Council declined to entertain this proposal. Huntly was conveyed to Edinburgh, and confined. He was tried for treason, but judgment was stayed. He was ordered to remain at Borthwick Castle and within six miles thereof, until the King returned from the north. Accordingly, on the return of the King to Edinburgh, in August, Huntly was liberated.

On the 17th of September, 1589, at Aberdeen, the Earls of Huntly and Erroll entered into a bond, because of the " changes and controversies daily falling out amongst the whole estates of this poor realm ; " considering these and their own peril, they resolved to bind their friendship as two brothers, and swore a great oath to maintain each other against all living men, save the King.

Huntly had many quarrels on his hands. He was at feud with the Earls of Moray and Athole, Lord Lovat, and their allies the Grants, Campbell of Cawdor, Stewart of Grantully, Sutherland of Duffus, the Dunbars of Moray, and the laird of Mackintosh. They met at Forres in the autumn of 1590, to devise measures against Huntly. The Gordons advanced to attack them, but they escaped to Darnaway Castle. Huntly sent John Gordon and others with a flag of truce to demand the surrender of the offenders, but they disregarded this, and a number of men issued from the castle and slew John Gordon, and wounded some of his company. Huntly complained to the Privy Council, but the quarrel continued. On the 5th of March, 1591, Huntly entered into a bond with Cameron of Lochiel, who engaged to support him against the Grants and Mackintoshes. There were fierce forays and bloodshed, and the Council issued an order commanding Huntly not to pass west of the Spey, the Earl of Moray not to cross east of the water of Findhorn, and the Earl of Athole to stay south of Skorkeith. These proceedings merely led to a temporary lull in the strife.

Francis Stewart, Earl of Bothwell and High Admiral of Scotland, was a cousin of James VI. He was for some time a powerful personage, and by his daring exploits often threw the King into a state of extreme alarm and terror. It was alleged that his cousin the Earl of Moray was one of his confederates. In January, 1592, the Earl of Huntly and the Duke of Lennox were commanded to apprehend the Earl of Bothwell; but he escaped to the island of Bute. The Earl of Moray was staying at Donibristle Castle, on the north bank of the Forth—a seat belonging to his mother. Huntly, having received a commission to apprehend him, proceeded with the Sheriff of Moray and a number of his own retainers, surrounded the Castle, and commanded the Earl of Moray to surrender. Naturally Moray declined to place himself in the hands of an enemy, and attempted a defence. The castle, however, was set on fire, and the inmates were forced to come out. Moray himself remained behind till nightfall, then, rushing through his enemies, he outran them all, and reached a rocky spot, where he thought that he would be safe. The pursuers, however, discovered his place of retreat, and cruelly murdered him. The untimely death of the "bonnie Earl of Moray" on the 7th of February was much lamented.

The King himself, on receiving tidings of the tragedy, showed little concern, and went out to hunt near Inverleith. On his return to the capital, the feeling and excitement of the citizens soon terrified him, and he removed to Glasgow with the Privy Council for a time. Huntly's commissions of Lieutenancy and Justiciary were withdrawn, and he escaped and retired to the north. But Captain Gordon, a brother of the Laird of Gight, was beheaded for his complicity in the tragedy of Donibristle. On the 10th of March, Huntly surrendered, and was confined for two weeks in Blackness Castle; and soon after he returned to the north.

The Earl of Athole and the Mackintoshes invaded

Huntly's territories and wasted them. The Gordons retaliated, and attacked the Grants in Strathspey and the Mackintoshes in Badenoch. The war spread, and there was much bloodshed and destruction of property; almost the whole country north of the Tay was in a state of actual war. So, on the 9th of November, 1592, the Earl of Angus received a Royal Commission of Lieutenancy and Justiciary to restore order in this region; and if necessary to charge the people "in the counties of Inverness, Cromarty, Nairn, Forres, Elgin, Banff, Aberdeen, Kincardine, Forfar, and that part of Perth lying north of the Tay, to muster in arms under the penalty of confiscation and death, and follow the Royal Lieutenant on such days and to such places, and for such space of time as he shall order by his proclamations; and if necessary he shall display His Majesty's banner, and summon all persons whom he shall think necessary to appear before him for finding of caution for their obedience, within such time as shall be fixed by him, under the penalty of rebellion and putting of them to the horn, and if they fail, to denounce them accordingly: with power to him also to charge the castles of disobedient persons to be surrendered under the penalty of treason, and in case of resistance to besiege them, raise fire and use all other warlike force for capturing them." There was the usual indemnity to the Lieutenant and his men for deaths or injuries inflicted in the execution of his commission, with all other powers usual in similar cases. On the 14th of December, Angus had succeeded in obtaining from the Earl of Athole, Grant and Mackintosh an assurance of peace, which included Huntly's allies.

On the 27th of December, Andrew Knox, minister of Paisley, having learned that George Kerr was ready to proceed to Spain, traced him to Glasgow, thence to the island of Cumbrae, and apprehended him on the ship in which he was about to sail. Kerr's baggage was searched, and some packets of letters being found, he was conveyed a prisoner to Edinburgh. Among the letters, several signatures of the Earls of Huntly, Erroll, and Angus were found at the bottom of blank slips of paper. Kerr was tortured, and on the first stroke of the boots confessed the conspiracy. Though this mode of extracting evidence destroys any degree of credit which might otherwise attach to the statements of the accused individual, yet it was enough, in the heated temper of the ministers and the people, to arouse their passions and feelings to a pitch of great excitement. The Lords of the Privy Council, after examining the letters, had no doubt of their authenticity. Huntly and his associates protested that they were innocent, and asserted that they had entered into no conspiracy. But they declined to obey the order to ward in St. Andrews, or to subscribe a bond touching religion; and they were then proclaimed rebels. The King mustered an army in February, 1593, and marched northward.

SECTION XI.

GEORGE, SIXTH EARL AND FIRST MARQUIS OF HUNTLY (CONTINUED)—THE KING IN THE NORTH—CASTLE OF STRATHBOGIE OCCUPIED.

THE King arrived in Aberdeen on the 20th of February, 1593, and stayed several weeks in the city. On the approach of His Majesty, Huntly and his chief allies went aboard a vessel at Rathbyhaven and sailed for Caithness. The Castle of Strathbogie was garrisoned by a body of men under the command of Archibald Carmichael. The Earl of Athole was appointed Lieutenant-General beyond the Spey, associated with Earl Marischal. Yet the King seems to have had no intention of proceeding to extremities against Huntly and the Catholic Earls. There were obvious reasons for this policy, as about one-third of the Scottish barons were still more or less firmly attached to the Roman Catholic religion. Thus the Countess of Huntly was courteously received at the Court, and interceded for her husband.

But many incidents and circumstances indicated that the King was much inclined to treat the Earl of Huntly and his associates with the utmost possible leniency. On the 16th of March Huntly was relieved from the horning proclaimed against him.

In September, Huntly proceeded to punish the Mackintoshes, who had ventured to invade Strathbogie during his absence. On his return, he pursued them, overtook and completely defeated them in the Cabrach, where sixty of them were slain. Yet the Earl was not satisfied. The following year, on the 30th of April, " Huntly made a raid against the Mackintoshes; burned their houses, slaughtered many people, and captured an immense booty."

In October, 1593, Huntly, Erroll, and Angus suddenly appeared at Fala, threw themselves upon their knees before the King, and entreated him not to condemn them unheard, and offered to enter ward whenever His Majesty should be pleased to command them. Those of the Council present were favourable to the Earls, and they were ordered to repair to Perth and stay there till arrangements could be made.

The Protestant clergy insisted on extreme measures against the Catholic Earls, and matters were running to a crisis. Both parties were mustering their forces throughout the kingdom. A committee of the Three Estates met at Holyrood, along with six of the leading ministers, to deliberate on the state of affairs. After some very animated debates, the King, on the 26th of November, 1593, pronounced what was called the "Act of Abolition" touching Huntly and his associates. This Act announced that the true religion established in the first year of His Majesty's reign should be the only one professed in Scotland; and that those who had never embraced it, and those who had declined from it, should either conform to it before the

11th of February, 1594, or depart from the country to such places as the King should direct, and there remain till they professed the truth and satisfied the Church. During their banishment, they were to retain the full possession of their estates. All accusations against Huntly and his friends were annulled. They were ordered to inform the King and the Church, before the 11th of January, which of the alternatives they meant to accept.

This Act pleased neither party. The Catholic Earls were not disposed to renounce their religion, nor to retain it only at the cost of exile; while the clergy were extremely annoyed at this temporising line of action, and immediately proclaimed their disapproval of it from their pulpits. The Earl of Huntly and his adherents were excommunicated in May.

In the beginning of June, Parliament met, and on the 4th an Act of Forfeiture was passed against Huntly and his associates, and they were proclaimed rebels. They still remained in the north; and the King issued a commission to the Earls of Argyle and Athole and Lord Forbes to muster their vassals and wage war against Huntly.

The young Earl of Argyle mustered his vassals and took the field, and advanced through the mountain passes in the direction of Strathbogie. He was joined on the march by the Macleans, Grants, Macgregors, and some of the Mackintoshes. Huntly and Erroll mustered their followers at Strathbogie, and marched through the parish of Glass; and on the way Gordon of Cairnborrow and his eight sons joined them. They advanced up the valley of the Deveron to the Cabrach, thence by the castle of Auchindoun to the Braes of Glenlivet. Argyle continued to advance toward Glenlivet, and pitched his camp in this district, near the Glenrinnes border. On perceiving the approach of Huntly's men, Argyle left his camp and drew up his men, numbering about 5000, in three divisions. Sir John Maclean commanded the right wing, which was posted on the shoulder of a mountain, terminating in an inclined plane; the left wing was partly protected by marshy ground, and Argyle himself commanded the reserve, which occupied the heights. Huntly's force consisted of about 900 well-armed men, and a few pieces of artillery, which opened fire on Maclean's line, and under cover of which the Earl of Erroll led the attack on the right wing and attempted a flanking movement; but his company was surrounded and placed in extreme peril. When Huntly observed this, he rapidly advanced with the main body of his men and horse, and assailed the right wing and centre of the enemy's line. After two hours' hard fighting, the centre of Argyle's line was thrown into confusion and driven back upon the reserve, which also became confused, and, in spite of his utmost efforts, fled from the field. But the right wing under Maclean fought with remarkable courage, and at last retired in good order. The battle was fought on the 13th of October, 1594. On Argyle's side, about 500 men were slain; on Huntly's side 20 men were slain, and many wounded. Among those slain was Sir Patrick Gordon of Auchindoun, a son of the fourth Earl of Huntly.

The King had advanced to Dundee when tidings of the defeat of Argyle reached him, and he immediately pushed forward. On the march he was joined by the Keiths, Forbesses, Irvines, and others, and arrived at Aberdeen.

The King, with his army, proceeded to Strathbogie, and the castle was dismantled and defaced. The Castle of Slains, the seat of the Earl of Erroll, and other mansions of the Gordons, were also dismantled. On returning to Aberdeen, the King caused a number of the Earl of Huntly's adherents to be executed, and then proclaimed a general pardon to those who had been with him at the Battle of Glenlivet, provided they paid the fines imposed by the council. After making some arrangements for preserving peace, and appointing the Duke of Lennox—

Earls of Huntly.   173

Huntly's brother-in-law—Governor of the North, the King disbanded the army, and in November proceeded to the south.

Huntly fled to Caithness. The sentence of forfeiture passed against him had never been acted upon; and the Duke of Lennox gave over the management of Huntly's estates to the Countess. In March, 1595, the Earl left Scotland, and made a tour through France and Germany. The Countess of Huntly made the utmost efforts to obtain her husband's pardon. In August, 1596, the Earl returned to Scotland, and there were indications that the Government would restore him. The Earl had forwarded overtures to the King, offering submission, and petitioning to be absolved from the sentence of excommunication. At a meeting of the barons and some of the clergy, it was agreed that, under certain conditions, to be drawn up by the King and the Privy Council, Huntly might be received, but the majority of the clergy were opposed to this proposal, and they engaged in a bitter struggle with the King.

At a General Assembly which met at Dundee on the 10th of May, 1597, the conditions prescribed for the absolution and admission of the Earls of Huntly, Erroll, Angus, and the Laird of Gight, were discussed, and a commission was appointed to receive them into the Church. The ceremony of their reconcilation to the church took place at Aberdeen in the Old Church. The church was crowded, many of the noblemen and gentlemen of the county were present. Immediately before the sermon, the Earls publicly subscribed the Confession of Faith. After the sermon, they rose and in a loud voice confessed their defection and apostasy, and professed their present conviction of the truth of the Protestant faith and their resolution to adhere to it. The Earl of Huntly then declared, before God, the King, and the Church, his penitence for the slaughter of the Earl of Moray. The three Earls were then absolved from the sentence of excommunication. They next communicated in the Prostestant form, and solemnly swore to keep order in all respects and to execute justice within their territories. The Laird of Gight appeared in the garb of a penitent, and threw himself upon his knees before the pulpit, and implored pardon for supporting the Earl of Bothwell, and prayed to be released from the sentence of excommunication; this was granted, and he was reconciled. The following day, the reconciliation of the Earls was proclaimed at the Cross on the Castlegate, amid a great assemblage of the people, who shouted joyfully, drank the health of the Earls, and tossed their glasses in the air.

The estates and titles of Huntly and the other Catholic Earls were restored to them by Parliament in December, 1597. On the 17th of April, 1599, he was created Marquis of Huntly, Earl of Enzie, Viscount of Inverness, &c. In 1601 he received a Royal Commission of Justiciary and Lieutenancy for the reduction of the Isles to order and obedience. About this time several projects touching the Western Isles were on foot.

A contract was entered into between the King on the one hand, and on the other James Learmonth of Balcomie, Sir James Anstruther, Captain William Murray, the Duke of Lennox, and others. They undertook to colonise the Island of Lewis, and develop its rich resources. The contract is dated 29th of June, 1598. On the 7th of July an Act of Council in favour of the new colonists was passed, to this effect:—" That a summons be raised to seek a declaration upon the late Act of Parliament against Highlandmen and Islesmen for non-production of their titles and rights, that they should be charged to appear before His Majesty and the Privy Council to find caution according to the acts and penalties contained therein, and being denounced rebels . . . That there shall be a process of forfeiture regularly deduced against these Highlandmen, and their goods given to the new colonising gentlemen. . . . That their lands shall by a new right and disposition be conveyed to the new colonisers, and to no others." The new colonisers or "gentlemen adventurers," as they are called in the record, took possession of the Island of Lewis, and in November, 1600, Parliament ratified their "infeftment of the island.

They did not long retain possession of Lewis. The tragic narrative is presented in the Register of the Privy Council thus:—" His Majesty, after good advice and deliberation, resolved to reduce that isle to obedience, and plant a number of good and dutiful subjects in it. For this purpose His Majesty disposed the right of that isle to certain barons and gentlemen, who enterprised the conquest of the isle, establishing religion and policy in it, and rooting out the barbarity and wickedness which were so common in it. Likewise, they having by force made a perfect conquest of that isle, and reduced it to as great obedience as any part of the mainland, so that all kind of traffic by sea was very frequent there, yet it is a truth that certain of the chiefs of the isle, confederated with the chiefs of the adjacent isles, under the pretence of friendship, conspired and devised the extermination and ruin of the gentlemen adventurers and their whole company. At last, in the winter of 1602, finding the proper time when these gentlemen expected no such hid treason, they then attacked them and slew them; and they have taken possession of the isle, intending by force to hold it against His Majesty's authority." Those of the adventurers not slain made terms with the islesmen, and departed from the island. The King was enraged, and ordered a muster of his subjects in the northern counties from the river Dee to the Orkney Islands—to reconquer the Island of Lewis. But the King had at the time too many irons in the fire, and the Isle of Lewis was not reconquered for a long time.

SECTION XII.

GEORGE, FIRST MARQUIS OF HUNTLY (CONTINUED)—THE MARQUIS RECONCILED TO THE EARLS OF MORAY AND ARGYLE—DEATH OF HUNTLY.

IN 1603 the Marquis of Huntly became reconciled to the Earl of Moray—the Earl of Moray in that year having married Lady Ann Gordon, the Marquis's eldest daughter. About the same time the Marquis was reconciled with the Earl of Argyle; and in 1607 the Earl of Enzie and Lord Gordon, the Marquis's eldest son, married Lady Anne Campbell, a daughter of Archibald, seventh Earl of Argyle. On the 25th of October, 1608, they were infefted in the Lordship of Badenoch, and other lands in Lochaber.

It appears that the Marquis and Marchioness were still much attached to the Roman Catholic faith. In 1606, the Marquis and his family were ordered to reside in Aberdeen for the benefit of advice and instruction from the ministers there. In the following year, he was ordered to live within eighteen miles of the city of Elgin, and to reside there ten days of every month, including two Sundays, and attend church every Sunday. In July, 1608, he was excommunicated by the General Assembly, and imprisoned in Stirling Castle. But he yielded in 1609, and the following year he was released on promising to subscribe the Confession of Faith.

On the 27th of February, 1617, the Marquis of Huntly appeared personally at a meeting of the Privy Council in Edinburgh, and presented His Majesty's letter, and, having taken the oath of allegiance and of Privy Councillor, was admitted to the Council. The King's letter was to this effect:—" Right trusty and well-beloved cousin, we greet you well. Whereas the Marquis of Huntly has now given full satisfaction in all matters concerning religion, we are well pleased to restore him to all dignities which at any time heretofore he enjoyed, or from which by reason of his recusancy he has hitherto been debarred, and especially to a place of our Privy Council in that our kingdom. Therefore it is our pleasure that you cause minister unto him the oaths usual in such cases and admit him to our Privy Council to enjoy all honours, dignities, privileges and immunities which any other of our ordinary Privy Councillors enjoys by reason of his place in our Council. Given at Newmarket, the 12th of December, 1616."

The Marquis seldom attended the meetings of the Privy Council. He chiefly directed his attention to the improvement of his estates. He rebuilt the Castle of Strathbogie, and repaired the Castles of Aboyne and Bog of Gight; he planted a considerable extent of ground, made roads and erected bridges.

But he was present in the Convention of Estates which met at Edinburgh on the 5th of March, 1617. At this meeting a vote of £200,000 was passed for His Majesty's expenses in his approaching visit to Scotland.

The Marquis attended the Parliament which met at Edinburgh on the 17th of June, 1617, and he was elected one of the Lords of the Articles. At the opening of this Parliament, the King, from the throne on which he was seated, delivered a long speech, explaining his own good intentions, his desire to see the Church settled, the whole nation in order, and necessary reforms passed for the good of his people.

The extraordinary and unprecedented preparations that were made for this visit of James VI. may be seen in the eleventh volume of the Register of the Privy Council of Scotland. The Marquis of Huntly when in Edinburgh had promised to the Council to send John Anderson, a painter, who attended to his works at Strathbogie, to attend on the works in progress at Falkland Palace, preparatory for the King's visit. "Yet John Anderson is not come here, so that His Majesty's works which were to be committed to his charge are like to be frustrated, highly to His Majesty's displeasure. Therefore the Lords of the Privy Council order letters to be directed charging George, Marquis of Huntly, to demit John Anderson from his work and service, and to set him forward on his journey hither within twenty-four hours, and also charging the said John Anderson to address himself, with his workloooms and other necessaries, to His Majesty's master of works at Falkland Palace, so that he may be employed by him in His Majesty's service, within six days, under the penalty of rebellion."

In 1629 the Marquis was deprived of the office of Sheriff of Inverness and Aberdeen for a composition of £5000, which was never paid. The following year he was much affected by the unfortunate and sad tragedy at Frendraught.

The old tower of Frendraught stands on a haugh on the north side of a streamlet, about a quarter of mile above the distillery of Glendronach, in the parish of Forgue. A fragment of the old tower still remains. Frendraught was a lordship and regality, and embraced a large part of the lands at Forgue, Inverkeithney, and Marnoch. At an early period it belonged to Dunbar, a branch of the Moray family of that name. But in the reign of James II. it came into possession of a son of Sir William Crichton, Lord High Chancellor of Scotland. About 1626, John Gordon of Cairnburrow, purchased the lands of Rothiemay from James Stewart, Lord of Ochiltree, and his son, William Gordon, became Laird of Rothiemay.

A dispute arose between Gordon of Rothiemay and James Crichton of Frendraught touching fishings in the river Deveron; Crichton carried the case before the Lords of the Privy Council, who decided in his favour. This appears to have greatly offended Gordon of Rothiemay; and he mustered a company of men, and attempted to waste the lands of Frendraught. But Crichton received a commission to apprehend him and his associates. Accordingly Crichton, accompanied by James Leslie, a son of the Laird of Pitcaple, John Meldrum of Reidshill, and others, proceeded toward Rothiemay on the 1st of January, 1630.

Gordon advanced and faced them, a conflict ensued, in which Gordon was seriously wounded, and died in a few days. The Marquis of Huntly intervened, and on Crichton paying 50,000 marks to the young Laird of Rothiemay, peace seemed to be restored. Yet John Meldrum apparently imagined that Crichton had not fully rewarded him for his service, for he carried off two of Crichton's horses. Crichton then took steps to apprehend Meldrum as a robber; on hearing this he took refuge with his brother-in-law at Pitcaple. When Crichton came in search of him, James Leslie, a son of the laird, came out and remonstrated with Crichton touching Meldrum. From words they soon came to blows, and Robert Crichton, a relative of Frendraught, shot Leslie through the arm.

Crichton of Frendraught immediately proceeded to Bog of Gight, and requested the Marquis of Huntly to terminate the feud. Leslie of Pitcaple also went and placed his case before the Marquis, but insisted that he could not agree to any terms with Crichton until he saw whether his wounded son would live or die. Fearing bloodshed between the two men, Huntly requested his son, Viscount Aboyne, and the Laird of Rothiemay, to escort Crichton home, which they did. On their arrival at Frendraught on the evening of the 18th of October, 1630, Crichton and his wife, to show their friendly feeling, desired them to stay overnight and enjoy themselves after their long ride. After supper they went to bed in one of the high chambers of the tower. About midnight the tower took fire, and Viscount Aboyne, the young laird of Rothiemay, and six attendants were burned to death. The scene is well described in a ballad, which appears to have been written shortly after the tragic event, of which a few verses may be quoted :—

> When mass was sung, and bells were rung,
> And a' men boun' for bed,
> Then good Lord John and Rothiemay,
> In ae chamber baith were laid,

> They hadna lang keist their claies,
>   And were but new asleep,
> When the weary smoke beguid to rise,
>   Likewise the scorching heat.
>
> "Oh! wauken, wauken, Rothiemay,
>   Oh! wauken, brither dear,
> And turn ye to oor Saviour—
>   There is strong treason here."
>
> When they were dressed in a' their claes,
>   And ready for to boun',
> A' doors and windows were secured,
>   The roof-tree burnin' doon.
>
> When he stood at the wire window,
>   Maist dolefu' to be seen,
> He did espy her Lady Frendraught,
>   Wha stood upon the green.
>
> Cried, "Mercy, mercy, Lady Frendraught,
>   Will ye not sink wi' sin?
> For first your man my father killed,
>   And noo ye burn his son."

The Gordons believed that the fire was wilful, and the Marquis of Huntly proceeded to prosecute Crichton. In 1631 he went to Edinburgh, accompanied by a number of his friends, and presented a petiton to the Privy Council. The council commissioned the Bishops of Aberdeen and Moray, Lord Carnegy, and Colonel Bruce to make inquiry into the matter. They met at the burnt Tower of Frendraught on the 13th of April, 1631. The Earl of Enzie, the Marquis's eldest son, Lord Ogilvie, Lord Deskford, and others were also present. They searched and investigated the burnt tower internally, and the vault below it; and came to the conclusion that the fire had been kindled inside the building, but by whom they could not discover. Huntly stayed in Edinburgh till the Commissioners presented their report to the Council, and then returned to the north.

The Gordons, however, were far from satisfied. They commenced a series of forays upon the lands of Frendraught and the Crichtons and their friends, and bloodshed and slaughter became almost a daily occurrence. At last the Government interfered, and summoned the Marquis of Huntly to appear before the Council and answer for not restraining his kinsmen and vassals. Having failed to appear, he was outlawed. Afterwards, the Marquis proceeded to Edinburgh, and was accused as the chief mover of the raids and depredations on the Crichtons. He pleaded innocence, and asserted that the rebels were neither his tenants nor servants, and, seeing that he was not then Sheriff, he had no right to interfere. The outlawry against him was withdrawn, on his giving assurance that he and his allies should keep the peace.

When he returned to the north, the disturbers of the peace dispersed for a time. In the winter of 1635, the Marquis was again summoned to appear at Edinburgh. Though no definite charge was brought against him he was imprisoned in the Castle of Edinburgh. Subsequently he received permission to live in his own lodgings, and to walk in the gardens of Holyrood. The Marquis felt himself to be approaching the end of his eventful career. In the beginning of June, 1636, he left Edinburgh to return to Strathbogie, and having reached Dundee, he died there on the 13th of June. He was interred at Elgin.

SECTION XIII.

GEORGE, SECOND MARQUIS OF HUNTLY—EARLY PART OF HIS CAREER—HIS LOYALTY TO CHARLES I.

THE late Marquis was succeeded by his eldest son, George, second Marquis of Huntly, who during the lifetime of his father was known as Earl of Enzie and Lord Gordon. As mentioned in the last section, he married Lady Anne Campbell, a daughter of the Earl of Argyle. In 1609 he was commissioned to suppress the "Knights of the Morter," otherwise "The Society of the Boyes," a secret organization of Aberdeenshire men, who were rather much inclined to use the dirk, pistol, and claymore upon the slightest occasion and to break the peace by their brawls. They were banded together by an oath to avenge their mutual wrongs, and roamed throughout the country and pillaged whoever they pleased. Their oppression and contempt of the laws attracted the attention of the Privy Council, who denounced them "as an infamous byk of lawlass lymmars and a foul reproach to any country." They were, however, very difficult to suppress, and Enzie's efforts against them were not very successful.

In March, 1618, he received a Commission of Justiciary to apprehend and try all persons suspected of murder, theft, and reset of theft, within the Lordship of Badenoch and Lochaber. In 1622, he received a commission to proceed against his relative, the turbulent Earl of Caithness; but his efforts were unavailing, and he petitioned to be relieved of the chief duty of his commission against the Earl of Caithness.

In the spring of 1623, he received a licence from the King to go abroad to any part of Christendom and stay for seven years. He was accompanied by a number of young gentlemen, and in 1624 he was appointed captain in the Scots Bodyguard of the King of France. He served with tact and distinction in Alsace and Lorraine, which was recognised and highly appreciated by the French King.

He was recalled by his father to assist in suppressing disorder in the north. He again went to France in 1633, where he stayed until after his father's death, and returned to Strathbogie on the 23rd of June, 1637, and was heartily welcomed by his friends and retainers.

The second Marquis of Huntly, on his return home, found the kingdom entering on a trying period of its history—the Covenanting struggle. Huntly continued loyal to Charles I., and exerted himself on his behalf. The

Covenanters made an effort to induce the Marquis to join them; it is said that they offered him the leadership of the movement, and also promised to discharge the family debt, which then exceeded £100,000. In the event of the Marquis refusing these offers, then they would adopt measures to ruin him and his family. This much is certain, that whatever proposals the Covenanters offered to the Marquis were rejected by him, as he avowed his intention to stand fast to the King's cause, as his ancestors had done.

He proceeded to Aberdeen and endeavoured to keep the citizens loyal, and encouraged them to take up arms against the Covenanters. On the 16th of March, 1639, the Marquis received a Royal Commission of Lieutenancy, and mustered his followers; and on the 25th of March, he was at Inverurie with a force of 5000 men. When he received tidings that the Covenanters were marching to the north under the command of the Earl of Montrose, he knew that, without assistance from England, he could not face the enemy. Montrose marched into Aberdeen on the 30th of March, at the head of an army of 6000 men; and the Covenanters of the surrounding country joined him with other 3000 men. Leaving a garrison in Aberdeen, he advanced on Inverurie, where he quartered his troops upon the opponents of the Covenant. Huntly, seeing no hope of aid from the south, sought an interview with Montrose, and they met at Inverurie. On the 5th of April a compromise was arranged, by which Huntly agreed to maintain the laws, liberties, and religion of the Kingdom, but his Roman Catholic friends were not to be pressed to sign the Covenant; Montrose agreed to withdraw from the north if Huntly disbanded his army, which he did, and returned to Strathbogie.

A few days after, the Marquis was invited to Aberdeen under a safe-conduct signed by Montrose and the other leaders of the army, and arrived at the city on the 12th of April. Montrose's object was soon manifested. He had entrapped Huntly, and made him a prisoner in a very treacherous manner. The Marquis and his eldest son, Lord Gordon, were immediately conveyed as prisoners to Edinburgh. On arriving at the capital, Huntly was pressed to take the Covenant, but he replied—" For my part, I am in your power ; and resolved not to leave that foul title of traitor as an inheritance upon my posterity. You may take my head from my shoulders, but not my heart from my sovereign." The Marquis and his son were imprisoned in Edinburgh Castle. Thus the King's hope of a rising in his favour in the North was blasted.

Yet, Huntly's second son, James, the young Viscount Aboyne, mustered the clan himself, with the object of preventing Montrose from wasting the lands of Strathbogie. He raised a considerable number of men, and took possession of Aberdeen. But he was soon forced to disband his army. He then went on board a ship and proceeded to the King, who promised him assistance, and appointed him to the office of Lieutenant held by his father. Aboyne returned to Aberdeen, and, being joined by the Farquharsons of Strathdee, he mustered a force of about 2000 men. He advanced to Kintore, and compelled the people to swear allegiance to the King. Shortly after his army was defeated by Earl Marischal in the vicinity of Stonehaven. A few days later a party of the Gordons defeated the advance guard of Montrose's army. Viscount Aboyne again resolved to make a stand and dispute the passage of the Bridge of Dee. On the 17th of June he ordered his men to muster. Only a small number assembled, but barricades were hastily thrown up at the south port of the bridge. On the following day Aboyne marched to the bridge with 200 musketeers and a small number of mounted men. He held the bridge against Montrose army for two days. But at last Montrose sent a body of men and horse up the south side of the river, moving as if they intended to ford it. This had the desired effect, Aboyne, with a company of the defenders, left the bridge and advanced up the north side of the river; then Montrose opened fire upon them, and at the same time redoubled the attack on the bridge. At four in the afternoon the bridge was taken. Montrose marched in triumph into the city. Aboyne managed with difficulty to escape to England.

Under the arrangements between the King and the Covenanters of the 18th of June, 1639, the Marquis of Huntly and his eldest son were liberated from prison on the 20th of the month. They proceeded to the King in England. During their absence their friends in the north had been subjected to very harsh treatment by the Covenanting generals—Argyle and Munro. While the Marquis was in prison his three daughters, Ann, Henrietta, and Jane, had been married respectively to the Earl of Perth, Earl of Haddington, and Lord Seton. These marriages were arranged by Argyle—Huntly's brother-in-law. Thus Argyle became bound for each of their tochers, and in 1641, to secure him, Huntly granted wadsets of Badenoch and Lochaber to him. The late troubles had involved the Marquis in many difficulties, from which he endeavoured to extricate himself.

When the struggle between the King and the Scottish Parliament recommenced in earnest, Huntly continued faithful to the Royal cause. In July, 1643, he was summoned to appear before the Scottish Parliament, but he did not appear, and the Committee of Estates—then the ruling body in Scotland—made the utmost efforts to capture him. He had an interview with Montrose in June, 1643. Acting under his commission of Lieutenant of the North, he ordered his clan and vassals to muster at Aboyne; and about 800 men on foot and 200 mounted men assembled. Thence he marched to Aberdeen, and issued a proclamation announcing that he was acting in self-defence. On the 24th of April, 1644, he was excommunicated. The Marquis was placed in an extremely trying position. It appears that he was averse to strong measures.

There is also evidence that the Earl of Argyle had in various ways contrived to hamper the Marquis's action. The hold that Argyle had acquired over portions of the Gordon estates was used to cripple the Marquis. Argyle managed to induce Lord Gordon and Lewis Gordon, Huntly's sons, to join the Covenanters and fight on their side. Thus, it was not surprising that on the approach of Argyle at the head of an army of 6000 men, Huntly disbanded his followers. How could he have fought against his own children?

A reward of 18,000 marks was offered for the capture of the Marquis of Huntly. He then fled to the wilds of Sutherland for refuge.

Argyle pillaged the Marquis's lands. He also wasted the lands of the young laird of Drum, whose wife was Lady Mary Gordon, Argyle's own niece.

The Earl of Montrose, who had been an ardent Covenanter, turned round to the King's side, was commissioned by his Majesty, and raised the Royal standard in Perthshire, in August, 1644. He was soon at the head of 3000 men, many of whom were Irish Roman Catholics. In a short time a number of the Highlanders rose at the call of Montrose to fight for the King. He concentrated his men at Blair-Athole. There were then three bodies of armed men in the field against him. Argyle was advancing from the west, another army was stationed at Aberdeen, and a third under Lord Elcho, consisting of the men of Fife and lower parts of Perthshire, to keep him in check if he attempted to advance along the valley of the Tay. Montrose resolved to attack Lord Elcho's force.

He drew up his men three deep and extended his line to the utmost, and presented a front as long as the enemy's. On the afternoon of September 1st, 1644, he attacked the Covenanters under Lord Elcho, and the first onset of the Highlanders threw them into confusion, and in an instant Elcho's army was routed and flying in all directions. Two thousand of the Covenanters were slain in the pursuit. In the evening Montrose was master of Perth.

On the 4th of September Montrose commenced his march on Aberdeen. The Marquis of Huntly could not make up his mind to join with Montrose, which was not surprising, seeing how he had before entrapped and betrayed him. The Covenanters, numbering about 2000 foot and 500 horse, were posted on rising ground on the westward side of the city. On the morning of the 13th of September, Montrose reached the vicinity of Aberdeen. He summoned the Magistrates to surrender the town, but they declined. He then prepared for battle, and placed his horse on the wings of his line. He began the attack, and, after a severe engagement, the Covenanters were completely defeated and fled in confusion. Montrose's army entered the town, massacred the unarmed citizens on the streets, and sacked the city. These cruel proceedings greatly heightened the hatred of the Lowland people against Montrose.

He appealed to the Gordons for assistance, but they refused to move; and he was forced to betake himself to the mountains. After a time, however, Lord Gordon, Viscount Aboyne, and many of the Gordon clan joined Montrose.

SECTION XIV.

GEORGE, SECOND MARQUIS OF HUNTLY—LORD GORDON, VISCOUNT ABOYNE, AND LORD LEWIS—BATTLE OF AULDEARN—BATTLE OF ALFORD—PROCEEDINGS OF HUNTLY—CAPTURED AND IMPRISONED—TRIED AND EXECUTED—LEWIS, THIRD MARQUIS.

ON the 2nd of February, 1645, Montrose completely defeated Argyle and all his clan at Inverlochy. He then marched northward by Inverness, and when he reached Elgin, Lord Gordon and his brother Lewis joined him, and Viscount Aboyne also joined the conquering hero. Montrose's career will be detailed afterwards, and only the battles in which the Gordons were engaged will be noticed here.

Montrose had reached the village of Auldearn on the evening of the 8th of May, intending to follow Hurry (the Covenanting general) the next day. But ere dawn on the morning of the 9th of May, Hurry had fronted round, and hoped by a rapid march to surprise Montrose; and, if an untoward incident had not occurred, it seems probable that he would have accomplished his object; but the night was rainy and wetted the powder in the muskets of Hurry's soldiers, some of whom fired a volley to clear their barrels. It so happened that Montrose's sentinels heard the sound of the firing, and thus gave him time to post his army in battle array, which he did admirably. The battle raged with the utmost fury, and was long and fiercely contested. Lord Gordon, Viscount Aboyne, and the rest of the Gordons, fought bravely. The greater part of Hurry's infantry stood their ground with remarkable courage, and were slain on the field.

But Montrose had soon to contend against forces more numerous than his own. General Baillie advanced from Athole northward, crossed the Dee with 2000 men, and was joined in Strathbogie by Hurry with 100 horsemen, the remnant of the army defeated at Auldearn. Montrose's force was greatly diminished, and, being unable to fight, he marched up the Valley of the Spey for safety. Baillie remained in the north and ravaged Huntly's lands.

After a time Montrose had again increased his force. He marched in search of Baillie, and found him in a strong position at Keith. Montrose did not venture to attack him, but marched southward, crossed the Don, halted at Alford, and Baillie followed him. On the 2nd of July, 1645, Montrose placed his men in battle array on an elevated position. Baillie crossed the river and prepared for battle. Lord Gordon commanded the right wing of Montrose's army; Viscount Aboyne fought on the left; and Glengarry led the centre, consisting of the Macdonalds and the Lochaber vassals of Huntly. The battle began and raged furiously with no apparent success on either side; at last Montrose brought up his reserve, and Lord Gordon attacked the Covenanters in flank; and they were completely defeated. Lord Gordon was slain, and many of the Gordons were wounded. A considerable number of the Covenanters were killed.

At the battle of Kilsyth, on the 24th of August, many of the Gordons fought under the command of Viscount Aboyne. Shortly after this battle, Viscount Aboyne left Montrose, and returned to the north.

The Marquis of Huntly, returned from his retreat in Strathnaver, was preparing to take the field, and led his men in person. Huntly had an interview with Montrose at Bog of Gight, but the Marquis declined to co-operate with him. Huntly proceeded to Aberdeen, and on receiving tidings that General Middleton was advancing against him with a large force, he marched up the valley of the Dee, and occupied the Castle of Kinnord. But Middleton turned aside in pursuit of Montrose; and Huntly then returned to Aberdeen. On the 14th of May, 1646, he defeated Colonel Montgomery and captured 350 prisoners. Shortly after, the King sent orders to Huntly and Montrose to lay down their arms.

Afterwards the King sent a secret message to the Marquis requesting him to take the field, and holding out the hope that he himself would join him. But their intentions were discovered. On the approach of General David Leslie and General Middleton, the Marquis retired to Badenoch. The Castle of Strathbogie was taken, and the other strongholds of the Marquis were successively reduced. The Marquis himself was pursued through Glenmoriston, Badenoch, and Lochaber, and had many narrow escapes. Surrounded by a few faithful and brave men, he lived in dens and sequestered spots. General Middleton lay at

Strathbogie, whence he sent out parties of troops to search for the Marquis. For some time he had been lying concealed at the farmhouse of Dalnabo, three miles below Inchroy, when his hiding place was discovered by the agents of the Government. Towards the end of December, 1647, Colonel Menzies, with a company of troops, at midnight surrounded Dalnabo. The Marquis had only ten of his faithful retainers around him, yet they made a heroic stand to protect their master against fearful odds. Six of them were killed and the rest wounded before Huntly was made prisoner. When the news of his capture spread, many of the Gordons and Grants rushed to the rescue. James Grant of Carron placed himself at the head of 400 men, and declared that he would rescue Huntly or die in the attempt. The Marquis thanked them for their devotion, but commanded them not to make any such attempt; and then said, "that now, almost worn out with grief and fatigue, he could no longer live in dens and hills, and hoped that his enemies would not drive things to the worst."

Colonel Menzies immediately conveyed the Marquis to Blairfinde in Glenlivet, and thence to Strathbogie. He was carried under a guard to Edinburgh, where he was imprisoned. When Charles I. heard of his capture, he wrote to the Earl of Lanark, and requested him to make the utmost effort to save the Marquis's life. The Marquis was confined in prison for 16 months. "During this time Argyle possessed himself of his brother-in-law's estate, and bought up all the comprisings which affected it; took up his residence in the Gordon castles, levied the rents, and left the Gordons to do as best they might." When in prison, the Marquis heard of the execution of Charles I., and also of the death of his own son, Viscount Aboyne.

The Marquis was brought to trial on the 16th of March, 1649, on a charge of treason. He was convicted, and sentenced to death. On the 21st of March, the Committee of Estates ordered the Magistrates of Edinburgh to receive the person of George Gordon, late Marquis of Huntly, from the constable of the Castle of Edinburgh, and to cause the aforesaid George to be brought to the place of execution, and there to see the sentence of Parliament executed. In his last moments Huntly manifested remarkable fortitude. He said to the people that he was going to die for having employed some years of his life in the service of the King, his master; that he was sorry he was not the first of his Majesty's subjects who had suffered for his cause, so glorious in itself that it sweetened to him all the bitterness of death. He declared that he forgave those who had voted for his death, although he would not admit that he had done anything contrary to the law; and, after embracing some of his friends, submitted his neck to the fatal instrument, at the Market Cross of Edinburgh, on the 22nd of March, 1649.

By Lady Ann Campbell the Marquis had five sons and five daughters. The sons were—George, Lord Gordon, who fell at the battle of Alford; James, Viscount Aboyne, who died at Paris in the beginning of February, 1649; Lord Lewis, who became third Marquis; Charles, who was afterwards created first Earl of Aboyne; Henry, who entered the service of the King of Poland, and who died at Strathbogie.

The late Marquis was succeeded by his third son, Lewis, third Marquis of Huntly. It is said that he was offered his father's estates if he satisfied the Church, but he declined to accept the family possessions on such terms. Thus, they continued in the hands of Argyle, who obtained from Parliament an order for the destruction of several of the Gordon strongholds.

During these troublous times Lord Lewis Gordon had sought refuge in a cave two miles from Castle Grant. When there his food was carried to him by Mary Grant, a young lady of such beauty and sympathy, that she obtained " possession of his soul against all the bewitching allurements of home-bred and foreign beauties whatsoever."

This lady was a daughter of Sir John Grant of Freuchie, and Lewis Gordon married her in November, 1644, and with her got 20,000 marks.

Lewis and his younger brother, Charles, continued to be loyal supporters of the Royal cause, and their loyalty to Charles II. was rewarded. On the 27th of March, 1651, the attainder passed on Lewis Gordon's father was reversed, and he was restored to the Marquisate of Huntly " with all the titles, honours, and dignities pertaining to his late father, as if there had been no forfeiture." The titles were to descend to him and his heirs male, whom failing to the next apparent heir male of his father.

On the 21st of August, 1651, the Marquis granted a discharge to the Magistrates of Aberdeen for ten men fully armed and equipped, as a part of the 90 men—the city's porportion of the levy. The Royalists were defeated at the battle of Worcester on the 3rd of September, and Charles II. fled to the continent.

Huntly was very anxious to come to terms with Argyle touching the family estates. Accordingly it was arranged that a meeting should be held at Finlarg Castle, Huntly to be accompanied by eighty men and Argyle by the same number. On the arrival of the Gordons at the appointed castle, whose company of eighty men were mostly Highlandmen, they found the whole district was in arms. Under these circumstances, Huntly's friends advised him to return home, and not enter into business ; but his escort was so surrounded by Argyle's men, " that it was impossible for him to recoil." Being thus constrained, at last Huntly entered upon the treaty, and signed several papers and writs, " to the great prejudice of his interest and family."— Miscellany of the Old Spalding Club, Vol. IV., pp. 166, 667.

The Marquis's lot was cast in troublous times. In September, 1653, he entered into negotiations with Colonel Morgan, one of Cromwell's officers, and agreed that the Lairds of Straloch and Lesmore should become sureties for his keeping the peace. This led to reports being circulated to his prejudice, which had reached the ears of Charles II., who was then abroad. Huntly died in the end of the year 1653, leaving a son, George, then a boy, who succeeded him, and subsequently was created Duke of Gordon.

In 1655 the late Marquis's widow wrote to the Marquis of Argyle, who then held the Gordon estates, requesting that she might get her portion, or at least a suitable maintenance. He replied that though her request was reasonable, it was not in his power to entertain it, "for the burdens of that family and others are like to bring me in great straits: for in truth I never yet had any annual rent paid in any year I received most, and many years I wanted near altogether, partly in your father-in-law's default, and likewise in your husband's. Yet, all that shall never make me fall short in my duty to the family without my own ruin; but yet these things disable me from doing many things which I would willingly do if I were able."

SECTION XV.

GEORGE, FOURTH MARQUIS OF HUNTLY, AND FIRST DUKE OF GORDON—HIS EARLY LIFE—MARRIAGE—CREATED DUKE OF GORDON—APPOINTED GOVERNOR OF EDINBURGH CASTLE—REVOLUTION OF 1688.—SURRENDER OF THE CASTLE.

AFTER the death of Lewis, third Marquis of Huntly, the interests and affairs of the family devolved on his younger brother, Lord Charles Gordon. He acted with remarkable judgment and tact during the period of Cromwell's government of Scotland, which was an exceedingly trying time for the Scottish nobles. In 1656, an intelligent and observant Scottish clergyman wrote thus:—"Our State is in a very silent condition. Strong garrisons over all the land, and a great army, both of horse and foot, for which there is no service at all. Our nobles—lying in prison, and under forfeitures or debts, private or public—are for the most part either broken or breaking."[1]

On the 3rd of September, 1658, Cromwell died. Shortly after, the Government of the three Kingdoms fell into the hands of the leaders of the armies of the Commonwealth, and they began a scramble for the summit of power; but Oliver's mantle had not descended upon any of them. General Monk was at the head of the army in Scotland, and he was on intimate terms with Charles, Lord Gordon. Monk collected his forces, and carefully prepared to march into England. On the 2nd of December, 1659, the landowners of Aberdeenshire met at Aberdeen, and elected Lord Gordon as commissioner to confer with General Monk at Berwick. He carried a letter from the barons and lairds of Aberdeenshire to Monk, in which they declared their unanimous resolution to keep the public peace. They also aided him with a sum of money.

Monk marched into England in the beginning of 1660. After various moves, he declared in favour of a free Parliament, which met in March, and resolved to recall the King. So Charles II. entered London on the 29th of May, amid the shouts and applause of the people.

On the 13th of February, 1661, the Marquis of Argyle was placed at the bar of Parliament, and accused of high treason. He was found guilty, condemned, and executed at Edinburgh on the 27th of May.

The Gordon property was restored to George, fourth Marquis of Huntly, who was still under age. His uncle, Charles, Earl of Aboyne, had the management of the Huntly estates—a very difficult and delicate task, owing to the late misfortunes of the family. The young Marquis was naturally much under the influence of his mother, and, in electing his curators, he disregarded the advice of his uncle. Aboyne, however, managed to effect a general settlement of the family affairs in 1665.

[1] Ballie's Letters and Journals, Vol. III. p. 317.

Earls of Huntly.

The Marquis travelled through a considerable part of Europe, and completed his education abroad. Afterwards he served in the French army, under Marshal Turenne; and also in the armies of the Prince of Orange.

He returned home in 1674. In November, 1676, he married Lady Elizabeth Howard, a daughter of the Duke of Norfolk, by whom he had issue, a son and a daughter.

On the 1st of November, 1684, Charles II. created him Duke of Gordon, with the power of regality over his own lands and vassals: This title did not affect the Earldom and Marquisate, or any other of the early titles of the family. In 1687 he was invested with the Order of the Thistle.

He was appointed Governor of Edinburgh Castle by Charles II.; and he held it at the Revolution of 1688 for James VII. In this crisis he acted with sound judgment and remarkable moderation.

Before the issue of the military operations in England was decided, disturbances arose in Edinburgh. The Roman Catholics were insulted on the streets; and placards were posted up threatening the ministers of the Crown. The Earl of Perth, Lord Chancellor, and head of the Privy Council, had been very servile to James VII., and therefore became an object of hatred, and fled to his own country seat. When at last it became clear that the King's cause was rapidly falling, crowds gathered on the streets, loud shouts was raised for a free Parliament, and the tumult increased. A few troops attempted to quell the mob, but they were soon overpowered. On Sunday, the 9th of December, a great number of students, apprentices, and others appeared on the streets; and, the Provost having refused to deliver to them the keys of the ports, they then threatened to burn his house. They next proceeded to the Market Cross, and proclaimed a reward of £400 sterling to anyone who should seize the Earl of Perth and bring him there dead or alive.

The following day the Town Council issued a proclamation prohibiting tumults on the streets, which was torn to tatters as soon as it was read, and the officers and drummer prevented from going through the town. All sorts of alarming rumours were rife. It was reported that an army of Irish Catholics was on the eve of landing upon the coast of Galloway, and some said it had landed. The people dreaded a massacre: As the Council had dissolved, the army had been marched into England, and there was an utter collapse of authority. The Duke of Gordon, the Governor of the Castle, though pressed by the extreme Jacobites to open fire upon the citizens of Edinburgh, firmly declined to do this, unless he received an explicit command from James VII.

In January, 1689, the Prince of Orange summoned a Convention of the Estates to meet at Edinburgh on the 14th of March. Preparations for this meeting were immediately commenced, all parties were anxious to return members to decide the future position of the nation. The Whigs secured a majority favourable to the Prince of Orange, though a number of the Barons and all the Bishops still clung to the cause of James VII. The Jacobites calculated on the support of the Duke of Gordon, who commanded the castle, and on Viscount Dundee, whose energy was well known and greatly feared, as they might attempt to intimidate or disperse the Convention. The Parliament House was well within the range of the guns of the Castle.

The Convention assembled at the appointed time. Nine of the Bishops appeared, 42 Peers, 49 members for the counties, and 50 for the burghs. The Bishop of Edinburgh opened the proceedings, and prayed that God would assist them and restore King James. The election of a President was then essayed. The supporters of James proposed the Marquis of Athole; the Whigs proposed the Duke of Hamilton, who was elected by a majority of 40. About 20 of the minority then deserted the cause of King James, and joined the majority. On the 16th of March a letter from the Prince of Orange was read, in which he expressed his desire that the Convention would settle the religion and liberties of the nation upon just grounds, and in harmony with the inclination of the people and the public good. The same day, after some debate, a letter from King James was read; but it contained nothing to raise the hopes of his adherents. He offered to pardon those who returned to their allegiance before the end of the month; while to others no mercy could be shown. His adherents in the Convention were mortified, his enemies were vehement, and the sitting closed in a scene of great excitement,

The Whigs had summoned the Duke of Gordon to surrender the Castle of Edinburgh, but he refused. He might at any moment, if he had thought fit, have opened a cannonade upon the Parliament House or the citizens. It was known that the Jacobites would not yield without a severe struggle, and might attempt some desperate move. Viscount Dundee and Sir George Mackenzie complained that their lives were in danger, alleging that the Covenanters had resolved to slay them, and they appealed to the Duke of Hamilton for protection.

When the Convention met on the 18th of March, tidings were brought into the House that Viscount Dundee was on the Stirling road with a troop of dragoons, and that he had been seen conferring with the Duke of Gordon at the Castle gate. This news threw the members of the Convention into a state of intense alarm, and Hamilton, the President, started to his feet and said—"It is high time that we should look to ourselves. The enemies of our religion and of our civil freedom are mustering all around us; and we may well suspect that they have accomplices even here. Lock the doors. Lay the keys on the table. Let no one go out but those Lords and gentlemen whom we shall appoint to call the citizens to arms. There are some good men from the west in Edinburgh, men for whom I can answer." The majority of the members shouted assent, and what the President proposed was immediately done. Lord Leven went out and ordered the drums to be beat. The Covenanters promptly answered to the call, and mustered in such numbers as overawed all the Jacobites in Edinburgh.

Viscount Dundee, in his brief interview with the Duke of Gordon at the gate of the Castle, had perhaps intimated his intention to attempt a rising on behalf of James VII., though on leaving Edinburgh he retired to his country mansion of Dudhope, in the vicinity of Dundee. He was summoned to appear in his place in Parliament, but he declined. A warrant was then issued for his apprehension, and the Earl of Leven, with 200 men, marched northward in pursuit of him. But Dundee took to the mountains and glens, crossed the Dee and entered the Duke of Gordon's territory, and concerted his intended rising.

After surmounting many difficulties, and outgeneraling his opponents, his career was terminated in the moment of victory on the field of Killiecrankie.

The Castle of Edinburgh was completely invested by the force appointed to protect the Convention, and all supplies of provisions for the garrison from the outside were cut off. The Duke of Gordon, however, refrained from firing on the Convention or the citizens of Edinburgh; yet held out until the store of provisions in the castle became exhausted. At last, on the 13th of June, 1689, he surrendered on honourable terms, and the garrison marched out of the castle. Afterwards he printed an account of the siege of the castle in French, for the information of the exiled court at St. Germains. He proceeded to London and made his submission to King William.

SECTION XVI.

GEORGE, FIRST DUKE OF GORDON—HIS DEATH—MARQUIS OF HUNTLY, SECOND DUKE OF GORDON, JOINED MAR'S RISING—HIS DEATH—COSMO-GEORGE, THIRD DUKE OF GORDON—LORD LEWIS JOINED THE RISING OF 1745—BALLAD TO HIS MEMORY.

SHORTLY after his submission to the new Government, the Duke went to Flanders. In 1691 he visited the court of James VII., but being somewhat coldly received by this personage, he retired to Switzerland. The Duke was arrested there, and conveyed to Scotland. During the reign of King William he was suspected of being a secret supporter of the exiled King, and consequently he was repeatedly imprisoned.

When George I. ascended the throne on the 1st of August, 1714, the Duke of Gordon was ordered to be confined to the city of Edinburgh on parole. He died at Leith on the 7th of December, 1716.

He was succeeded by his only son, Alexander, Marquis of Huntly, and second Duke of Gordon. In 1706 he married Lady Henrietta Mordaunt, a daughter of the famous general, Charles, Earl of Peterborough and Mordaunt, and had issue.

In his father's lifetime he travelled abroad, and visited some of the Courts of Europe. He was on intimate terms of friendship with the Grand Duke of Tuscany, Cosmo III. A fine bust of this Duke of Tuscany, which he presented to Alexander, Marquis of Huntly, is still preserved amongst the treasures in Gordon Castle.

It appears that he was a Jacobite. When Marquis of Huntly in his father's lifetime he was present at the great Jacobite meeting in Braemar on the 26th of August, 1715. Afterwards he joined Mar's army at Perth, and commanded a body of cavalry. He was present at the battle of Sheriffmuir. But shortly after this event he returned north; and in April, 1716, he surrendered to the Government. He was conveyed to Edinburgh, and imprisoned in the castle for a time. No further proceedings, however, were instituted against him.

The second Duke of Gordon was a very kind-hearted man. He had the character of being a good landlord, and friendly and obliging to his neighbours. He died from an attack of inflammation on the 22nd of November, 1728.

By his Duchess, Lady Henrietta, he had four sons and seven daughters. He was succeeded by his eldest son, Cosmo-George, third Duke of Gordon, who received the name Cosmo owing to the friendly relations of his father with the Grand Duke of Tuscany. He was born in 1719; and in 1741 he married Catherine, a daughter of William, second Earl of Aberdeen, and had issue.

Lord Lewis Gordon had a remarkable career, of which some account will be presented in the sequel.

Lord Adam Gordon entered the army and rose to the rank of general. He was appointed Commander-in-Chief of the forces in Scotland. On the second of September, 1767, he married Jane, a daughter of John Drummond, Esq., and widow of James, second Duke of Athole. He died in 1801.

Lady Anne married William, second Earl of Aberdeen, and had issue. Lady Catherine married Francis, Earl of Wemyss.

The third Duke of Gordon was an accomplished gentleman. He studied law in the University of Leyden. He was elected one of the Representative Peers of Scotland; and was created a Knight of the order of the Thistle.

Lord Lewis Gordon had been an officer in the navy. He was a very fine-looking young man, with a remarkable mild and characteristic expression of intelligence in his face. His countenance also betokened warm feeling and earnestness. He joined the rising of 1745, and entered into it

Earls of Huntly.   201

with the utmost zeal and enthusiasm. He endeavoured to persuade his brother, the Duke of Gordon, to join the rising but in this he failed; the Duke declined to join Prince Charles, or to contribute anything to the Jacobite exchequer. Nevertheless the example and energy of Lord Lewis induced many of the Duke's tenantry to join the rising.

Lord Lewis was appointed Lord Lieutenant of the counties of Aberdeen and Banff, and Governor of the city of Aberdeen; and he then appointed William Moir of Lonmay to be deputy-lieutenant and governor of the city of Aberdeen. Thus Lord Lewis was empowered to hold the counties of Aberdeen and Banff, and the city of Aberdeen, to collect taxes and to raise men. Accordingly, the provost and town council were ordered "to make payment to us or to William Moir, our deputy-governor of the town, for the service of His Royal Highness, before the 12th of December, 1745, of the sum of £2847 16s, being the amount of His Majesty's subsidy, free of all charges, payable out of the town of Aberdeen, from Martimas, 1744, to Martimas, 1745, as appears from the taxation book." The citizens had to pay this sum under the penalty of military execution. The city also had to equip its proportion of armed men—one man for each £100 of valued rent, or pay a sum of £5 in lieu of each man, under the penalty of military execution. For this demand the authorities made an arrangement with Moir, the deputy-governor of the town, to pay £1000.

It appears that James Chalmers, the printer, had issued the manifestoes of the leaders of the insurgent army for some time; and also printed sheets giving the details of the progress of the rebellion. At last, however, Chalmers deemed it necessary to leave the town, and owing to this, his house and premises were greatly damaged by the insurgents.

Events were rapidly running to a crisis. The march of Prince Charles upon London had failed, and his army was returning northward. But Lord Lewis Gordon continued to exert himself to the utmost on behalf of the Prince's cause. He had a considerable body of armed men in Aberdeen and its neighbourhood. A force under the command of Macleod of Macleod was advancing for the relief of Aberdeen. Lord Lewis immediately mustered his men and marched to Inverurie, where he met Macleod on the 23rd of December, and completely defeated him. Four days after the action, Lord Lewis wrote the following letter to the vanquished chief:—

" Sir,—I received your letter by express last night, dated Castle Gordon the 24th. All the care in our power has been and shall be taken of your wounded men; and all the prisoners that were taken under their arms shall meet with all the civility in our power. But for Regent Chambers, Forbes of Echt, and Maitland of Pitrichie, who have acted the infamous part of spies and informers, and the two last especially, who have given a great deal of bad advice to a certain great man who shall be nameless, (the Duke of Gordon) it is neither consistent with my honour nor inclination to treat them as prisoners of war. I shall take care to order supplies to be given to all the prisoners who want them, and the wounded men are as well taken care of as our own. I shall send you a list of the prisoners and wounded, with any useless papers and letters as soon as possible; and any other thing that we can reasonably agree to shall be done with pleasure."

This letter needs no comment—it is complete in itself.

The Duke of Cumberland and his army entered Aberdeen on the 25th of February, 1746, and stayed till the 8th of April. During this time the Duke lived in the Guestrow, and held his levees in the Marischal College Buildings.

After the battle of Culloden, though it was reported at first that Lord Lewis Gordon was captured, he was one of those who escaped. Yet he endured much suffering in his efforts to keep out of the clutches of the emissaries of the Government—sometimes hiding in the secret recesses of

Gordon Castle, the Castles of Strathbogie and Aboyne, or at other times finding refuge in the glens and forests of Birse and Braemar. At last, after many adventures and hairbreadth escapes, he got aboard a friendly vessel which carried him to France. But the hardship and suffering which he had endured brought on sickness, and almost broke his noble spirit.

He became very anxious to return home, and longed for the refreshing air of the hills and glens of his native land. From Sens, on the 30th of November, 1751, he wrote to his brother, the Duke of Gordon, thus :—

"My dear Lord Duke,—The very bad state of health I have been in for a year has given me a great inclination to return home. Since I had the happiness of seeing you in Paris I have been 16 or 17 times blooded for violent fevers, and now I am subject to violent cholicks and pains in the stomach. Neither dare I take any severe exercise for fear of having one of these terrible fevers; and I assure you that my constitution is become so tender that I am not fit to follow any public business. Now, my Lord Duke, I shall begin with humbly begging pardon of you for my foolish behaviour, which I beseech you to forget; and I hope, my dear brother, in consideration of my misfortune, and the melancholy state of my health, you will have the goodness to apply to His Majesty for leave to me to come home. I am not so ambitious as to think of the attainder being taken off, and all I want is just to live peaceably in Scotland without ever meddling with public affairs. I am ready to make all the submissions that His Majesty and the Ministry ask of anybody; and whatever your grace promises them in my name I assure you on honour and conscience I shall perform."

He again wrote to the Duke on the 17th of January, 1752, and restated, almost in the same words, his desire for leave to return home. But his touching letters never reached his brother the Duke—they were all intercepted by officials in the service of the British Government. The unhappy young man was not aware of this, and, not receiving any replies from his friends, he began to think they had forsaken him, while his friends in Scotland were amazed at his long silence. At last, worn out with sorrow and sickness, this noble-minded young man died at Martreuil in 1754. A Jacobite song was composed to his memory :—

> "Oh ! send Lewie Gordon hame,
> And the lad I daurna name ;
> Though his back be at the wa',
> Here's to him that's far awa'.
>
> Och hon ; my Higlandman,
> Och my bonny Highlandman ;
> Weel would I my true love ken,
> Amang ten thousand Highlandmen.
>
> Oh ! to see his tartan trews,
> Bonnet blue, and laigh-heel'd shoes ;
> Philabeg aboon his knee ;
> That's the lad that I'll gang wi'.
> The princely youth of whom I sing
> Is fitted for to be a king ;
> On his breast he wears a star ;
> You'd tak' him for the god of war."

. . . . . .

SECTION XVII.

DEATH OF COSMO-GEORGE—ALEXANDER, FOURTH DUKE OF GORDON—HIS MARRIAGE—CREATED A BRITISH PEER—HE RAISED TWO REGIMENTS—THE REEL O' BOGIE—THE DUKE AS A LANDLORD—HIS DEATH.

IN 1752 the Duke of Gordon went on a tour through France. While near Amiens he died on the 5th of August, in the thirty-third year of his age. His body was embalmed in France, and thence conveyed to the chapel near Gordon Castle, and afterwards interred in Elgin Cathedral.

He left three sons and three daughters ; and was succeeded by his eldest son, Alexander, Fourth Duke of

Earls of Huntly. 205

Gordon, then a boy of nine years. Lord William Gordon joined the army at an early age, and served in the East Indies. Subsequently he was appointed a deputy-keeper of St. James's Park. On the 1st of March, 1781, he married Frances, a daughter of Charles, ninth Viscount of Irvine. He died in May, 1824. Lord George died unmarried on the 1st of November, 1792.

Lady Susan Gordon married, first, John, Earl of Westmorland; and, secondly, Lieutenant-Colonel John Woodford. She died on the 11th of December, 1814. Lady Catherine married Thomas Booker, Esq. She died on the 3rd of January, 1797. Lady Anne married the Rev. Alexander Chalmers, minister of the parish of Cairnie.

Alexander, Fourth Duke of Gordon, was born on the 18th of June, 1743. In 1761 he was elected one of the Representative Peers of Scotland. He was created a Knight of the Order of the Thistle in 1775. It appears that Professor Ogilvie, of Aberdeen, acted as travelling tutor to the Duke, who in 1761 visited Italy, and stayed for some time in the country of the Grand Duke of Tuscany.

He married, first, in 1767, Lady Jane, a daughter of Sir William Maxwell, Bart., of Moreth, by whom he had two sons and five daughters. He married, secondly, Mrs. Christie, in 1820, by whom he had no issue.

On the 12th of February, 1784, he was enrolled amongst the British Peers, under the title of Baron Gordon of Huntly and Earl of Norwich, which he inherited through Lady Elizabeth Howard, his great-grandmother. He also inherited the baronies of Beauchamp and Mordaunt, and the lands of Durris, as heir-general of the Earl of Peterborough.

The Duke was a man of great energy and public spirit. His wife, the Duchess of Gordon, was also a highly-gifted lady, with fine personal attractions and remarkable talents. Many of her husband's enterprises were admirably supported by her active and enthusiastic efforts.

In 1778 he raised a regiment of Fencibles, numbering 960 men. They were recruited on the Duke's estates in the counties of Aberdeen, Banff, Moray, and Inverness. This regiment was embodied at Aberdeen, and continued in service till 1783, when it was reduced. During the five years that the regiment was embodied only 24 men died.

In 1793, the Duke, assisted by the winning manner and efforts of the Duchess, raised another regiment of Fencibles. He raised over 300 men on his own estates of Badenoch, Lochaber, and Strathspey; and nearly the same number was enlisted on the neighbouring estates; while about 150 were recruited on the Lowlands of the counties of Moray, Banff, and Aberdeen. The uniform of the men consisted of the Highland garb. This regiment was embodied at Aberdeen. In 1794 the regiment was removed to England, and was reviewed by George III. in Hyde Park. The regiment, with other fencible regiments, was disbanded in 1799.

The Duke was an accomplished and exceedingly genial gentleman. On the 20th of February, 1793, he was elected Lord Chancellor of the University and King's College, Aberdeen. The minute records that:—" His Grace is of all others the most natural choice, several of his predecessors having held that office, and his father and many of that family and their connections having been educated here." The Duke continued Chancellor till his death.

When Burns, on the 7th September, 1787, visited Gordon Castle, he wrote the following note:—" Fine palace, worthy of the noble, polite, and generous proprietor. The Duke makes me happier than ever great man did—noble, princely; yet mild, condescending, and affable, gay and kind—the Duchess charming, witty, and sensible—God bless them." Burns greatly admired the Castle and its surroundings, and wrote:—

"Give me the stream that sweetly laves
The banks of Castle Gordon."

The Duke of Gordon himself is the reputed author of a

popular version of the song called "The Reel o' Bogie." It is a characteristic song, and has been long associated with the dance tune of the same name. A few verses may be quoted:—

> "In foursome reel's the Scotch delight,
>   At threesomes they dance wond'rous light.
> But twasomes ding a' out o' sight,
>   Danced to the reel o' Bogie.
>
> Come, lads, and view your partners well,
>   Wile each a blythesome rogie;
> I'll tak' this lassie to mysel,
>   She looks sae clean and vogie.
>
> Now, piper lad, bang up the spring;
> The country fashion is the thing—
> To pree their mou's ere we begin,
>   To dance the reel o' Bogie.
>
> Now, ilka lad has got a lass,
>   Save yon auld doited fogie,
> And ta'en a fling upon the grass,
>   As they do in Stra'bogie.
>
> But a' the lassies look sae fain,
> We canna think oursel's to hain,
> For they maun hae their come-again,
>   To dance the reel o' Bogie.
>
> Now a' the lads hae done their best,
>   Like true men o' Stra'bogie.
> We'll stop a while and tak' a rest,
>   And tipple out a cogie.
>
> Come now, my lads, and tak' your glass,
> And try ilk other to surpass,
> And wishin' health to every lass,
>   To dance the reel o' Bogie."

William Marshall, who was born in Fochabers on the 27th of December, 1748, was engaged as house stewart and butler to the Duke of Gordon till 1790; and afterwards he acted as factor to the Duke till 1817. Marshall was a famous violin-player, and an able and assiduous composer. Two hundred and eighty-seven of his tunes have been published, in three collections, the first of which appeared in 1793, containing 36 tunes; the second in 1822, embracing 170 tunes; and the third in 1847, which was issued after his death. It is said by eminent authorities on Scottish dance music, that his second collection is the finest ever published by any Scottish composer. Many of his strathspeys were very spirited and popular in the north, such as " The Bog o' Gight," " The Duke of Gordon's Birthday," " Gordon Castle," "Craigellachie Bridge," " The Marchioness of Huntly," " The Marquis of Huntly," " Huntly Lodge," " The Duchess of Richmond," and many others.

Marshall was a faithful and trusted servant of the Duke, and a highly-respected man. He died on the 29th of May, 1833, in his seventy-fifth year.

The Duke of Gordon was Lord Superior of the town of Huntly—a burgh of barony—as his predecessors had been for three centuries. He was appointed keeper of the Great Seal of Scotland and Lord-Lieutenant of Aberdeenshire.

He was a very kind and considerate landlord. He was one of those who fully recognised that property and wealth have many responsibilities and important duties attached to them. Thus his example and great influence had a beneficial effect upon others.

He died on the 17th of June, 1827. He had two sons and five daughters, and was succeeded by his eldest son, George, fifth and last Duke of Gordon, Alexander, his second son, joined the army, and died in 1808.

Lady Charlotte Gordon married Charles, fourth Duke of Richmond; and their son afterward inherited the estates of the Dukedom of Gordon.

Lady Madelina married first, Sir Robert Sinclair, Bart.; and, secondly, Charles F. Palmer, of Lockly Park, Berks. Lady Susan married the Duke of Manchester. Lady Lousia married the second Marquis of Cornwallis. Lady Georgina married the Duke of Bedford.

SECTION XVIII.

GEORGE, FIFTH DUKE OF GORDON—HE JOINED THE ARMY—HE RAISED THE 92ND HIGHLANDERS, WAS APPOINTED COLONEL COMMANDANT OF THE REGIMENT—SKETCH OF THE SERVICES OF THE 92ND—THE REGIMENT IN EGYPT, PORTUGAL, AND SPAIN—HEROIC ACTION OF THE 92ND AT QUATRE BRAS AND WATERLOO.

GEORGE, fifth Duke of Gordon, was born in 1770. He joined the army in his 20th year; and in 1791 he was a captain in the famous 42nd Highlanders. He was present at the engagements connected with the Duke of York's expedition to Flanders in 1793.

Afterwards the Marquis of Huntly (as he then was) exchanged and became a captain in the 3rd Foot Guards. While in this regiment he offered to raise a regiment for general service; and on the 10th of February, 1794, he received a commission for this purpose. The young Marquis's zeal and spirit for the service were admirably seconded by his father and mother, the Duke and Duchess of Gordon; and both of them, along with the Marquis himself, actively engaged personally in the work of recruiting. Such were their combined efforts that within four months, the requisite number of men was raised. On the 24th of June, the regiment was inspected by Major-General Sir Hector Munro at Aberdeen, and embodied under the name of the Gordon Highlanders. About three-fourths of the men were Highlanders, mainly drawn from the estates of the Gordon family; and the other fourth came from the Lowlands of Aberdeenshire and the neighbouring counties. The Marquis of Huntly was appointed Lieutenant-colonel commandant of the regiment. A few of the other original officers may be mentioned:—

Major Charles Erskine of Cardross was killed in Egypt in 1801. Amongst the captians Alexander Napier of Blackstone was killed at the battle of Corunna in 1809, when commanding officer of the regiment. Captain John Cameron, who had risen to the rank of colonel, was killed at Quatre Bras on the 16th of June, 1815. Captain William Mackintosh of Aberarder, was killed in the battle of Bergen, in Holland, on the 2nd of October, 1799.

On the 9th of July, 1794, the regiment embarked at Fort-George, and joined the camp at Netley Common in August, and then placed on the list of numbered corps as the 100th Regiment. On the 5th of September the Gordon Highlanders embarked for Gibraltar, where they continued till the 11th of June, 1795, when they were ordered to the Island of Corsica. In the following year the regiment returned to Gibraltar; and in the spring of 1798, they embarked for England, and landed in the middle of May.

In a short time the regiment was ordered to Ireland. The duties of the service in that distracted country were very arduous, as the men were kept almost constantly moving. On one occasion the regiment marched on three successive days a distance of 96 Irish miles, with arms, ammunition, and knapsacks. Yet the Gordon Highlanders in the execution of their duties won much respect in Ireland. When the regiment was about to leave one of its stations, the magistrates and people of the district presented an address to the Marquis of Huntly, the commander, in which they remarked that "peace and order were re-established, rapine had disappeared, confidence in the Government was restored, and the happiest cordiality subsisted since his regiment came among them."

The Gordon Highlanders left Ireland in June, 1799, proceeded to England, and joined the expedition then preparing for the coast of Holland. At this time the number of the regiment was changed to the 92nd.

The Marquis of Huntly, as colonel in command, accompanied his regiment. He led the 92nd at the battle of Bergen, fought on the 2nd of October, 1799, and in which he was severely wounded. The Gordon Highlanders were in General Moore's brigade, and he was exceedingly pleased with their heroic efforts in this battle.

In the summer of 1800 the Gordon Highlanders disembarked on the island of Minorca, and they formed a part of the expedition against Egypt. In the battle of the 13th of March, 1801, against the French in Egypt, the 92nd greatly distinguished themselves. They not only firmly maintained their ground against the repeated attacks of the enemy, supported by a park of artillery, but also drove them back. In this action the regiment suffered severely—their commanding officer, Lieutenant-Colonel Charles Erskine, died of his wounds, other four officers, and nineteen rank and file, were killed; 6 officers, 10 sergeants, and 100 rank and file wounded.

At the memorable battle of Alexandria, on the 21st of March, in which the noble and brave General Abercromby, the Commander-in-Chief of the expedition, was fatally wounded, the 92nd was not much engaged, owing to their reduced condition. But the other Highland regiments were encouraged by General Abercromby, who called out to them—" My brave Highlanders, remember your country, remember your forefathers!":—

> When smoke of cartridge filled the air,
> And cannons loud did shake the plain,
> Many a hero brave fell there,
> That never will come back again.

The battle was won, though the loss of the British in killed and wounded was heavy. In September the French, numbering 27,000 men, capitulated and re-embarked for France.

On leaving Egypt the 92nd sailed for Ireland, and landed at Cork on the 13th of January, 1802. Shortly after they were removed to Glasgow, where they stayed till the renewal of the war in 1803. Then they were marched to Leith, and embarked for the camp at Woeley. The regiment formed a part of the expedition against Copenhagen, which sailed in 1807, and they served in Sir Arthur Wellesley's brigade. In this campaign, by a spirited charge with the bayonet, they drove back a greatly superior force.

In 1808 the Gordon Highlanders embarked for Sweden, and immediately after the return of the expedition, the troops employed were ordered to Portugal, under the command of Sir John Moore. The 92nd accompanied all the movements of General Moore's army, and were engaged in the Battle of Corunna, in which their commanding officer, Colonel Napier, was killed. Sir John Moore fell in the Battle of Corunna—one of the ablest and bravest generals that ever led a British army. [My father fought in the battle of Corunna, also in the battles of Vimiera, Badajoz, Salamanca, and Vittoria, in which he lost the thumb of his left hand, which he buried with the aid of his bayonet on the battlefield.] The Gordon Highlanders returned to England in the spring of 1809, and were quartered at Woeley.

The regiment was next employed in the expedition to Walcherin, which sailed in the end of July, 1809. In this expedition the Marquis of Huntly, being then a lieutenant-general, had command of a division of the force.

On the 21st of September, 1810, the Gordon Highlanders embarked for Portugal, and in October joined the British army under Lord Wellington at the lines of Torres Vedras. On the service of the regiment in the Spanish Peninsula and the south of France I cannot here enter, and it has only to be remarked that in all the battles in which they were engaged, they maintained their high character and bravery in the hour of peril.

At Quatre Bras the 92nd fought heroically. Though their brave commander, Colonel Cameron, was killed, they drove back a strong body of the enemy, and pursued them for a quarter of a mile.

The service rendered by the Gordon Highlanders at a

critical moment in the battle of Waterloo was so important that it should be narrated at some length.

On the day of the battle the Gordon Highlanders were commanded by Major Donald Macdonald. They were in the 9th Brigade, with the Royal Scots, the 42nd Highlanders, and the 44th Regiment. This brigade was placed on the left wing on the crest of an eminence, forming one side of the low valley which separated the two hostile armies. A brigade of Belgians, another of Hanoverians, and General Ponsonby's Brigade of 1st Dragoons, Inniskillings, and the Scots Greys, were also posted on the left. About ten o'clock in the morning Bonaparte opened a severe cannonade upon the whole line of the British and their allies, and made a determined attack upon the post at Hougoumont. At two o'clock the enemy, covered by a strong fire of artillery, advanced in a close column of infantry towards the position of the Belgians. The fire of the Belgians and a few cannon checked the advance of the column for some time; but the troops of Nassau fell back and retired behind the crest of the eminence, leaving an open space to the enemy. The third battalion of the Royal Scots and the second battalion of the 44th Regiment were ordered up to occupy the abandoned ground; and there a severe conflict occurred, in which the two regiments lost many men and spent all their ammunition. The enemy's column still continuing to advance, General Park ordered up the Highlanders, calling out—"Ninety-second, now is your chance. Charge!" This order was repeated by Major Macdonald, and the Highlanders gave a ringing shout. Though the regiment then only numbered 250 men, they instantly formed two men deep and rushed forward to charge a column ten men deep and 3000 strong. The enemy seemed appalled at the daring and rapid advance of the Highlanders, stood a few moments motionless, then panic seized the great column, and they fled in the utmost confusion, throwing away their arms. Swift as the Highlanders were, they were unable to overtake them. But the cavalry pursued them at full speed, slew many, and took 1700 prisoners. It was on observing this scene that Napoleon exclaimed—" Les braves Ecossais, qu'ils sont terribles ces chevaux gris!" when he saw a small body of Highlanders causing one of his favourite columns to flee, and the Greys charging almost up to his line.

From the date of the embodiment of the Gordon Highlanders to the battle of Waterloo—a period of twenty-two years—the regiment had fought in twenty-six battles. In this period they had 12 officers killed and 100 wounded, and 238 rank and file killed, and 1261 wounded—making a total loss of 1499.

Since the battle of Waterloo the Gordon Highlanders, on every battlefield where they have been engaged, have admirably upheld their character of brave and faithful soldiers.

SECTION XIX.

GEORGE, FIFTH DUKE OF GORDON—APPOINTED LORD-LIEUTENANT OF ABEEDEENSHIRE—HIS DEATH—THE DUCHESS OF GORDON—RETURN TO HUNTLY LODGE—HER DEATH—DUKES OF RICHMOND AND GORDON AS LANDLORDS.

THE Fifth Duke of Gordon attained the rank of full General in the army. He was also Colonel of the Scots Fusilier Guards. In 1820 he received the honour of the Grand Cross of the Bath.

In 1813 he married Elizabeth, only daughter and heiress of Alexander Brodie of Arnhall. Shortly afterwards he settled at Huntly Lodge—a modern mansion which stands on a fine elevated site, near the edge of the forest of Binn, about a quarter of a mile from the old Castle of Strathbogie, and on the opposite side of the river Deveron. In this mansion the Marquis and Marchioness of Huntly resided for fourteen years. During this period they became much respected and beloved by the people of Huntly and the surrounding district.

On the death of his father, in 1827, he became fifth Duke of Gordon, and Earl of Norwich. The Duke and his Duchess then removed from Huntly Lodge to Gordon Castle. He was appointed Keeper of the Great Seal of Scotland, Governor of the Castle of Edinburgh, and Lord Lieutenant of Aberdeenshire.

The Duke discharged all the functions and duties of his high position with unaffected dignity, friendliness, and hospitality. He was an exceedingly genial gentleman, and was implicitly trusted and universally respected. He was a very kind and considerate landlord, and won the gratitude of all classes.

He died on the 28th of May, 1836, at the age of 66. His death was deeply regretted over the north of Scotland. Indeed, there was much heartfelt grief when the last male representative of the Dukes of Gordon departed. Having left no issue by his Duchess, who survived him, the title of Duke of Gordon and Earl of Norwich became dormant. But all the Gordon estates of the Dukedom were inherited by Charles, fifth Duke of Richmond, a grandson of Alexander, fourth Duke of Gordon, who then assumed the surname and the arms of Gordon.

After the death of the last Duke of Gordon (of the male line), his widow, the Duchess of Gordon, returned to Huntly Lodge, the residence associated with the early period of her married life. There the Duchess lived a remarkably unaffected, charitable, and Christian life; and she was much respected and beloved by all classes in the locality.

Shortly after the death of her husband, the Duchess resolved to erect a memorial to his memory and her own in the place where they had spent many happy days, amongst a community warmly and deeply attached to them. Her sentiment and conception assumed the form of an institution which would confer benefit on the people of Huntly and the surrounding district. Accordingly, to realise this she built and endowed "The Gordon Schools," a chaste and characteristic building, standing at the north end of the town. It consists of a central clock-tower with an archway in it, through which runs the avenue to the old castle and to Huntly Lodge, and a school and teachers' houses on each side. Busts in marble of the Duke and Duchess are placed in niches on either side, within the archway. On the outer and reverse sides are placed the following inscription :—

Gordon Schools, erected in memory of George, fifth Duke of Gordon, by his widow.

Founded 1839—Opened 1841.

These memorials of George, fifth Duke of Gordon, and his widow, Elizabeth, Duchess of Gordon, are placed here in testimony of the respect and affection of an attached tenantry and a faithful people.

The Duchess of Gordon in the later years of her life took much interest in religious movements. For a number of years a series of large religious meetings were annually held at Huntly, in which the Duchess manifested a special and warm interest. She died in 1862.

The fifth Duke of Richmond died in 1860, and was succeeded by his son, Charles Henry Gordon Lennox, Duke of Lennox, Earl of Darnley, Baron of Torbelton, Duke of Richmond and Gordon, &c. He was born in 1818, and educated at Oxford. In 1841 he was elected member of Parliament for West Sussex, and continued to represent this constituency till 1860. He was appointed Lord Chancellor of the University at Aberdeen in 1861.

On the suggestion of the late Lord Beaconsfield, he was created Duke of Gordon, on the 13th of January, 1876.

Having made some reference in preceding sections to the fourth and fifth Dukes of Gordon as landlords, it seems right to state some facts and circumstances which came within my own recollection and observation. In the glen of Clunymore, in the parish of Mortlach, Banffshire, there are five crofts on the territory of the Duke of Richmond and Gordon, which the original occupiers reclaimed from moorland and moss. These crofts had been given off in the time of the fourth and fifth Dukes of Gordon. Fifty-six years ago the cultivated portions of these crofts ran from about six to fifteen acres; and the rents of them varied from 10s to £1. Strange to say, the one with the largest extent of arable land was the lowest rent—10s. Although the cultivated land of these crofts has since been much increased, the rents are the same now as they were 56 years ago; the Dukes of Richmond and Gordon have never raised the rents, nor in any way disturbed the successive tenants.

About the year 1841 a large number of the farms on the Huntly and Gordon estates of the Duke of Richmond were relet. At that time it was resolved that a number of small farms adjacent to each other should be formed into one large farm. In such circumstances the usual way of proceeding is to warn the tenants to remove, and if they decline, to evict them. In this instance, however, the procedure was different. It was thus:—the tenants whose farms were to be annexed to make a large farm, were informed of what was intended to be done, and if they could not find suitable farms on some of the other estates of the Duke, or elsewhere, or if they still wished to remain, then they were permitted to reside in the dwelling-house of the farm, with their kailyard—rent-free and five pounds a year for the remainder of their life. As might have been expected, a considerable number of old tenants gladly accepted this kind and generous arrangement. Not a single tenant was evicted.

When a boy, I have sat at the fireside of one of these who accepted the above arrangement—a hale and hearty old man, in the parish of Mortlach, Banffshire. His small farm was one of five which were annexed to Keithmore. His house stood on a bank on the south side of the Water of Fiddich, near the bridge which there spans this beautiful stream, a little below the Milltown of Auchindoun.

Having concluded the eventful history of the Earls and Marquises of Huntly, and the Dukes of Gordon, of the lineal male line, the Aboyne Peerage has yet to be treated. On the death of the fifth Duke of Gordon, the fifth Earl of Aboyne became Marquis of Huntly.

SECTION XX.

ABOYNE BRANCH OF THE HUNTLY FAMILY.

Commencement of Aboyne Peerage—Viscount Aboyne—Lord Charles Gordon Created Earl of Aboyne—Lands Incorporated into an Earldom—His Death—Charles, Second Earl of Aboyne—Charles, Third Earl—Charles, Fourth Earl—George, Fifth Earl and Ninth Marquis of Huntly—Charles, Tenth Marquis—Charles, Eleventh Marquis.

The Aboyne Peerage commenced in 1627, when Charles I. created Lord John Gordon, second son of the first Marquis of Huntly, Viscount of Aboyne and Lord Melgum. Unhappily, as stated in a preceding section, the Viscount was burned to death in the tower of Frendraught, on the 8th of October, 1630. Having left no male issue, the Peerage in his person terminated. In 1632, George, Lord Gordon, eldest son of the first Marquis, was created Viscount of Aboyne in his father's lifetime; and, if he should survive his father and succeed to the Marquisate, the title of Viscount should descend to his second son, James, and his heirs male. On the death of his father in 1636, he succeeded as second Marquis of Huntly, while the Aboyne Peerage descended to his second son, James, who then became second Viscount of Aboyne.

His action and proceedings in the Covenanting struggle have been noticed in a preceding section. He died at

Earls of Huntly.

Paris in the spring of 1649, and, leaving no issue, the Viscounty of Aboyne became extinct.

After the Restoration, Charles, the fourth son of the second Marquis of Huntly, was created Earl of Aboyne, Lord Strathavon and Glenlivet, on the 14th of September, 1660. This was granted to him "on account of the great services rendered by the late Marquis of Huntly and his predecessors to the Kings of Scotland; and in consideration of the fidelity and singular activity in the Royal service of Charles Gordon, uncle of the Marquis of Huntly. His Majesty grants to the said Charles, and the heirs male of his body for ever, the title, dignity, and honour of an Earl and Lord of Parliament, as that in all time coming he shall be styled Earl of Aboyne, Lord Strathavon and Glenlivet; with all the other honours, privileges, immunities, and precedence due and suitable to an Earl."

By a charter under the Great Seal, dated the 14th April, 1662, Charles II. incorporated the Lordships of Aboyne, Glentanner, Glenmuick, Cabrach, Strathavon, and other lands, into one free earldom, lordship, and barony, "to be called now and in all time coming the Earldom, Lordship, and Barony of Aboyne. To be held of the King and his successors in fee heritable, free Earldom, Barony, and Lordship for ever."

In 1676, Charles II. granted a long charter in favour of Charles, first Earl of Aboyne, who had resigned the lands of the Earldom for new infeftment because they were claimed by the Marquis of Huntly; but the Marquis resigned his rights. In this charter the lands embraced in the Earldom of Aboyne are given in minute detail, and the deed was of much topographic and local interest.

Charles Gordon, the first Earl of Aboyne, was a man of great energy, ability, and sound judgment. It was stated in a preceding section, that during the minority of his nephew, the fourth Marquis of Huntly and first Duke of

Gordon, Aboyne had the management of the Huntly estates.

He married, first, Margaret Irvine, a sister of the Laird of Drum, by whom he had an only daughter. Margaret Irvine was a lady of great attractions, and was poetically commemorated as "Bonnie Peggy Irvine." She died in 1664, and her daughter, Lady Ann Gordon, was served heir to her mother on the 17th of June, 1665. The Earl married, secondly, Lady Elizabeth Lyon, a daughter of John, Earl of Kinghorn, by whom he had issue.

The Earl of Aboyne occasionally indulged in writing verses, and several of his pieces occur in manuscript collections of the period. He wrote a satire on the Duke of Lauderdale.

About the year 1671 he built the west wing of Aboyne Castle.

He died in 1681. By his Countess, Lady Elizabeth Lyon, he had three sons and one daughter. His daughter, Lady Elizabeth, married John, the eldest son of the Earl of Cromartie.

He was succeeded by his eldest son, Charles, second Earl of Aboyne. He married Lady Elizabeth, a daughter of Patrick, Earl of Strathmore, and had issue. He died in 1702, and was succeeded by his son, Charles, third Earl of Aboyne.

The Earl married Grace, a daughter of Sir George Lockhart of Carnwath—a well-known Jacobite, and a keen opponent of the Union. Aboyne joined Mar's Rising, which involved the family in many difficulties. He died in 1732, and left three sons.

He was succeeded by his eldest son, Charles, a boy of six years, fourth Earl of Aboyne. The young Earl acquired strong Jacobite feelings, and probably he would have joined the Rising of 1745, if his friends had not wisely conveyed him to France under the colour of completing his education.

On attaining his majority, he found the lands of the Earldom heavily burdened; and in order to clear off the debt, in 1749 he sold the lands of Glenmuick to John Farquharson of Invercauld. He then became afraid that, owing to the limits of his estates, he would be unable to live in Scotland and keep up his equipage. Accordingly he sent his baggage to Paris, intending shortly to follow and live abroad. His love for the land of his birth, however, ultimately prevailed, and he ordered his baggage to be brought back.

The Earl then earnestly directed his attention to the improvement of his lands. He planted woods, erected about 40 miles of stone fences, and endeavoured to induce his tenants to adopt improved methods of agriculture; and he cleared his estates of debt.

In 1759 he married, first, Lady Margaret Stewart, a daughter of the sixth Earl of Galloway, and by her he had a son and two daughters. His Countess died at Aboyne Castle on the 12th of August, 1762. In 1774 he married, secondly, Lady Mary Douglas, a daughter of the ninth Earl of Morton, by whom he had a son, who eventually succeeded to his cousin's estates in Forfarshire, and then assumed the name of Hallyburton.

After a very active and upright life, the Earl died at Edinburgh, on the 28th of December, 1794. He was succeeded by his eldest son, George, fifth Earl of Aboyne. He was born in Edinburgh on the 28th of June, 1761. At an early age he joined the army. Subsequently he was engaged in France at the Court of Louis XVI.; and returned home shortly before the Revolution.

In 1794 he was elected one of the representative Peers of Scotland, and acted in this position for 18 years. He was created a British Peer in 1815, under the title of Baron Meldrum of Morven, in virtue of which he had a seat in the House of Lords. On the death of the fifth Duke of Gordon in 1836, the Earl of Aboyne claimed the title of Marquis of

Huntly, and the Committee of Privileges admitted his claim. The Committee announced that the Earl of Aboyne had a right to the title of Marquis of Huntly, Earl of Enzie, Viscount Melgum and Aboyne, Lord of Badenoch and Aboyne.

The Earl in 1801 built the east wing of the Castle of Aboyne. In 1831 he erected the suspension bridge which spans the Dee a short distance above Charlestown of Aboyne solely at his own expense. In 1791 he married Catherine, a daughter of Sir Charles Cope of Brewern, and by her he had six sons and three daughters. His third son, Lord John Frederick, was born in 1799. He was a captain in the navy; and represented Forfarshire in Parliament for several years. When he succeeded to his uncle's estate of Pitcur, he assumed the name of Hallyburton. Lord Henry was born in 1802, and entered the service of the East India Company. Lady Catherine married the Hon. Charles Compton Cavendish; and Lady Mary married Frederick William Seymour.

The Marquis died on the 17th of June, 1853, at the great age of 93 years. He was succeeded by his eldest son, Charles, tenth Marquis of Huntly and sixth Earl of Aboyne. He was born in 1792; and was educated at the University of Cambridge, and graduated in 1812.

In 1826 he married, first, Lady Elizabeth Henrietta, a daughter of the first Marquis of Conyngham, by whom he had no issue; and secondly, in 1844 he married Marian Antoinette, only daughter of the Rev. Peter William Pegus, and by her he had six sons and seven daughters.

While Lord Strathavon, he was elected member of Parliament for East Grinstead, which he represented for twelve years. He was one of the Lords in waiting, and a deputy-lieutenant of Aberdeenshire. The Marquis died on the 18th of September, 1863, in his seventy-first year.

He was succeeded by his eldest son, Charles, eleventh Marquis of Huntly and seventh Earl of Aboyne. He was born on the 5th of March, 1847, and on the 14th of July, 1869, he married Amy, eldest daughter of Sir William Cunliffe Brooks, of Barlow Hall and Glen Tana.

CHAPTER IV.

Earldom and Earls of Erroll.

SECTION I.

TRADITION OF THE HAYS—EARLY NOTICE OF THE HAYS—WILLIAM HAY OF ERROLL—SIR GILBERT HAY.

IT may not be amiss to touch briefly on an early tradition associated with the Hays, which is to the following effect:—

In the reign of Kenneth III., about the end of the tenth century, the Danes, with a large fleet, anchored near "Red Head" in Angus. Shortly after, they sailed for the mouth of the South Esk, where they landed their army. They seized and plundered the nearest town on the coast, dismantled the castle, slew the inhabitants without distinction of age or sex, and devastated Angus to the Firth of Tay. Tidings of this having reached the King, who was staying at Stirling, he immediately mustered the men in the locality, and proceeded to watch the movements of the enemy and prevent pillage by them. He pitched his camp at the confluence of the Tay and the Earn. Intelligence came to the King, that the enemy had marched along the Tay, and was besieging Perth. The King was aroused at the imminent danger, and at once marched on Perth. On coming in sight of the Danes, the Scots formed in order of battle in the plain, and advanced against the enemy. The Danes were strongly posted upon a hill opposite, where it was difficult to attack them; but the Scots were forced to attack. A severe battle ensued at the foot of the heights, in which many on both sides fell; but at last both wings of the Scots line gave way and fled, and the battle seemed to be lost.

But a countryman of the name of Hay, with his two sons, happened to be ploughing in a neighbouring field, over which a number of the Scottish fugitives were running. The farmer and his sons, being men of daring minds and great personal strength, and influenced by a warm love of their native land—the father seized the yoke and the sons whatever implements came readiest to their hands, and placed themselves in a narrow path through which many of the fugitives were running, and endeavoured by reproaches and threats to stop them. When this failed, they struck down those nearest, exclaiming that they would be Danes to the runaways. Thus the more timid were stopped, while the braver men, who had been carried away by the disorderly crowd of their followers, joined with them, and shouted that assistance was at hand. Then the whole body of the men turned upon the enemy, and pressed the foremost of the Danes back upon their companions in a confused mass. At this moment the Scottish camp followers raised a shout, as if a fresh army was approaching, which greatly animated the Scots and raised their spirits to the highest pitch of enthusiasm; and they pressed upon the Danes with the utmost fury, and in a short time utterly routed them. This is that victory which was won near the village of Luncarty, "which was celebrated with the greatest rejoicing during many days, and the fame of which will extend to the latest posterity."

After the battle, Hay was the object of universal applause. Many noblemen attested that wherever he and his sons attacked, there the Scottish ranks were restored, and those of the enemy overthrown. Hay, when introduced to the King, spoke modestly of his service; and when offered robes for himself and his sons, to render their entrance into Perth more glorious, he declined the honour, and only shook off the dust from the garments which he wore every day, and retained the yoke which he used in the battle. Thus he entered the city, preceded by an advance guard and followed by a numerous train appointed by the King. The attention of all who had assembled to see this unusual spectacle was turned upon him, and only he appeared to carry the triumph of the day. The first question mooted was as to what honours and rewards should be given to Hay and his sons. "An estate was bestowed upon them, one of the most fertile in Scotland, which his posterity—now increased to many families—enjoy even to this day." So much for the tradition associated with the battle of Luncarty.

The Hays appear in the records of Scotland in the twelfth century, during the reign of William the Lion. The King granted to William de Hay a charter of the lands of the barony of Erroll, which are situated in the parish of Erroll, Perthshire, and consists of a portion of the well-known Carse of Gowrie. Erroll lies near the centre of the Carse of Gowrie, along the banks of the Tay, about seven miles from Perth, and nine from Dundee. The King also granted to him some land in the burgh of Forfar.

William de Hay married a daughter of Randolph, Lord of Liddlesdale, by whom he had issue. His second son, Robert, became the ancestor of the Earl of Tweeddale. William was succeeded by his son, David de Hay of Erroll.

He married Helen, a daughter of the Earl of Strathearn, and had issue. William the Lion by charter confirmed all the lands of the barony of Erroll to David de Hay, son of William de Hay, with all the rights and privileges of a free barony. Alexander II. also granted a charter to David, confirming to him the lands of the barony of Erroll.

David was succeeded by his son, Gilbert de Hay of Erroll. William, Earl of Mar, granted to him all the lands of Dronlaw, which was confirmed by a charter of Alexander III. in 1251. Gilbert was succeeded by Nicholas Hay, Lord

Earls of Erroll.

of Erroll. In 1294 King John granted a charter confirming to him the barony of Erroll, and other lands of considerable extent, to be held in free ward. Donald, Earl of Mar, granted a charter to Nicholas de Hay, of all the lands of Dronlaw, which Earl William had before given to his predecessor.

In the closing years of the thirteenth century, Scotland was in a very critical state. The opportunity of the Hays of Erroll to take an active part in the affairs of the nation was approaching. Nicholas de Hay died about the year 1302, and was succeeded by his son, Sir Gilbert Hay of Erroll. In the spring of 1306, Sir Gilbert and his brother, Hugh, joined Robert Bruce, and were amongst the small party who then formed the forlorn hope of the Scottish nation.

Sir Gilbert Hay of Erroll was one of the bravest and most faithful of all King Robert's followers. He was the King's steadfast and inseparable companion in arms throughout all his wanderings and severe privations, cheerfully travelling with Bruce over mountains, moors, and forests by night and day. As mentioned in a preceding chapter, he was wounded and had his horse killed under him in the severe encounter with the Lord of Lorne at the head of the Tay. He was engaged along with the King in many a desperate struggle, and had many narrow escapes. He was present and fought heroically on the memorable field of Bannockburn.

When the hour of victory at last came Robert Bruce was exceedingly grateful. He rarely failed to remember and reward those who had faithfully adhered to him, when his back was at the wall. Accordingly, Sir Gilbert Hay was well worthy of any distinction and reward which Bruce had at his disposal. The King, therefore, appointed him Hereditary Lord High Constable of Scotland shortly after the battle of Bannockburn.

The office of Lord High Constable dates from the reign

of Alexander I., and it became hereditary in the family of De Morvill. It was by inheritance through the De Morvill line, and the old Lords of Galloway, De Quinci, Earl of Winchester, that the office of Lord High Constable became vested in John Comyn, Earl of Buchan. After the forfeiture of Comyn, Bruce granted the office of Constable to David de Strathbogie, Earl of Athole, but this noble soon joined the English, and he was forfeited. Thus King Robert had the office of Constable again at his disposal.

The charter by King Robert, conferring the office of Constable on Sir Gilbert Hay, is dated the 12th of Nov., 1314, at Cambuskenneth. Amongst the witnesses to the charter were Bernard, Abbot of Arbroath, who was then High Chancellor of Scotland; Thomas Randolph, Earl of Moray; Sir Robert Keith, Great Marischal of Scotland; James Douglas, and others. The charter, in brief, conveyed to Sir Gilbert and his heirs all the privileges and liberties, the duties and functions which constitutionally pertained to the office. These will be explained in the next section.

SECTION II.

OFFICE OF HIGH CONSTABLE—DEATH OF SIR GILBERT—SIR DAVID, SECOND HIGH CONSTABLE OF THE ERROLL LINE—SIR THOMAS, THIRD HIGH CONSTABLE—WILLIAM, FOURTH HIGH CONSTABLE—WILLIAM, FIFTH HIGH CONSTABLE, AND FIRST EARL OF ERROLL.

THE following duties and privileges were attached to the office of Lord High Constable of Scotland:—

I. In early times he had precedence next to the Lord High Chancellor, and before all other officers. It appears that this precedence had been recognised and given to the Constable till the reign of James VI., when, in 1601, he appointed Sir George Home of Sprott Lord High Treasurer, and, in March, 1605, created him Earl of Dunbar, and then ordered that the Treasurer, in right of his office, should have precedence next to the Lord Chancellor.

II. In the royal army and expeditions the High Constable, in right of his office, was Lieutenant-General and supreme officer next to the King. He had command and direction of the army, and was sole judge in all military affairs, and in actions touching the captains, lieutenants and their officers and companies during their employment in the King's service.

III. The Constable was supreme judge in all matters of riot, disorder, bloodshed, and murder, committed within a circuit of four miles of the King's person, or of the Parliament and Council representing the Royal authority in His Majesty's absence. The trial and punishment of persons committing such crimes and offences came properly within the jurisdiction of the courts of the Constable and his deputies; while the magistrates and other judges of the city or burgh within the limits of the circuit were obliged to rise and assist the constable and his officers in apprehending such offenders and criminals. The High Court of Constabulary continued to hold its sittings until the Union, and its functions were usually discharged by deputies. When Parliament was sitting, the court often had many cases.

IV. When Parliament was sitting the High Constable had the charge of guarding the King's person. The keeping of the Parliament House was committed to him, and the keys of the House were delivered to him. He also had the chief command of the guards and men-at-arms attending upon the King's person at such times. In time of Parliament the High Constable rode on the King's right hand and carried a white baton in token of command, and accordingly sat apart from the rest of the nobility upon the King's right hand, having the honours lying before him.

V. The High Constable presided at tournaments and passages-at-arms. On such occasions he had the privilege of right to apartments in the King's palace. It appears also that he had a right to all the materials of which the fences or "barrars" were formed, within which the tourney was fought.

VI. In early times the High Constable and his deputies had a right to take custom, in name of fees, of all kinds of goods brought to the markets for sale, wherever the Parliament or the Session was sitting. But in 1456 an Act of Parliament was passed which ordered that this should in future be discharged.

It also appears that in some instances, there was a piece of land attached to the office of High Constable in the royal burghs, for a lodging to himself and his officers. In 1456 the Constable granted a lease of his land to Thomas Cuthbert, a burgess of Inverness, who says—"I by my letters oblige myself to an high and mighty lord, William, Earl of Erroll and High Constable of Scotland: That for his constable land given to me by charter in fee and heritage, I, my heirs and assignees, shall find yearly to the said Lord William and his heirs, a sufficient stable upon the said ground for the number of twelve horses during the time of their residence in the burgh of Inverness, together with six pennies Scots yearly, if it be asked by the said lord or his heirs.

Interesting instances of the exercise of the duties and functions of the High Constable will occur in the succeeding sections.

The first High Constable of the Erroll family, Sir Gilbert Hay, received a grant of the barony of Slains from the Crown. After an active and honourable life in the service of his country, he died in 1333, at Aberdeen, and was interred in the Abbey Church of Cupar.

He was succeeded by his son, Sir David Hay, Second High Constable of the Erroll line. He accompanied David II. and the army that invaded England in 1346, and in the disastrous battle of Durham the High Constable was slain.

Sir David was succeeded by his son, Sir Thomas, third High Constable. He married the Princess Elizabeth Stewart, a daughter of Robert II., by whom he had two sons and two daughters. One of his daughters married Sir George Leslie, the ancestor of the Earl of Rothes. His other daughter married Andrew Leslie of that ilk, who received as her dowry two hundred pounds sterling on the 12th of July, 1376.

In 1368, Sir Thomas Hay, High Constable, made an agreement with William Fenton of Fenton, by which he granted to Fenton twenty mercates of land in the barony of Slains. Robert III., in 1392, promised not to ratify any grants of lands made by Sir Thomas Hay, High Constable of Scotland, the father of William Hay, the King's nephew.

Sir Thomas died at an advanced age, on the 6th of July, 1406, and was interred at the Abbey Church of Cupar. He was succeeded by his son, William, fourth High Constable. In 1406, Albany, the Governor of Scotland, granted to him relief of all his lands held in chief of the King for a payment of two hundred merks. Albany also granted to him the lands of the barony of Cowie in the Sheriffdom of Kincardine.

Sir William died at Furvie in 1437, and was succeeded by his son, William, fifth High Constable, and First Earl of Erroll. He was created Earl of Erroll in 1452. He married Beatrice, a daughter of James Douglas, third Lord of Dalkeith, and had issue. In 1454, he purchased the lands of Petilyell, in Forfarshire, from Alexander Ogilvie of Ouchterhouse.

The Earl died at Slains on the 19th of August, 1460, and was interred in the Abbey Church of Cupar. He was succeeded by his eldest son, Nicholas, second Earl of Erroll. In 1465 he married Elizabeth, a daughter of Alexander, first Earl of Huntly. On the 26th of January, 1466, he entered into a bond of alliance with George, Lord Gordon, Master of Huntly, his brother-in-law, in which they agreed to defend each other against all living men. "And, if it seems to be advisable to either of the Lords or their counsel to add to or reform this agreement, they shall be ready to put it in the best form without fraud or guile, for the honour and advantage of both the Lords."

Earl Nicholas died in 1470, leaving no issue. He was succeeded by his brother, William, third Earl of Erroll. He married, first, Lady Isabel Gordon, a daughter of George, second Earl of Huntly, by whom he had two sons, William and Thomas, and a daughter—Lady Beatrix. Secondly, in 1485, he contracted a marriage with Lady Elizabeth Leslie, a daughter of the first Earl of Rothes, and by her he had a daughter, Lady Mariana. She married David Lindsay, seventh Earl of Crawford.

The Erroll family obtained extensive estates in Buchan in the parishes of Slains, Cruden, Turriff, and others; and the Earls of Erroll attained much influence and power both in the south and north of Scotland.

On the 17th of June, 1472, Erroll received a bond of manrent from Alexander Mackintosh, Thane of Rothiemurcus, who became "riding man to my Lord, William, Earl of Erroll, Lord the Hay, and Constable of Scotland, for all the days of my life. That I shall give my Lord leal and true counsel, according to my knowledge, when he asks it; I shall conceal his when he shows it to me; whenever I hear of or see any scath to my Lord, I shall inform him, and to the utmost of my power endeavour to prevent it. And I shall be with my Lord in war and in peace before and against all living men, excepting my allegiance to the King and my Lord Huntly. In witness hereof I have affixed my seal to this letter at Perth."

In 1477 the Earl received a bond of manrent from Master William Scheves, coadjutor of St Andrews, who undertook by the faith in his body that he and his friends and servants would support Erroll to the utmost of their power.

At the Castle of Slains, on the 17th of April, 1483,

Alexander Irvine of Lonmay, son and heir-apparent of Sir Alexander Irvine of Drum, "became true man and servant to a noble and mighty lord, William, Earl of Erroll, Lord the Hay, and Constable of Scotland; in true manrent and service, in peace and in war, with my person and goods against all that live or die may, my allegiance to the King only excepted. And, if I see or hear of any hurt or peril to his person, friends, goods, or heritage, I shall warn him thereof, and to the utmost prevent it. If he asks me any advice, I shall give the best I can; and if any counsel be shown to me, I shall conceal it without fraud or guile . . . At the end of seven years my fee to be considered and modified by the persons undernamed:— Mr Gilbert Hay of Ury, Mr David Hay, Mr John Hay, prebender of Cruden; Alexander Fraser of Durris, Robert Blynsall, alderman of Aberdeen; and Alexander Irvine of Belte, or such-like persons."

At Aberdeen on the 29th of November, 1484, the Earl received a bond of manrent from John Keith of Ludquhairn. The same year, at Aberdeen, on the 24th of November, the Earl of Erroll had a bond of manrent from William Keith of Ythan.

In 1487 William Kynidy, Constable of Aberdeen, gave his bond of manrent to the Earl of Erroll, "for all the days of my life." The same year William Crawford, Laird of Federat, gave his bond of manrent to Erroll—"to serve him in peace and in war," In the following year the Earl received a bond of manrent from William Scott of Flawcrag, who "became man and servant to a mighty and noble Lord, William, Earl of Erroll, Lord Hay, and Constable of Scotland." On the 15th of January, 1489, Alexander Fraser, Lord of Philorth, "became true man to a noble and mighty Lord, William, Earl of Erroll . . . and to render true service to him in peace and in war." This bond is witnessed by Alexander Irvine of Lonmay, William Reid of Colliston, John Panton of Petmeithand, and others.

On the 11th of September, 1499, John Cheyne of Essilmount gave his bond of manrent to the Earl of Erroll—"for all the days of my life. . . . And I shall ride and go with my lord in peace and in war, as ready as any man serving his lord within the realm, with my kin, men, and friends that will do for me." At Aberdeen, on the 3rd June, 1504, Alexander Bannerman of Wattertown "became man and servant to a right noble man, William, Master of Erroll, for all the days of my life. And I shall ride and go with him at all times when I am charged."

SECTION III.

A Combat between a Frenchman and a Scotsman—Death of Earl William—William, Fourth Earl of Erroll—Erroll Slain at Flodden—William, Fifth Earl of Erroll—William, Sixth Earl—George, Seventh Earl.

In 1501, a Frenchman, called John Coupante, came to Scotland and challenged any man to fight him. Lindsay of Pitscottie says that the Frenchman desired fighting and jousting in Scotland with the Lords and barons—"but none was so apt and ready to fight with him as Sir Patrick Hamilton, a brother of the Earl of Arran, being then a young man, strong of body, and able in all things; yet for lack of exercise he was not so well practised as need were, though he lacked no hardiment, strength, nor courage in his proceedings. At last, when the Frenchman and he were assembled together, both on great horses, within the lists, under the castle wall of Edinburgh, so after the sound of the trumpet, they rushed rudely together, and broke their spears on each side on other, and afterward got new spears and re-encountered freshly again. But Sir Patrick's horse uttered with him, and would nowise encounter his marrow, so he was forced to light on foot, and give this

Frenchman battle, and therefore, when he lighted, cried for a two-handed sword, and bade the Frenchman light from his horse, and end out the matter, saying to him—' A horse is but a weak weapon when men have most ado.' Then, when both the knights were lighted on foot they joined pertly together with awful countenances, and each strake maliciously at the other, and fought long together with uncertain victory. At the last, Sir Patrick Hamilton rushed manfully upon the Frenchman, and strake him upon the knees. Meantime, the Frenchman being at the earth, the King threw his hat over the castle wall, and caused the judges and men-at-arms, to redd and sunder them ; and the heralds and trumpeters blew, and cried that the victory was Sir Patrick Hamilton's."

This Sir Patrick was a nephew of James IV. He was the father of Patrick Hamilton, Abbot of Ferne, the protomartyr of the Reformation in Scotland. Sir Patrick himself was slain in a skirmish on the High Street of Edinburgh, in 1520, called "Cleanse the Causeway."

It was stated in a preceding section, that the High Constable had duties in connection with combats, and that he had a right to the materials of which the lists and fences were formed. Accordingly, touching the combat described above, on the 13th of July, 1501, the provost, magistrates, treasurer, and some of the burgesses of Edinburgh, appeared before a noble and Mighty Lord, William, Earl of Erroll and High Constable of Scotland, who had caused them to be summoned before the King and his Council, for their intromission and detention from him, of timber and other materials of the ring called "The Barras," in which the Frenchman and Sir Patrick Hamilton fought. They were, however, unwilling to appear in Court against the High Constable, and paid to him a sum of money for the materials of the enclosure. At the same time, they promised to support the High Constable in the right of his office in such cases, and in others touching his office of Constabulary.

The Earl died on the 14th of January, 1506, and was interred at the Abbey Church of Coupar. He was succeeded by his son, William, Fourth Earl of Erroll.

On the 18th of January, 1507, James IV. made a gift of the dues to William, Earl of Erroll, of the non-entry and relief of all his lands which were in the hands of the Crown, owing to the death of his father, the late Earl.

The Earl married Elizabeth, a daughter of William, first Lord Ruthven, and had issue.

On the 17th of February, 1508, the provost, magistrates, and town council of Edinburgh bound themselves faithfully "to a noble and mighty Lord, William, Earl of Erroll, Lord Hay, and High Constable of Scotland." At this time Erroll constituted the provost and magistrates of Edinburgh as his deputies in the office of Constabulary for a term of three years, and thereafter during his will; and, therefore, the magistrates and council undertook to support the High Constable in the duties, privileges, and honour of his office to the utmost of their power.

At Aberdeen on the 8th of January, 1511, Ranald Udny of Udny gave his bond of manrent to the Earl of Erroll, and High Constable of Scotland. "And I shall be leal and true to my Lord, and serve him with my kin, men, and friends for all the days of my life."

The Earl of Erroll was present in his post at the battle of Flodden. He fell while fighting heroically by the side of the King:—

> "No thought was there of dastard flight,
> Linked in the serried phalanx tight.'

He was succeeded by his only son, William, fifth Earl of Erroll. He married Lady Helen Stewart, only daughter of John, third Earl of Lennox, by whom he had issue.

On the 16th of February, 1515, William Lesk, burgess of Aberdeen, rendered homage "and became man to a noble and potent Lord, William, Earl of Erroll, Lord Hay, and

High Constable of Scotland ; that I shall be leal and true to him and his heirs. . . . Because my good Lord and Master has admitted and affirmed me tenant in the half of the lands of Lesk, with pertinents, which my deceased father, William Lesk, held in heritage, of which the said Lord is superior."

In May, 1516, the Earl of Erroll, on account of the bond of manrent before received from Patrick Chyne of Essilmont —" Therefore we bind and oblige us and our heirs, that we shall supply, maintain, and defend the said Patrick in all his righteous causes and quarrels, moved and to be moved. And be and do for him all things as we ought to do for our own man, kinsman, and servant. . . . And this to endure as well for his kin, friends, and servants, as for himself."

Earl William died at Edinburgh on the 28th of July, 1522, and was interred at the Abbey Church of Coupar. He was succeeded by his son, William, an infant. Alexander Hay, a canon and commisssary of Aberdeen, was tutor to the young Earl.

On the 22nd of April, 1538, James V. granted a special licence for serving William heir to his father as sixth Earl of Erroll, Lord High Constable of Scotland, and Sheriff of Aberdeen, notwithstanding his minority. Accordingly, he was served heir, and became sixth Earl of Erroll. He died on the 11th of April, 1541, in the twentieth year of his age.

The Earldom then reverted to George Hay of Logie-Almond, a son of Thomas Hay, a brother of the fourth Earl of Erroll; thus he became seventh Earl of Erroll. Earl George first married Margaret, a daughter of Alexander Robertson of Strowan, by whom he had four sons and two daughters; and secondly, he married Helen, a daughter of Walter Bruce, of Pitcullen, and by her he had a daughter, Jean.

At Slains, on the 22nd of May, 1543, Alexander Chalmers of Balnacraig gave his bond of manrent to the

Earl of Erroll—"For certain gratitudes and favours conferred on me by his lordship as his bond of maintenance made to me thereupon purports. To be a true servant to the Earl for all the days of my life, and shall serve his lordship in peace and in war, no man being excepted saving our Sovereign Lady and Lord when God provides us thereof. . . . And generally all other things I shall do for my lord which the law and constitution of this realm permits a servant to do for his lord and master." This was witnessed by William Hay, a brother of Alexander Hay of Delgaty; John Rattary of Kinward; Sir William Hay, chaplain; Mr. Gilbert Chalmers, and others. Then follows the Earl's bond:—"By this writ, we, George, Earl of Erroll, Lord Hay, and Constable of Scotland, to be bound and obliged, and by the faith and truth in our body leally and truly binds and obliges us, to our servant, Alexander Chalmers of Balnacraig for as much as he is become man and servant to us for all the days of his life. . . . To maintain and defend the said Alexander, his servants and friends in all his and their just actions and quarrels against all deadly. And is content that the said Alexander at Whitsunday next enter and labour with his own stock the half of Ordlethin lying in the barony of Slains and Sheriffdom of Aberdeen, being instantly in his hands by reason of the alienation thereof. And if we happen to redeem it from him, then he shall have a take of it for five years, besides the takes contained in his reversion; but, if there be no takes in the reversion, immediately after the redeeming thereof—paying yearly therefor four pounds of money, eight bolls of meal and beir equally, four sheep, four geese, six capons, and two dozens of poultry."

The same year, in November, John Cochrane of Pitfour gave his bond of manrent to the Earl of Erroll. The following year, George Meldrum of Fyvie, and Patrick Mowat of Boquholle also gave their bonds of manrent to Erroll. In 1545 Alexander Buchan of Auchmacoy entered into a bond of manrent with Erroll, "for gratitudes, profit, and maintenance done and to be done to me, as his Lordship's bond made to me purports."

In 1546 the Earls of Huntly and Erroll entered into an agreement for maintaining themselves against all persons. At the same time it was agreed between the Earls of Huntly and Erroll, that John Gordon, also called Ogilvie, third son of the Earl of Huntly, should marry Lady Margaret Hay, second daughter of the Earl of Erroll. This contract was not realised, as John Gordon married Elizabeth Gordon, widow of Alexander Ogilvie of Findlater, and was executed at Aberdeen in the beginning of November, 1562.

It appears that the High Constable had duties in connection with the punishment of offending officers at arms. At Edinburgh on the 16th of January, 1555, the Lyon-King-at-Arms (Sir David Lindsay of the Mount) and the other heralds met, and having considered the many oppressive actions of William Crarar, messenger, upon the people, and especially upon the poor tenants and workmen of the Abbey of Coupar and the surrounding district, which were notoriously known to the Lyon-King and the heralds, and partly confessed by the offender himself: Therefore they ordered the said William's arms to be taken from him, and his person to be delivered to the Lord High Constable to be punished at the Queen's pleasure as an example to others.

SECTION IV.

EARL GEORGE APPOINTED LIEUTENANT—HIS DEATH—ANDREW, EIGHTH EARL OF ERROLL—DEATH OF EARL ANDREW—FRANCIS, NINTH EARL.

IN 1559 Francis and Mary, King and Queen of Scots, appointed the Earl of Erroll Lieutenant between the Water of Erne and the North Water. He was invested with ample power to suppress disorder and rebellion.

Earl George died in January, 1573, and was interred at Erroll. He was succeeded by his eldest son, Andrew, eighth Earl of Erroll.

He married, first, Lady Jane Hay, only surviving child of William, fifth Earl of Erroll, by whom he had three sons and one daughter. He married, secondly, Lady Agnes Sinclair, a daughter of George, fourth Earl of Caithness; and by her he had issue.

While he was Master of Erroll, on the 14th of November, 1572, he entered into an agreement with Andrew Tulidef, son and heir-apparent of Alexander Tulidef of Rancistoun. The agreement was to the effect—" That Andrew Tulidef, of his own free will and by the advice of his dear father and friends, became man and servant, and also with him another riding man, for all the days of his lifetime to the said noble lord. And shall be ready upon horse and foot to serve, upon his lordship's expenses. And shall be sufficiently equipped with armour and weapons, according to his rank. And shall be leal and true in word and deed, as becoming a faithful servant to his lord and master, and should defend his lord in all cases. For these services his lordship shall be thankfully content to pay each year to Andrew Tulidef sixteen bolls of good oatmeal, to be yearly uplifted and paid out of his lordship's land of Neder Ardlethin—or, failing this, out of any other lands within the barony of Slains; and the meal to be carried to the said Andrew's house of Mostoun or Raneistoun between Yule and Candlemas. And, if the sixteen bolls of meal be not paid to the said Andrew, then he shall be free of his servitude and promises. Further, if it happens that the said Andrew's horse dies or is killed in his lordship's company or service, then the said lord shall give to him another horse as good as the one lost." This agreement was witnessed by George Hay of Newraw, Neil Neilson, John Storie, and others.

On the 23rd of January, 1580, James VI. addressed a letter charging the provosts and magistrates of Edinburgh, Linlithgow, Stirling, Glasgow, Ayr, Perth, Cupar-in-Fife, St Andrews, Dundee, Aberdeen, and all other burghs in the kingdom, "wherever our presence and palace of honour shall be for the time. Forasmuch as the punishment of trespassers, invaders, and shedders of blood within four miles of our presence, it has pertained and pertains to our High Constable and his deputies to take inquisition of all such persons, who commit crimes, to put them before an unsuspected jury, and any person whatsoever apprehended and being convicted, to be imprisoned and kept in prison until they make satisfaction for their crimes, according to the laws and constitution of the realm. For the effective execution of this, it is necessary that all our prisons and warding-houses in our burghs and other parts of the kingdom, wherever we happen to be for the time, be made patent to our High Constable, his deputes and officers, for incarcerating all persons who commit slaughter or crimes of violence. And your assistance and support is requisite for this, so that such criminals and trespassers may receive due punishment for their crimes and offences as an example to others, who disturb us and our right trusty Councillors daily attending and awaiting upon us for the welfare of us and our realm and people. Therefore our will is, and we charge and commend ye and each of you by yourselves and your officers, in your name as ye shall be required herein, to concur, fortify, and assist our right trusty Councillor, Andrew, Earl of Erroll, our High Constable, and William Henderson, his deputy, and their officers in the execution of the office in all time coming, according to the privilege and jurisdiction thereof, of old use and wont in all points."

Earl Andrew in the later years of his life had unhappily serious domestic troubles, which seem to have arisen from his second marriage. It appears that there was a suspicion of the influence of the second Countess over her husband, which might be turned to the prejudice of the children of the first marriage. He died at Slains on the 8th of October, 1585, and was interred there.

He was succeeded by his son, Francis, ninth Earl of Erroll. He married Lady Elizabeth Douglas, a daughter of William, sixth Earl of Morton, by whom he had issue.

On the 17th of September, 1589, the Earl of Erroll entered into a bond of friendship with the Earl of Huntly, which proceeded on the ground—" That, seeing and considering the changes and controversies daily occurring among all classes of this poor realm, to the great disturbance of His Majesty's good estate and the grief of all his good subjects, and thereby perceiving our own peril and danger in particular, and how necessary it is for us two to knit up a sure friendship, to continue between us as two brothers born of one mother, in all time coming during our lifetime : We therefore become bound to act faithfully to each other, having sworn the great oath and touched the Holy Book, that we shall keep and observe our sure and infallible affection, goodwill, and friendship to each other, in such a way that any of our actions and causes whatsoever—criminal or civil—shall be alike common to us both ; to assist, fortify, and defend in the law and by the law against all other persons, the King's own person only excepted." Further, it was stipulated that no deadly feud should be reconciled or pacified by one of them without the special consent and advice of the other ; that no new friendship should be contracted by either of them with any person without the mutual consent of both of them. And in case it should be thought necessary to receive any other noblemen into this bond of friendship, " the same to be done by both of us." And, generally, that nothing shall be done by either of us in prejudice " of this particular bond, under the pain of dishonour, and defamation for ever." This bond is dated at Aberdeen, signed by the two Earls, and witnessed by John Leslie of Balquhain, John Gordon of Buckie, and Captain Thomas Ker.

The part played by this Earl of Erroll along with Huntly in the reaction against Protestantism, was indicated in the preceding chapter. In common with Huntly, he was subjected to persecution, repeatedly excommunicated and confined in prison. After the battle of Glenlivet, in 1594, the old Castle of Slains was almost demolished.

On the 8th of December, 1591, James VI. issued a letter to the Provost and Magistrates of Edinburgh, commanding them not to encroach upon the rights and duties of Francis, Earl of Erroll, High Constable of Scotland; but to assist the Constable and his deputies in the execution of the functions and duties of the office, when required: "Commanding and charging them to readily answer and obey our High Constable and his deputies in all things concerning their office in time coming, under the penalties aforesaid as ye will answer to us thereupon."

In 1596 the King sharply rebuked the baillies of Leith for encroaching on the High Constable's privileges. It appears that the baillies had tried a man named John Shanks, who should have been tried in the Constable's Court, and had declined to obey a messenger sent by the King himself. His Majesty therefore wrote:—"We command and charge every one of you, and those that shall be for the time in your places, as ye will answer to us upon your obedience and under the penalties that thereafter may follow. That ye nor your successors in any time hereafter hold court to examine or put to trial any person or persons whatsoever for such crimes committed within the four-mile limit, without a licence from our High Constable or his deputies and substitutes. And if any of you hereafter interpose your authority to stop or impede the same, we will see that you be punished for your contempt."

In February, 1601, the Earl of Erroll received a bond

of service from Andrew Hering of Little Blair, upon the special consideration of a free remission, "granted to me by Francis, Earl of Erroll, Lord Hay, and High Constable of Scotland, for the slaughter of the late James Hay, son of the late William Hay of Gourdie, committed by me—thereby finding myself for ever obliged to this noble lord's clemency. Therefore, of my own accord and free will, I have become a servant to the said noble lord and his heirs and successors for all the days of my life. And faithfully promise henceforth to honour, reverence, serve, and obey him and his heirs and successors, whom I acknowledge as my only lord and master. And I will take part with them in all their actions, quarrels, and affairs whatsoever to the utmost of my power against all persons, excepting the King. This bond is dated at Perth, and witnessed by David Hering, fier of Glasclune; James Ogilvie, fier of Cloway; Sir James Stewart of Ballequhain; and Henry Drummond, tutor of Blair.

One of the most remarkable of this class of documents is that in which the Clan Donachie came under bond to the Earl of Erroll to be faithful to their chief, Robertson, Laird of Strowan. The bond proceeds thus:—" Forasmuch as we understand the loving favour and regard entertained by a noble and potent Lord, Francis, Earl of Erroll, Lord Hay, and High Constable of Scotland, to Robert Robertson of Strowan, our chief, and his house, whereof we are descended: And being most willing for our part to defend our chief to the utmost of our power: Therefore we bind and oblige ourselves faithfully to the said noble Lord, that we shall by his lordship's advice concur and assist the Laird of Strowan, and maintain his house and estate as far as possible, under the pain of infamy and defamation." The document is dated at Perth on the 19th of May, 1612, and signed by eight of the leading men of the clan.

SECTION V.

FRANCIS, NINTH EARL OF ERROLL—FEUD BETWEEN THE GORDONS AND THE HAYS, GORDON OF GIGHT'S PROCEEDINGS—HIS TRIAL ADJOURNED, RESUMED, AND AGAIN ADJOURNED—SETTLEMENT OF THE FEUD.

SOMETIMES rather serious differences arose between the Lord High Constable and Earl Marischal touching the respective functions and duties of their offices. This usually occurred on points of duty when Parliament was sitting. On the 2nd of July, 1606, the Privy Council passed an Act touching the "privilege and liberty claimed by either of them to the keeping of the keys of the Parliament House. And the Lords of the Council, being well advised, and having heard all that was proposed and alleged by both the parties in this matter, and having heard the statements of several persons regarding the form and order observing by them in preceding Parliaments: The Lords of the Council find and declare —That the keeping of the keys of the Parliament House and the guarding of the utter bar and gates thereof appertains to the Constable."

It appears, however, that George, fifth Earl Marischal, was not satisfied with above decision. In July, the following year, the Privy Council passed another Act touching this matter:—"Forasmuch as a motion has been made to the Lords of the Privy Council, alleging some prejudice done to him, by the Lords of Council in the privilege of his office of Marischalship, during the last Parliament, held at Perth, by finding that the keys of the Parliament House ought to be delivered and kept by the Lord High Constable, which the Marischal alleges to be due to him by the privilege of his office and bygone custom: And touching an ambiguous word in the last act, that the guarding of the utter bar of the Parliament House appertains to the Lord High Constable: and William Hay, agent to the Lord

Constable, being called and heard in the matter, and all that the Earl Marischal and he had to say or allege being heard by the Lords of Council and considered: The Lords of Council for avoiding heat, strife, and contention between Earl Marischal and the High Constable, and their deputies, and for explanation of their first Act—declare, as before, that the keeping of the keys of the Parliament House appertains to the High Constable, and the guarding and keeping of the utter gates of the Parliament House also appertains to the High Constable; and that he and his deputies have the charge and command of all outside the gates of the Parliament House: That the meaning and intention of the word utter bar, was nothing else but the utter gates: And declare that the guarding of the inner bar and the charge of all within the gates and doors of the Parliament House appertain to Earl Marischal."

In spite of the bond of friendship so carefully formed between the first Marquis of Huntly and Francis, ninth Earl of Erroll, a feud arose between the Gordons and the Hays of the north. The feud was caused by George Gordon of Gight. The Gordons of Gight were descended from Sir William Gordon, third son of George, second Earl of Huntly. Of all the branches of the Gordons, the Gight family was the most turbulent and violent.

George Gordon of Gight was a remarkably headstrong and unruly individual, and firmly attached to the Roman Catholic Church. A brother of his was slain in a quarrel with Francis Hay, and in revenge for this, Gordon seized Hay, and under a guard conveyed him to Aberdeen, in December, 1615. There Francis Hay underwent a mock trial before John Gordon, sheriff-depute of Aberdeen, and a packed jury connected with the Gordons, He was condemned, of course, and then carried to the back green of a private house in the Gallowgate, and there beheaded.

The following year, in the month of February, Gordon of Gight proceeded with an armed force of men, on horse and foot, to a field near the burn of Cruden, and there attacked three young brothers—known as the Hays of Brunthill—and two of them were severely wounded. They were relatives of the late Francis Hay, who was executed in the Gallowgate by the Gordons.

The trial of the Laird of Gight for these crimes was fixed to take place in Edinburgh on the 28th of August, 1616. All the Gordons of the north, with the Marquis of Huntly as their chief, ranged themselves on one side of the feud, and all the Hays of the north with the Earl of Erroll as their chief, placed themselves on the other side. Thus, it was to be a very important "day of law" in Edinburgh. The utmost precautions had to be taken to preserve the peace in and around the Tolbooth of Edinburgh.

On the appointed day the trial commenced, and the Earl of Erroll and other representatives of the Hays appeared. There were long preliminary statements made and arguments presented by counsel on both sides; but after these proceedings, the case was indefinitely adjourned.

The case was resumed the following year. On the 16th of January, 1617, George Gordon of Gight appeared before the Lords of the Privy Council and complained that he had been wrongfully put to the horn for not entering into ward to answer these charges—1, the persuit of William, George, and Patrick Hay; 2, the slaughter of Francis Hay; and 3, his not appearing to answer the complaint touching the trouble between him and the brethren of Brunthill. "As he was never lawfully charged to enter his person or to appear, and as he had found caution in 6000 merks to appear this day, and will make payment of 200 merks to the treasurer for his escheat, he pleaded that the hornings should be suspended." The pursuer and the King's Advocate appeared personally, and the Lords in respect of the Laird of Gight's appearance before them, suspended the letters of horning. They ordered him to find caution in a sum of 5000 merks to keep the peace and appear before them to answer for his crimes, and to find caution in the books of adjournal for his appearance before the Justice, under the penalty of 5000 merks. Caution to be found within 48 hours.

The 26th of February, 1617, was fixed for the trial of Gordon of Gight. Five of the Lords of the Privy Council were appointed assessors to the Justice who was to try the case.

At this "day of law" the Government anticipated that there would be present in Edinburgh a number of noblemen, barons, and gentlemen—friends of either party, between whom there was already heart-burning, private grudge, and discontent, and, so it was likely enough that some trouble might arise:—

"Therefore the Lords of the Privy Council command letters to be directed charging the officers at arms to proceed to the Market Cross of Edinburgh, and there by open proclamation to command and charge George, Marquis of Huntly, as chief of the said Laird of Gight, and Francis, Earl of Erroll, as chief of the late Francis Hay, and the brothers (Hays) of Brunthill, as also the parties themselves, and all the noblemen, barons, and gentlemen of their name, and all their servants, followers, and dependants, who are already come to this burgh or shall come to attend and wait upon the said day, for assisting and backing of any of the parties—that they immediately proceed to their lodgings within this burgh and continue therein, and noways come forth therefrom without licence of the Lords of Council sought and obtained. And that the parties themselves in noways presume to come to the Justice Court until the magistrates of Edinburgh come and make convey to the court, under the pain of rebellion. . . . And, suchlike to command, charge, and inhibit all persons, that none of them be found walking upon the streets of this burgh after the ringing of the ten o'clock bell at night, under the penalty of being apprehended, imprisoned, and punished."

The court held eight sittings on the trial of the Laird of Gight. Able counsel were engaged on both sides, and many technical objections and long arguments were adduced. But on the 13th of March, the Lords of the Council ordered the trial to be posponed to the 18th of June. It seems that the King had intervened, as he was on grounds of policy very anxious to put an end to this great feud between the Gordons and Hays, and perhaps he wished to save the Laird of Gight.

When the 18th of June came, it appeared that the King had taken the matter into his own hands. Accordingly, letters were sent to the Marquis of Huntly and the Earl of Erroll, directing them to come to Edinburgh on the 8th of September, in a peaceable manner, accompanied only by their household servants; the Marquis of Huntly to bring Gight and John Gordon with him, and Erroll to bring the brethren of Brunthill.

On the 10th of September, 1617, George, Marquis of Huntly, George, Lord Gordon, William Gordon of Gight, Sir Alexander Gordon of Cluny, Gordon of Abergeldie, and John Gordon of Buckie, on the one side, and Francis, Earl of Erroll, Lord Hay, Hay, a brother of the Earl, and the Hays of Brunthill on the other side, appeared before the Privy Council. And it was intimated to them that the King had pronounced his decree arbitral on the matters in question between them; and that it was the King's will that, before disclosing to them the terms of his decree, they should be reconciled, agreed, and promise to abide by the King's decree. They were then asked if they were all content to submit to his Majesty's decree? They declared that with all reverence and humility they would acquiesce to his Majesty's will and pleasure. Therefore, to show their willing obedience to the King, they shook hands with one another and promised to bury all former enmity standing amongst them. Thus ended the feud between the Gordons and the Hays.

SECTION VI.

FRANCIS, NINTH EARL OF ERROLL—A DISPUTE BETWEEN LORD KEITH AND LORD HAY—DEATH OF EARL FRANCIS—WILLIAM, TENTH EARL—CORONATION OF CHARLES I.—DEATH OF EARL WILLIAM—GILBERT, ELEVENTH EARL.

THE Earl was excommunicated for non-conformity to the Protestant religion. He had been for a considerable time confined to his residence of Erroll and a certain distance round it. But in the spring of 1617 the King issued a warrant to relieve the Earl from confinement and the sentence of excommunication: Seeing that he had "given satisfaction to the fathers of the Church concerning matters of religion, there was now no reason to restrain his natural liberty in any way." Yet, on the 28th of March, 1620, the Earl of Erroll was charged to appear before the Lords of the Privy Council for sending his son in company with Patrick Con (younger of Auchrie) to France, "who was known to be a Papist."

On the 20th of January, 1620, the Earl of Erroll received a commission to hold Justice Courts within the bounds of the barony of Slains and the parish of Turriff. The following year, this commission was renewed to the Earl and his son, Lord Hay, for the suppression of the crimes of theft and reset of theft, with power to them and their baillies to apprehend, imprison, and try offenders for such crimes.

The Erroll family had extensive estates in the parish of Turriff, which included the barony of Delgaty and its fine old castle. The Earls of Erroll frequently resided in this ancient baronial mansion, which stands on a beautiful site amid extensive woods, about three-quarters of a mile from the town of Turriff.

Earls of Erroll. 251

For a period of nearly 350 years, the family of Erroll were superiors of the town of Turriff. It also appears that the Earls of Erroll had a lodging in the town, which stood on a bank on the east side and at the top of the road leading from the town to the railway station.

A dispute arose between William, Lord Hay, son of Francis, Earl of Erroll, High Constable of Scotland, and William, Lord Keith, son of George, fifth Earl Marischal, touching their respective rights and privileges when Parliament was sitting. The dispute came before the Lords of the Privy Council on the 25th of July, 1621. It was then alleged for the High Constable that the guarding and keeping of the Parliament House pertained to the Constable, and that the Marischal ought not to have a guard within the House, and that he has power only to marshal the estates, and, if he have a guard, that its number should be prescribed by the Constable. To this Lord Keith replied that the Marischal, by the privilege of his office, ought to have and always had had a guard within the House, that his office is not subaltern, but as free as any office in the kingdom, and that the Constable ought not to prescribe a number to him. The Lords, having heard both parties, and considered their reasons and allegations, ordered them both to serve in that Parliament as they did in the last Parliament; and advised the Marischal not to bring a confused number of persons as a guard within the house to disturb the Parliament.

On the 2nd of May, 1627, Charles I. issued a commission to inquire into the honours and privileges of the office of the High Constable. The members of the commission named by the King, with full power given to them, were Sir George Hay of Kinfauns, Lord High Chancellor of Scotland; John, Earl of Mar, High Treasurer; James, Marquis of Hamilton; George, Marquis of Huntly; George, Earl of Winton; Alexander, Earl of Linlithgow; John, Earl of Wigton; Sir Archibald Napier of Merchiston, subsequently first Lord Napier ; Sir John Skene, President of the Court of Session ; Sir Henry Bruce, General of his Majesty's artillery, and a few others. Along with the Earl of Erroll, and Lord Hay, his son, the commissioners or any six of them were directed to meet and " To examine the laws and Acts of Parliament, the order and custom touching the office of High Constable which prevailed in the kingdom in former times, or from ancient monuments, registers, rolls, and records, also any right, title, or evidence whatsoever that the Earl of Erroll or his son could produce ; or otherwise make clear what had been the ancient and accustomed honours, privileges, fees, and immunities belonging to the office of High Constable. . . And especially to consider the honours, privileges, and immunities belonging to the office both in time of peace and war, and the privileges and honour due thereunto about His Majesty's person, or where the Royal authority is represented either in Parliament, Convention, Council or otherwise. . . And, finally, with power to them to examine and consider such orders, privileges, and immunities which for the credit of the kingdom may be best fitted for the present estate of the time to be added unto the office of High Constable."

It appears the commissioners made no report ; and, on the 23rd of June, 1630, another commission was issued by the King, in the same terms as the one quoted from above. In compliance with this, the Lord Chancellor and other officers of the Privy Council prepared a report, which was presented to the King in the beginning of August, 1631. This document has usually been considered as authoritative on the functions and duties of the High Constable's office ; but it is unnecessary to quote it, as the principal parts of it were embraced in a preceding section.

Earl Francis died on the 16th of July, 1631. Dr Arthur Johnston, a distinguished scholar and writer of Latin verse, wrote a funeral lament for Earl Francis, which has been translated thus :—

"Erroll, chieftain of the Hays, is gone, the world's regret, who was once its pride. He was enrolled among the Peers through his stem of Royal line, ennobled by the blood-red 'yokes.' Martial virtue and a thousand trophies, won by his lightning-hand, linked him to the shades of his forefathers. Picty well proved, bequeathed him to heaven. Is there ought beyond this, either for men to win or for Heaven to give?"

He was succeeded by his son William, tenth Earl of Erroll. He married Anne Lyon, only daughter of Patrick, first Earl of Kinghorn, by whom he had issue.

In the summer of 1633, preparations were made for the visit of Charles I. to Scotland, and for his coronation at Edinburgh. In a letter to the Lords of the Privy Council, dated the 11th of May, the King expressed his approval of the report of the commissioners touching the honours, privileges, and functions belonging to the office of the Lord High Constable, but he recommended to them further consideration of the honours and functions of the office, and especially on the coming occasion of the King's coronation at Holyrood. The Lords of the Council, in a further report to the King, stated very clearly what the duties of the Lord High Constable were in connection with the coronation.

On the 18th of June, 1633, the coronation of Charles I. took place. The King on that eventful morning was conducted from his chamber of presence to the hall of the Castle of Edinburgh by the Lord High Constable on the right hand and Earl Marischal on the left. The whole day the Constable and Earl Marischal carried their batons of office in their hands. In the procession from the castle to Holyrood, the High Constable rode immediately before the King, on the right hand of the Earl of Angus, who bore the Crown, on account of his hereditary privileges of giving the first vote and taking the first seat in Parliament, of leading the vanguard of the King's army on the day of battle, and of bearing the King's Crown in the Riding of Parliament.

After the service in the chapel of Holyrood, the Archbishop of St Andrews, the High Constable and Earl Marischal, and the Lyon King, presented the monarch to his people. After the King was crowned and anointed, the High Constable then girt the Sword of State upon His Majesty's side. Then the Lord Chamberlain loosed the King's sword, and the King taking it in his hand, offered it, and the Archbishop laid it on the communion table; then the High Constable redeemed it with an offering, and drawing it out of the sheath, he carried it naked before the King.

Earl William died in 1636, and was succeeded by his only son, Gilbert, eleventh Earl of Erroll—a boy of five years. The Earl of Kinghorn was his tutor.

The young Earl, though a minor, was commanded by a committee of Parliament sitting at Perth in December, 1650, to attend at the coronation of Charles II. at Scone, on the 1st of January, 1651. And the part which he acted as Lord High Constable on this occasion is interesting, and may be briefly narrated thus:—The King, robed as a Prince, was conducted from his bedchamber by the High Constable on his right hand and Earl Marischal on the left, to the chamber of presence, and there placed in a Chair of State by Lord Angus, Chamberlain. After a short repose, the noblemen and the commissioners of the barons and burghs entered the hall, and presented themselves before the King. After the reception, the nobleman and the commissioners of the barons and burghs accompanied His Majesty to the Church of Scone; in the procession the High Constable rode on the right hand of the King and Earl Marischal on the left. When the sermon was over, the King solemnly swore the National Covenant, and the League and Covenant, and the King's oath. After this the King went to the platform and sat down in the Chair of State; and the High Constable and Earl Marischal went to the corners of the platform, and the Lyon King-at-Arms, going before them, spoke to the people, saying—" I do present unto you the King, Charles

II." . . . Then the King, supported by the High Constable and Earl Marischal, came down from the platform, and sat down in the chair in which he heard the sermon. The coronation oath was administered to the King. He was next divested of his princely robes, and then invested with his royal robes. The King was conducted to a chair on the north side of the church, the sword was brought by Sir William Cockburn of Langtown, gentleman usher, from the table, and delivered to the Lyon King-at-Arms, who gave it to the Lord High Constable, and he put it in the King's hand, saying—" Sir, receive this kingly sword, for the defence of the Faith of Christ and the protection of His Church, and of the true religion as presently professed within this kingdom, and according to the National Covenant and the League and Covenant, and for executing equity and justice, and for punishment of all iniquity and injustice." Then the High Constable received the sword from the King, and girt it upon His Majesty's side. The Crown was placed on the King's head, and, the nobles and people having sworn fealty to him, then the Lord High Chamberlain loosed the sword from the King, and drew it out, and delivered it into the King's hands. And the King placed it in the hands of the High Constable, who carried the naked sword before the King. After the King was installed in the throne, he arose, and, supported by the High Constable and Earl Marischal, and accompanied by the Lord High Chancellor, he went out at a door prepared for the purpose, to a platform ; and showed himself to the people outside, "and they clapped their hands and shouted for a long time—' God save the King.'" Amen.

SECTION VII.

GILBERT, ELEVENTH EARL OF ERROLL—FINE IMPOSED ON HIM BY CROMWELL'S COMMISSIONERS—HIS DEATH—SUCCEEDED BY SIR JOHN HAY, TWELFTH EARL—REVOLUTION IN 1688—HIS DEATH—CHARLES, THIRTEENTH EARL—SERVED HEIR TO HIS FATHER.

EARL GILBERT was subjected to much trouble for the part that he had taken in connection with the coronation of Charles II., and for attending meetings of Parliament, by the commissioners of the Commonwealth appointed under Cromwell's Government of Scotland. By the ordinance of pardon and grace to the people of Scotland, issued under Cromwell's rule, certain parties were excluded, and enormous fines were imposed upon them. A fine of £2000 sterling was imposed on the Earl of Erroll. But, in 1654, the Earl addressed a petition to these English Commissioners under Cromwell, in which he clearly explained his position. He pointed out that he was not at the battles of Dunbar, Preston, nor Worcester, and did not invade England in the years of 1648, 1650, or 1651, and that he was not engaged in any war against England during these years, as he was under age and tutors, and at school. He had not attained the age of 21 years until July, 1652, and therefore he was not qualified by the law of the nation to sit as a member of Parliament.

"But the truth is, that the petitioner being, by his birthright and by succession of many ages, High Constable of Scotland, an office of great enimence and trust in this nation, was several times during his minority brought by his tutors and curators from the schools to be present at some Parliaments and committees only for preserving his office, and to sit there in the Constable's chair, and to look upon the guarding and ordering of the House of Parliament, as properly belonging to the High Constable's office. This he humbly conceives can infer no guilt upon him as he had no vote in Parliament nor any accession to the carrying out of any designs therein. Though the Parliament did sometimes (in his minority) give him the name colonel or member of committee, yet that cannot be a ground to infer any guilt upon the petitioner, because he was all that time a minor; so he never owned nor acted in any charge in the armies, nor followed the court nor armies during the King's abode in Scotland; save that he once came to Stirling in July, 1651, and stayed there only a few days, where your petitioner refused the charge of a regiment of horse to which the Parliament had named him. This was looked upon with an evil eye by all those then in power, whereupon your petitioner immediately retired to his own house, where ever since he has lived peaceably.

"Since the present authority was established in this nation, the petitioner has been constant in submission and obedience to it. . . . And his submission and peaceable conduct has had no small influence upon many persons of all ranks in this quarter of the country. . . . So he has deserved by his good conduct to be taken into favourable consideration.

"As to the petitioner's estate, when the rental of it and the specification of the vast burden left upon it by his father (who died in 1636, when your petitioner was but five years of age) shall be exhibited to be considered by your honours, it will be evident how far his condition has been mistaken, and how unable the petitioner is to pay the fine imposed on him, or any part thereof, without utter ruin to himself and family."

In general, Cromwell's Government was very hard on the Scottish barons. Indeed, some of them were ruined by the heavy fines extorted from them, and many were crippled.

Earl Gilbert married Lady Catharine, a daughter of James, Earl of Southesk. The Earl took a keen interest in the restoration of Charles II. After this event, Erroll was made a Privy Councillor. He died at Slains in 1674 leaving no issue.

The Earldom then reverted to the descendants of the fourth son of Earl Andrew, Sir George Hay of Killour. He married Elizabeth, a daughter of Sir Patrick Cheyne of Essilmont, and they had a son, Sir Andrew Hay of Killour. He married Margaret, a sister of the first Lord Kinnaird, and had a son, Sir John Hay. This Sir John then became twelfth Earl of Erroll, and sixteenth High Constable of Scotland.

Earl John married Lady Anne Drummond, only daughter of James, third Earl of Perth, by whom he had issue, three sons and two daughters.

The Earl and Countess of Erroll took a great interest in the Revolution of 1688, more especially as Drummond, Earl of Perth, was Lord Chancellor and head of the Government of Scotland when the revolutionary movement began. The following letter, dated at Leith on the 12th of December, 1688, was addressed to the Countess of Erroll :—" Upon Monday last (there having been a tumult the night before), my Lord Chancellor called all the councillors in town, and others of the nobility to Holyrood House : and after he had spoken with them, went away towards Drummond, having with him about ten gentlemen of his own friends and 40 militia horsemen. That night he went to the Earl of Callendar's house of Almond, between Linlithgow and Falkirk. And in Edinburgh, after he was gone on the Monday night, there was a terrible tumult, and his lodgings were entirely rifled ; and all those of the Roman persuasion were used in the same manner, even old Lady Margaret Hay, Lady Lucie Hamilton, and Mr Andrew Hay, the Laird of Niddrie. And towards the morning they came to Blair's lodging and ruined everything within the house, broke his cabinets to shivers, treated his children very barbarously, and burnt his papers on the floor of one of his rooms, and all other papers they got. Himself and his lady had withdrawn, and now he is out of town and his family to follow. I was fully of your ladyship's mind as to my lord's being here, but it was both the King's service and my Lord Chancellor's security that he should stay; and though in resisting of tumults there is much danger and little honour to be won, as your ladyship very rightly says, yet even that danger cannot at some times by persons of quality be well declined. However, now my lord is on his way towards your ladyship, yet going by Drummond, which is the reason I have troubled you with this account, because himself thought the post would be at Aberdeen before him. . . . So, wishing God to comfort your ladyship for this affliction of your dearest and nearest friends, I shall add no more."

The Earl of Erroll, along with his friends, was inclined to the side of the Stuart line of Kings. But, at the crisis of the Revolution he acted with singular moderation and judgment.

On the 5th of February, 1700, the Earl of Erroll was elected Chancellor of University and King's College, Aberdeen. He held this office till his death, which occurred on the 30th of December, 1704. He was succeeded by his eldest son, Charles, thirteenth Earl of Erroll. His two brothers, John and Thomas, died without issue.

Earl Charles was elected Chancellor of University and King's College, Aberdeen, on the 12th of February, 1705. He held this office for 11 years, and resigned it on the 14th of May, 1716.

On the 24th of April, 1705, he was served heir to his father, as Earl of Erroll, Lord Hay and Slains, and High Constable of Scotland, and also served heir to the lands of the barony of Slains, along with the patronage of the churches of the parishes of Cruden and Turriff. Also the castles, towers, and manor houses, mills, and fishings—" as well in salt as in fresh water. . . . The lands of Leask and Garnhill, in the parish of Slains; the lands of Artrochies,

Tipperty, and Tartie, in the parish of Logie; the lands of
little Arnadge, in the parish of Ellon; the lands of Pitmedden and mill of Torrie, in the parish of Udny; the lands of
Wester Auchquharnie and Earlescat, in the parish of
Cruden; the lands of Kininmonth, of Haddo and Rattray,
in the parish of Crimond, in the county of Aberdeen; and
the lands of Elsick, in the parish of Fetteresso and county
of Kincardine, along with the donation of church benefices
and chaplainaries all lying in the lordship and barony of
Slains. And also the lands and barony of Essilmont, with
tower, fort, and manor place thereof. . . With salmon
fishing on the water of Ythan . . . the towns and lands
of Aberdour and Pennan, lying in the parish of Aberdour,
and the manor places and houses, all in the barony of
Essilmont and county of Aberdeen. . . And also the
lands and barony of Crimond with castle, tower, fort, and
manor places thereof—the dominical lands of Crimond,
mill, lands of Blairmarmouth, Cairnekempsie, Tilliekeirries,
and the lands of Crimondhayhills, with the meal mill thereof; the lands of Crimondgorth, with the meal mill of Loch-
hills; the lands of Crimondmogate, with the meal mill and
dye mills; the lands of Cairnlob, Blairquhattan, and
Berribrae, all lying in the parishes of Crimond and Lonmay
and in the barony of Crimond, and county of Aberdeen.
Also the lands and barony of Delgaty, with the manor
place, meal and dye mills. . . . The lands of Udoch
Coupland, called the dominical lands of Udoch and manor
place, with the flower gardens. . . With the superiority
of the shady half of the lands of Ardein and the pertinents
lying in the parish of Turriff. . . . And likewise the
town and lands of Meikle and Little Auchrys, with the
tower, fort, and manor place; the town and lands of Nether-
wood and Hairmoss; the lands of the shady half of Greeness,
and Grayston, Mill of Hairmoss, and mill lands. . . .
And also the towns and lands of Over and Nether
Kinmissities, and Corssgeldie . . The lands of Muriefauld,

Assogills mill and lands. . . . Whiterashes, Wraes, Skatertie, Claymyres, along with the fishing on the water of Deveron, all lying in the barony of Delgaty, and the parishes of Turriff and Monquhitter. Also the towns and lands of Leasyde, Haughmuir, Leys, Ross, Chapelhill, Pollcalk, Cassingray, and Gourdies, lying in the shires of Fife and Perth. Further, in the lands and barony of Mountblairy, with the tithes, rectorial and vicarage, lying in the parishes of Alva and Forglen, and the county of Banff. . . . The lands of Turriff and Knockinsch, Hillhead and Knockiemill, with the mill of Turriff, and mill lands and pertinents, which lands are held of the Queen, as coming in place of the late rectors of Turriff, for a yearly payment of three pounds." The barony of Slains was held in free regality; the barony of Essilmont was held in free blench from the Crown; and the baronies of Crimond and Delgaty were held of the Crown in taxed ward.

SECTION VIII.

Charles, Earl of Erroll, Opposed to the Union—Coronation of George I.—Mary, Countess of Erroll.—Coronation of George II.

EARL Charles was strongly opposed to the union between England and Scotland. He dissented to most of the articles of the Treaty, and finally entered a protestation in the following terms:—

"I, Charles, Earl of Erroll, Lord High Constable of Scotland, do hereby protest—that the office of High Constable, with all the rights and privileges of the same, belonging to me heritably, and depending upon the Monarchy, Sovereignty, and ancient constitution of this Kingdom, may not be prejudiced by the Treaty of Union between Scotland and England, nor any article, clause, or condition thereof, but that the said heritable office, with all the rights and privileges thereof, may remain to me and my successors, entire and unhurt by any votes or Acts of Parliament whatever relating to the said Union ; and I crave that this, my protestation, may be recorded in the registers and rolls of Parliament."

The office of Lord High Constable was not abolished by the Union, though, owing to the changed circumstances and the extinction of the Scottish Parliament, the duties of the office were very limited.

In April, 1708, the Earl of Erroll was conveyed prisoner to London, on suspicion of his being connected with the attempted French invasion in favour of the exiled King.

There is a report by the Lords of Committee for the coronation of George I. in 1714, which touched on the precedence due to the Lord High Constable of Scotland and Earl Marischal, and made the following statement :—" Their Lordships have agreed to offer it as their humble opinion to His Majesty that the Constable of Scotland do in the procession at his Majesty's coronation walk on the right hand side of the High Constable of England, and Earl Marischal on the left hand of the Marshal of England. The High Constable and the Marshal of England being nearest the Sword of State."

But it does not appear that Erroll, the Lord High Constable, took his place in person at the coronation of George I.

Earl Charles died unmarried in 1717. The Earldom then devolved on the late Earl's eldest sister, Lady Mary, who became Countess of Erroll. She married Alexander Falconer, second son of Sir David Falconer of Newton, Lord President of the Court of Session in 1682.

The Countess's sister, Lady Margaret, married James, fifth Earl of Linlithgow, and fourth Earl of Callander, and by him had a son, who died young, and an only daughter, Lady Anne Livingstone. This lady married William, fourth Earl of Kilmarnock, and by him had three sons—James

Lord Boyd, who eventually became Earl of Erroll; Charles, and William.

In 1727, on the occasion of the coronation of George II., Mary, Countess of Erroll, claimed her right to act by deputy, and the claim was admitted. On the 2nd of October it was intimated—" That, whereas His Majesty was pleased by his Order in Council of the twentieth of last month to allow of the claim of the Countess of Erroll as Hereditary High Constable of Scotland to walk at the coronation of Their Majesties, and to order that she should nominate to His Majesty some proper person to be her deputy; and whereas the said Countess of Erroll did this day nominate His Grace John, Duke of Roxburgh, to His Majesty to walk in her stead: His Majesty in Council is pleased to approve of the said nomination, and accordingly hereby to appoint the said Duke of Roxburgh to walk as the said Countess of Erroll's deputy at the coronation, and to take the same place as was allowed at the last coronation—on the right hand of the High Constable of England; the said High Constable of England being nearest to the Sword of State."

On the 30th of September an order was issued to this effect:—"Whereas Mary, Countess of Erroll, is allowed by the King in Council to have the right of the office of High Constable of Scotland vested in her, and she, having nominated, with the King's approbation, His Grace John, Duke of Roxburgh, to officiate for her at the ensuing coronation: These are to signify the same, and that you cause to be provided and made a truncheon or staff of silver, gilt at each end, of twelve-ounces weight, of the same fashion and goodness as was made at the last coronation for the High Constable of England, with His Majesty's arms at one end, and the arms of the Countess of Erroll at the other, both engraved; and deliver the same to the above named John, Duke of Roxburgh, to be used at Their Majesties' coronation."

On the day of the coronation of George II., the Duke of

Roxburgh acted instead of the Countess, as indicated above, and took his place on the right hand of the High Constable of England.

Mary, Countess of Erroll, died in 1758, and, leaving no issue, the Earldom reverted to a son of her neice, the Countess of the unfortunate Earl of Kilmarnock, and, as indicated in a preceding paragraph, James, Lord Boyd, became fourteenth Earl of Erroll.

His father, the fourth Earl of Kilmarnock, having joined the Rising of 1745, and, according to his own account, surrendered himself immediately after the battle of Culloden, he was conveyed a prisoner to England. When he was confined in the Tower of London, after his trial, and under sentence of death, he wrote a few letters to the Duke of Hamilton, and to his son, Lord Boyd. Shortly before he was beheaded, the condemned Earl was naturally very anxious to see his son, but the authorities refused to grant his request. His last letter to his eldest son, Lord Boyd, is preserved, and it has a peculiar though a sad interest. The condemned man wrote thus :—

" To the Right Honourable the Lord Boyd.

" Dear Boyd,—You may easily believe it gave me a great deal of uneasiness that you did not get leave to come up here, and that I would not have the pleasure of taking a long and last farewell of you.

Besides the pleasure of seeing you and giving you the blessing of a dying father ; I wanted to have talked to you about your affairs more than I have strength or spirit to write. I shall therefore recommend you to George Menzies in Falkirk, and Robert Paterson, in Kilmarnock, as your advisers in them, and to a state of affairs I sent to my wife, of which you will get a copy, which I recommend to you in the same manner as to her. I desire you to consult with her in all your affairs. I need hardly recommend it to you —as I know your good nature and regard for her—to do all you can to comfort her in the grief and affliction I am sure she must be in when she has the accounts of my death. She will need your assistance, and I pray you may give it her.

"I beg leave to say two or three things to you as my last advice. Seek God in your youth, and when you are old he will not depart from you. Be at pains to acquire good habits now, that they may grow up and become strong in you. Love mankind and do justice to all men. Do good to as many as you can, and neither shut your ears or your purse to those in distress whom it is in your power to relieve. . . . Live within your circumstances, by which means you will have it in your power to do good to others and create an independence in yourself, the surest way to rise in the world.

"Above all things, continue in your loyalty to his present Majesty and the succession to the Crown as by law established. Look on that as the basis of the civil and religious liberty and property of every individual in the nation. Prefer the public interest to your own wherever they interfere. Love your family and children, when you have any, but never let your regard for them drive you on the rock I have split upon, when on that account I departed from my principles, and brought the guilt of rebellion and public and particular desolation on my head, for which I am now under the sentence justly due to my crime. Use all your interest to get your brother pardoned and brought home as soon as possible, that his circumstances, and the bad influence of those he is among, may not induce him to accept of foreign service, and lose him both to his country and his family. If money can be found to support him, I wish you would advise him to go to Geneva, where his principles of religion and liberty will be confirmed, and where he may stay till you see if a pardon can be procured for him. As soon as Commodore Barnes comes home, inquire for your brother Billie, and take care of him on my account. I recommend to you the payment of my debts, particularly the servant's wages, as mentioned in the state of affairs. I must again recommend to you your unhappy mother. Comfort her, and take all the care you can of your brothers. And may God of his infinite mercy preserve, guide, and conduct you and them through all the vicissitudes of this life, and after it bring you to the habitations of the just, and make you happy in the enjoyment of Himself to eternity, is the sincere prayer of your affectionate father,

"WILLIAM BOYD.

"Tower of London, August 17th, 1746."

Charles Boyd, mentioned in the above letter, was the second son of Kilmarnock. He joined the Rising, but escaped to France, and resided abroad for many years. He eventually returned home, and lived at Slains Castle. He died at Edinburgh in 1782, leaving a son and a daughter. The son mentioned as "Billie," was William Boyd, an officer in the Royal Navy at the time of his father's death.

Lady Anne, Kilmarnock's wife, did not long survive the death of her husband. She died in 1747.

SECTION IX.

JAMES, LORD BOYD, AND FIFTEENTH EARL OF ERROLL—HIS DEATH—GEORGE, SIXTEENTH EARL OF ERROLL—WILLIAM, SEVENTEENTH EARL—WILLIAM GEORGE, EIGHTEENTH EARL—VISIT OF GEORGE IV.—WILLIAM HARRY, NINETEENTH EARL—CHARLES GEORGE, TWENTIETH EARL.

THE Boyds were an old family. Robert Boyd of Kilmarnock was one of the small party who joined Bruce in the spring of 1306—the forlorn hope of the Scottish nation. The Boyd family possessed the Lordship of Kilmarnock from an early period. In the fifteenth century they had attained considerable influence and power. Sir Robert Boyd of Kilmarnock was created a Lord of Parliament in

1459; and William, ninth Lord, was created Earl of Kilmarnock in 1661.

James, Lord Boyd, fifteenth Earl of Erroll, and nineteenth Lord High Constable of Scotland, was a nobleman of striking personal form and stature, distinguished also for his amiable mind and high and generous spirit.

He was born on the 20th April, 1726. In 1749 he married Rebecca, a daughter of Alexander Lockhart, a Lord of the Court of Session, by whom he had an only daughter, Mary. She married General John Scott of Balcomie. Secondly, in 1762, his lordship married Isabella, a daughter of Sir William Carr, Bart., of Etal, Northumberland, by whom he had three sons and nine daughters. His third son, James, was accidentally drowned in 1797. Lady Charlotte married the Rev. William Holwell Carr. She died in 1800. Lady Augusta married the Earl of Glasgow, and died in 1822. Lady Maria Elizabeth married the Rev. George Moore, a son of the Archbishop of Canterbury, and died in 1804.

Earl James, as Lord High Constable of Scotland, was present and officiated at the coronation of George III., on the 22nd of September, 1761. The functions of the High Constable of Scotland at this ceremony were much the same as those described at the coronation of George II. in a preceding section. It may be remarked that on this occasion Erroll made an excellent appearance.

In 1770 he was elected one of the representative peers of Scotland. He died in 1778, and was succeeded by his eldest son, George, sixteenth Earl of Erroll. His lordship married Elizabeth, a daughter of Joseph Blake, Esq. of Ardfry, Galloway. He died on the 14th of June, 1798, leaving no issue.

The Earldom then reverted to his brother William, seventeenth Earl of Erroll. He was born on the 12th of March, 1772.

Earl William married first Jane, a daughter of Matthew

Bell, Esq., by whom he had an only daughter ; his countess died in 1793. Secondly, his lordship married Alicia, youngest daughter of Samuel Eliot, Esq., of Antigua, by whom he had three sons and four daughters. Thirdly, his lordship, on the 14th of October, 1816, married Lady Harriet Somerville, a sister of Lord Somerville, by whom he had a son and two daughters.

In 1805 Erroll was appointed Knight-Marischal of Scotland. He was elected one of the representative peers of Scotland in 1806. For several years he was Lord High Commissioner to the Church of Scotland.

His eldest son, James, Lord Hay, entered the army. He was present and engaged in the battle of Waterloo, and fell on that memorable field. The Earl's third son, Samuel, was born on the 9th of January, 1807. He also joined the army. On the 2nd of April, 1832, he married Louisa, only daughter of Vice-Admiral Duncombe-Pleydell Bouverie. He died on the 25th of November, 1847.

Lady Isabella married Lieutentant-General Wemyss on the 14th of April, 1820. She died on the 28th of July, 1868. Lady Caroline Augusta married John Morant, Esq. of Brokenhust, Hants, in 1823, and had issue. She died on the 19th of August, 1877.

Earl William died on the 26th of January, 1819, and was succeeded by his eldest-surviving son, William George, eighteenth Earl of Erroll. He was born on the 21st of February, 1801.

On the 4th of December, 1820, his lordship married Lady Elizabeth Fitzclarence, a natural daughter of King William IV., by whom he had a son and three daughters.

His eldest daughter, Lady Ida Harriet Augusta, married the Earl of Gainsborough on the 1st of November, 1841. She died on the 22nd of October, 1867. Lady Agnes Georgina Elizabeth married James Duff, fifth Earl Fife, on the 16th of March, 1846, and had issue. She died on the 18th of December, 1869. Lady Alice Mary Emily

Earls of Erroll. 269

married the Count Charles Edward d'Albanie, only son of Charles Edward Stuart, Count d'Albanie.

When King George IV. visited Scotland in August, 1822, the Earl of Erroll, as Lord High Constable, attended His Majesty and discharged the functions of the office. On this interesting occasion, the High Constable was accompanied by eight esquires on horseback, four pages, ten grooms, and 25 marshal-men on foot; and also a large company of Highlanders, placed at his disposal by the Duke of Argyle, the Earl of Breadalbane, the Countess of Sutherland, Sir Evan Macgregor, and Macdonald of Glengarry. Thus the High Constable's officers and suite presented a striking appearance. Whenever the King landed at Leith all criminal jurisdiction within four miles of the Royal presence became vested in the High Constable of Scotland. And in order that justice might be administered, the Sheriff of Midlothian, the magistrates of Edinburgh and Leith, and the Bailie of Holyrood were appointed the Constable's deputies in the office of constabulary. A great concourse of people turned out to welcome and see His Majesty on Scottish ground.

In the procession from Leith to Holyrood the Lord High Constable took precedence immediately before the King, carrying the baton of his office. The Constable claimed apartments in Holyrood Palace. Accordingly, rooms were set apart for his use, adjoining the private chambers occupied by the King. In the procession from Holyrood to the Castle of Edinburgh, the Constable rode on the right hand side of the King's carriage, carrying his baton. At the grand banquet in the Parliament House he sat on the left hand of the King, and the Lord Provost of Edinburgh sat on His Majesty's right hand.

On the 31st of May, 1831, Erroll was created a British Peer, under the title of Baron Kilmarnock of Kilmarnock, in virtue of which he had a seat in the House of Lords. The following year he was appointed Knight-Marischal of

Scotland. He was created a Knight of the Thistle and a Knight Commander of the Guelphs of Hanover. He was one of the Lords of the Royal Household, and also Lord-Lieutenant of Aberdeenshire.

He died in 1846, and his Countess died on the 16th of January, 1856. He was succeeded by his son, William Harry Hay, nineteenth Earl of Erroll. He was born in 1823. In 1848 he married Eliza-Amelia, a daughter of the Hon. General Sir Charles Gore, by whom he had issue, three sons and two daughters.

When Lord Kilmarnock, in his father's lifetime, he joined the army. In 1854, he was a major in the Rifle Brigade. He was engaged in the battle of the Alma, fought on the 20th of September, 1854, in which he was wounded in the hand.

His lordship died in 1891, and was succeeded by his eldest son, Charles Gore Hay, twentieth Earl of Erroll, Baron Kilmarnock of Kilmarnock, and twenty-fourth Lord High Constable of Scotland, of the Erroll line.

He was born in 1852. He entered the army; and was an aide-de-camp to the Commander-in-Chief, and late Lieutenant-Colonel commanding the Royal Horse Guards.

In 1874 he married Mary Caroline, youngest daughter of Edmund L'Estrange, Esq., of Tynte Lodge, and has issue. The same year he was appointed a Deputy-Lieutenant of Aberdeenshire. In 1895, the University of Aberdeen conferred on him the honorary degree of LL.D.

CHAPTER V.

Keiths, Great Marischals of Scotland, and Earl Marischals.

SECTION I.

LEGEND AND TRADITION OF THE KEITHS—NOTICE OF EARLY GREAT MARISCHALS—HERVEY DE KEITH—SIR PHILIP—SIR HERVEY—SIR JOHN—SIR ROBERT—SIR ROBERT—SIR EDWARD SIR WILLIAM—DUNNOTTAR CASTLE—SIR WILLIAM.

THE legend and tradition associated with the Keiths stretches far back into bygone ages. Tradition brings the Keiths to Scotland from the province of Hesse, in Germany, which was the home of the Catti until they were conquered by the Roman legions. After leaving Germany, they landed on the northern extremity of Scotland, where they secured a settlement, and gave the name of Caithness to the territory which they had conquered. According to the legend, their chief married a daughter of the Pictish King, Brude, who had his seat on the south side of the river Ness, on or near the old Castle Hill of Inverness; and consequently they became involved in the misfortunes which befell the Picts in succeeding generations. At length they were driven out of Caithness and into Lochaber, where many tragic scenes and deeds have been enacted. But eventually they emerged from Lochaber, and appeared in another quarter of the country.

Robert, the chief of the Catti in 1010, fought against the Norsemen, and slew Comus, the leader of the invaders, and thus gained a complete victory, for which Malcolm II.

gave him the lands of Keith in East-Lothian. He was succeeded by his son Robert, who also fought against the Norsemen in Fife.

In the period of transition from legend to records there is usually some confusion and inconsistency. Accordingly, the lists of the names of the early Great Marischals of Scotland show some discrepancy.

Hervey de Keith was Great Marischal of Scotland in the reign of William the Lion. He witnessed several charters between 1189 and 1195, and died before 1196. He was succeeded by his grandson, Sir Philip Keith, Great Marischal of Scotland. He died before 1219, and was succeeded by his son, Sir Hervey. On the 15th of July, 1220, he officiated as Marischal of Scotland at the marriage of Alexander II. to Joan of England, at York.

He died before 1250, and was succeeded by his son, Sir John Keith, Great Marischal of Scotland. As Marshal he witnessed a charter of Alexander II. He married a daughter of Alexander, Earl of Buchan, and had issue. He was succeeded by his son, Sir Robert, Great Marischal of Scotland. Before the end of the thirteenth century the Keiths had become numerous in Scotland, and a discrepancy in the family succession appears.

But in 1294 Sir Robert Keith, Great Marischal of Scotland, received a charter from King John. He was a man of great energy and ability, and took an active part in the affairs of the nation and the War of Independence. He joined Robert Bruce, and fought in the battle of Inverurie, in which he greatly distinguished himself. Shortly after this event he received a grant of lands in Aberdeenshire, including the seat called "Hall Forest" in the parish of Kintore.

At the Battle of Bannockburn Sir Robert, Great Marischal, had a very important duty to discharge. The King gave him the command of the Scottish cavalry—numbering only 500, and held in reserve for a special movement. After the English cavalry had many times furiously charged the Scottish spearmen, but were repelled, then the English bowmen and archers supported the cavalry charges by showers of arrows and stones, which severely galled the ranks of the Scottish spearmen. It was at this critical moment that Sir Robert Keith, with his 500 cavalry, advanced round the Milton Bog and charged the left flank of the archers, and, as they had no weapons with which to defend themselves at close quarters, they were instantly broken and scattered in all directions, and so utterly cowed that they declined to return to their posts, in spite of all the efforts of their leaders to rally them and restore order. They dispersed and fled headlong.

There is no reasonable doubt that the dispersion and dispiriting of the English bowmen by Sir Robert Keith's small body of cavalry was one of the main causes which contributed to the complete overthrow of the great English army on the field of Bannockburn.

Sir Robert was present at the meeting of Parliament in the Abbey of Arbroath in April, 1320, in which the memorable address to the Pope was drawn up. In this spirited and constitutional address, the following, amongst other very important sentences, occur:—" For, so long as one hundred of us remain alive, we will never consent in any way to subject ourselves to the English; since it is not for glory, nor riches, nor honours, but liberty alone that we fight and contend for, which no good man will lose but with his life."

On the 7th of November, 1324, Robert I. granted a charter of the lands of Keith Marischal to Sir Robert Keith and his heirs, and the office of Great Marischal of Scotland.

The Marischal married Barbara Douglas, by whom he had two sons, John and William. John, the elder, died in his father's lifetime, leaving a son, Sir Robert Keith. The Marischal was engaged in the battle of Dupplin, and fell on that disastrous field, on the 11th of August, 1332.

He was succeeded by his grandson (mentioned above) Sir Robert Keith, Great Marischal of Scotland. He was a man of much energy, and a warm supporter of the young King David II. against the claims and pretensions of the adventurer, Edward Baliol; and he exerted himself to the utmost to expel this intruder and disturber of the nation. He also showed an aptitude for administrative work, and was appointed Sheriff of Aberdeen.

Sir Robert married Margaret, a daughter of Sir Gilbert Hay, First High Constable of the Erroll line.

He accompanied David II. and the army which invaded England in 1346, and was engaged in the battle of Durham, on the 17th of October, and fell on the field. He was succeeded by his kinsman, Sir Edward Keith, Great Marischal of Scotland.

Sir Edward first married Isabel Keith, by whom he had two sons, Sir William Keith and John. Secondly, he married Christian, only daughter of Sir John Menteith and Ellen of Mar, by whom he had a daughter, Janet, who married Sir Thomas Erskine, ancestor of the Earls of Mar of the surname of Erskine.

The Marischal's second son, John Keith, married Mariot, a daughter of Sir Reginald Cheyne of Inverugie, and with her he obtained the lands and barony of Inverugie. Sir Edward died about 1350, and was succeeded by his eldest son, Sir William, Great Marischal of Scotland.

He married Margaret, only daughter and heiress of Sir John Fraser, eldest son of Sir Alexander Fraser, High Chamberlain of Scotland. By this lady the Great Marischal of Scotland obtained extensive estates—embracing the lands and baronies of Cowie, Durris, Strachan, and others in Kincardineshire; the lands and baronies of Aboyne, Cluny, Glentanner, Tullich, and Glenmuick in Aberdeenshire.

In 1357, the Marischal was appointed one of the Commissioners to treat with the English Government for the liberation of David II. The following year he was sent to

England touching the King's affairs. Again, in 1369, he was one of the Commissioners appointed by the Scottish Parliament to treat with England for a truce, which was arranged for a term of 14 years.

He was present and officiated at the coronation of Robert II. at Scone, on the 26th of March, 1371. He was also present at the meeting of Parliament, held at Scone, on the 4th of April, 1373, when an ordinance limiting the succession to the Crown and Kingdom to the male line was passed, "by all the bishops, earls, and barons, which ordinance was also confirmed by the consent and assent of a multitude of the people assembled in the Church of Scone, before the great altar."

Sir William gave lands in Fifeshire to William Lindsay, Lord of Byres, in exchange for the lands and Lordship of Dunnottar in Kincardineshire. He afterwards erected the Castle of Dunnottar, which became one of the chief seats of the family. The Castle was associated with interesting events and incidents which will be narrated in succeeding sections.

By Margaret, his wife, he had three sons and four daughters. His eldest son, John, married a daughter of King Robert II., by whom he had an only son, Robert; but John died before his father, and his son Robert also died before his grandfather, leaving an only daughter, Lady Jane Keith. The Marischal's second son, Sir Robert, married the heiress of Urquhart, of Troup, and had issue two sons, William and John; but Sir Robert also predeceased his father.

The Marischal's eldest daughter Muriel, married the Duke of Albany, Regent of Scotland, and by her he had a son, John Stewart, Earl of Buchan and Constable of France; his second daughter, Janet, married Philip Arbuthnott of Arbuthnott; his third, Christian, married Sir James Lindsay, Lord of Crawford; and his fourth, Elizabeth, married Sir Adam Gordon of Strathbogie—and through her, as stated in a preceding chapter) Lord Gordon inherited the Aboyne estates.

Sir William died about 1412, and was succeeded by his grandson, mentioned above, Sir William Keith, Great Marischal of Scotland. He married Mary, a daughter of Sir James Hamilton of Cadzow, by whom he had four sons and two daughters.

He was a man of remarkable ability and energy. During the minority of James II. the Marischal rendered important service to the country. When the factions of the Crichtons, Livingstons, and the Earl of Douglas were distracting the southern quarters of the kingdom, he endeavoured to secure order and peace in the north. When the King attained his majority he recognised and rewarded the Marischal's services.

Owing to so large a portion of the Keith estates having passed into the hands of Lord Gordon of Huntly, a dispute arose between him and Sir William, Great Marischal of Scotland. On the 1st of August, 1442, a meeting to settle this matter was held at Cluny, at which Sir William and Lord Gordon, and others were present. After discussion and careful consideration of the matter, an amicable agreement between the parties was concluded.

SECTION II.

WILLIAM, FIRST EARL MARISCHAL—WILLIAM, SECOND EARL MARISCHAL—WILLIAM, THIRD EARL MARISCHAL—THE MARISCHAL APPOINTED GUARDIAN OF THE KING'S PERSON—WILLIAM, FOURTH EARL—HE JOINED THE REFORMERS.

IN 1457, James II. created Sir William Keith, first Earl Marischal. He was present at the Court held in Aberdeen on the 15th of May, 1457, when Lord Erskine's claim to the Earldom of Mar was rejected.

His youngest daughter, Lady Egidia, married John, second Lord Forbes. Sir Robert, his eldest son, died in

Earl Marischals.

his father's lifetime; and the Marischal himself died in 1475. He was succeeded by his second son, William, second Earl Marischal.

In the strife and rebellion of the southern barons against James III., the Marischal acted with sound judgment and moderation. He officiated in the Parliament of 1488, in which his duties were to keep guard and order within the House when Parliament was sitting.

He married Mariota, a daughter of Thomas, Lord Erskine, by whom he had issue—four sons. From his youngest son, John, the Keiths of Craig were descended.

He was succeeded by his oldest son, William, third Earl Marischal. In 1481 he married Lady Elizabeth Gordon, second daughter of George, second Earl of Huntly, by whom he had four sons and two daughters.

His eldest son, Robert, Lord Keith, married Lady Elizabeth, a daughter of John, second Earl of Morton, by whom he had two sons, William and Robert. On the 8th of January, 1506, Lord Keith and his wife received a charter of Auchincloich, Tortoll, and other lands. His daughter Lady Elizabeth, married George, fourth Earl of Huntly, in 1530.

In 1512 Earl William received from James IV. a charter as Marischal of Scotland. His two eldest sons—Robert, Lord Keith, and William—accompanied the army mustered by James IV. in August, 1513, which crossed the Tweed on the 22nd and invaded England. But valuable time was lost in besieging and taking the English border castles of Norham, Wark, Etal, and Ford, which gave the enemy an opportunity of mustering his forces and advancing against the Scots. The English army, under the command of the Earl of Surrey, was advancing northward, and messages passed between him and James IV. Although the King was exceedingly brave and determined, as general of an army he had no qualifications whatever; his idea of leadership was simply to make a stand-up fight.

The King, in person, and on foot, led the centre of the Scottish army at the Battle of Flodden on the afternoon of the 9th of September, 1513. He himself fought with the utmost fury and bravery, till he fell mortally wounded in the head by a ball; and many of his barons, knights, and spearmen were slain around him, amongst whom were Lord Keith and his brother William.

When the tidings of this great national disaster became known in Scotland, there was mourning and lamentation among all classes throughout the kingdom. Early in October a Parliament met at Perth, at which Earl Marischal was present. It at once proceeded to the coronation of the infant King, James V., and the ceremony, in which the Marischal officiated, was performed at Scone.

At this trying time the Marischal showed a fine patriotic loyalty to the throne of his country. During the Regency of the Duke of Albany the Marischal supported his government. In 1515 he was appointed guardian of the young King's person, along with Lord Fleming and Lord Borthwick. When Albany, the Regent, visited France in 1517, the young King was conveyed from Stirling Castle to Edinburgh Castle and entrusted to the keeping of Earl Marischal and Lord Erskine.

The Marischal died in 1530, and was succeeded by his grandson (son of Lord Keith, who fell at Flodden), William, fourth Earl Marischal. He was one of the suite of Earls and Barons who accompanied James V. on his matrimonial visit to France in 1536. The marriage of the King of Scots with the Princess Magdalen, the only daughter of Francis I., was celebrated amid great pomp in the church of Notre Dame, on the 1st of January, 1537. The Kings of France and Navarre, many distinguished foreigners, and seven Cardinals, were present at the ceremony. The King stayed in France over eight months. At last he embarked at Dieppe, and landed at Leith with his beautiful Queen on the 28th of May, amid great rejoicings.

In 1541 Earl Marischal was appointed an extraordinary Lord of the Court of Session. James V. appears to have had implicit confidence in the ability and integrity of the Marischal.

The Parliament which assembled on the 12th of March, 1543, selected Earl Marischal and the Earl of Montrose, with the Lords Erskine, Lindsay, Ruthven, Livingston, and Seton, to be the keepers of the infant Queen Mary's person. The Marischal was at the same time appointed a member of the Privy Council to the Regent.

At this time the English Ambassador, Sadler, described the Marischal of Scotland "as a goodly young gentleman, and well inclined to the project of the marriage of Queen Mary with Prince Edward." He further says that "the Marischal has ever borne a singular good affection to Henry VIII."

It appears that from an early period of his life he was inclined to favour the Reformation movement. In 1544, when George Wishart, the martyr, had preached in Dundee, and was interdicted by the magistrates from preaching there again, Earl Marischal and a few other noblemen were present, and endeavoured to induce him to go with them, but he proceeded to Edinburgh.

The Marischal married Margaret, daughter and heiress of Sir William Keith of Inverugie, by whom he had two sons and seven daughters. Thus he united the Inverugie branch to the main line of the family.

He was present with his followers and friends at the battle of Pinkie on the 10th of September, 1547, in which his eldest son William, Master of Marischal, was taken a prisoner. He was confined in England until a ransom of £2000 sterling was paid for his liberation.

The Master of Marischal married Lady Elizabeth Hay, a daughter of George, seventh Earl of Erroll, and had issue, four sons and three daughters. The Marischal's second son, Robert, was made Commendator of the Abbey of Deer, which was erected into a temporal lordship; and in 1587 he was erected Lord Altire.

Mary the Queen-Mother aspired to the position of Regent of Scotland, and to promote this aim she resolved to visit the French Court. She selected Earl Marischal, the Earls of Huntly, Sutherland, Cassillis, and a number of other barons to accompany her; she embarked at Newhaven for France, and landed at Dieppe on the 19th of September, 1550. She immediately proceeded along with her suite to the French Court at Rouen, and they were received with great distinction. The Queen-Mother attained the aim of her visit to France, and returned to Scotland in the end of November, 1551. In April, 1554, she was proclaimed Regent of Scotland amid public rejoicings.

Although Earl Marischal joined the Reformation movement, it appears that he did not approve of extreme measures. He had won the respect, and even the affection of the Queen-Regent, who on her death-bed in the Castle of Edinburgh requested an interview with the leaders of the Reform movement; and the Duke of Chastelherault, the Marischal, the Earls of Argyle and Glencairn, and Lord James Stewart, Prior of St. Andrews, proceeded to the Castle, and entered her bed-chamber, and were welcomed by the dying Queen with an expression of kindness which touched their hearts. She advised them to send both the French and English armies out of the kingdom: she expressed her grief that matters had been pushed to such extremities, and ascribed this to the instructions of the French Cabinet, which she was forced to obey, though she herself would have been glad to agree to the proposals of the Scottish Lords. She advised them to adhere to the league with France. Further, she uttered many touching expressions, and asked pardon of all whom she had in any way offended, and declared that she herself freely forgave any injuries she might have received. She embraced and kissed the noblemen one by one, and extended her hand to those of lower rank, as a token of dying charity. The barons were deeply moved, and earnestly requested her to send for some godly and learned man, who might instruct and console her. The following day she received a visit from John Willock, the Reformed preacher, and she cheerfully listened to his exhortations. The succeeding day— 10th of July, 1560—the Queen Regent expired.

SECTION III.

WILLIAM, FOURTH EARL MARISCHAL—HE MOVED THE ADOPTION OF THE CONFESSION OF FAITH IN PARLIAMENT—GEORGE, FIFTH EARL MARISCHAL.

EARL MARISCHAL was present in the Parliament which met at Edinburgh in the beginning of August, 1560. This Parliament had important work before it. All those who had a right by law or custom to a seat in the House were summoned, and there was an unusually large attendance. On the 17th of August the Reformed Confession of Faith was read in Parliament. Only two of the Peers and three of the Bishops dissented; they said that time had not been given to examine the book. Earl Marischal rose and called upon the Bishops to defend the tenets of their Master: he then said :—" It is long since I had some favour for the truth, and was somewhat jealous of the Roman Catholic Religion, but this day has fully resolved me of the truth of the one and the falsehood of the other, for, seeing my lords the Bishops, who by their learning can, and for their zeal they should, hold to the truth, would, as I suppose, gainsay anything repugnant to it, yet say nothing against the Confession we have heard, I cannot but think it is the very truth of God, and the contrary of it false doctrine."

In 1562, his eldest daughter, Lady Anne Keith, married Lord James Stewart, afterwards Earl of Moray and Regent of Scotland.

Not long after, the Marischal retired to his Castle of Dunnottar, where he enjoyed a pretty quiet life. He continued, however, to administer justice in the Mearns.

In 1580 his eldest son William, Master of Marischal, died. The succeeding year the Earl Marischal himself died at an advanced age. He was succeeded by his grandson, George (eldest son of William, Master of Marischal), fifth Earl Marischal.

He was born in 1553, and studied at King's College, Aberdeen. Afterwards he was sent to France with his brother William, where he stayed for some time, and extended his studies and the scope of his mind. Thence he proceeded with his brother to Geneva, and George became a pupil of the distinguished classical scholar Theodore Beza. It is stated that he formed a very favourable opinion of the abilities of his pupil. After the two brothers had stayed a considerable time in Geneva, a very sad incident happened, for in a tumult amongst the citizens William Keith was killed. After the death of his brother, who was a youth of great promise, George left Geneva. He then travelled in Italy and in Germany, and returned to Scotland.

After he succeeded to the Marischalship he took an active part in public affairs. He took an interest in Church matters and the work of the General Assembly. In 1582 he was appointed a member of the Privy Council.

James VI. became exceedingly anxious to get married and have a queen of his own. Queen Elizabeth desired to counsel and advise the young King as to whom he should marry. But he thought that in so important a matter he should have the liberty of choice, and act on his own feeling and judgment. Accordingly, in July, 1589, the King sent Earl Marischal accompanied by a grand suite, to Copenhagen to conclude the matrimonial match between His Majesty and the Princess Anne of Denmark, and convey her across the sea to Scotland.

When the Scottish Ambassador arrived in Denmark, he found that the Danish Court was exceedingly anxious touching the marriage, and it was soon arranged. For a time great bustle prevailed in the Court. The Princess's mother, the Queen, was especially active—buying silk, cheapening jewellery, or "urging on a corps of 500 tailors, who sat daily stitching and getting up the most princely apparel." Women, guards, and pages, who were to form the suite of the royal bride, were ordered to hold themselves in readiness. A fleet of twelve vessels, with brass cannon, was fitted out to transport the Princess to Scotland. King James forwarded to his Ambassador a mild remonstrance touching the smallness of the Princess's dowry. The Danish Court, however, declined to add anything to it. At last the squadron, with the young Princess on board of one of the ships, sailed for Scotland; but a terrific storm arose, which disabled the ships, and forced them to land on the coast of Norway, and the voyage for a time was abandoned. When tidings of this reached James VI., he was excited and disappointed. Indeed he felt strongly inclined to punish and execute all the Scottish witches, who, he said, by their unlawful rites and incantations had raised the tempest which delayed his bride. He was in extreme anxiety; and finally he resolved to brave the waves of the ocean himself.

Accordingly, on the 22nd of October, 1589, he embarked at Leith, accompanied by a select suite of his nobles and his favourite minister, Rev. David Lindsay. He landed at Upsal on the 27th, and immediately rode to the palace where his bride awaited him, and "hurried, booted and spurred, into her presence, and, in the fashion of Scotland, attempted to kiss her." The marriage was celebrated in the church of Upsal, on the 23rd of November, 1589, and the ceremony was performed by the Rev. David Lindsay. The King was easily persuaded not to risk himself and his new Queen to the dangers of a winter voyage, and he remained over eight months in Denmark. In the spring he embarked on his voyage home, accompanied by his Queen and a retinue of Danish nobles and ladies, and arrived at Leith on the 1st of May, 1590.

The Marischal's uncle Robert, Lord Altire, for whom the Abbey lands of Deer were erected into a Lordship, having died in 1589, leaving no male issue, his nephew thus became heir to the Lordship. Accordingly, the King regranted it to Earl George—"as a perpetual monument of his service in connection with the marriage of His Majesty."

In 1593 Earl Marischal and the Earl of Athole were appointed Lieutenants-General of the north. At this time the conflict between the Government and the Roman Catholic Earls was going on, and there was much disturbance and disorder in the north.

In 1604 he was one of the Scottish Commissioners nominated to treat with the English Commissioners touching a union of the two kingdoms. He was appointed Royal Commissioner to the Scottish Parliament, which met at Edinburgh in June, 1609. This Parliament restored the consistorial courts to the bishops.

On the 14th of January, 1619, a commission was given to George, Earl Marischal; William, Lord Keith; the Sheriff of Kincardine and his deputies, the Sheriff of Aberdeen and his deputies, the Captain of the Guard and his company, Sir Robert Arbuthnott of Arbuthnott, Sir Thomas Menzies, and the Provost of Aberdeen, "to apprehend Duncan Forbes, and his servant, James Abirdour, who were put to the horn at the instance of Nicolace Horne as relict, George and William Keith as sons, Margaret, Geillis, and Sara Keith as daughters, John Bannerman, spouse of the said Geillis; John Forbes, spouse of the said Sara; and the remaining kin of the late Gilbert Keith of Loristoun, for not finding caution to appear to answer the charge of having murdered the said Gilbert Keith.

The Marischal was Sheriff of Kincardineshire, and, on

the 18th of January, 1820, a commission was given to him and Lord Ogilvie, the Sheriff of Forfarshire and their deputies; and to the magistrates of Dundee and Brechin, each to act within his jurisdiction—to apprehend and try Thomas Bowman, "a common sorner and vagabond, haunting for the most part within the bounds of Glenesk," who was on the 1st of January denounced as a rebel at the instance of Margaret Blacklaw, relict, Alexander Brockie, son, and Christian, Margaret, Isobel, and Janet Brockie, daughters, with the rest of the kin and friends of the late William Brockie of Craigeouthill, for failing to find caution to appear before the Justice for stealing from the said William Brockie a milk cow, and for the cruel and odious slaughter of him.

On the 14th of June, 1621, Earl Marischal was charged by the Lords of the Privy Council to keep the peace, some disputes having arisen between him and neighbouring landlords. The matter is stated in the register thus :—" Forasmuch as it is understood by the Lords of Council that there is great appearance of trouble and unquietness likely to fall out between George, Earl Marischal, on the one side, and Alexander Irvine of Drum on the other; and also between Earl Marischal and Douglas of Glenbervie, touching the casting of petes, and building of houses, and pasturing upon lands controverted, and such matters, which might receive a civil decision before the ordinary judge : But the said parties, disdaining the ordinary course of law prosecution, and maintaining of their right and possession, they intend by the convoking and assistance of their kin and friends, and in a violent manner, to do their turn : Whereupon great inconvenience cannot fail to occur, the break of His Majesty's peace, and disturbing of the country : Therefore the Lords of Council ordain letters to be directed charging the said parties to appear personally before the Council and answer to the premises, and abide by such order as shall be taken for the peace and quietness of the country, under the penalty of rebellion : And in the meantime to command and charge the said parties to observe our Sovereign Lord's peace, keep good rule and quietness in the country, and that none of them presume to molest one another, nor attempt anything hurtful to the peace, under the following penalties :—viz., Earl Marischal under the penalty of 10,000 merks, and each of the other parties under the penalty of 5000 merks."

SECTION IV.

GEORGE, FIFTH EARL MARISCHAL—HIS FOUNDATION OF MARISCHAL COLLEGE—HIS DEATH—WILLIAM, SIXTH EARL MARISCHAL—ACTED AT THE CORONATION OF CHARLES I.—WILLIAM, SEVENTH EARL—HE JOINED THE COVENANTERS—HOW THE REGALIA WAS PRESERVED.

ALTHOUGH George, fifth Earl Marischal, was occasionally embroiled in the feuds of the time, yet he served his King and country admirably. He was a man of the world, as we have seen in a preceding section. Among the Scottish barons of his time he was reputed the wealthiest and most distinguished for learning and culture. Having himself experienced the advantages of education, and keenly felt the blessing which it would impart to the nation, he resolved to found a new educational institution in his native country.

During the last forty years of the sixteenth century great and memorable efforts were made to improve and extend the blessing of education to all classes of the people, and with this movement the name and fame of the fifth Earl Marischal is honourably and justly associated.

His foundation charter of Marischal College is dated the 2nd of April, 1593. It indicated the advantages of education, which, in the northern quarters of Scotland, was then deficient. He expressed his desire to found at New Aberdeen a public gymnasium, in which young men might be thoroughly trained and instructed in the humane arts, and also in philosophy and a purer piety, "under the charge of competent and learned teachers, to whom shall be given from our endowment such salaries as may be required."

The original endowment consisted of—"The manse and offices, glebes, yards, cloisters, church, and walls, which formerly belonged to the Franciscan Friars, commonly called the Grey Friars, of Aberdeen, as they are bounded and marked off by walls lying on the east side of the street called the Braid Gate; all the lands, crofts, roods, rigs, orchards, barns, dovecots, tenements, houses, buildings, yards, acres, annual rents, feu-duties, kilns, offices, and others whatsoever, belonging to the Preaching and the Carmelite Friars of Aberdeen, commonly called the Black and White Friars; and the estates and lands belonging to us in Bervie, once the Chaplainry of Bervie, and also the Chaplainry of Cowie, commonly called St. Mary's, belonging to us. . . To be held of us and our successors, Earls Marischal, in pure and perpetual alms, rendering therefor only the offering of pious prayers."

At the end of the foundation charter, the Marischal says:—"We forbid any perpetual leasing out of land or feus, whether on pretext of augmentation or improvement, or for any other reason, or under any name whatsoever." In this he showed his remarkable sagacity, and the only regret is that his wise provision was not adhered to.

Earl Marischal married, first, Lady Margaret, a daughter of Alexander, Lord Home, by whom he had a son, William, and two daughters. Lady Anne Keith married William, Earl of Morton, and Lady Margaret married Sir Robert Arbuthnott of Arbuthnott. Secondly, he married Margaret, a daughter of James, Lord Ogilvie of Airlie, by whom he had a son, Sir James Keith of Benholm.

In the latter years of his life he lived in retirement at the castle of Dunnottar. But, sad to say, the evening of the Marischal's life was clouded by domestic troubles. Sir

James Keith of Benholm behaved extremely ill to his aged father, who was forced to complain against him to the Lords of the Privy Council. The Marischal died at Dunnottar Castle on the 2nd of April, 1623.

He was succeeded by his eldest son, William, sixth Earl Marischal. In 1623 he issued a charter ratifying his father's provisions to Marischal College; but recalled the important grants of the Chaplainry of Bervie and the Chaplainry of Cowie.

The Marischal was called by a letter from the Privy Council to attend a meeting at Edinburgh on the 9th of July, 1623. This meeting was to consider the ways and means of establishing manufactures in Scotland, especially the woollen manufacture. He was appointed a member of the Privy Council by Charles I.

Touching the report of the Commissioners on the privileges, functions, and duties of the High Constable, presented to Charles I. in July, 1631: on the 21st of the month Robert Keith, writer to His Majesty's signet, appeared before these Commissioners as counsel for William, Earl Marischal, and in name and behalf of the earl protested:—" That nothing to be done by the said Commissioners in the trial and report to be made by them to His Majesty touching the privileges due and belonging unto the office of Constabulary, should be prejudicial to the Earl Marischal—touching the rights, liberties, and privileges due and belonging unto him in right of his office as Marischal of the Kingdom, whereof he and his predecessors have been in possession, or which has been controverted and not decided, and whereunto it shall be found, after lawful trial, that the said Earl has just right. This protestation the Commissioners thought reasonable; whereupon Robert Keith, in name and behalf of the Marischal, asked and took instruments in the hands of me, Mr. Gilbert Primrose, clerk of His Majesty's Privy Council, and to the Commissioners before mentioned."

The Marischal officiated at the coronation of Charles I. at Edinburgh on the 18th of June, 1633, and in the ceremony performed the part which belonged to his office. He walked and rode on the left hand of the King.

He married Lady Mary Erskine, a daughter of John, Earl of Mar and High Treasurer of Scotland, by whom he had four sons, William, George, Robert, and John (who eventually became Earl of Kintore), and three daughters. Lady Mary married John, Lord Kilpont, son and heir of William, Earl of Menteith and Airth; and Lady Jean married Alexander, Lord Pitsligo.

The Marischal died on the 28th of October, 1635, and was succeeded by his eldest son, William, seventh Earl Marischal. He was in France when his father died. Returning through England, he stayed for some time at the Court of Charles I. When he arrived in Scotland the nation was in a state of great excitement, and shortly after entered on the momentous Covenanting Struggle.

The Marischal was then a youth in his 20th year, animated with all the glowing feelings and aspirations which entrance the mind of the young and vigorous man. In the winter of 1639, he hospitably entertained a committee of the Covenanters at Dunnottar Castle, who were returning south from a meeting held at Turriff on the 14th of February. The Marischal then joined the Covenanters. In the month of March he accompanied the Covenanting army under the command of the Earl of Montrose, which marched northward toward Aberdeen. The Marquis of Huntly held Aberdeen for the King, but on the approach of Montrose at the head of a superior force, he rode out of the city with 100 horse to Inverurie, where 5000 Royalists had mustered. A party of the Covenanters took possession of Aberdeen, and visited the colleges. A number of the leading citizens fled from the town and offered their services to the King, while others sought refuge in houses in the neighbourhood of the city. The main body of the army under Montrose and Earl Marischal, advanced to Kintore, and encamped at Tilty.

The Marquis of Huntly sought an interview with Montrose, and they met on the 4th of April, and the following day a compromise was arranged between them. But a few days later Huntly was invited to Aberdeen, and entrapped by Montrose, and conveyed a prisoner to Edinburgh.

Afterwards, Earl Marischal mustered the Covenanters of Angus and Mearns; while the Aberdeenshire Covenanters mustered and encamped in the vicinity of Aberdeen. Earl Marischal and the Forbeses took possession of Aberdeen; and on the 25th of May they were joined by the Earls of Montrose, Kinghorn, and Athole, Lord Drummond, the Master of Gray, and the Constable of Dundee. Their combined force numbered over 6000 men. Yet the position of parties in Aberdeen and the north again changed. Early in June, 1639, the Covenanters retired from Aberdeen, and the city fell into the hands of the Royalists.

The Marischal continued to act on the side of the Covenanters till 1645, when he joined the Royalists and supported the cause of the King.

After the surrender of Charles I. to the English Parliament, the Scots sent Commissioners, in the end of December, 1647, to make a last attempt to treat with the King, then a captive in the Isle of Wight. He now promised to be the Covenanted King of the Presbyterians, and entered into a treaty with the Scots, but it came too late; and it was regarded as an act of treachery to the Long Parliament and the English army, with whom the King was at the same time openly treating. This underhand treaty with the Scots is known in history as "the Engagement."

Parliament met at Edinburgh in March, 1648, and agreed to the Engagement, and commissioned an army to aid the King. The commission of the General Assembly opposed this, and proclaimed that the King's concessions were incomplete. They demanded that the King should take the Covenant himself, and immediately establish Presbyterianism in England. Parliament, however, ordered the army to muster and fight for the King, and the Duke of Hamilton was placed in command of the force.

Earl Marischal raised a troop of horse and joined the army, and his brother George also accompanied it. The army marched into England in several divisions, at too long distances from each other. Cromwell attacked the Scots at Preston on the 17th of August, 1649, and completely defeated them. Earl Marischal and his brother escaped with difficulty from the disastrous field. But the Duke of Hamilton was taken prisoner; and, shortly after, he was tried and beheaded.

On the 23rd of June, 1650, Charles II. arrived at the mouth of the Spey. There he signed the Covenant and Solemn League and Covenant, and landed the following day. Thence he proceeded southward, and was met by Earl Marischal, who entertained the King at Dunnottar Castle.

The Marischal officiated at the coronation of Charles II. at Scone, on the 1st of January, 1651. On this occasions as usual, the Marischal was on the left hand side of the King, and the High Constable on the right. As part of the coronation ceremony, the King again swore to maintain the National Covenant and the Solemn League and Covenant.

As the Scots were unable to drive back the English army in Scotland under Cromwell, they resolved to make a raid across the Border. But Earl Marischal was hereditary custodier of the Crown jewels (Regalia), and after being used at the coronation, the Earl placed them for safety in the Castle of Dunnottar, and the King forbade the Marischal to leave his charge of the castle. But his brother, George Keith, accompanied the King and the Scottish army into England. Cromwell, with a part of his force, followed the Scottish army, and on the 3rd of September, 1651, a battle ensued at Worcester, in which the Scots and English Royalists were defeated. The Marischal's brother, George, was taken prisoner, sword in hand, fighting heroically. The King escaped and fled to the Continent.

Earl Marischal himself was taken in Scotland, by Cromwell's officers, conveyed to England, and imprisoned in the Tower of London for nine years. His estates were seized by Cromwell's Commissioners, and the rents and revenues lifted by them. So, during the nine years that the Marischal was imprisoned, his mother had to supply the means of his support.

Shortly before he was imprisoned, he appointed George Ogilvie of Barras Governor of the Castle of Dunnottar. As Cromwell's force was rapidly subduing the kingdom, it was feared that he would seize and carry off the Regalia. But Mrs. Ogilvie devised a plan to get it removed out of the castle, without the knowledge of her husband, that he might not be compromised when it was missed. The castle was besieged before she got the scheme carried into effect. She took into her counsel the Rev. James Grainger, minister of Kinneff, and his wife. One day the minister's wife went past Dunnottar, on horseback, to Stonehaven for flax to spin, accompanied by a servant woman to carry the flax. When returning, she asked leave of the commanding officer of the beseiging army to visit Mrs. Ogilvie in the castle, and was permitted to pass followed by her servant with the bag of flax. On reaching the Governor's quarters, the servant was relieved of her burden and sent to another apartment, until the two mistresses transacted their business, which was to place the regalia in the bag of flax. When Mrs. Grainger returned from the castle, through the lines, the officer on duty kindly assisted her to mount her horse; while the servant knew nothing of what had occurred, or that she was carrying the crown, sceptre, and sword of the kingdom of Scotland in her flax-bag. On reaching the manse of Kinneff, the mistress took the bundle. That very night the minister and his wife made a receptacle for the regalia beneath the pulpit of the church. Sometimes it was hid there and at other times in a double-bottomed bed in a room in the manse until the Restoration in 1660, when it was returned to George Ogilvie of Barras, who restored it to the Court.

SECTION V.

WILLIAM, SEVENTH EARL MARISCHAL—LIBERATED FROM PRISON—HIS DEATH—GEORGE, EIGHTH EARL—HIS DEATH—WILLIAM, NINTH EARL—AN OPPONENT OF THE UNION—GEORGE, TENTH EARL—HE JOINED MAR'S RISING—EARL MARISCHAL ABROAD—SKETCH OF THE CAREER OF FIELD-MARSHAL KEITH.

WHEN the Restoration came, in 1660, Earl Marischal was liberated from the Tower of London. Charles II., appointed him a member of the Privy Council, and in other ways conferred on him many marks of respect.

The Marischal married Elizabeth, a daughter of George, Earl of Winton, by whom he had four daughters:—Lady Mary married Sir James Hope of Hopetoun; Lady Elizabeth married Robert, Viscount Arbuthnott; Lady Jane married George, Lord Banff; and Lady Isabel married Sir Edward Turner, an English Baronet.

He died at Inverugie in 1661, and was succeeded by his brother, George, eighth Earl Marischal. He married Lady Mary Hay, a daughter of George, Earl of Kinnoull, by whom he had an only son.

Earl George was a man of much energy, and had suffered a long period of exile on account of his adherence to the cause of Charles II. He was one of the members of the Commission appointed by Parliament to visit the Scottish Universities in 1690. He was one of the committee selected to make inquisition of the University of Aberdeen; and this committee met at King's College on the 15th of

October, 1690. Professor Garden declined to recognise their jurisdiction, appealed to the General Assembly, and refused to sign the Confession of Faith.

The Marischal died at Inverugie in 1694, and was succeeded by his son, William, ninth Earl Marischal. He was an exceedingly kind and open-handed nobleman.

On the 8th of August, 1700, he endowed a Chair of Medicine in Marischal College—"Taking into our consideration the weal, utility, and profit of our said College, and resolving to advance and promote the good thereof, and to encourage the profession and teaching of all sciences therein."

He was a firm opponent of the Union between England and Scotland, and entered a protest against it in the following terms:—"I do hereby protest that whatever is contained in any article of the Treaty of Union between Scotland and England shall in no way derogate from, or be prejudicial to, me or my successors in our heritable office of Great Marischal of Scotland, in all time coming, or in the full possession and exercise of the whole rights, dignities, powers, and privileges thereto belonging, which my ancestors and I have possessed and exercised as rights of property these 700 years. And I do further protest that the Parliament of Scotland and constitution thereof may remain and continue as heretofore. And I desire that this my protestation may be inserted in the minutes and records of the books of Parliament."

In 1710 he was elected one of the Representative Peers of Scotland.

He married Lady Mary, a daughter of James Drummond, Earl of Perth, and High Chancellor of Scotland, by whom he had two sons and two daughters:—Lady Mary married John, Earl of Wigton; and Lady Anne married Alexander, Earl of Galloway.

He died on the 27th of May, 1712, and was succeeded by his eldest son, George, tenth Earl Marischal.

Earl Marischals.

In the reign of Queen Anne, Earl Marischal was appointed Captain of Her Majesty's Guards. After the accession of George I. he was removed from his post. He had doubtless taken offence at this treatment, being a young and high-spirited nobleman; while his mother was a daughter of the Earl of Perth, one of the great Jacobite families, and no doubt she had influenced the action of her sons. Accordingly the Marischal joined Mar's rising with a troop of horse, mostly raised in Buchan; and his only brother, James Francis Edward Keith, also joined the rising.

On the 20th of September, 1715, Earl Marischal, accompanied by a number of noblemen, entered Aberdeen and proceeded to the Cross and there proclaimed the accession of James VIII. to the throne of his ancestors. The depute-sheriff read the proclamation, at night the city was illuminated, and the bells of St. Nicholas Tower were rung in honour of the new king. On the succeeding day, Earl Marischal and his party were hospitably entertained by the members of the Incorporated Trades; and in the afternoon they accompanied him to his mansion of Inverugie. The professors and regents of the two colleges were nearly all Jacobites; but the magistrates were inclined to continue loyal to the Government. The majority of the citizens of Aberdeen of that day, however, appear to have been Jacobites, and they took the command of the city.

Earl Marischal returned to Aberdeen on the 28th of September, and arrangements were immediately made for the election of a Jacobite Town Council. In the new Church of St. Nicholas a head court of the burgh was held, and the election of a council proceeded. Those nominated by Earl Marischal were installed in the offices, and Patrick Bannerman assumed the functions of Lord Provost of the city in the name of James VIII.

On the 2nd of October the kirking of the new council came off in the West Church, in which the King's loft was.

Special care was taken to place well-disposed ministers in the pulpits. In the forenoon Dr George Gordon officiated, in the afternoon the Rev. Robert Blair preached, and both of them prayed for King James.

Earl Marischal commanded two squadrons of cavalry at the battle of Sheriffmuir. His brother James was wounded in this engagement; and shortly after he made his escape to France. On the failure of the rising, the Marischal also escaped to France; but he was attainted, and his estates forfeited to the Crown.

Cardinal Alberoni was at the head of the Government of Spain, and promised to declare war against England. Spain recognised the Pretender as King of Great Britain; and the Cardinal undertook to land a force in Scotland. Earl Marischal and his brother were invited to serve in the Spanish army. A fleet consisting of ten ships of war was equipped, and a number of transports, which had on board a force of about 6000 men, many of whom were Irish. The fleet sailed for Scotland on the 7th of March, 1719, and the Duke of Ormond had command of the expedition, as captain-general for the King of Spain.

But a storm off Cape Finisterre dissipated the Spanish fleet, and only a small force effected a landing in the Western Highlands, and a few Seaforth Highlanders joined them. Earl Marischal intended to surprise Inverness and capture it; but the Government was well prepared, and the capital of the Highlands was defended by loyal troops. The small army took up a position in the pass of Glenshiel, and attempted to make a stand. They were soon attacked by the Government troops, driven from height to height, and defeated. Earl Marischal and other officers retired to the Western Isles, and after lying concealed for some time, he escaped to Spain. He resided a number of years in Spain, and was sometimes employed in the service of the Spanish Government. In 1745 he left Spain and visited Vienna. Shortly after, he went to

Prussia, where he was kindly received and employed by Frederick the Great.

This seems to be the proper place to present a brief sketch of the remarkable career of Earl Marischal's brother, James Francis Edward Keith—Field-Marshal, and one amongst the greatest men of his time in Europe. He was born in the Castle of Inverugie, in the parish of St Fergus, Aberdeenshire, in 1696. As stated in a preceding paragraph, he joined the rising of 1715, and, after the battle of Sheriffmuir, escaped to France. For some time he studied military tactics in Paris. He went to Spain in 1719, and joined the Spanish army, in which he attained the rank of colonel. But on account of his religion (being a Protestant) there was little hope of further promotion in the Spanish army. Accordingly he resolved to seek another country where military abilities and personal merit alone would determine the rank of an officer.

Colonel Keith fixed his mind on Russia, and only requested the court of Madrid to give him a recommendation to the court of St. Petersburg, which was readily granted. He arrived in Russia in 1729, and immediately received the brevet of major-general. He soon gained the favour of the young Emperor Peter II., who gave him a lieutenant-colonel's commission in a newly raised regiment of guards. Shortly after, he was made colonel of the regiment.

The revolution, which occurred in Russia in 1730, did not effect Keith's promotion. After the death of Peter II., Anne, a daughter of Ivan IV., was made Empress, and she was very favourable to Colonel Keith.

In 1733 the election of a King of Poland caused a war, in which Russia took the side of Augustus, a son of the late King, against Stanislaus. General Lacy (a Scotchman) was ordered to enter Lithuania with a Russian army. On the 12th of September, Stanislaus was elected King, and the Russian troops then advanced into Poland. Keith served under his distinguished countryman General Lacy, who had complete confidence in him. The Russian army forced Stanislaus and his followers to abandon Warsaw on the 22nd of September. On the 5th of October, Augustus was elected King of Poland, and on the 10th Lacy and his army entered Warsaw. Fifteen thousand men were left in Poland; while Lacy marched into Prussia with the main body of the army. Dantzic and other towns were besieged. On the 7th of July, 1734, Dantzic surrendered on terms. Keith greatly distinguished himself at this siege; and in November he was made a lieutenant-general.

SECTION VI.

GENERAL KEITH'S CAREER IN RUSSIA—HE ENTERED THE SERVICE OF FREDERICK THE GREAT—MADE FIELD-MARSHAL—HIS DEATH AND CHARACTER—EARL MARISCHAL IN THE SERVICE OF PRUSSIA—HIS VISIT TO SCOTLAND—HE BECAME HEIR TO THE EARLDOM OF KINTORE—AGAIN VISITED SCOTLAND—RETURNED TO PRUSSIA—HIS DEATH.

IN 1736 a war arose between Russia and the Porte, owing to the incessant raids and ravages of the Turks and Tartars into Russian territories. In the end of March, General Munich, with a strong Russian force, was before Asoph. The Tartars advanced to relieve it, but Munich marched to meet them. Another large army, under the command of Lacy and General Keith, reached Asoph on the 4th of May; the siege was vigorously pushed on, and the place surrendered on the 20th of June. Munich defeated the Tartars in several battles, and advanced into Crim-Tartary. In this region he had many skirmishes, and took a number of strong positions.

Afterward he returned to the Ukraine, and placed his army in winter quarters along the Dnieper. Munich then left to General Keith the chief command of all the Russian forces in the Ukraine, and proceeded himself to St Petersburg. Thus Keith was entrusted with very difficult service, which showed the implicit confidence placed in his abilities. He had to preserve the troops from a contagious malady, to protect them from the continual raids of the Turks and Tartars, and also to prepare everything for the campaign in the succeeding spring. Keith performed his difficult work effectively, and had everything ready for the opening of the campaign of 1737, much earlier than usual.

Munich, the Commander-in-Chief, joined the army in March. He resolved to fight the Turks himself, and General Keith accompanied him; while General Lacy was to handle the Tartars. Munich crossed the Dnieper early in May, and the Hypanis on the 20th of June, and advanced upon Ockakow, in which there was a garrison of 20,000 men. It was invested on the 30th of June; the approaches were pushed on with the utmost vigour, and the town was taken by assault on the 2nd of July. In this action General Keith distinguished himself, and was severely wounded. This disabled him from serving in the army for a considerable time.

General Keith's health was for a time broken by his wounds, and in the hope of restoring it, he went to France. But he was charged with the management of some State affairs, relating to the war between Russia and Sweden. He had also orders (as soon as his health permitted) to proceed to England and conduct important State affairs. He arrived at London in February, 1740, and on the 15th he was presented to His Majesty, George II., who received him very graciously. He was no longer regarded as a Scottish rebel. He was received as a great general, and as the Minister of a great Power. On the 14th of May he had his audience of leave, and he left London on the 18th, and thence proceeded directly to St Petersburg.

While Keith was in London, peace was concluded between Russia and Turkey. This event was celebrated in St Petersburg on the 25th of February, 1740. The Empress gave presents to all the great officers, and General Keith, though absent, was not forgotten. He received a gold-hilted sword valued at £1500 sterling. Yet his services were not considered adequately rewarded, and he was appointed Governor of Ukraine. In July he left St Petersburg, and proceeded to the province entrusted to his charge.

On the 28th of October, 1740, the Empress Anne died. The Government then fell into the hands of Biron, but General Keith declined to recognise his authority. The governor of the Ukraine was beloved by a numerous people, and it would have been difficult to reduce him by force. Biron's rule, however, only continued 22 days. Then the mother of the young Emperor took the administration into her own hands as Regent; and presented to Keith another sword more valuable than the former one.

In 1741 war broke out between Russia and Sweden. In August, Field-Marshal Lacy appeared before Wyburg with an army of 80,000 men; and among the ablest generals in the army was Keith. A strong body of the Russian army, under Wrangel, advanced to attack the Swedish van, and on the 3rd of September a battle ensued. The Swedes fought bravely, but the Russians defeated them. General Keith was much admired for his conduct and courage in this battle; and his annual income was increased by the Government.

After the battle, Lacy took Williamstraud, and then returned to the camp at Wyburg. Afterward he marched the greater part of the army to the vicinity of St Petersburg, leaving General Keith before Wyburg with the rest of the troops, and Generals Stoffel and Fermor under him. This showed the confidence which Marshal Lacy had of the military abilities of General Keith.

Meantime there was a revolution in St Petersburg. On the 25th of November, 1741, Elizabeth, a daughter of Peter the Great, mounted the Throne. General Keith immediately recognised the new Empress, and took the oath of allegiance.

General Keith was engaged in several other battles against the Swedes. But, on the 7th of July, 1743, peace was concluded between Russia and Sweden.

But Denmark threatened war against Sweden, and the Swedish King demanded aid from Russia. The Empress Elizabeth granted 10,000 men, and gave the command of them to General Keith. He embarked in Finland with his force, and appeared before Stockholm in October, 1744, and was treated with much distinction. He was then acting as Commander-in-Chief of the Russian forces, and as plenipotentiary for his Sovereign at the Court of Sweden. "He acquitted himself in each of these characters entirely to the satisfaction of both Courts." He was highly esteemed by the King of Sweden; and on New Year's Day His Majesty presented to him a very fine sword. After he had brought all the affairs entrusted to him, to a satisfactory issue, and had his audience of leave on the 23rd of June, 1745, he received another sword, the prince's portrait, and £1000 sterling. The Russian troops commenced their march homeward on the 2nd of August, and, on arriving at St Petersburg, the Empress gave an exceedingly gracious reception to her General and Ambassador.

In 1747 Earl Marischal, visited his brother in Russia, and they then resolved to spend the remainder of their lives together as far as possible. Accordingly General Keith asked his dismission, and obtained it. He left St Petersburg, passed through Copenhagen, and arrived at Berlin. As stated in a preceding section, his brother, Earl Marischal, was at this time in Prussia.

At his first interview with Frederick the Great, His Majesty quickly realised the great abilities of General Keith. The King immediately seized the opportunity of gaining him to his service. On the 18th of September, 1747, the King made him Field-Marshal; in October, 1749, he appointed him Governor of Berlin, and conferred on him the Order of the Black Eagle. The Marshal's income then was 12,000 crowns—£2400 sterling.

The Marshal was much esteemed and greatly admired in Berlin. The Royal Academy of Berlin enrolled his name in the list of its honorary members. Thus he enjoyed a few years of quiet life, almost the only ones throughout his illustrious career.

In August, 1756, the King of Prussia took possession of Saxony, and Marshal Keith accompanied him. The column which Keith commanded joined the other divisions of the army before Pirna; thence they advanced into Bohemia. Keith reached the camp at Aussig on the 19th of September, and took the command-in-chief. The King arrived on the 28th, and the Battle of Lowositz was fought on the 1st of October, in which Marischal Keith was by the King's side. The King returned to Saxony on the 13th of October, and Keith retained the chief command in Bohemia.

On receiving orders from the King, Keith marched the army back into Saxony, and on the 23rd of October, joined the King at Linay. The army was then placed in winter quarters.

In the campaign of 1757, the Prussians advanced into Bohemia through four different passes. Marshal Keith was with the King, and after various marches, the army reached the White Mountains before Prague. On the 6th of May, a great battle was fought under the walls of Prague. The Prussians gained a complete victory, and the vanquished Austrians fled into the city. Prague was besieged. But strong and desperate sallies were made against the besiegers. On the night, between the 23rd and 24th of May, a strong and furious attack was made on the quarter where Marshal Keith commanded. The engagement was fiercely contested for several hours, but at last the enemy was driven back to within 300 yards of the fortifications. It was mainly by the admirable command and valour of Keith that the victory was won.

The siege was continued, though there was little hope of taking a city so well fortified, and defended by a force of 40,000 men. A retreat was resolved on, which Marshal Keith successfully executed, in spite of the attempts of the enemy to harass him, without losing any of his men. On the 22nd of June he reached Baden, thence he marched into Saxony, and joined the King on the 12th of August in Lusatia.

A French army was approaching Saxony, and the King advanced to cover it, and Marshal Keith accompanied him. They had a comparatively small army, while French and Austrian armies were in the field against them. Marshal Keith marched to Leipsic, carefully observing the movements of an army greatly superior in numbers to his. Having received reinforcements, he continued to advance, and joined the King at Roseback on the 3rd of November. On the 5th a great battle was fought, in which the Prussians—numbering about 20,000 men, under the command of the King and Marshal Keith, completely defeated the combined armies of the French and Austrians—numbering 60,000 men. Many of the French and Austrians were slain.

In the beginning of 1758, the King conferred with Marshal Keith touching the operations of the ensuing campaign. Keith took part in this campaign until he was attacked by sickness. When partly recovered, he joined the King at Breslau, and shortly after the King defeated the Russians.

The Prussians were encamped between Bantzen and Hochkirchen. On the night of the 14th of October, the Austrians, under the command of Marshal Daun, surprised the Prussians in the quarter where Marshal Keith commanded. The noise of the cannon alarmed Keith, who instantly mounted his horse and hastened where his presence was most necessary—in the midst of danger. The battle raged with terrible fury. Marshal Keith received two wounds in the groin, and a cannon ball brought down his horse. Efforts were made to place him again on horseback, but he fell down among the hands of those who were assisting him, and expired on the battlefield. General Lacy descried the body of the Marshal in the midst of the slain, and it was interred on the field with military honours. Afterward the King had his remains disinterred and conveyed to Berlin, where, on the 3rd of February, 1759, new obsequies were performed, amid great funeral pomp and solemnity.

A fine statue of the Field-Marshal was erected in Berlin. Some years after his death, a monument was erected to his memory in the churchyard of Hochkirchen, by Sir Robert Murray Keith.

Although it was chiefly in military affairs that Field-Marshal Keith excelled, yet, in many other respects he was a very accomplished gentleman. "He spoke English, French, Spanish, Russian, Swedish, and Latin, and was able to read the Greek authors. . . He had seen all the Courts of Europe, great and small, from that of Avignon, to the residence of the Khan of Tartary, and accommodated himself to every place, as if it had been his native country. . . But that which ought to render his memory for ever precious is that he was a hero extremely humane; never omitting to do anything in his power that might soften and alleviate the calamities of war, lessen the number of its miseries, and in some measure relieve those whom it had rendered wretched." Amen.

Resuming the sketch of Earl Marischal's life abroad. In 1751 Frederick the Great, King of Prussia, appointed him Ambassador to France. In 1752 he received from the King the Order of the Black Eagle, and was appointed Governor of the principality of Neufchatel, in Switzerland. He was appointed Ambassador from Prussia to Spain in 1759. When at the Spanish Court he discovered the secret of "The Family Compact," by which the branches of the House of Bourbon bound themselves to assist and defend each other to the utmost of their power. He communicated this intelligence to the British Cabinet, and shortly after left Spain and returned to Prussia.

On the 29th of May, 1759, the Marischal received a pardon from George II. The same year an Act of Parliament was passed to enable him to inherit any estates that might devolve to him. His own estates had been sold, but the Government gave him an equivalent of over £3000.

The Marischal arrived at London in June, 1760, and on the 15th he was presented to His Majesty George II., who graciously received him. He visited Scotland. On arriving at Peterhead he proceeded to the Bridge of Inverugie, but could go no further, and sent his secretary to examine the state of the castle, who found it to be in ruins. The recollections of his childhood and youth overpowered the brave man, and he wept over the ruins of his once stately residence.

On the death of the fourth Earl of Kintore, and the failure of male issue in 1761, Earl Marischal became heir to the estates of the earldom. He stayed for some time in Scotland, but was back to Prussia in 1762. He again returned to Scotland in August, 1763, and repurchased some of his estates with the intention of settling in his native land. But Frederick the Great was extremely anxious that Keith would return to Prussia. Accordingly, on the 15th of May, 1764, the silver plate belonging to Earl Marischal at Keithhall — consisting of household utensils and articles, were packed up, to be sent to Hamburg by his orders, and the Marischal himself returned to Prussia. He was greatly esteemed by Frederick the Great, and spent the evening of his days in peace and comfort. On the 28th of May, 1778, he died unmarried in his 86th year. Thus terminated the main lineal line of one of the oldest and most illustrious families of Scotland.

CHAPTER VI.

Earldom and Earls of Findlater, and Seafield.

SECTION I.

TERRITORY OF THE EARLDOM—EARLY NOTICE OF THE OGILVIES— SIR WALTER OGILVIE OF AUCHLEVEN—HIS SON, SIR WALTER —SIR JAMES—HIS FAMILY—SIR JAMES—SIR ALEXANDER, HIS SETTLEMENT OF THE ESTATES TO SIR JOHN GORDON—QUARREL BETWEEN THE GORDONS AND OGILVIES, JAMES OGILVIE—SIR WALTER, FIRST LORD DESKFORD—JAMES, SECOND LORD.

THE lands of the Earldom of Findlater originally consisted of the baronies of Findlater and Deskford, in the parishes of Deskford and Fordyce. Subsequently the territory of the earldom was considerably increased. In 1517, by a charter from the Crown, the baronies of Findlater, Deskford, Keithmore, Auchindoun, Glenfiddich, and other lands, with the constabulary of Cullen, fishings on the river Deveron, the lands of Ballhall and others in Forfarshire, were incorporated into one free barony, to be called the barony of Ogilvie. On the accession to the title and the estates of the earldom by Sir Lewis Alexander Grant of Grant, of course, the possessions of the historic chief of the Grants greatly extended the territories of the earldom.

The Earls of Findlater and Seafield were descended from a branch of the Airlie family. At an early period the Ogilvies appear to have settled in Forfarshire, and their surname occurs in the national records about the middle of the thirteenth century. Before the end of the fourteenth century Sir Walter Ogilvie of Aucherhouse was high sheriff of Forfar. He was a man of much energy and ability. While endeavouring to maintain law and order, he lost his life in the following circumstances:—Duncan Stewart, a natural son of Alexander, Earl of Buchan and Lord of Badenoch, led a party of his followers across the mountains which divide the counties of Aberdeen and Forfar, and plundered the lowlands of Forfarshire. Again, in 1392, Duncan appeared with a company of his followers on a pillaging raid; but the landed gentry, headed by Sir Walter Ogilvie, the sheriff, mustered and met him at Gasklune, near the water of Isla. A fierce encounter ensued, in which the lowland party were completely defeated, and the sheriff, his brother, and 50 of their followers were slain on the field.

Sir Walter Ogilvie of Lintrathen was the second son of Sir Walter of Auchterhouse. He was Lord High Treasurer of Scotland in 1425, and Master of the King's Household in 1430. He married Isabel Durward, the heiress of Lintrathen, by whom he had two sons—Sir John, who succeeded to his father's estate, and Sir Walter, the direct ancestor of the Earls of Findlater.

This Sir Walter Ogilvie held the lands of Auchleven, in the parish of Premnay, of the Earl of Mar. In 1437 he married Margaret, a daughter and heiress of Sir John Sinclair, laird of Deskford and Findlater, who was killed at the battle of Harlaw. Thus, through his wife, he obtained these two baronies, and added the arms of Sinclair of Deskford to that of Ogilvie. In 1440 he received two charters from James II. of the lands and baronies of Findlater and Deskford.

By his wife he had two sons and one daughter. His second son, Sir Walter Ogilvie of Boyne, was the ancestor of Lord Banff, and of William Ogilvie of Strathearn, Lord High Treasurer of Scotland.

He was succeeded by his eldest son, Sir James Ogilvie

Earls of Findlater.

of Deskford and Findlater. In 1473, he got a charter of the lands of Blairshinnoch from James III. Subsequently he received charters of other lands; and he purchased the constabulary of Cullen from John Hay, on which he obtained a charter from James III. in 1481.

Sir James married Mary, a daughter of Sir Robert Innes of Innes, by whom he had four sons and five daughters. His second son, Gilbert, became laird of Glassaugh; the third, Alexander, was killed at the battle of Flodden; and the fourth, George, entered the Church. His eldest daughter, Margaret, married James Abercromby of Birkenbog; Marian married Partick Gordon of Haddo; Catherine married William Crawford of Fedderate, Aberdeenshire; Elizabeth married John Grant of Freuchie; and Mary married Alexander Urquhart, sheriff of Cromarty.

He died about 1489, and was succeeded by his eldest son, Sir James. In 1490, he received a charter of the lands and barony of Keithmore, in the parish of Mortlach, and afterwards charters of Langmuir and other lands.

He married a daughter of George, second Earl of Huntly, by whom he had five sons and two daughters. His eldest daughter, Elizabeth, married Sir James Dunbar of Westfield; and the second married the laird of Mackintosh, and had issue.

Sir James died in 1510, and was succeeded by his eldest son, Sir Alexander. In 1517 he received a charter from the Crown by which the baronies of Findlater, Deskford, Keithmore, Glenfiddich, Auchindoun, and other lands, with the fishings on the Deveron and the water of Ythan, the constabulary of Cullen, in the counties of Banff and Aberdeen, and the lands of Ballhall and others in Forfarshire, were all incorporated into one free barony, called the barony of Ogilvie—"To him and the heirs male of his body; whom failing, to his brothers, James, John, Patrick, and George; whom failing, to Gilbert Ogilvie, his uncle; whom failing, to his own nearest heirs male, whatever."

He married, first, Lady Janet Abernethy, a daughter of James, third Lord Saltoun, by whom he had a son, James, and a daughter, Elizabeth, who married Sir Alexander Irvine of Drum; secondly, he married Elizabeth Gordon, a daughter of Adam Gordon, Dean of Caithness, third son of Alexander, first Earl of Huntly.

As indicated by the charter quoted above, his son, James Ogilvie of Cardell, was the lawful heir-apparent to the barony of Ogilvie. But his father thought fit to disinherit him, and probably his second wife, who was a Gordon, had influenced her husband in such conduct. In 1546, Alexander settled the whole lands of the barony on Sir John Gordon, third son of George, fourth Earl of Huntly, only reserving his own and wife's life-rent. Sir John Gordon was to assume the name and arms of Ogilvie, and, failing his male issue, the succession to the barony was to devolve to his brothers, William, James, and Sir Adam; whom all failing, then to revert to Sir Walter Ogilvie of Boyne, Sir Walter Ogilvie of Dunlugus; whom all failing, to James, fifth Lord Ogilvie of Airlie.

After the death of Alexander Ogilvie, Sir John Gordon married his widow, Elizabeth Gordon, and took possession of the estates. Naturally, James Ogilvie, the lawful heir, considered that he was unjustly disinherited, and a bitter quarrel arose between the Gordons and the Ogilvies, which contributed considerably to the eclipse of the Huntly family.

The Queen Regent, Mary of Lorraine, attempted to settle the matters in question between Ogilvie and Gordon, but she failed. James Ogilvie was Steward of Queen Mary's household, and he raised an action in the Court of Session to recover the estates from Sir John Gordon. The case was to come before the court in July, 1562, and Sir John Gordon was in Edinburgh and met James Ogilvie in the street. A fight ensued, in which Ogilvie was wounded, and Gordon was imprisoned. On the 25th of July Gordon escaped from prison. He persistently declined to surrender himself, and his action tended much to bring matters to a crisis against the Earl of Huntly.

James Ogilvie accompanied Queen Mary in her progress to the North in 1562; and he was very active in bringing the Ogilvies from Angus and the Mackintoshes in Inverness-shire to her assistance. But Sir John Gordon, when summoned by the Queen to surrender the castles of Findlater and Auchindoun, declined to comply; he also refused to admit the Queen to Findlater Castle. So a company of troops under the command of Captain Stewart was sent to take possession of Findlater Castle; but on the 21st of October Sir John Gordon attacked and defeated them. Sir John Gordon, however, surrendered after the battle of Corrichie, and shortly after he was executed at Aberdeen.

The estates of Findlater and Deskford, and others were forfeited to the Crown, but Sir Adam Gordon, in virtue of the deed of settlement of Alexander Ogilvie, then claimed the estates. But, on the 8th of February, 1563, Queen Mary granted a charter of the whole of the lands and baronies of Findlater, Deskford, and others to James Ogilvie of Cardell, the lawful heir. In spite of this charter, the Gordons still claimed part of Ogilvie's lands; but, on the 23rd of March, 1566, the matters in question between Ogilvie and Gordon were settled by a submission to a decret-arbitral, which assigned to James Ogilvie the land and baronies of Findlater and Deskford, and to Sir Adam Gordon the lands of Auchindoun and Keithmore.

James Ogilvie married Mary Livingstone, of the Livingstone family, one of the ladies who attended Queen Mary to France, by whom he had a son, Alexander. He married Barbara, a daughter of Sir William Ogilvie of Boyne, by whom he had a son, Sir Walter. Alexander died before his father, thus Sir Walter succeeded James Ogilvie, his grandfather.

He was a favourite of James VI. In 1594 the King

granted to him a charter of the lands and barony of Keithmore and Auchindoun. Notwithstanding this charter, the Gordons retained possession of these lands, which still form a part of the estates of the Duke of Richmond and Gordon.

He married, first, Agnes, a daughter of Robert, Lord Elphinstone, by whom he had an only daughter, Christina, who married Sir John Forbes of Pitsligo: Secondly, he married Lady Mary Douglas, a daughter of William, Earl of Morton, by whom he had a son and two daughters. Margaret married James Douglas, Earl of Buchan; and Mary married Sir John Grant of Grant.

On the 4th of October, 1616, Sir Walter Ogilvie was elevated to the peerage under the title of Lord Ogilvie of Deskford. He was succeeded by his son James, second Lord Deskford.

He married Lady Elizabeth Leslie, a daughter of Andrew, Earl of Rothes, by whom he had two daughters. Lady Elizabeth married Sir Patrick Ogilvie of Inchmartin, and had issue; and Lady Anne married William, Earl of Glencairn.

On the 20th of February, 1638, Lord Ogilvie of Deskford was created Earl of Findlater by Charles I., by a patent limited to his heirs male.

SECTION II.

JAMES, FIRST EARL OF FINDLATER—HE JOINED THE COVENANTERS—HE OBTAINED A NEW PATENT—PATRICK, SECOND EARL OF FINDLATER—JAMES, THIRD EARL—HIS FAMILY—JAMES, FOURTH EARL OF FINDLATER AND FIRST EARL OF SEAFIELD—A DISTINGUISHED NOBLEMAN—SECRETARY OF STATE, PRESIDENT OF PARLIAMENT, LORD HIGH CHANCELLOR.

IN the early stage of the Covenanting struggle, the Earl of Findlater appeared in company with the Marquis of Huntly on the Royal side. But on the 16th of March, 1639, the Marquis published his Commission of Lieutenancy, and

Earls of Findlater.

summoned by proclamation all the King's loyal subjects, between the ages of 16 and 60, to muster and meet him at Inverurie on the 25th, with 15 days' provisions. The Earl of Findlater failed to appear, and shortly after, he joined the Covenanters.

He was appointed one of the committee for considering the national debt in November, 1641 ; and in 1644, one of the Committee of the North for prosecuting those opposed to the Covenant. In 1645, he was elected a member of the Committee of Estates — the body who controlled the government of the Kingdom when Parliament was not sitting.

In 1641 he received a charter of the lands of the Earldom from the Crown, and in 1644 he obtained a ratification of the bailiary of Strathisla.

Earl James having no male issue, obtained a new patent from Charles I. on the 18th of October, 1641, which conferred the succession to the earldom on his son-in-law, Sir Patrick Ogilvie of Inchmartin, and to their heirs male. Accordingly, after the death of Earl James, Sir Patrick Ogilvie of Inchmartin, in Perthshire, became second Earl of Findlater. Sir Patrick's ancestors had been in possession of the estate of Inchmartin since the middle of the 14th century. On the 30th of May, 1623, he received a commission of justiciary from the Privy Council to try John Smyth, miller in Craigdaylie, who had cruelly slain John Morton in Westerton of Inchmartin. The criminal being apprehended red-handed, he was handed over to Sir Patrick Ogilvie, who was the lord of them both.

Sir Patrick was a member of the Standing Commission appointed by the King and the Privy Council on the 18th of July, 1625, for the introduction of new manufactures into Scotland, and the improvement of the existing manufactures, especially the woollen manufacture. He was also a Justice of the Peace for Perthshire and the Stewartries of Menteith and Strathearn.

When he succeeded to the Earldom of Findlater, and came to the North, he was a firm supporter of the Royal cause; and, consequently, he was exempted from pardon by Cromwell, and fined a sum of £1500 sterling.

Earl Patrick died in 1658, and was succeeded by his son James, third Earl of Findlater. He married first Lady Anne Montgomery, only daughter of Hugh, seventh Earl of Eglinton, by whom he had three sons and one daughter. His eldest son, Lord Deskford, died before his father, unmarried. His third son, Colonel James Ogilvie of Lonmay, married Elizabeth, a daughter of Francis Montgomery of Giffen and had issue. His daughter, Lady Anne, married George Allardyce of Allardyce, and had issue. Secondly, his lordship married Lady Mary, a daughter of William, second Duke of Hamilton, by whom he had no issue.

He died in 1711, and was succeeded by his eldest surviving son, James, fourth Earl of Findlater. He was born in 1664. He studied law, and sojourned abroad for a considerable time completing his education. In 1685 he returned home, and was called to the Scottish Bar. He was a man of remarkable energy and ability, and soon attained distinction. He was elected member for the burgh of Cullen to the Convention of Estates, summoned by William of Orange, which met at Edinburgh on the 14th of March, 1689. He distinguished himself by a vigorous speech in favour of King James VII., and he was one of the five members who dissented from the resolution which declared the throne of Scotland vacant. Yet his adherence to James VII. did not prejudice him in the eyes of William of Orange; on the contrary, he soon became a favourite of the new King. In 1693 he was appointed Solicitor for the Crown and Sheriff of Banff, and also received the honour of knighthood.

In 1695 he was appointed Secretary of State for Scotland. He was appointed President of Parliament in

1699, and in the same year he was created Viscount Seafield. On the 24th of June, 1701, he was created Earl of Seafield and Viscount Reidhaven, with remainder in default of direct heirs male, then to heirs general.

He was appointed Royal Commissioner to the General Assembly of the Church of Scotland in 1700, and he was thrice reappointed to this high honour. In 1703 he was created a Knight of the Thistle.

In 1704 he was appointed Lord High Chancellor of Scotland, and held this office till the Union between England and Scotland was completed. In 1705 he was nominated by Queen Anne one of the Scottish Commissioners to treat with the English Commissioners touching a Union between England and Scotland. These Commissioners numbered 62, being 31 for England and 31 for Scotland. They met at Whitehall on the 16th of April, 1706, and sat for three months, discussing and framing the articles of the important Treaty of Union.

The Earl of Seafield also presided in the session of the Scottish Parliament which passed and ratified the Treaty of Union. While he was Lord Chancellor he presided in the Court of Session. As a Senator of the Supreme Court, it is recorded that he manifested eloquence, great legal ability, and a remarkable faculty of despatching business.

In 1708 Seafield was appointed Chief Baron of the Exchequer Court in Scotland, with a salary of £3000 per annum. He was elected one of the sixteen Scottish Representative Peers in the first Parliament of the United Kingdom of Great Britain, and he was re-elected to the four succeeding Parliaments.

On the death of his father, in 1711, he became fourth Earl of Findlater and first Earl of Seafield. In 1713 he was again appointed High Chancellor and Keeper of the Great Seal of Scotland.

It is a notable circumstance that the Earl, who had taken so active a part in promoting the passing of the Treaty of

Union, by his own effort placed it in some danger of being dissolved. When, in 1713, the Malt Tax was extended to Scotland, he considered this was an infringement of the Articles of the Union. And, on the 1st of June, he delivered a vigorous speech in the House of Lords upon the grievances of the Scottish nation, which he presented under four heads :—(1) The abolition of the Privy Council of Scotland : (2) the introduction of the treason laws of England into Scotland ; (3) the prohibition of the peers of Scotland from being created peers of Great Britain ; (4) the introduction of the Malt Tax, which would be more oppressive on the Scottish people now, seeing that it was not imposed on them during the war, and therefore they had every reason to expect the benefits of peace. In concluding he said, since the union had not been followed by the beneficial effects which were expected, he moved that leave should be given to introduce a bill for dissolving it and securing the Protestant succession in the House of Hanover, preserving the Queen's prerogative in both kingdoms and a good understanding between England and Scotland. A division was taken on the motion. There were 108 peers present, who were equally divided—54 in favour of the motion and 54 against it ; there were 30 proxies, and 13 voted for the motion and 17 against it. Thus his lordship's motion was only defeated by the narrow majority of four votes.

There was a bitter and determined feeling amongst the great majority of the Scottish people against the Malt Tax. For many years, in spite of all the efforts of the excise officers, the sum collected from this tax in Scotland fell short of the expense connected with it, and not a fraction from the Malt Tax in Scotland reached the Imperial Exchequer.

Earl James cleared off all the burdens and debts on the family estates, and considerably extended the possessions of the house.

He married Anne, daughter of Sir William Dunbar of

Earls of Findlater and Seafield.

Durn, Bart., by whom he had two sons and two daughters. His eldest, daughter, Lady Elizabeth, married Charles, Earl of Lauderdale, and had issue. Lady Janet married Hugh Forbes, son and heir-apparent of Sir William Forbes of Craigievar; secondly, she married William Duff of Braco, afterwards first Earl Fife.

His Lordship died in 1730, in the sixty-sixth year of his age, and was succeeded by his eldest son, James, fifth Earl of Findlater and second Earl of Seafield.

In 1734 he was elected one of the representative peers of Scotland to the British Parliament, and he was re-elected to the three succeeding Parliaments. In 1737 he was advanced to the post of Vice-Admiral of Scotland, an office which he held for a period of 27 years. He was a loyal and stedfast supporter of the King and the Government throughout his life.

Indeed, he suffered much loss for his loyalty in the rising of 1745-6. On the 8th of April a party of the insurgents arrived at Cullen House and ransacked it thoroughly. They broke into the rooms and closets, forced open the presses, trunks, and cabinets, and the big charter chest. They carried off a number of papers and a great deal of booty. The Earl estimated the loss which he had suffered from the insurgents at £8000 sterling, and in a petition to Parliament craved redress; but there is no evidence that he received anything.

SECTION III.

JAMES, FIFTH EARL OF FINDLATER AND SECOND EARL OF SEAFIELD—HIS FAMILY, MARRIAGE OF HIS DAUGHTER TO THE LAIRD OF GRANT—HIS DEATH—JAMES, SIXTH EARL—HIS EFFORTS TO INTRODUCE IMPROVEMENTS—HIS DEATH—JAMES, SEVENTH EARL—SIR LEWIS ALEXANDER GRANT—DEATH OF EARL JAMES—SUCCESSION OF SIR LEWIS ALEXANDER GRANT.

EARL James married Lady Elizabeth Hay, a daughter of Thomas, sixth Earl of Kinnoull, by whom he had a son and two daughters. His eldest daughter, Lady Margaret Ogilvie, married Sir Ludovick Grant of Grant, Bart., on the 31st of October, 1734. This was a very important marriage, and some details associated with it are quite in character. The marriage gave much satisfaction to the Earl of Findlater, who on the occasion wrote to the chief of the Grants thus :—

"The constant and uninterrupted friendship which has always been between our families, and the great esteem I justly have both for you and your son, makes the honour you do me of proposing a third alliance between our families most agreeable, and it is with great pleasure that I renew our ancient ties of relation and friendship." After the consummation of the marriage, the Earl again wrote :—"I have the pleasure to acquaint you that your son was married on Monday last. We made all possible despatch, because of his being obliged to be so soon in Edinburgh. . . I have great satisfaction in this alliance, because it strengthens and renews the ancient friendship which has constantly been between our families, and which the instructions of my father and grandfather had made habitual to me from my infancy. There is sincerely nothing I wish more heartily than the prosperity of your family, and that my daughter may have the happiness of contributing to it according to her duty. My wife and my son join with me in offering you their humble services, and I am, with the greatest truth and esteem, dear sir, your most faithful and obedient humble servant,

FINDLATER AND SEAFIELD."

On the same occasion the famous Lord Lovat, who was related to the Chiefs of Grant through marriage, wrote to Sir James Grant as follows:—

"My Dear Sir James,—It is with inexpressible joy that I congratulate you on the marriage of your eldest son to the Earl of Findlater's daughter, whom I believe is the best match in Scotland. She is a young lady not only beautiful in her person, but much more by her good sense and understanding, and by her sweet and even temper, which I hope will make him as happy as he was before, and I could not wish him better. He sent me an express to go and solemnise the infer at Castle Grant with the Earl and Countess of Findlater and his other friends; but my chariot-wheels being broke I could not go but on horseback, and that I durst not venture without the imminent danger of my life—which would be no service done him or to your family—which I am resolved to stand by while there is breath in me. . . . I got here last night and my best friends of the Aird and Stratherick, and put on a very great bonfire on the castlehill, and there drank heartily to the bridegroom and bride and your health and my Lord Findlater's, and, in short, to all the healths that we could think of that concerned the family of Grant, and then had a ball, and concluded with most of the gentlemen being dead drunk. We fired a random platoon at every health that was drank at the bonfire, where I stood an hour and a half, and drank my bottle without water—and while the bonfire was burning. I having sent my officers to the three parishes, all the country of the Aird and Great Barony of Beauly was, I am sure, better illuminated than London was on the 30th of October. . .   I had at once in this country about 200 bonfires, which made as pretty a figure as ever I saw of fireworks. . . . After our earthly rejoicings we should all thank heaven for this happy event. May God bless them and give them a very numerous offspring, and may you see their grandchildren. . . —

Yours against all quarrels,

LOVAT."*

The descendants of this marriage eventually succeeded to the Earldom of Seafield.

Earl James died in 1764, and was succeeded by his only son, James, sixth Earl of Findlater and third Earl of Seafield. He was born in 1714, and completed his education by travelling abroad.

In 1761, when Lord Deskford, he was appointed Chancellor of the University and King's College, Aberdeen, and held the office for nine years.

He was appointed one of the Commissioners of Custom in Scotland in 1754; he was one of the trustees for the improvement of manufactures and fisheries; and also a member of the Board of Commissioners for the management of the forfeited estates in Scotland. He directed his attention to the business of these boards with much energy and commendable assiduity. Through his efforts linen manufacture was introduced in Cullen in 1748, and in 1752 he established a bleachfield at Deskford.

His lordship made many efforts to introduce improved methods of agriculture on his estates in the lower district of Banffshire. Until the later part of the last and the first quarter of the present centuries there was no regular rotation of cropping, while all the agricultural implements and appliances in use were of a very primitive description. The Earl, while Lord Deskford, introduced the alternate method of cropping, and he was also among the first to introduce the culture of turnips.

* "The Chiefs of Grant," by Wm. Fraser, LL.D., voi. ii., pp. 125, 428, 337.

Earls of Findlater and Seafield.

He married Lady Mary Murray, a daughter of John, First Duke of Athole, by whom he had issue. Earl James died at Cullen House, on the 3rd of November, 1770, in his 56th year, and was succeeded by his only surviving child, James, Seventh Earl of Findlater and Fourth Earl of Seafield.

At Brussels, in 1779, he married Christina Teresa, a daughter of Joseph, Count Murray of Melgum, but had no issue.

On the 6th of September, 1787, Burns stayed a night in Cullen when on his Highland tour. On the 14th of December, 1788, Sir James Clark, Bart., M.D., was born in Cullen House, where his father was butler. He received the elements of education in the parish of Fordyce, and became a distinguished physician.

It appears that the Earl was on the best terms with his heir-apparent, Sir Lewis Alexander Grant, who, in the beginning of March, 1789, visited the Earl at Cullen House. On the occasion of the first appearance of Lewis at the Scottish Bar, in January, 1789, the Earl of Findlater wrote to Sir James Grant (Lewis's father) thus :—" I cannot delay congratulating you on the brilliant appearance which Lewis has made on his entry to the Bar. Mr. Mackenzie wrote me wonders about it, and Mr. Davidson wrote me that nothing had ever been heard equal to it for wit, judgment, and eloquence . . . I thought it proper to write Lord Henderland, acknowledging my gratitude for the public commendations he had given of it . . ." The Earl in another letter says :—" I wrote my young friend not to go on as he had began, otherwise the vanity of belonging to him would prolong my life 20 years beyond its natural course."

Earl James died at Cullen House on the 5th of October, 1811, leaving no issue, and the titles of Earl of Findlater and Viscount of Seafield, which were limited to heirs-male, then became extinct. But the titles of Earl of Seafield and

Viscount Reidhaven, created by the patent of 1701, were not so restricted, and accordingly devolved with the whole of the family estates on Sir Lewis Alexander Grant of Grant, Bart., a grandson of Sir Ludovick Grant of Grant, and his wife, Lady Margaret Ogilvie. Thus Sir Lewis Alexander Grant became fifth Earl of Seafield, Viscount Reidhaven, and Lord Ogilvie of Deskford and Cullen, and assumed the surname of Ogilvie.

At this stage it is requisite to present a brief account of the Chiefs of Grant prior to their succession to the Earldom of Seafield. This will form the subject of a few sections.

SECTION IV.

EARLY NOTICE OF THE GRANTS—THEIR TERRITORIES—CHIEFS OF GRANT—PATRICK GRANT—JOHN GRANT—SIR DUNCAN GRANT OF FREUCHIE—JOHN GRANT OF FREUCHIE—JAMES OF FREUCHIE—JOHN OF FREUCHIE—DUNCAN GRANT—JOHN OF FREUCHIE—LANDS OF ROTHIEMURCHUS—SIR JOHN OF FREUCHIE—JAMES GRANT OF CARRON—DEATH OF SIR JOHN.

THE Grants appear in the national records about the middle of the 13th century. They do not claim a Celtic origin, though they became a great clan; and they were at one time or other associated with many of the Highland clans.

Sir Laurence the Grant and Sir Robert Grant appear as witnesses to a deed dated 1258. Sir Laurence the Grant was Sheriff of Inverness in 1263, which then embraced an extensive and important jurisdiction, including the counties of Inverness, Ross, Sutherland, and Caithness. He was also Baillie of Inverquoich; and in 1266 he rendered an account for it to the Crown.

The Grants have been connected with Strathspey for a period of over six centuries, and it was and still is their main district. Yet it was not in Strathspey that the

Chiefs of Grant. 323

Grants first appeared in Scotland. So far as has been ascertained, their original possession was Stratherrick, a district in Inverness-shire, lying on the south-eastern side of Loch Ness. In 1357 Patrick Grant was Lord of Stratherrick, and probably it had been possessed by his grandfather, Sir Laurence Grant, Sheriff of Inverness. The lands of Stratherrick continued in the possession of the Grants till 1419, when they passed into the hands of the Frasers.

In the reign of Robert I. John Grant had acquired possession of the lands of Inverallan, in Strathspey, the first territory which the Grants obtained in this region. And gradually by grants from the Crown, by purchase, and in other ways, they acquired possession of the greater part of the lands in Strathspey—from Laggan, to a considerable distance beyond lower Craigellachie, which stands near the confluence of the Fiddoch with the Spey. Upper Craigellachie marks the boundary between Badenoch and Strathspey, and was the meeting-place for the Clan Grant in time of war. The war-cry of the clan was—" Stand fast, Craigellachie"; and the onset of Craigellachie was not easily withstood.

Sir Duncan Grant was called Laird of Freuchie in a precept addressed to him on the 31st of August, 1453, touching the infeftment of John Hay in certain lands in the earldom of Moray. He was the first Grant called Laird of Freuchie, and his successors became the recognised chiefs of Grant. He was a man of energy and ability, and extended the possessions of the family.

He married Muriel, a daughter of Malcolm, tenth chief of the Mackintoshes, by whom he had issue, one son and two daughters. His eldest daughter, Catherine, married Lachlan Mackintosh of Badenoch, and had issue. Muriel married Patrick Leslie of Balquhain, and had issue.

Sir Duncan Grant died in 1485, and was succeeded by his grandson, John Grant of Freuchie. He was an able and determined man, and played his part well for a period of 43 years.

He was on intimate terms with the second and third Earls of Huntly, and had several transactions with them touching the lands of Urquhart and Glenmoriston, in Inverness-shire, and other matters.

In January, 1494, he resigned all his lands into the hands of the king, who regranted them to him and his heirs, incorporating them all into a barony, to be called the Barony of Freuchie. On the 8th of December, 1509, James IV. granted a charter of the lands and barony of Urquhart and Glenmoriston, to John Grant, laird of Freuchie, and his sons.

He married Margaret Ogilvie, a daughter of Sir James Ogilvie of Deskford, in 1484, by whom he had two sons and five daughters. His daughter Anne married Hugh Fraser, Master of Lovat; Agnes married Donald Cameron, the chief of Clan Cameron.

John Grant, second laird of Freuchie, died in May, 1528, and was succeeded by his son James, third laird. He also extended the family possessions.

He married twice, his first wife being a daughter of John, sixth Lord Forbes, and his second was Christina Barclay, and by these wives he had four sons and five daughters. He died on the 26th of August, 1553, and was succeeded by his eldest son John, fourth laird of Freuchie.

On the 30th of October, 1554, he was appointed baillie of the Abbey of Kinloss, an office which his father had held. He was present at Holyrood with the Earl of Huntly on the night of the 9th of March, 1566, when David Rizzio was slain. He joined Queen Mary's party after her flight into England, and acted with the Earl of Huntly. In 1569 he received from the Earl of Huntly a gift of the Abbey of Kinloss, with all its pertinents.

He married, first, Lady Margaret Stewart, a daughter of John, third Earl of Athole, on the 19th of February,

1539; and, secondly, he married Lady Janet Leslie, a daughter of the Earl of Rothes, and by his two marriages he had two sons and seven daughters.

His eldest son, Duncan Grant, married Margaret, daughter of William Mackintosh of Dunnachton, by whom he had issue, five sons and two daughters. In 1578 Duncan Grant acquired the lands of Ardneidlie, Corsairtly, and Cowperhill, in the parish of Keith. He died at Abernethy in the spring of 1582, and was interred in the family vault at Duthil.

John Grant died on the 3rd of June, 1585, at Ballachastell, and was interred at Duthil. He was succeeded by his grandson, John Grant (son of Duncan, noticed above) fifth Laird of Freuchie.

The possession of the lands and barony of Rothiemurchus had long been a matter of dispute between the Mackintoshes and the Grants. On the 14th of June, 1586, the Laird of Mackintosh entered into an agreement with the Laird of Freuchie, by which Mackintosh resigned all rights he had to the lands and barony of Rothiemurchus; and he also became bound to assist in guarding the lands of Urquhart, Glenmoriston, and other lands belonging to the Grants, against the raids of the Clan Cameron, Clan Donald, or others. On the other hand, the Laird of Freuchie undertook to infeft Mackintosh in certain lands in Lochalsh and Kessoryne, and in the castle of Strome, with office of constable, which had come into the possession of the Lairds of Freuchie. The Laird of Freuchie further undertook to uphold the Laird of Mackintosh in peaceable possession of Lochaber against the Clan Cameron and all others, excepting the King and the Earl of Huntly.

John Grant greatly extended the territory of the family. In 1606 he acquired the lower portion of the lordship of Abernethy from George, First Marquis of Huntly, by exchanging for it the lands of Blairfindy and others in Strathavon. And in 1609 he made arrangements with the Earl of Moray, by which he obtained a charter of the lands and lordship of Abernethy, and in return for it paid the earl a sum of money. The same year he purchased the lands and barony of Cromdale from Thomas Nairn.

He married Lady Lilias Murray, a daughter of Sir John Murray of Tullibardine, by whom he had a son and four daughters. Agnes was born in 1594; she married Sir Lachlan Mackintosh of Dunnachton, and had issue. Her tocher was 10,000 merks. Jean married William Sutherland of Duffus, and had issue. Lilias married Sir Walter Innes of Balveny, and had issue.

The laird died on the 20th of September, 1622, and was interred at the Church of Duthil. He was succeeded by his only son, Sir John Grant, sixth laird of Freuchie. He was born on the 17th of August, 1596.

In his time there was often strife and disorder in the north, and Sir John was frequently involved in these troubles. He was convener of the Justices of the Peace in the counties of Inverness and Cromarty, and he was also sometimes entrusted with special and general commissions of justiciary in his own and other districts. He exerted himself to keep order in his own territories.

But one of his own clan, James Grant of Carron, locally called James an Tuim (of the Hill), was an extremely turbulent character. His acts of violence caused much trouble to Sir John Grant. At last James an Tuim was captured, conveyed to Edinburgh, and imprisoned in the Castle. His trial, however, was postponed for some time, and one night he made his escape from Edinburgh Castle, and returned to Strathspey. He was proclaimed an outlaw, and great efforts were made to capture him dead or alive. He committed more deeds of violence, and eluded all the attempts to capture him. Eventually, through the influence of the Marquis of Huntly, James an Tuim obtained a remission of all his crimes from Charles I. in 1639, and afterwards he entered the service of the Marquis against the Covenanters.

Sir John Grant married Mary, a daughter of Sir Walter Ogilvie of Findlater, and afterwards Lord Ogilvie of Deskford, by whom he had seven sons and three daughters. His eldest daughter Mary married Lord Lewis Gordon, afterwards third Marquis of Huntly, and had issue, George, who was created first Duke of Gordon, and two daughters.

In March 1637, he went to Edinburgh, and on his arrival he was imprisoned on a charge of not pursuing the Clan Gregor, but shortly after he was liberated. He died at Edinburgh on the 1st of April, 1637, and was interred in the Chapel of Holyrood.

SECTION V.

JAMES GRANT, SEVENTH LAIRD--JOINED THE COVENANTERS—LUDOVICK GRANT OF FREUCHIE—HIS MARRIAGE—A MEMBER OF PARLIAMENT—SUMMONED FOR NONCONFORMITY—AN ACTIVE MEMBER OF THE REVOLUTION—CONVENTION, RAISED A REGIMENT—BATTLE OF CROMDALE—REGALITY OF FREUCHIE—CASTLE GRANT—DEATH OF LUDOVICK—COLONEL ALEXANDER GRANT OF GRANT—ONE OF THE UNION COMMISSIONERS—A MEMBER OF PARLIAMENT.

SIR JOHN GRANT was succeeded by his eldest son, James Grant of Freuchie. He was born on the 24th of June, 1616. He joined the Covenanters, which caused him much loss. Owing to the district in which his estates lay, they were often traversed by the contending armies. When Montrose raised the Royal Standard, and mustered an army, Grant, with the aim of saving his lands from pillage, promised to support him. But after the Restoration in 1660, he was excluded from the Act of Indemnity, and the Govenment imposed on him the enormous fine of £18,000 Scots.

On the 24th of April, 1640, he married Lady Mary Stewart, only daughter of James, Earl of Moray, by whom he had two sons and three daughters. He died at Edinburgh in the end of September, 1663, and was interred in the Chapel of Holyrood.

He was succeeded by his eldest son, Ludovick, eighth laird of Freuchie. He was a minor at the time of his father's death; but in virtue of a dispensation from the King, on the 23rd of May, 1665, he was retoured heir to his father in all the lands of Freuchie, Mulben, Urquhart, and others in accordance with the Royal precept. For some time after, he was engaged in settling matters connected with his estate.

On the 16th of December, 1671, he married Janet, only daughter and heiress of Alexander Brodie of Lethen, by whom he had five sons and four daughters. One of his daughters, Margaret, married the famous Simon Fraser, Lord Lovat, and had issue.

The Laird of Freuchie was elected one of the members of Parliament for the county of Elgin, and was present in the Parliament which was opened by the Duke of York at Edinburgh on the 28th of July, 1681. Grant ventured to vote against a clause in the Test Act. Four years later, in 1685, the laird and his wife were summoned to appear before the Commission appointed to prosecute all persons guilty of non-conformity and other crimes, between the bounds of the Spey and the Ness. They appeared before the Commissioners and were examined at length. They were both found guilty of having withdrawn from the Parish Church, and of hearing and countenancing unlicensed ministers. Therefore the Commissioners fined the laird for his own and his wife's irregularities in the sum of £40,000 Scots, and ordered him to render payment to His Majesty's cash keeper before the 1st of May next. A few days after the sentence was pronounced he was charged to make payment of the fine within 15 days, under the penalty of being put to the horn. Grant, however, resolved to make an effort to have the fine remitted. Reasons for the reconsideration and reversal of the sentence were framed and presented to the Privy Council, with a petition for review of the decree. Afterwards he sent a petition to James VII., who took a favourable view of the case, and, on the 9th of January, 1686, he addressed a letter to the Privy Council discharging the laird of the whole amount of the fine.

In the autumn of 1688 the Revolution was drawing nigh. In October the chief of the Grants was summoned to Edinburgh to receive the orders of the Privy Council; and on the 2nd of November he received a letter from the Duke of Gordon, governor of Edinburgh Castle, desiring him to raise a company of men for the service of King James. It seems probable that Grant did not respond to these letters.

He was elected a member of the Convention of Estates, which assembled at Edinburgh on the 14th of March, 1689. He signed the minute, which declared the convention to be "a free and lawful meeting of the estates of the realm." He was appointed a member of the committee to consider means for securing the peace of the kingdom.

On the 23rd of March he signed the address to King William. On the 26th he was elected a member of the Committee for settling the Government. This Committee consisted of eight peers, eight representatives of the counties, and eight representatives of the burghs; and they immediately proceeded to discuss and frame the decisive resolution. This resolution of the estates declared—" That James VII. had assumed the Royal power, and acted as king without ever taking the oath required by law; and by the advice of evil counsellors he had invaded the fundamental constitution of the kingdom, and altered it from a limited monarchy to an arbitary and despotic power; and did exercise the same to the subversion of the Protestant religion and the violation of the laws and liberties of the kingdom, whereby he forfeited his right to the crown, and the throne has become vacant."

He took an active part in raising men to assist General

Mackay to overcome Viscount Dundee, and to restore peace and order in the Highlands. On the 24th of April, 1689, he was appointed, for the time, sheriff of Inverness-shire, and along with the other northern sheriffs, was commissioned to call a meeting of the heritors and fencible men within his jurisdiction, and to disperse any rebel forces.

He raised a regiment mainly consisting of the men of his own clan; but it appears that at first they were not well equipped. They were engaged at the Battle of Cromdale. The royal troops, under the command of General Livingstone, numbering about 1000 men, and 300 of the Grants were posted in Strathspey. The insurgents, under the command of General Buchan, and numbering about 800 men, marched through Badenoch and down Strathspey, and encamped on the Haughs of Cromdale. When tidings of Buchan's advance reached Livingstone, he immediately resolved to march his force up the valley of the Spey, and on the 1st of May, 1690, at the break of day, attacked the enemy by surprise. The Highlanders were completely defeated, and a considerable number of them slain and taken prisoners, but, in the pursuit, the mist on the hills favoured their escape. This engagement brought the civil war, arising from the Revolution, to a close. The event was celebrated in a ballad which was long popular in the north, "The Haughs of Cromdale," beginning thus :—

>
As I came in by Auchindoun,
>A little wee bit frae the town,
>When to the Highlands I was bound,
>>To view the Haughs of Cromdale.
>
>I met a man in tartan trews;
>I speer'd at him what was the news;
>Quo' he "The Highland army rues
>>That ere we came to Cromdale.
>
>"We were in bed, sir, every man,
>When the English host upon us came,
>A bloody battle then began
>>Upon the Haughs of Cromdale.

> "The English horse they were so rude,
>   They bathed their hoofs in Highland blood,
>   But our brave clans, they boldly stood,
>   Upon the Haughs of Cromdale.
>
> "But, alas! we could no longer stay,
>   For o'er the hills we came away,
>   And sore we do lament the day
>   That ere we came to Cromdale."

Before the date of the battle, the laird of Grant himself had returned to Edinburgh, and resumed his duties in Parliament. He took the oath of allegiance to the Government on the 15th of April, 1690. On the 14th of July, he was appointed one of the commissioners for visiting the universities and schools. In 1696 he signed the document which declared that William III. was truly and lawfully king, and bound the subscribers to defend His Majesty. In 1705 he joined in the protest against the union of the two kingdoms, unless the English Alien Bill was repealed.

On the 28th of February, 1694, he received from William III. a charter incorporating all the lands of Freuchie and other lands into a regality, to be called the Regality of Grant, and the castle and manor place of Freuchie to be henceforth called the Castle of Grant. At this time the Laird of Freuchie changed his designation to that of Laird of Grant—"Grant of Grant."

Castle Grant stands on an elevated site, one of the finest in Strathspey, and commands a wide and varied view of the surrounding country. The castle is a large structure, and was erected at different periods. A part of it was built by John Grant of Freuchie about 1525, and Sir Ludovick Grant, in the middle of the last century, made alterations and extensive additions to the castle. The dining hall is 47 feet in length and 27 in breadth. The park and the pleasure grounds are very extensive and varied.

The laird died at Edinburgh in November, 1716, and was interred in the Abbey Chapel of Holyrood. He was succeeded by his eldest surviving son, Colonel Alexander Grant of Grant. He was one of the Scottish Commissioners appointed to treat with England in 1706. He was a member of Parliament for Inverness-shire from 1703 till the last session of the Scottish Parliament in 1707. He usually voted with the Government.

He entered the army and attained the rank of brigadier-general. In 1708, at the first election in Scotland of members of the British Parliament, he was elected member for the county of Inverness. On the 24th of September, 1713, he was elected member of Parliament for the counties of Elgin and Nairn. He retired from the army in 1717.

In the spring of 1719 he was seized with a severe illness when in England. Although he recovered somewhat, and left London for Scotland in the beginning of August, and arrived at Leith on the 18th, the following day he died, and was interred in the Chapel of Holyrood.

General Grant was twice married, but he left no surviving issue, and he was succeeded by his brother, Sir James Grant, third son of Ludovick Grant of Grant.

SECTION VI.

SIR JAMES GRANT OF GRANT, BART.—HIS MARRIAGE—SUCCESSION TO THE GRANT ESTATES—A MEMBER OF PARLIAMENT—HIS DEATH—SIR LUDOVICK GRANT OF GRANT—HIS MARRIAGE—A MEMBER OF PARLIAMENT—RISING OF 1745—SIR JAMES GRANT OF GRANT—HE FOUNDED GRANTOWN—HE RAISED TWO REGIMENTS—HIS DEATH—TRIBUTES TO HIS MEMORY.

SIR JAMES GRANT was born on the 28th of July, 1679. On the 29th of January, 1702, he married Anne, only child and heiress of Sir Humphrey Colquhoun, fifth baronet of Luss, by whom he had six sons and eight daughters. His second daughter, Jean, was born on the 28th of September, 1705. She married William Duff of Braco in 1722, who was elevated to the peerage of Ireland in 1735, and to him she had seven sons and seven daughters. Anne Drummond was born on the 2nd of May, 1711. She married Sir Henry Innes of Innes in 1727.

Sir James Grant assumed the surname of Colquhoun. His father-in-law desired that, failing heirs-male, the title of Baronet should be inherited by his son-in-law and the heirs-male of his marriage. Accordingly, he resigned the baronetcy into the hands of the Crown for a new patent. On the 29th of April, 1704, Queen Anne, by a new patent, granted, renewed, and conferred on Sir Humphrey and his sons to be born; whom failing, on James Grant and his heirs-male of his marriage with Anne Colquhoun, only daughter of Sir Humphrey; whom failing, on the other heirs named, with the hereditary title and rank of knight-baronet. So on the death of Sir Humphrey in 1718, his title descended to his son-in-law, who then became Sir James Colquhoun of Luss, baronet.

But on the death of his brother, General Alexander Grant, in 1719, without surviving issue, Sir James succeeded to the lands of Grant. He then dropped the name of Colquhoun, and resumed his name of Grant. Sir James's second son, Ludovick, then became laird of the barony of Luss, the eldest son being the heir-apparent to the Grant estates.

On the 12th of April, 1722, Sir James was elected member of Parliament for the county of Inverness; and he was twice re-elected, in 1727 and 1734, and he continued to represent the county till 1741, when he resigned. The same year he was elected member for the Elgin burghs, which he represented till his death in 1747.

During the rising of 1745, he was opposed to the scheme of the Government of forming the loyal clans into independent companies. He thought that the best way for securing the effective assistance of his own clan or any clan, was to follow the Highland custom and summons each clan to muster under their respective chiefs, and thus engage them in active service. In this way an effective force could have been raised for active service on the side of the Government.

Sir James died in London on the 16th of January, 1747. "He was a gentleman of very amiable character, justly esteemed and honoured by all ranks of men."

He was succeeded by his second son, Sir Ludovick Grant of Grant, Baronet. He was born on the 13th of January, 1707. On the 6th of July, 1727, he married Marion Dalrymple, a daughter of the Hon. Sir Hew Dalrymple, Bart., and President of the Court of Session, by whom he had a daughter, who died unmarried in 1748, and her mother died in January, 1734. Secondly, on the 31st of October the same year, he married Lady Margaret Ogilvie, eldest daughter of James, fifth Earl of Findlater and second Earl of Seafield (as stated in a preceding section), and by her he had a son and seven daughters.

He studied law, and was called to the Scottish bar in 1728. But, in 1738, when he became heir-apparent to the estates of Grant of Grant, he retired from the practice of the profession of law, and mainly directed his attention to the management of the Grant estates, which his father had entrusted to him.

In 1741 he was elected member of Parliament for the counties of Elgin and Nairn, which he represented till 1761, when his son, Sir James, was elected member.

During the rising of 1745, Sir Ludovick did his utmost in support of the Government. It appears that the Government of George II. had no confidence in the loyalty of the Highland clans who had openly declared themselves on the side of the House of Hanover. This suspicious policy hampered the action of the chief of the Grants and others. This was extremely unfortunate for the loyal cause, for the Clan Grant, if called upon, would have mustered a considerable force.

Grant still resolved to assist the Government, but to remain in his own territories and defend them against the insurgents, unless the Government openly ordered him and his clan to join the Royal army in the field. In the winter and spring of 1746, however, he rendered important service to the Government.

A party of insurgents, under the command of Lord George Murray and Lord Nairne, with two pieces of cannon, marched into Strathspey; and on the 14th of March they proceeded to Castle Grant, and threatened to batter the castle down if any resistance was offered. The garrison surrendered, and opened the gates, and Lord Nairne took possession of the castle. But, on receiving tidings of the retreat of the insurgents from Strathbogie, Lord Nairne immediately withdrew from Castle Grant.

Sir Ludovick continued to attend to his duties in Parliament till 1761, when failing health caused him to resign his seat. His son James was elected member of Parliament, and succeeded his father in the representation of the constituency.

He died at Castle Grant on the 18th of March, 1773, and was interred in the family aisle at Duthil Parish Church. His death was much regretted, and touching tributes to his memory were rendered in verse and prose.

He was succeeded by his only son, Sir James Grant of Grant, baronet. He was born on the 19th of May, 1738. His father being a member of Parliament, often resided in London, and James was educated at Westminster School; thence he went to Cambridge, and studied under Dr Beilby Porteus, afterwards Bishop of Chester. In January, 1758, he left Cambridge and went to travel abroad. On the 20th of December he was at Geneva. Subsequently he travelled in Italy and Naples, and sojourned for some time in Rome. He left Rome in May, 1760, and proceeded homeward by Verona, Munich, and northwards to Scotland.

On the 4th of January, 1763, he married Jane Duff, only

daughter and heiress of Alexander Duff of Hatton, by Lady Anne, eldest daughter of Willian Duff, first Earl of Fife, by whom he had seven sons and seven daughters.

After his marriage he usually lived at Castle Grant, and mainly directed his attention to his extensive estates and numerous tenantry. He was exceedingly anxious to improve agriculture on his lands, and endeavoured to introduce the best method of tillage.

In 1766 he founded the town of Grantown, usually called the capital of Strathspey. The original site of the village was a barren moor; and before 1792, he had expended £5000 sterling in promoting the extension and welfare of Grantown. Efforts had been made to introduce trade and manufactures into the place. A linen manufactory had been started, and wool-combing and stocking-making. He erected a Town House, made roads, built a stone bridge, and introduced a supply of water into the town. He also drew up a series of regulations for the inhabitants of Grantown, touching proper cleansing, fencing of the different holdings, repair of broken windows, and likewise rules against immorality, which was to be punished by fines. In 1792 the population of the village was upwards of 300.

In 1793 Sir James made an offer to George III. to raise a regiment of fencibles, which was immediately accepted. Within three months the regiment was raised, mainly in Strathspey, and consisted of 500 men, exclusive of commissioned officers. On the 5th of June, the regiment was inspected and embodied by Lieutenant-General Leslie. In August they were marched to Aberdeen; and afterwards they were quartered in most of the chief towns in the south of Scotland—Glasgow, Paisley, Linlithgow, Dumfries, and other places. The appearance of the Grant fencibles was represented in an etching by John Kay, a well-known miniature painter and caricaturist, who lived in Edinburgh in the latter part of the last century. The regiment was disembodied in 1799.

Sir James raised another regiment for general service, which was embodied at Elgin, and numbered the 97th. They served for some time as marines on board Lord Howe's fleet in the English Channel; and, in 1795, the two flank companies, consisting of the best men, were incorporated with the 42nd—the famous Black Watch—and the rest of the men and officers were drafted into other regiments.

He was appointed Lord Lieutenant of Inverness-shire in 1794. The following year he was appointed to the office of general cashier of the Excise of Scotland. He was member of Parliament for Banffshire from 1790 to 1795.

Sir James died at Castle Grant on the 18th of February, 1811, and was interred at the Parish Church of Duthil. He was a man of high character and sterling worth. The "Edinburgh Evening Courant," in a notice of his death, made the following among other remarks:—" The virtues of Sir James, as an individual, will be long cherished in the recollections of his friends; the excellence of his public character will be not the less remembered in the district over which he presided . . . He had all the affections, without any of the pride or any of the harshness of feudal superiority, and never forgot, in attention to his own interests, or in the improvements of his extensive estates, the interests or the comforts of the people. Amidst the varied situations, and some of the severe trials of life, he was uniformly guided by rectitude of principle, benevolence of disposition, and the most fervent, though rational piety."

Mrs. Grant of Laggan issued a volume of poems in 1803, in which there is one on Sir James Grant, a few verses of which may be quoted:—

> "The patriot chief, who dwells belov'd
> Among the race his fathers sway'd;
> Who, long his country's friend approv'd,
> Retires in peace to bless the shade.

"Who when the dreadful blast of war
 With horror fill'd the regions round,
His willing people call'd from far
 With wakening pipe of martial sound.

"The valiant clan, on every side,
 With sudden warlike ardour burns,
And views those long-lov'd homes with pride,
 Who's loss no exil'd native mourns.

"From every mountain, strath, and glen
 The rustic warriors crowded round;
The chief who rules the hearts of men,
 In safety dwells, with honour crown'd.

"For thee (they cried), dear native earth,
 We gladly dare the battle's roar;
Our kindred ties, our sacred hearth,
 Returning peace will soon restore.

. . . .

"And when each tender pledge we leave,
 Our parent chief, with guardian care,
Shall soothe their woes, their wants relieve,
 And save the mourners from despair."

SECTION VII.

Sir Lewis Alexander Grant of Grant, Fifth Earl of Seafield, Viscount Reidhaven, and Lord Ogilvie of Deskford and Cullen—His Death—Sir Francis William, Sixth Earl of Seafield—A Member of Parliament—A Kind Landlord—Cullen House—Improvements—Rebuilding the Town of Cullen—A Representative Peer—His Death—Sir John Charles, Seventh Earl of Seafield.

Sir James Grant was succeeded by his eldest son, Sir Lewis Alexander Grant, a grandson of Margaret Ogilvie, and heir of the Earl of Findlater and Seafield. He was born on the 22nd of March, 1767. He studied for the bar, and entered the University of Edinburgh in 1784, and attended the requisite course. In 1789 he was called to the

Scottish Bar. His first appearance in the Court of Session made a favourable impression on the presiding judge, as noticed in a preceding section.

In 1790 he was elected member of Parliament for the county of Elgin. He made his first speech in the House of Commons on the impeachment of Warren Hastings, and supported the constitutional side of the question. His speech received the attention and applause of the House. But, unhappily, in the succeeding year his health began to fail, and he was forced to retire from public life.

On the death of the Seventh Earl of Findlater and Fourth Earl of Seafield in 1811, the title of Earl of Findlater, which was limited to direct male heirs, became extinct; but the title of Earl of Seafield, and the other titles created by the patent of 1701, and all the estates of the earldom, devolved on Sir Lewis Alexander Grant of Grant, Bart., who accordingly succeeded as Fifth Earl of Seafield, Viscount Reidhaven, and Lord Ogilvie of Deskford and Cullen.

After his succession to the estates of Grant and the title and estates of Seafield, it appears that he lived in retirement with his sisters at Grant Lodge in Elgin, and occasionally visited the other seats of his wide territories. His brother, Col. Francis William Grant, was intrusted with the management of the earl's estates.

The earl died at Cullen House on the 26th of October, 1840, in his 74th year, and, leaving no issue, he was succeeded by his brother, Colonel Sir Francis Willliam Grant of Grant, Bart. and Sixth Earl of Seafield.

He was born on the 6th of March, 1778. He entered the army at the early age of 15, and obtained his first commission as lieutenant in the Strathspey Fencibles, raised by his father.

In 1802 he was elected member of Parliament for the Elgin and Banff district of burghs, which he represented for four years. In 1806 he was elected member of Parliament for the Inverness Burghs; in the following year he was elected member for the county of Elgin, which he represented till 1832. In 1833 he was elected member of Parliament for the united counties of Elgin and Nairn, which he continued to represent until 1840, when he succeeded to the Earldom of Seafield. Thus he was a member of Parliament for 38 years; and in politics he was a Conservative of a mild type.

He was a very considerate and kind landlord, and was much respected by the tenantry throughout the extensive estates of Grant and Seafield. He made great and successful efforts to improve his estates and the welfare of his numerous tenants. It is recorded that under his direction 8223 acres had been planted with Scotch firs, larch, and hardwoods on his territories of Seafield, Strathspey, Moray. and Glen Urquhart.

The earl enlarged Cullen House, and rearranged and greatly extended the pleasure grounds around the mansion. New gardens and hothouses were formed and admirably stocked. New avenues and walks were made, ponds were formed, and many thousands of young trees, ornamental plants, and shrubs were planted. Thus Cullen House and its surroundings was rendered a charming residence.

He also directed attention to, and made special efforts to improve, the harbours of Cullen and Portsoy. The harbour of Cullen was reconstructed, enlarged, and deepened at a cost of £10,000. On the harbour of Portsoy a sum of £17,000 was expended.

Further, in his time the town of Cullen was almost rebuilt on a new site, mainly through the earl's efforts. "In 1813 the town occupied a position more to the west, and royal burgh though it was, presented a miserable contrast as regards cleanliness, comfort, and indeed, in every respect, to the present handsome town. The entire burgh consisted only of one street, towards which the gables of the houses (mostly covered with thatch), were turned, while noxious gutters yawned on either side. The place was also poor. . . . Under the auspices of his lordship, the old town was gradually removed, and on the present site there was laid out a new town, consisting of a handsome square and several spacious streets, crossing each other at right angles. . . . Building proceeded rapidly, until the burgh attained its present appearance, which, as respects architectural elegance and cleanliness, may vie with any town in the North." The first house was erected in 1820, and by 1830 the old town was removed and the new one erected.

It is said that the decay in the linen manufacture had led to the decay of the town. This offered an opportunity for improving the amenities of Cullen House. The earl usually resided at Cullen House, and his improvements, enterprise, and expenditure in the locality tended to promote the prosperity of the people.

On the 5th of August, 1841, he was elected one of the representative peers of Scotland to the Imperial Parliament, and he held this position till his death. He was a supporter of Sir Robert Peel in the early part of that statesman's career; but, like a number of others, he seceded from Sir Robert at a later period.

The earl was twice married. He married first, on the 10th of May, 1811, Mary Anne, only daughter of John Charles Dunn of Higham House, Sussex, by whom he had six sons and one daughter. She died on the 27th of February, 1840. Secondly, he married Louisa Emma, a daughter of Robert George Maunsell, of Limerick, in 1843, by whom he had no issue.

His lordship died at Cullen House on the 30th of July, 1853, in his 76th year, and was interred at Duthil Parish Church. His funeral was a public one, and was attended by a large number of people. I will quote a few sentences from a notice of his death which appeared in the "Banffshire Journal," on the 2nd August, 1853 :—" He instinctively recoiled from severe measures; and even when these would have been necessary, and where prudence might have counselled a resort to them, his lordship invariably refused to adopt them. The consequence was, that throughout his wide estates no nobleman was more truly beloved by his tenantry, who felt that they could always rely upon his indulgence. A prominent feature of his character was his love of justice and respect for his word . . . . He was ever conscious of the responsibility of his high position, and sought consistently to perform its duties . . . . In person, he was tall and of a commanding appearance. His disposition was gentle, and his manners retiring. His attainments in knowledge were of a high order, and tempered and modified by an enlarged practical acquaintance with the world and with human nature, acquired not merely at home, but during frequent residences for lengthened periods in various countries on the continent. These qualities rendered his conversation peculiarly fascinating."

He was succeeded by his eldest surviving son, Sir John Charles Grant Ogilvie, Seventh Earl of Seafield. He was born on the 4th of September, 1814. He joined the navy as a midshipman at the age of 15, and served for some time on board the ship commanded by Sir John Franklin. After the death of his eldest brother in 1840, he retired from the navy, and by his father's succession to the Earldom of Seafield, he had the courtesy title of Lord Reidhaven and Master of Grant.

In 1841, Lord Reidhaven contested the representation of Banffshire against Mr. James Duff, afterwards Fifth Earl of Fife. Lord Reidhaven came forward as a Conservative, and fought the election with remarkable energy and vigour. The contest was very keen, but Duff carried the seat by a majority of 43 votes.

SECTION VIII.

JOHN CHARLES GRANT OGILVIE, SEVENTH EARL OF SEAFIELD—A REPRESENTATIVE PEER—CREATED BARON OF STRATHSPEY, GREAT REJOICINGS—HE MADE IMPROVEMENTS—HIS MARRIAGE—HIS DEATH—TRIBUTES TO HIS MEMORY—IAN CHARLES GRANT OGILVIE, EIGHTH EARL—REJOICINGS ON ATTAINING HIS MAJORITY—HIS DEATH—JAMES, NINTH EARL—FRANCIS WILLIAM, TENTH EARL—JAMES, ELEVENTH EARL.

IN 1853 the Earl of Seafield was elected one of the representative peers of Scotland to the Imperial Parliament, and he held this position for five years. On the 14th of August, 1858, he was elevated to the Peerage of the United Kingdom under the title of Baron Strathspey of Strathspey. Under this inspiring title he continued to sit in the House of Lords.

When it was announced that this honour had been conferred on the 20th chief of the Grants and seventh Earl of Seafield, there were great rejoicings throughout his wide territories, and many bonfires blazed on the hills of Strathspey. A few verses from a poem composed on the event may be quoted:—

>"Why are the hills of proud Strathspey
>   Crowned with a blaze of light?
>Why do the dazzling fires burst forth
>   Amidst the calm of night?
>
>Is it the beacon's warning gleam?
>   Is the invader near?
>And doth the land call forth her sons
>   To aid with sword and spear?
>
>The chieftain of their ancient line
>   Has won another name—
>A title dearer to his clan
>   Than any he can claim.
>
>The bells are ringing far and near;
>   The throng came forth to-day,
>To render homage to their lord,
>   The Baron of Strathspey.

> He's richer in these loyal hearts,
>   Than in his princely lands,
> They're true and constant as their rock,
>   Which ever firmly stands.
>
> . . . . .
>
> But now the bonfire's ruddy glow
>   Streams all the country o'er,
> From Tullochgorum's lofty heights,
>   On Freuchie and Craigmore.
>
> On Cromdale's Hill, on Garten's crest,
>   The rival flames ascend,
> In honour of the Lord Strathspey,
>   The chieftain and the friend."

The earl took a warm interest in the welfare of his numerous tenantry, and made extensive improvements on his estates. He erected new farm steadings, encouraged the reclamation of waste land, and made roads. He was an excellent landlord, and won the esteem and affection of his tenants.

He directed special attention to the breeding of Highland cattle, and in this he attained remarkable success. His herd of Highland cattle at Castle Grant was at that time the best in the north of Scotland. He encouraged agricultural and cattle shows, and frequently presided at such meetings.

He planted a considerable extent of ground on his estates, and it was stated that the plantations and woods on the estates in his time extended to upwards of 40,000 acres. He also made many important improvements on Cullen House and its surroundings. During the 27 years which he held the Grant and Seafield estates he expended a sum of over £200,000 sterling on improvements.

He took a keen interest in all questions touching the welfare and progress of the country.

In 1879 he was invested with the Order of the Thistle by the Queen.

On the 12th of August, 1850, he married Lady Caroline

Stuart, a daughter of Robert Walter, eleventh Lord Blantyre, by whom he had an only child—Ian Charles Grant Ogilvie.

The Earl died at Cullen House on the 18th of February, 1881. His death was universally regretted. His funeral took place on the 25th and 26th of February, and was attended by a great assemblage of mourners and friends; and his body was laid to rest with his father's in the mausoleum at Duthil.

"Lord Seafield's death, before attaining the three score and ten, produced a feeling of mourning, as if for a dear friend, among all parties and classes throughout the counties of the north with which he was more immediately connected by property and residence. We have received—and we doubt not our contemporaries have also received—many communications seeking to give expression to the deep and general sense of loss and bereavement. Elsewhere, too, the tributes of commemoration, due to one whose life has been beneficial to his country and honourable to himself, have been freely bestowed by the organs of public opinion. Not only in the northern counties, where he lived, worked, and was best known, but broad Scotland feels with sorrow that a great chief and noble Scotsman has departed from our midst . . . . ."

> "Firm as Craigellachie he stood,
> Aye holding by the right;
> That which was just, and true, and good,
> Weighed more with him than might." Amen.

. . . .

He was succeeded by his only child, Sir Ian Charles Grant Ogilvie, Eighth Earl of Seafield, and Second Baron Strathspey of Strathspey. He was born in Edinburgh on the 7th of October, 1851. He was taught by tutors at home, and afterwards he studied for several years at Eton. He joined the army, and on the 8th of December, 1869, received a cornet's commission in the 1st Regiment of Life Guards. In 1871 he was promoted to lieutenant; and he retired from the army in 1877.

On the 7th of October, 1872, when he attained his majority, there were great rejoicings throughout the Grant and Seafield estates. On this occasion he received a portrait of himself from the tenants of the Strathspey estates, which was painted by the late Sir Francis Grant. The portrait was presented to his lordship by General Sir Patrick Grant in name of the tenantry.

He died on the 31st of March, 1884, at Claridge's Hotel, London, unmarried. He bequeathed his estates entirely to his mother, which were valued at £80,000 per annum, but charged with nearly £800,000. On his death, the peerage of the United Kingdom Baron Strathspey of Strathspey became dormant; but the other Scottish titles (without the estates) devolved on James Ogilvie Grant, Ninth Earl of Seafield—the uncle and heir of the preceding Earl.

He was the fourth son of Francis William, sixth earl, and was born on the 27th of December, 1817. He was educated at Harrow; joined the army, and was a captain in the 42nd Foot Regiment. He was elected member of Parliament for Morayshire in 1868, and represented the county for six years. He was Lieutenant-Colonel of the Morayshire volunteers. Shortly after his succession to the title of Earl of Seafield he was created a peer of the United Kingdom as Baron Strathspey of Strathspey, in the counties of Inverness and Moray, on the 17th of June, 1884.

He was thrice married. On the 6th of April, 1841, he married Caroline Louisa, a daughter of Eyre Evans of Askill Towers, county of Limerick : she died on the 6th of February, 1850. Secondly, on the 13th of April, 1853, he married Constance Helena, a daughter of Sir Robert Abercromby, fifth baronet of Birkenbog; she died on the 12th of February, 1872. Thirdly, on the 15th of December, 1875, he married Georgina Adelaide, a daughter of

Earls of Seafield.

Frederick Nathaniel Walker, K.C.H., Bushey Manor House, Herts.

The Earl died on the 5th of June, 1888, and was interred in the mausoleum at Duthil. His countess survived him, and she is one of the three Dowager Countesses of Seafield now living.

He was succeeded by his eldest son, Francis William Ogilvie Grant, tenth Earl of Seafield and fourth Baron Strathspey of Strathspey. He was born on the 6th of March, 1847, and educated at Harrow. On the 24th of December, 1874, he married Ann Trevor Carry, a daughter of George Thomas Evans, of Otago, in New Zealand. He died suddenly of heart disease on the 3rd of December, 1888, at his residence in Oarvarn, New Zealand, and was interred there. His widow, who was born on the 24th of July, 1847, is still living.

He was succeeded by his eldest son, James Ogilvie Grant, eleventh Earl of Seafield, Viscount Reidhaven, Lord Ogilvie of Deskford and Cullen, and Fifth Baron of Strathspey. He was born on the 18th of April, 1876. His lordship is a young man of great promise, and it may be hoped that there is a bright future before him. If he should return to the home of his fathers, he would receive a hearty Highland welcome.

The address which was presented to him in New Zealand on the occasion of attaining his majority, emphatically showed the respect and esteem in which this ancient and honorable family is still held in Strathspey and the North of Scotland, notwithstanding all adverse eventualities and circumstances.

In 1883 the family estates consisted of 160,224 acres in Inverness-shire, 96,760 acres in Morayshire, and 48,946 acres in Banffshire—making a total of 305,930 acres.

INDEX.

Aberchirder, 20, 125.
Abercorn, 115.
Abercromby, General Sir Ralph, 211, James, 309, Sir Robert, 5th Bart. of Birkenbog, 346.
Aberdeen, 19, 26, 34, 35, 39, 41, 65, 67, 68, 69, 90, 95, 117, 124, 126, 142, 144, 146, 147, 149, 156, 158, 165, 166, 169, 172, 173, 176, 183, 184, 185, 187, 189, 194, 201, 202, 205, 206, 209, 230, 233, 234, 236, 241, 246, 259, 274, 289, 290, 295; University of, 67, 68, 206, 216, 259, 293; Cathedral of, 37; Synod of, 70.
Aberdeen, Earl of, 200.
Aberdeenshire, 49, 73, 95, 100, 110, 114, 130, 168, 182, 194, 201, 206, 208, 209, 215, 222, 260, 270, 274, 290, 308, 309.
Abergairn, 118.
Abergeldie, 116, 249.
Abernethy, 28, 325, 326.
Aboyne, Earl of, Charles, first Earl, 193, 194, 219, 220; Charles, second Earl, 220; Charles, third Earl, 220; Charles, fourth Earl, 220, 221; George, fifth Earl, 221, 222; Charles, tenth Marquis of Huntly and sixth Earl of Aboyne, Charles, eleventh Marquis, 222, 223; Viscount of, John, 179, 218; George, 218; James, 184, 185, 187, 188, 189, 191.
Aboyne, 65, 66, 114, 274.
Ada, 83.
Aden, 122.
Albany, Duke of, Robert, 33, 34, 35; Murdoch, 35, 36, 102; Alexander, 47, 123; John Regent, 133, 134, 278.
Alexander I., 19, 78.
Alexander II., 21, 22, 80, 226, 272.
Alexander III., 22, 23, 79, 80, 87, 88, 226.

Alford, 70, 71; Battle of, 188, 189.
Allardyce, Thomas, 42, 44, 45; George, 314.
Alloa, 40.
Alva, Duke of, 157.
Angus, Earl of, Thomas, 27; George, 28, 30; Margaret, Countess of, 28, 29, 30; Archibald, 133, 135; William, 168, 170.
Annabella, Princess, 119.
Anstruther, Sir James, 174.
Arbroath, 69.
Arbuthnott, Robert, 122, Philip, 275, Sir Robert, 284, 287, Robert Viscount, 293.
Argyle, Earl of, 128, 132, 138, 144, 151, 155, 156, 157, 162, 171, 172, 176, 181, 185, 186; Marquis, 181, 186, 190, 193, 194; Duke, 68, 69, 71.
Armada, 163.
Arran, Earl of, Regent, 138, 139, 142, [149.
Asoph, 298.
Aswanley, 112, 117.
Athole, Earl of, 22, 94, 97, 99, 111, 120, 131, 148, 162, 166, 167, 169, 171, 228; Duke of, 68, 321.
Auchindor, 37.
Auchindoun, 158, 161, 172, 307, 309, 311, 312; Castle of, 147, 148, 171.
Auchinhamper, 137.
Auchinhove, 136.
Auchleven, 308.
Auchrie, 250, 260.
Auchterhouse, 103, 308.
Auldbar, 65.
Auldearn, Battle of, 188.
Ayr, 241, Castle of, 98.
Ayrshire, 97.
Badenoch, 19, 36, 116, 128, 138, 140, 162, 168, 182, 189, 323, Lord of 79, 81, 82, 83, 86, 87, 89, 90, 91, 92, 93, 94, 100, 101, 116, 118, 120, 123, 125, 130, 137, 138.
Baillie, General, 188; Rev. Robert, 193-4.

Index.

Balfour, Sir James, 151, 155.
Baliol, King John, 82, 83, 84, 85, 86, 272; Edward, 99, 100, 111.
Ballebeg, 48.
Ballindalloch, 139.
Balnabooth, 49.
Balnacraig, 237, 238.
Balnacrief, 128.
Bane, Donald, 79, 94.
Banff, 35, 78, 90, 314, 339.
Banff, Lord, 293, 308.
Banffshire, 34, 80, 260, 309, 342, 347.
Bannerman, Patrick, 67, 68; Alexander, 234.
Bannockburn, Battle of, 110, 272, 273.
Barclay, Walter, 42, 43, 45.
Barton, Captain Robert, 127.
Beaton, James, Archbishop, 135; David, Cardinal, 138, 139.
Beaumont, Henry, Earl of Buchan, 99, 100.
Berwick, 84, 85, 97, 141.
Birse, 203.
Blair, 162.
Blairfindie, 190, 325.
Blairshinnoch, 309.
Bog of Gight, 12, 179, 189.
Borthwick, Lord, 278; Castle of, 154.
Bothwell, Earl of, 124, 151, 152, 153, 154, 155, 167.
Boyd, Robert, 94; James, Lord Boyd, 264, 266, 267.
Braemar, 30, 50, 57, 65, 66, 71, 72, 203.
Boyne, 308, 311.
Brechin, 26; Castle of, 86, 90, Battle of, 117, 159.
Brigham, Treaty of, 82.
Brodie, Alexander, 214.
Bruce, Robert of Annandale, 82, 83, 84; Robert, Earl of Carrick, 86, 87, 89, 93; Nigel, 97.
Brude, 271.
Brux, 33.
Buchan, Earl of, Colbain, 78, 79; Roger, 79; Fergus, 79; Marjory, Countess, Comyn, William, 79, 80; Alexander, 80, 81, 82; John, 82, 85, 86, 87, 88, 89, 91, 92; Beaumont, Henry, 99, 100; Stewart, Alexander, 100, 101; John, 101; Murdoch, 102; James Stewart, created Earl of, 103, 104; Alexander, Second Earl, 104; John, Third Earl, 104, 105; Christian, Countess of Buchan, James Douglas, Fifth Earl, 105; Mary, Countess of Buchan, 105; James Erskine, Sixth Earl, 105; James, Seventh Earl, 105; William, Eighth Earl, 105; David, Ninth Earl, 105; Henry David, Tenth Earl, 105, 106, 107; David Stewart, Eleventh Earl, 107; Henry David, Twelfth Earl, 107; David Stewart, Thirteenth Earl, 107.
Buchan, Andrew, 42, 43, 45.
Buchanan, George, 81, 119.
Buckie, 249.
Burns, Robert, 206, 321.
Burnett, of Leys, 59, 60.
Byres, Lord of, William, 275.
Cabrach, 37, 130, 170, 171.
Caithness, 169, 173, 271.
Caithness, Earl of, 182.
Calder, 117.
Callander, Earl of, 262.
Calloquhy, 128.
Cambuskenneth, 128, 228.
Cameron, Ewan of Lochiel, 139, 140, 166; Donald, 224.
Cantyre, 96, 120.
Carberry, Hill, 155.
Cardross, Lord, 105.
Carmichael, Archibald, 169.
Carnborrow, 171, 178.
Carnegie, Lord, 180.
Carnegie, Robert, 137.
Carnwath, Earl of, 65.
Carron, 190, 326.
Cassillis, Earl of, 155, 280.
Chalmers, James, 201; Alexander, 237, 238; Gilbert, 238.
Charles I., 182, 184, 185, 186, 189, 190, 251, 253, 254, 288, 289, 290, 313.
Charles, II., 192, 193, 194, 195, 254, 255, 257, 291, 293.
Cheyne, Ranald, 42, 43, 45; John, 234; Patrick, 237; Sir Reginald, 258, 274.
Cluny, 114, 115, 274, 276.
Clunymore, 216.
Colliston, 233.
Colquhoun, Sir Humphrey, 332, 333.
Comyn, William, 79; Richard, 79, John, 99.
Corrichie, Battle of, 148.
Corsairtly, 325.
Coull, 20.
Covenanters, 182, 183, 185, 186.
Craig, 277.
Craigellachie, 323, 344, 345.
Craigievar, 156.

Index.

Craigmillar Castle, 47, 151.
Crawford, Earl of, 42, 53, 55, 59, 62, 116, 117, 120, 129, 132, 137, 138, 139, 164.
Crichton, Sir William, 40, 41, 44, 45, 46, 115; James, 178, 179, 180, 181.
Crimond, 260, 261.
Cromar, 26, 48, 49.
Cromdale, Lands of, 326; Battle of, 330, 331.
Crome, Alexander, 130.
Cromwell, 193, 194, 257, 291, 292.
Cruden, 232, 247, 259.
Cruickshank, Elizabeth, 112.
Culblean, Battle of, 111.
Cullen, 321, 340, 341.
Cullen House, 317, 340, 341, 345.
Culloden, Battle of, 202, 264.
Culquhony, 48.
Cumberland, Duke of, 202.
Cumnock, 97.
Cupar, Abbey church of, 230, 231, 236, 237.
Cushnie 71.
Cuthbert, Thomas, 230.
Daach, 113.
Dacre, Lord, 134.
Dalfour, 162.
Dalkeith, Lord, 113, 231.
Dalnabo, 190.
Danes, 19, 24, 25.
Darnaway Castle, 147, 149.
Darnley, 150, 151, 152, 153.
Davachindore, 33.
David I., 19, 21, 79.
David II., 25, 26, 27, 111, 112, 230, 274.
David, Earl of Huntingdon, 21, 83.
Davidson, William, 71; John, 130; Duncan, 137.
Dee, 19, 20, 111, 161; Bridge of, 184.
Denibristle Castle, 167.
Denmark, 282-84.
Dempster, David, 45.
Deskford, 307, 308, 309, 311, 320.
Dingwall, 80, Castle of, 120, 134.
Donald, Lord of the Isles, 33, 34, 35.
Douglas, Earl of 27, 28, 116, 276.
Douglas, Sir James, 94, 97; Sir James, 50; Sir William, 109, 111; Sir Robert, 105.
Dronlaw, 226, 227.
Drum, 33, 38, 233.
Drumlanrig, 50.
Drummond, Sir Malcolm, 28, 29, 30, 31; Robert, 50; Margaret, 132.

Drummond, Lord, 65.
Duffus, Lord, 65.
Dumbarton Castle, 39, 158.
Dumfries, 54, 93, 336.
Dunaverty Castle, 96.
Dunbar, Battle of, 24, 85, 109; Castle of, 151, 153, 154.
Dunbar, Jerome, 71.
Dunblane, 68.
Dundarg Castle, 81, 100.
Dundee, 53, 69, 181, 198, 226, 279.
Dundee, Viscount, 196, 197, 198.
Dunfermline, Abbey of, 19.
Dunideer, 21, 51.
Dunkeld, 67, 157.
Dunlugus, 145, 310.
Dunnottar Castle, 275, 282, 288, 289, 291, 292.
Dupplin, Battle of, 25, 100, 273.
Durham, Battle of, 230, 274.
Durris, 205, 233, 274,
Durward, Thomas, 20; Alan, 22, 23, 80.
Duthil, 325, 326, 335, 337, 341, 345.
Edinburgh, 142, 145, 149, 150, 151, 152, 153, 158, 163, 165, 167, 177, 180, 190, 191, 195, 196, 234, 235, 237, 241, 243, 247, 249, 253, 267, 269, 328; Castle of, 129, 145, 149, 155, 164, 181, 184, 190, 197, 198.
Edward I., 24, 26, 82, 83, 84, 85, 86, 87, 88, 90, 91, 93, 95, 97, 99.
Edward II., 110.
Edward III., 112.
Edward IV., 119.
Eglington, Earl of, 160.
Elgin, 101, 118, 119, 131, 139, 140, 149, 161, 181, 187, 204, 337.
Elizabeth Queen, 157, 160, 167, 282.
Ellon, 78, 260.
Elphinstone, Sir John, 48; Sir Alex. 48, 49.
Elphinstone, Alexander, first Lord Elphinstone, 49; Robert, third Lord, 56, 57; Alexander, fourth Lord 58, 59.
Enzie, Earl of, 174, 181.
Erroll, Earl of, William, first Earl, 231, Nicholas, second Earl, 231, 232, William, third Earl, 232-236, William, fourth Earl, 236, William, fifth Earl, 236, 237, William, sixth Earl, 237, George, seventh Earl 237-240, Andrew, eighth Earl, 240-242, Francis, ninth Earl, 242-253, William, tenth Earl, 253, 254, Gilbert, eleventh Earl, 254-258,

John, twelfth Earl, 258-259, Charles, thirteenth Earl, 259-262, Margaret, Countess of Erroll, 262-264, James, Lord Boyd, Fifteenth Earl of Erroll, 264-267, George, sixteenth Earl, 267, William, seventeenth Earl, 267-268, William George, eighteenth Earl, 268-270, William Harry, ninteenth Earl, 270, Charles Gore, twentieth Earl, 270.

Erskine, Sir Thomas, 24, 29, 30, Sir Robert, Lord Erskine, 37-40, 45, 46, Thomas, Lord Erskine, 40, 41, 42, 44, 45, 46, 47, John, Lord Erskine, 278, 279.

Erskine, James, Lord Grange, 73, David, of Dun, 73, Henry, 106, Thomas, 106, 107.

Essie, 113.
Esslemont, 113, 160, 234, 237, 260.
Eton, 345.
Fala, 170.
Falconer, Alexander, 262.
Falkirk, battle of, 68.
Farquharson, John, 66, 68, 221.
Fenton, William, 27, William, 231.
Ferguson, Dr. Adam, 68, Francis, 71.
Fidlemouth, 33, 39.

Findlater, and Seafield, Earl of, James first Earl of Findlater, 312, 313, Patrick, Second Earl, 313, 314, James, Third Earl, 314; James Fourth Earl, 314; created Earl of Seafield, 315, 316, 317; James, Fifth Earl of Findlater, and Second Earl of Seafield, 317-320; James Sixth Earl of Findlater, and Third of Seafield, 320-321; James, Seventh Earl, 321; Sir Lewis Alexander Grant, Fifth Earl of Seafield; Chiefs of Grant, 322-338; Sir Francis William, Sixth Earl of Seafield, 339-342; John Charles, Seventh Earl, and first Baron of Strathspey, 342-345; Ian Charles, Eighth Earl, 345-346; James, Ninth Earl, 346-347; Francis William, Tenth Earl, 347, James, Eleventh Earl, 347.

Fleming, Lord, 155, 278.
Fleming, Robert, 94, Malcolm, 102.
Flodden, Battle of, 132, 236, 277, 278.
Forbes, Lord, 59, 104, 115, 118, 122, 136, 171.
Forbes, Sir John, 38, Sir William, 38, Duncan, 47, Alexander, 47, William, 57, Patrick, Bishop of Aberdeen, 58, Sir William, Arthur, Archibald, 71, Thomas, 71, Duncan, 284, John, 284. Sir John, of Pitsligo, 312, Hugh, 317, Sir William, 317.

Forfarshire, 101, 307, 308.
Forres, 142, 166.
Foulis, 156, 162.
France, 32, 47, 69, 73, 85, 87, 88, 89, 101, 133, 134, 144, 161, 182, 278, 282, 296, 297, 299, 301.
Fraser, Sir Simon, 91, 97, Alexander, 94, Sir John, 274, Sir Alexander, 274, Alexander, 233, Alexander, Lord Philorth, 233.
Frendraught, 178-180.
Freuchie, 323, 324, 325, 327, 328, 331.
Fyfield, 127.
Fyvie, 38, 238.
Fyvie, Lord of, 61.
Galloway, Lord of, 82, 228; Earl of, 76, 294.
Galloway, 160.
Garioch, Earl of, David, 21; John, 21; Lordship of, 24, 26, 41, 48, 50, 51, 59.
Gasklune, Battle of, 101.
Geneva, 265, 282.
George I., 64, 199, 262, 295.
George II., 263, 264, 299.
George III., 267, 305.
George IV., 269.
Gight, 136, 167, 173, 174.
Glamis, Master of, 53, 164, 165.
Glasgow, 151, 156, 168, 211, 336.
Glass, 112, 171.
Glencairn, Earl of, 155, 280.
Glencourse, 33.
Glenfiddich, 307, 309.
Glenlivet, Battle of, 171, 172.
Glenmoriston, 139, 140, 324, 325.
Glenmuick, 115, 219, 221, 274.
Glennochty, 48.
Glentanner, 115, 174.
Gordon, Richard, Sir Thomas, 108; Alice, 109; Sir Adam, Sir Adam, 109; Sir Adam, 109, 110; Sir Adam, 110, 111, 112, Sir John, 112, Sir John, 112, John and Thomas, 112, 113, Sir Adam, 113, Sir John, Elizabeth, 113; Alexander Seton, Gordon, 113, 114.
Alexander of Midmar, 115; George of Gight, 136; George, 246, 247, 248, 249; Sir John, 145, 146, 147, 148, 149, 239, 310, 311; Sir Adam

of Auchindoun, 158, 159, 160, 310, 311; Sir Patrick, 172; William, of Rothiemay, 178, 179, 180; Lord Lewis, 200, 204; Sir Alexander, 249; John, 249.
Gordon, Duke of, George, first Duke, 194, 199; Alexander, second Duke, 199, 200; Cosmo George, third Duke, 200, 201, 204, 205; Alexander, fourth Duke, 205, 208; George, fifth Duke, 209, 211, 212, 214, 215; Duchess of Gordon, 215, 216; Duke of Richmond and Gordon, 216, 218.
Gordon Highlanders, 92nd, 209, 214.
Gormson, Donald, 143.
Gowrie, Earl of, 52, 53; Countess of, 53, 54.
Graham, David, 91.
Grant, Sir Lawrence, Sir Robert, 322, 323; Sir Patrick, 323; John, 323; Sir Duncan of Freuchie, 323; John, 323, 324; James, 324; John, 324, 325; John, 325, 326; Sir John, 326, 327; James, 327, 331; Alexander, 331, 332; Sir James, 332, 334; Sir Ludovick, 334, 335; Sir James, 335, 337, 338; Sir Lewis Alexander, 321, 338, 339.
Grant, John, 139; James, 326.
Gray, Master of, 290.
Haco, 80.
Haddington, Earl of, 185.
Haddo, 309.
Hailes, Lord, 124.
Hamilton, Duke of, 196, 197, 198.
Hamilton, Lord, 158.
Hamilton, Archbishop, 158; Sir Patrick, 234, 235; Sir James, 276.
Harlaw, Battle of, 33-35.
Hastings, John, 82, 83.
Hay, Sir Gilbert, 38; Hugh, 94; John, 156; George, 237; Alexander, 238, Sir William, 238; Francis, 246; Sir George, 258; Andrew, 258.
Hay, of Erroll, William, David, 226; Gilbert, 226; Nicholas, 226, 227; Sir Gilbert, created hereditary Lord High Constable, 227, 228, 230; Sir David, Second High Constable, 230, 231; Sir Thomas, Third High Constable, 231; William, Fourth High Constable, 231; William, Fifth High Constable, 231.
Henderson, William, 241; Robert, 149.
Henry, III., 22, 23.

Henry VIII., 134, 138, 139.
Home, Alexander, 123.
Home, Lord, 132, 133; George, 137, 155.
Huntly, Alexander, First Earl of, 114-119, 145, 231; George, Second Earl of, 119-128, 232; Alexander, Third Earl of, 128-134; George, Fourth Earl of, 134-140-141-146-147-149, 277; George, Fifth Earl of, 149-152-152-161; George, Sixth Earl of, 161-163-164-169-169 174; George, First Marquis of, 174-181; George, Second Marquis of, 181-187-187-191; Lewis, Third Marquis of, 191-193; George, Fourth Marquis, 193-195; Alexander, Fifth Marquis of, 199, 200; Cosmo George, Sixth Marquis of, 200; Alexander, Seventh Marquis of, 204; George, Eighth Marquis of, 209, 210, 211, 212, 214, 215, 218; George, Ninth Marquis of, 221, 222, Charles, Tenth Marquis of, 222; Charles, Eleventh Marquis of, 222, 223.
Hurry, General, 188.
Inchmartin, 312, 313.
Innes, Alexander of Aberchirder, 125; Robert of Invermarkie, 130; Robert, 136; Robert, 156; James, of Draunie, 156; Sir Walter of Balveny, 326; Sir Robert, 309; Sir Henry of Innes, 333.
Inverlochy, Battle of, 36, 187; Castle of, 130, 138.
Inverness, sheriffdom of, 130, 131, 132, 178; Castle of, 121, 130, 138, 147.
Inverness, 140, 147, 230, 296.
Invernethy, 48.
Invernochty, 48.
Inverugie, 67, 274, 279, 293, 297, 305.
Inverurie, 98, 183, 202, 289.
Irvine, Sir Alexander of Drum, 33; Sir Alexander, 38; Sir Alexander, 137, Sir Alexander, 186; Alexander of Coull, 137; Alexander of Belte, 233.
Isabel, Countess of Mar, 28, 29, 30, 31, 32.
Isles, Lord of, Donald, 33, 34, 35; Alexander, 35, 114; John, 125.
Jacobites, 64, 65, 66, 196, 197, 198, 199, 202-204, 295, 296.
Jaffery, minister, 70.
James, I., 35, 36, 37, 46, 102, 114, 119.
James, II., 39, 40, 41, 42, 43, 44, 46, 47, 116, 117, 118, 276.

23

Index.

James III., 47, 47, 48, 103, 104, 118, 120, 122, 123, 277, 309.
James, IV., 123, 125, 126, 127, 128, 129, 132, 235, 236, 277, 278.
James V., 51, 135, 137, 138, 237, 278, 279.
James VI, 51, 52, 53, 56, 58, 61, 163, 164, 165, 166, 167, 169, 170, 171, 172, 174, 175, 176, 177, 241, 249, 282, 283, 284.
James VII., 105, 195, 196, 197, 198.
James VIII., Pretender, 65, 67, 68, 69, 70, 73, 295, 296.
Jesuits, 163, 165.
Johnston, Gilbert, 47; John of Johnston, 54; Dr. Arthur, 252, 253.
Justiciary, 22, 80, 110, 121.
Kay, John, 336.
Keith, 188, 325.
Keith, Great Marischals of Scotland; Hervey, Sir Philip, Sir Hervey, John, 272; Sir Robert, 272-274; Sir Robert, 274; Sir Edward, 274; Sir William, 274-276; Sir William, First Earl Marischal, 276, 277; William, Second Earl Marischal, 277; William, Third Earl Marischal, 277, 278; William, Fourth Earl Marischal, 278-282; George, Fifth Earl Marischal, 282-288; William; Sixth Earl Marischal, 288, 289, William, Seventh Earl Marischal, 289-293; George, Eighth Earl Marischal, 293, 294; William, Ninth Earl Marischal, 294. George, Tenth Earl Marischal, 294-297, 304, 305, 306.
Keith, James Francis Edward, Field-Marshal, 295, 296, 297, 301, 302, 303, 304.
Keith, Robert, Lord Altire, 279, 280, 284; John, first Earl of Kintore, 289; Sir Robert M., 304; Sir William, 279.
Keithmore, 217, 307, 309, 311, 312.
Kelso, 53; Abbey of, 108, 109.
Kent, Edmond, Earl, 32.
Keppoch, 140.
Kildrummy Castle, 25, 26, 27, 31, 32, 39, 40, 49, 50, 51, 58, 59, 95, 96, 97, 111; Lordship of, 59, 71.
Killiecrankie, Battle of, 198.
Kilmarnock, William, Earl of, 264, 266.
Kilpatrick, 93.
Kilpont, Lord, 289.
Kilsyth, Battle of, 189.
Kincardineshire, 260, 275, 282.
Kinghorn, Earl of, 220.
Kirk-of-Field, 152.
Kirkcaldy, Sir William, of Grange, 156.
Knapdale, 120.
Laggan, 323, 337.
Lamberton, Bishop of St. Andrews, 86, 87, 93, 94.
Lauder Bridge, 122.
Lauderdale, 220.
Leith, William, 26.
Leith, 145, 243, 278, 283, 284, 332.
Lennox, Earl of, 96, 135, 158, 236.
Leslie, Sir Andrew, 31, Margaret, Countess of Ross, 33; Sir William, of Balquhain, 42, 45; Alexander, of Arderay, 156; John, of Leslie, 156; Alexander, of Pitcaple, 156; Sir George, 231; Andrew, 231; John, of Wardes, 125.
Lesly, John, Bishop of Ross, 144.
Lesmore, 113.
Leven, Earl of, 198.
Lewis, Island, 174, 175.
Lindsay, Walter, 42; Rev. David, 283.
Lindsay, Lord, 155, 158.
Linlithgow, 163, 258.
Linlithgow, Earl of, 65, 262.
Livingstone, Lord, 155.
Livingstone, General, 330.
Lochaber, 120, 128, 129, 139, 140, 182, 189, 271.
Lochalsh, Alexander, 125.
Lochiel, Chief of the Camerons, 140.
Lochindorb Castle, 90, 92.
Lochleven, 155.
Lochmaben Castle, 93.
Lockart, Sir George, 64.
Lorne, Lord of, 95.
Lovat, Lord, 139, 145, 166, 319, 320, 324, 328.
Lumphanan, 136.
Lumsden, David, of Cushnie, 71.
Lundin, Malcolm, 20.
Luss, 332, 333.
Mabuisson, Sir Edward, 110.
Macdonald, Ranald, 140; Major Donald, 213.
Macgregor, of Glenstrae, 162.
Mackenzie, John, of Kintail, 125, 139, 162.
Mackintosh, Duncan, 121; Hector, 136; William, 139, 140, 142; Lachlan, 156, 162; William, Captain, 210; Malcolm, 323; Lachlan, of Badenoch, 323; William, 325; Lachlan, 326;

Laird of, 166, 309, 325; Mackintoshes, 145, 167, 168, 170, 171.
Maclean, of Lochbuy, 129, Hector, of Duart, 136.
Macleod, of Lewis, 129, 162; of Macleod, 202.
Macneil, of Barra, 128.
Maid of Norway, 23, 81.
Maitland, of Lethington, 145, 151, 156.
Malcolm II., 78, 271.
Malcolm III., 79.
Mar, Earl of, Ruadri, First Earl of Mar, 19; Morgund, Second Earl, 19, 20; Gilchrist, Third Earl, 20; Gratney, Fourth Earl, 20; Duncan, Fifth Earl, 20, 21, 22; William, Sixth Earl, 22, 23; Donald, Seventh Earl, 23, 24; Gartney, Eighth Earl, 24; Donald, Ninth Earl, 24, 25; Thomas, Tenth Earl, 26, 27; Margaret, Countess of Mar, 27; James Douglas, Twelfth Earl of Mar, 27, 28; Isabel, Countess of Mar, 28, 29, 30, 31, 32; Robert, Lord Erskine, Fourteenth Earl, 37-41; John, Nineteenth Earl of Mar, 49-51; John, Twentieth Earl, 51-60; John, Twenty-first Earl, 60, 61, 62, 63; John, Twenty-second Earl, 63; Charles, Twenty-third Earl, 63, 64; John, Twenty-fourth Earl, 64-69, 72, 73; John Francis, Twenth-seventh Earl, 74; John Thomas, Twenty-eight Earl; John Thomas Miller, Twenty-ninth Earl, 74; John Francis, Thirtieth Earl, 74, 75, 76, 77.
March, Earl of, 82.
Mary, Queen Regent, 142, 143, 144, 280.
Mary, Queen of Scotland, 145, 146, 147, 148, 150, 151, 152, 153, 154, 155, 156, 157, 158, 159.
Maule, Sir Thomas, 90.
Maxwell, Lord, 54, 55.
Meldrum, Alexander, 38; George, 238.
Melville, Sir James, 54.
Menteith, Earl of, 289.
Menzies, Gilbert, 43; Andrew, 45.
Methven, Battle of, 94.
Migvie, 20, 23, 26, 51.
Moidart, John, 142, 143.
Moigne, Sir Walter, 27.
Monk, General, 194.
Monymusk, 20.
Moore, General, 211, 212.

Moray, Sir Andrew, 100, 111.
Moray, Earl of, 25, 99, 117, 119, 147, 148, 155, 156, 166, 167, 176.
Montgomery, Alexander, 45.
Montrose, Marquis of, 183, 184, 185, 186, 187, 188, 189.
Mortimer, John, of Craigievar, 156.
Morton, Earl of, 151, 155, 158, 159, 160, 312.
Mowat, John, of Loscragy, 42, 44.
Munro, General, 209.
Murray, Sir John, of Tullibardine, 326.
Murray, Lord George, 335.
Musselburgh, 155.
Nairne, Lord, 335.
Nairn, 168, 332, 334, 340.
Nairn, Thomas, 326.
Neilson, Neil, 240.
Ness, 21, 22.
Newburgh, 80.
Nicolson, Thomas, 58.
Nithsdale, Earl of, 65.
Norfolk, Duke of, 195.
Norham, 82.
Norsemen, 271.
Northumberland, 127.
Norway, 23, 82.
Ochiltree, Lord, 179.
Ogilvie, Sir Walter, 101, 308; Sir John, of, Lintrethan, 42, 45; Sir Walter of, Deskford, 42, 45, 308; Sir James, 308, 309; Sir Alexander, 309, 310; James, 310, 311; Sir Walter, 311, 312.
Oliphant, Sir William, 91; James, 58.
Orkney Isles, 138.
Ormond, Earl of, 117.
Otterburn, Battle of, 27, 28, 112.
Panton, John, 233.
Paterson, Robert, 264.
Peebles, 87.
Pembroke, Earl of, 94, 97, 98.
Perkin Warbeck, 125-127.
Perth, 67, 68, 69, 90, 100, 121, 124, 126, 187.
Perth, Earl of, 195, 258.
Peterhead, 68, 305.
Philworth, Lord, 233.
Pinkie, Battle of, 140, 279.
Pitcur, 222.
Pitfour, 238.
Pitmedden, 156.
Pitsligo, Lord, 289.
Poland, 60, 191, 297, 298.
Prague, 302, 303.
Preston, Battle of, 68, 71.
Pretender, 68, 69, 295, 296.

Index.

Primrose, Gilbert, 288.
Prussia, 297, 301, 302, 303, 305.
Quhitecrose, 121.
Raits Castle, 92.
Ramsay, of Preston, 111.
Ranaldson, Doul, 131.
Randolph, Thomas, 110.
Redesdale, Earl of, 76.
Regent, Arran, 138, 139, 141, 142.
Reid, Alexander, 130.
Richmond, Duke of, 215, 216, 217.
Rizzio, David, 150.
Robert, I., 26, 92, 93, 94-99, 227, 228, 272, 273.
Robert, II., 28, 100, 112, 231, 275.
Robert, III., 28, 29, 30, 231.
Robertson, of Strowan, 130, 237, 244.
Rollo, Lord, 65.
Roseback, Battle of, 303.
Ross, Earl of, 33, 34, 35, 114, 116, 117, 120.
Rothes, Earl of, 137, 155, 232.
Rothiemay, 145, 178, 179.
Rothiemurcus, 162, 232, 325.
Roy Castle, 92.
Rutherford, Sir John, of Tarland, 123;
Roxburgh, Duke of, 263, 264.
Russia, 297, 298, 299, 300, 301.
Ruthven, 113; Ruthven, Lord, 150.
Sadler, 279.
St. Petersburg, 297, 299, 300, 301.
Saltoun, Lord, 139.
Sauchie, Burn, Battle of, 104.
Scone, 17, 29, 69, 94, 254, 255, 275.
Scott, Sir William, 130.
Scroggs, 42, 43, 45.
Scrymgeour, James, 104.
Seton, Christopher, 94 ; Sir William, of Seton, 113; Alexander of Meldrum, 125, Alexander, 166.
Seton, Lord, 157, 185.
Sinclair, Sir John, 308,
Skene, James, of Skene, 42, 43, 45 ; Sir John, 61, 252.
Somerset, Duke of, 140, 141.
Somerville, Sir John, 94.

Soulis, John, 86, 88, 89, 91.
Southesk, Earl of, 65. 257.
Spain, 164, 212.
Spey, 34, 117, 188.
Stewart, Sir Thomas, 36, 37, Robert, 51 ; Lewis, 58; James, 103.
Stirling, 39, 40, 55, 86, 103, 128, 154, 158, Castle of, 91, 146.
Stirling, James, of Keir, 50.
Stonehaven, 184, 292.
Stormont, Lord, 65.
Strachan, John, 130.
Strathbogie, David, 110, 228,
Strathbogie, 34, 98, 110, 117, 136, 147, 161, 165, 169, 170, 171, 183, Castle of, 172, 177, 189.
Strathfillan, 95.
Strathspey, 188, 206, 222, 323.
Swinton, Sir John, 29.
Tay, 86, 95.
Tarland, 19, 23, 123.
Thomson, Duncan, 131.
Towie, 161.
Tullibardine, Marquis of, 65.
Tulidef, Andrew, 240.
Turenne, Marshal, 195.
Turriff, 232, 250, 251.
Tweeddale, Marquis of, 64.
Udny, Ranald, of Udny, 236.
Ukraine, 298, 300.
Urquhart, William, 126.
Umfraville, Ingram, 89.
Wade, General, 72.
Wake, Lord, 99.
Wallace, William, 86, 87, 91, 97, 109, 110 ; Malcolm, 87.
Wark Castle, 277.
Watterton, 234,
Wemyss, Lord, 59.
White Mountains, 302.
Wigton, Earl of, 251, 294.
Williamstraud, 300.
Winton, Earl of, 251.
Wishart, Bishop of Glasgow,
Worcester, Battle of, 291, 292.
Wyburg, 300.

THE END.

www.ingramcontent.com/pod-product-compliance
Lightning Source LLC
Chambersburg PA
CBHW030254240426
43673CB00040B/971